THE
COMPLEAT
TENNESSEE
ANGLER

Everything You Need to Know about Fishing in the Volunteer State

VERNON SUMMERLIN
& DOUG MARKHAM

RUTLEDGE HILL PRESS®

Nashville, Tennessee

Published by Rutledge Hill Press®, 211 Seventh Avenue North, Nashville, Tennessee 37219.
Distributed in Canada by H. B. Fenn & Company, Ltd., 34 Nixon Road, Bolton, Ontario
L7E 1W2.

Cover photo by Jack Bissell
Cover and page design by Karen Phillips
Typography by Roger A. DeLiso, Rutledge Hill Press®
Photos by the authors unless otherwise noted.

Library of Congress Cataloging-in-Publication Data:
Summerlin, Vernon, 1943–
        The Compleat Tennessee Angler / Vernon Summerlin and Doug Markham.
                p. cm.
        Includes index.
        ISBN 1-55853-741-4 (pbk.)
        1. Fishing—Tennessee—Guidebooks. 2. Tennessee—Guidebooks.
I. Markham, Doug, 1959–. II. Title.
SH549.S85 1999
799.1′2′09768—dc21   98–32122
                                CIP

Printed in the United States of America
1 2 3 4 5 6 7 8 9—00 99

Dedications

This book is dedicated to every sportsman, whose financial contributions and support help make Tennessee one of America's great fishing states, and to fishery biologists, technicians, creel clerks, secretaries, and others, whose dedication to fish management deserves every sportsman's admiration and confidence.

—Doug

More than half a century past, I owe much to the four strongest influences in my angling history: my grandfather Charles William Collier, who had the patience and encouragement to make my earliest fishing experiences fun; my father Vernon Summerlin Sr., who added discipline to the sport; my dear friend Joe Bakes, who became my angling mentor; and my beloved wife Cathy, who helped me transform my hobbies of fishing and writing into an outdoor profession.

—Vern

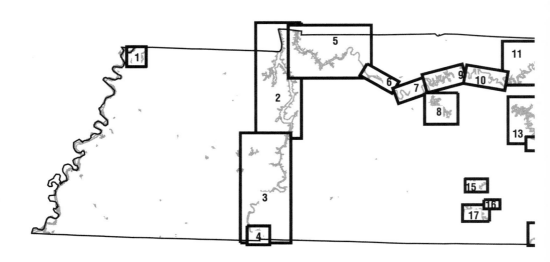

1   Reelfoot Lake
2   Kentucky Reservoir (Tennessee River)
3   Kentucky Reservoir (Tennessee River)
4   Pickwick Reservoir
5   Lake Barkley
6   Cheatham Reservoir
7   Cheatham Reservoir
8   J. Percy Priest Reservoir
9   Old Hickory Reservoir
10 Old Hickory Reservoir
11 Cordell Hull Reservoir
12 Dale Hollow Reservoir
13 Center Hill Reservoir
14 Great Falls Reservoir
15 Normandy Reservoir

Reservoir Locations

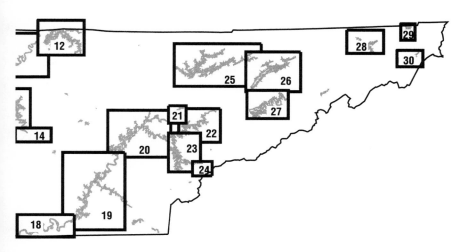

16   Woods Reservoir

17   Tims Ford Reservoir

18   Nickajack Reservoir

19   Chickamauga Reservoir

20   Watts Bar Reservoir

21   Melton Hill Reservoir

22   Fort Loudoun Reservoir

23   Tellico Reservoir

24   Chilhowee and Calderwood Reservoirs

25   Norris Reservoir

26   Cherokee Reservoir

27   Douglas Reservoir

28   Boone and Ft. Patrick Henry Reservoirs

29   South Holston Reservoir

30   Watauga Reservoir

Contents

PART III: EAST TENNESSEE

APPENDICES

Acknowledgments

Besides meeting great fishermen while researching this book, I met good people and experienced several unforgettable outings. Many old friends provided help. I thank:

My wife Dian Markham for helping me with various book projects. I also appreciate her patience with my computer grumpiness and hope that one day she publishes her own good book about life.

Gina and Tracy Boyd, our married map makers, who worked with Rutledge Hill Press to give readers an idea of reservoir size, shape, and location.

TWRA's Cliff Whitehead, who heads several sharp people in the agency's division for geographic information.

TWRA creel clerks Paul Shaw, Sonny Pool, Tim Pool, and Darrell (Bones) Bernd. These guys led me to some of Tennessee's best fishermen.

TWRA fish crew members Brian James, Jerald Bryson, and Pat McInturff for helping with a much-needed photograph, and the late Lewis Land, who for many years was a part of this hard working fishery team.

TWRA reservoir biologists Doug Pelren, John Riddle, Doug Peterson, Anders Myhr, and Tim Broadbent for sharing information and working hard for many years.

Gene Austin, one of Tennessee's best fishermen and nicest guys. Ask Gene to help and he will be there.

The Rutledge Hill Press staff that helped create a book which I believe will benefit fishermen for decades. I especially appreciate Clay White, our friendly editor with a bright future.

My friends Jimmy Holt and Glenn Smith, who have done as much as anyone and much more than most to promote fishing with their long-running television show *Tennessee Outdoorsmen*. I also thank Nashville's WDCN Channel 8 for letting me be a part of this unique broadcast.

Tennessee Radio Network, which lets Vernon and I talk fishing each week on stations across the state.

All the people who took the time to talk with me (some even took me fishing) and then read my chapters to correct mistakes.

Herman Waddell, a pioneer in Tennessee's television outdoors industry and the father of my Rutledge Hill friend, Hugh Waddell.

My parents Jim and Delores. My dad taught me to fish; my mom encouraged it with many gifts.

Cathy Summerlin, who like my wife, provided encouragement and help during this project. She always sees a glass as half full.

And finally, my partner Vernon Summerlin, whose idea for this book has been one of many great ideas during his distinguished career as an outdoors communicator.

—Doug

Neither this book nor my career would have happened if my wife Cathy hadn't bought me a computer and said, "Start writing." She has been, and continues to be, my source of encouragement and happiness.

For many years I have picked the brains of TWRA fisheries biologists across the state. They deserve thanks, not only from me, but from all anglers because they study and implement management techniques to ensure excellent fishing in the years to come.

A special thanks to Joe Bakes, Gene Austin, Stan Warren, John Cates, Jim Duckworth, David Woodward, Bob Latrendresse, Jim Moyer, Sherrill Smith, Harold Morgan, Benny Hull, Dayton Blair, Tom Waynick, Yank Kramer, Garry Mason, Steve McCadams, William Emerton, Tom Richards, Jack Christian, Jimmy Bunch, Dr. Woodson Carter, Pete James, George Gregory, Larry and Emily Shaffer, Billy Hurt Jr., Jeff Hudson, Roy Foster, Don Winstead, Glen Stubblefield, Ron Tuberville, Donny Hall, Doug Plemons, Terry Sherfield, and the famous *Tennessee Outdoorsmen* Jimmy Holt and Glenn Smith for wetting a line with me—friends all. It has been one of life's extraordinary gifts to share my passion with these fine Tennessee anglers.

My thanks to Larry Stone, publisher of Rutledge Hill Press, for providing the opportunity to write another fishing book, and to our superb editor Clay White, who made sure the i's were dotted and the t's crossed, among many other essential responsibilities.

Finally, my coconspirator in finding yet another way to spend time on the water, Doug Markham, has become my best friend, fishing buddy, and partner. He is an exceptional outdoors communicator with a wealth of talent. I'm proud to have spent the last year writing this book with him. Thanks, friend.

—Vern

Introduction

You are holding more than 1,000 years of angling knowledge—the experience attained by dozens of first-rate, freshwater anglers during their collective lifetimes. No other book exists like *The Compleat Tennessee Angler*, which contains numerous ideas for catching fish from every major reservoir in this famous fishing state.

This book will interest anyone who wants to learn as much as possible about catching a variety of fish with a variety of methods tested and proven by veteran sport anglers. Our sources are well-known anglers in their region. Some have statewide fame, others have national recognition, a few are world fishing champions, and several even have their own television programs. Guides, tournament competitors, and serious, year-round fishermen are this book's primary sources.

Many of our sources take between 100 and 250 fishing trips each year. Where applicable, they discuss methods used year-round on their favorite lakes. In cases where fishing is seasonal, they address the best months to be on the water. We urge anglers to read all the methods described for their desired species. A technique that catches bass, crappie, striper, sauger, walleye, bluegill, or other fish in one section of Tennessee stands a good chance of attracting them in other sections—even from freshwater impoundments in other states.

Take advantage of all the information within, even if a featured angler's style does not necessarily interest you. How someone catches fish is important, but so is where he catches his fish during a particular time of the year. Countless fishing lures, numerous angling techniques, and a myriad of fishing styles exist; however, there are only so many places inhabited by your favorite fish.

We hope each chapter's boxed notes, game fish ratings, and map give you important additional information. Although we rate quality of fishing in each chapter, assessing a lake is somewhat subjective. We primarily base our judgment on a fish's population, but if the average size of a fish in a particular species increases its appeal on a given lake (even if there isn't an abundance of fish), we recognize its importance. Our ratings are also based on the opinions of local expert anglers and guides, and on the opinions and research of TWRA fishery biologists. Each featured fish is rated on a scale from one to five (five being the best) and indicated by fish symbols. Our omission of a particular species from the ratings list does not necessarily indicate poor angling, but inclusion of a species does indicate that we find it more worthy of pursuit.

How to obtain maps is included in the book's appendices, along with telephone numbers of local guides, a list of family fishing lakes operated by the Tennessee Wildlife Resources Agency, descriptions of various rigging styles, and telephone numbers where anglers can obtain daily lake news. We also include a glossary of fishing terms.

Finally, *The Compleat Tennessee Angler* gives novice fishermen a strong starting position on the water, but it can also make accomplished fishermen much better. Remember, however, that this book—heavy with experience and full of ideas—cannot hook, fight, or net fish for you. It takes time for anyone to acquire skills. That means you must, and should, fish often.

We selected the word *Compleat* for the book title for its literal meaning and as a play on words. *Compleat* describes someone with highly skilled abilities. It also evokes the word *complete*, which means something done in its entirety. We believe we have written a *complete* fishing book based on the advice of *compleat* anglers.

We wish you the best of luck and hope that one day we can come calling on you when we write this book's sequel and seek your advice as a *compleat* angler.

—Vern and Doug

PART I
West Tennessee

CHAPTER 1

Reelfoot Lake

Mother Nature's Incredible
Earthquake Lake

When a major earthquake along the New Madrid Fault shook Tennessee late in the fall of 1811, the state's northwestern region suffered considerable damage. The land buckled, and the Mississippi River, mighty as it was, actually flowed backward. At the time no one could have foreseen that Mother Nature's act of violence would one day make many inhabitants of this area financially dependent on crappie, bluegill, bass, and a unique gathering of wildlife that includes the American bald eagle. But that is exactly what happened. History is full of ironies, and Reelfoot Lake is one of them.

As the Mississippi reeled from the earthquake, its waters poured into an abyss where a cypress forest had stood. The resulting lake, Reelfoot, has never been deep, and it has steadily become shallower since its turbulent birth. Despite the silt that has settled into it over the years, Tennessee's only large natural impoundment continues to provide some of the best fishing in the South.

Reelfoot is a series of shallow basins, the largest of which are Upper Blue Basin, Buck Basin, and Lower Blue Basin. The lake has abundant cover; stumps, logs, live cypress, and vegetation—lily pads, grass, moss, and numerous other aquatic plants—are everywhere. The lake's shallowest water, averaging only a few feet in depth, is in Upper Blue Basin; the deepest is in Lower Blue Basin, where the bottom reaches 18 to 20 feet. Buck Basin, located between the Upper and Lower Blue Basins, is also shallow.

Unlike most Tennessee lakes where game fish often suspend

GAME FISH RATINGS

Largemouth Bass	🐟🐟🐟🐟
Crappie	🐟🐟🐟🐟🐟
Bluegill	🐟🐟🐟🐟🐟

around river or creek channels and drop-offs, Reelfoot has few of these features. It is primarily fed by rain, springs, and an occasional gush from the Mississippi River flood waters. Though unlike other Tennessee lakes, Reelfoot's fish must still spawn and eat. Thus, finding fish requires locating appropriate cover, which might seem like a difficult task with so many places to look. That task, however, is made easier with help from a top Reelfoot guide and from a world champion crappie angler.

LARGEMOUTH BASS

Guide Billy Blakley counts television angler Bill Dance as both a friend and an occasional fishing partner. While Blakley primarily fishes Reelfoot Lake, Dance has tested countless bass waters. Blakley knows that Reelfoot is an excellent largemouth bass lake, but has few lakes with which to compare it. On the other hand, Dance has many, and Blakely says, "I've heard him say that Reelfoot is one of his favorite places."

Blakley began fishing Reelfoot as a kid and began guiding as a youngster. He has many years of largemouth experience—enough expertise, in fact, to gain the confidence of America's most famous angler.

REELFOOT AT A GLANCE

Location:	Lake and Obion Counties
Size:	15,500 acres
Length:	12 miles
Shoreline:	Not available
Normal pool:	282 feet
Featured species:	Largemouth Bass, Black Crappie, White Crappie, Bluegill
Other species:	Yellow Bass, Hybrid (Cherokee Bass), Channel Catfish, Flathead Catfish
Description:	Tennessee's only large natural lake, much of Reelfoot resembles a wetland. The lake bottom is mucky from years of siltation. Stumps, live cypress, and aquatic vegetation are abundant, especially lily pads.
Main tributary:	Bayou Du Chien
Landmarks:	Reelfoot is situated near the Lake County seat of Tiptonville. Nearby routes include TN 22, 21, and 78. The closest interstates are I-40 and I-155.

See Appendix C for map information

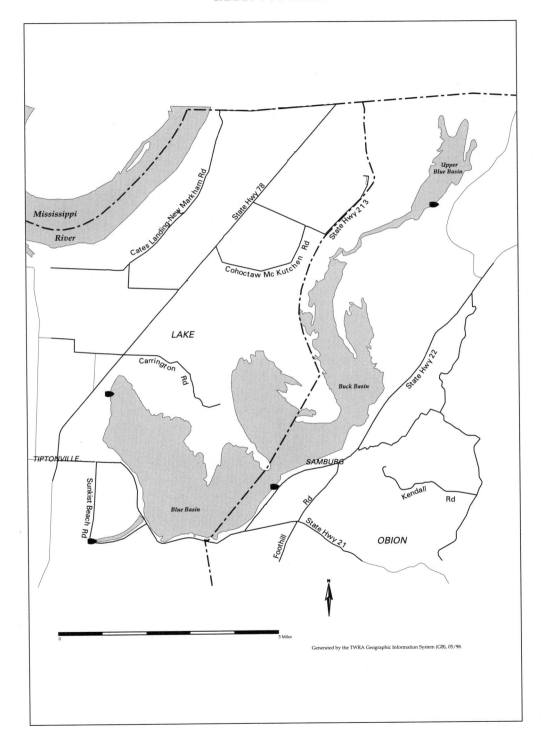

Generated by the TWRA Geographic Information System (GB), 05/98.

Guide Billy Blakely is among anglers who realize what an excellent largemouth lake Reelfoot is. He has learned that only a few lures are needed to help him catch big fish throughout the year.

Winter

Cold-weather fishing begins for Blakley in mid-February when he tosses jerk-baits, spinnerbaits, and spoons. He spends most of his time in the shallow Upper Blue Basin, where the water heats up quickly on sunny days and during warm fronts. Shallow water and lily roots provide his best fishing spots. "When it's cloudy, I'll usually throw a spinnerbait because of the flash, but if it's sunny, I'll go with a jerkbait," says Blakley.

Blakley's favorite jerkbait is a Rattlin' Rogue Shallow Diver with green sides, black back, and orange underbelly. "I make sure the ripples clear away from the lure before I start retrieving," explains Blakley. "Then I jerk it back to the boat." When not tossing a Rogue, he favors a 3/8-ounce white spinnerbait made by Strike King.

Blakley fishes alongside lily roots that in winter are minus their big leaves. "I fish around roots that are anywhere from the size of someone's leg to the size of a living room if a bunch of them are wadded together," notes Blakley, who uses baitcasting gear and 14-pound-test monofilament this time of year. Shallow water is the most important feature to locating winter bass, emphasizes the guide.

Johnson Silver Minnows are among Blakley's favorite winter lures. He threads his spoons with a white twin-tailed plastic grub. "I fish this 9 or 10 inches under the surface and give it a steady retrieve," says the guide. Fishing early is not necessary. Blakley has his best luck on most days throughout the year between 10 A.M. and 2 P.M.

Spring

As spring approaches, Blakley moves out of Upper Blue Basin and into Buck Basin, where the average water depth is deeper and where he finds large-mouth suspending 4 to 5 feet above stumps. "This is when I catch big fish while other people catch little ones," says Blakley. "Most fishermen stay in shallow water and go after numbers instead of size. I fish deeper stumps that get overlooked because I know that's where the big sows are. I catch bass that weigh 5 pounds and more."

Blakley catches many fish with spinnerbaits that he retrieves over stumps, but 7½-inch black- and blue-plastic worms are his favorite early spring bait. "I like laying my worm right in the middle of their eggs," says Blakley, who increases his line strength to 17-pound test and fishes worms Texas style on a 3/0 hook tied below a ¼-ounce sinker. Reelfoot has countless stumps and Blakley covers them quickly.

After the spawn, which usually occurs from mid-April to mid-May, Blakley fishes 6 to 7 feet deep alongside living cypress. This is when he catches his biggest bass, even larger on average than spawning sows.

Blakley has his best success with a pig and jig combination, particularly a black and blue Rattlin' Bootlegger Jig. "Most of the time I'll let the jig hit the bottom beside a tree, then jerk it up fast and let it fall," he explains. "Some-times I'll bounce it across the bottom, just barely moving it. I find out what the fish want and then I give it to them."

Reelfoot bass don't often reach 8 pounds, but many do exceed 5 pounds, says Blakley. Mid-April to mid-May is when Blakley catches his best fish, including 7- to 7½-pound largemouth. Because fish are big and cover is dense, Blakley uses 25-pound-test monofilament this time of year.

Summer and Fall

Brook silverside (better known by anglers as pin minnows) spawn on top of lily pads in June, making this a perfect time to pull buzzbaits, spoons, or plas-tic frogs over the pads, or to work spinnerbaits around them. Solid white is Blakley's favorite lure color. He even threads white twin-tailed grubs on his spoons. Pin minnows are tiny and Blakley matches the hatch by tossing small lures. He catches many hungry bass at about 3 feet deep.

Largemouth feed aggressively by July. "I fish around grass this time of year, especially grassy points," says Blakley. "I cast a ¼-ounce white spinner-bait, but I also use black- and blue-plastic worms on a Texas rig." When sum-mer gets hot, Blakley stays in the Lower Blue Basin and catches bass as shallow as 2 feet.

Blakely says that August is an excellent month to fish "what we call moss seeds." "The wind blows these seeds against banks and shad get under them for shade," says the guide. "Largemouth get under them for shad. I make sure to fish moss seeds, especially when I see them in the mouths of ditches."

Blakley's favorite summer lures are either silver spoons with white grubs, or white plastic frogs. He uses 14-pound-test monofilament on a baitcasting outfit to toss light lures.

In July, August, and "for the remainder of the year," Blakley often fishes next to protruding logs. "When I fish a log, I cast toward its lower end and retrieve toward the upper end," he says. "I fish parallel to it."

In September and until he starts hunting in October, Blakley fishes logs, lily pads, stumps, and live cypress. "This is when I catch bass all over the lake," he says. Largemouth become more aggressive as the water temperature cools and "Reelfoot Lake gets real exciting."

CRAPPIE

Ronnie Capps is a world champion crappie angler and one of America's best tournament fishermen. He and partner Steve Coleman won the 1995 Crappie-thon Classic held in Missouri; two years later, they won the same tournament in Ohio under its new ownership name, Crappie USA. Much of what Capps knows about crappie angling he learned from his great grandfather, who adored Reelfoot Lake.

Whether anglers duplicate Capp's favorite crappie technique or modify it, he assures that it will catch fish anywhere most any time of the year.

"This technique works perfect on structure lakes like Reelfoot," says Capps. "My partner and I have been all over the United States and have won tournaments in Florida, Michigan, South Carolina, and Oklahoma using the same technique. We have caught crappie using it as shallow as 4 feet on Reelfoot Lake and as deep as 65 feet on Percy Priest Reservoir."

Probably no one knows for sure where this technique developed, but the rig that helps make Capps and Coleman successful requires a three-way swivel, two hooks, one sinker, and—on Reelfoot Lake—minnows about 2½ inches long.

Tennessee River anglers call this setup—or one similar to it—the Kentucky Lake Double-Hook Bottom Bumping rig, but in northwest Tennessee, fishermen refer to it as the Reelfoot Lake rig. (*The Compleat Tennessee Angler* refers to it simply as the Reelfoot rig in this chapter.)

Important in this setup are 12-foot graphite rods, rod holders, small reels, and a trolling motor.

Reelfoot Lake is a stump-infested impoundment that damages boats navigated clumsily, but fishing vessels of all sizes operate efficiently here if carefully handled. Many Reelfoot anglers use johnboats, but Capps and Coleman prefer a modern fiberglass boat.

Capps and Coleman troll slowly and use wind as an ally. "Sometimes we move less than 1 mile per hour, but we make sure to have forward move-

Learning to slowly troll a minnow or a jig on the "Reelfoot Rig" has made Ronnie Capps (left) one of the top tournament crappie anglers in America.

ment," says Capps. He and Coleman achieve better control over their path of movement by pointing their boat upwind.

They also sit abreast in the boat's bow behind a rack of rod holders. On Reelfoot, they each use three 12-foot graphite rods that spread their bait presentation almost in a semicircle from port to stern. The rod length places bait far enough ahead of their vessel that fish aren't spooked by its approach.

Both anglers use B 'n' M poles because "they're real sensitive," says Capps. All six poles rest in rod holders. "I don't touch a pole until I get a hit or start to get hung up," notes Capps. "I watch line movement. It gets pretty easy after a while to tell the difference between strikes and stumps."

Capps remembers when Reelfoot anglers twisted line around the tips of cane poles, untwisting whatever length they needed to fish the Reelfoot rig. Nowadays, Reelfoot anglers use spinning or closed-face reels on graphite rods. Capps and Coleman favor closed-face Johnson reels spooled with 8-pound-test monofilament.

The Reelfoot rig consists of a three-way swivel (No. 6 or 8 swivels work well) with two leaders. The most vertical of these lines is approximately 28 inches long with an egg sinker (⅜-ounce to ½-ounce, depending on the wind) looped 16 inches below the swivel and a wire hook tied 12 inches below the weight.

The other leader is tied to the remaining swivel ring. Capps uses No. 2 Eagle Claw wire hooks (214EL), which he says are sharp and strong but bend easily when snagged. Many Reelfoot rig fishermen tie both hooks above the sinker; however, Capps believes that minnows move more freely below it.

Minnow color is important. Capps buys 2½-inch pink tuffy minnows (which actually have an orange hue) when the lake is clear, and he purchases darkly colored shiners when it's murky. He hooks his minnows through the mouth.

Winter

Lower Blue Basin is Reelfoot's deepest area and is where Capps and Coleman spend most of their time throughout the year, including winter. Crappie inhabit all of Reelfoot, but Capps believes the largest fish reside in Lower Blue. He notes that black crappie are the predominant crappie species in Upper Blue Basin's shallow water, while white crappie are more numerous in the deeper lower basin.

Regardless of where they fish—in deep or shallow water—the two anglers troll and make whatever adjustments are necessary in their rig for a perfect bait presentation. In winter they fish deep water, at least deep for Reelfoot. "We find water that is about 15 feet deep, drop our lines to the bottom, and then give them two or three cranks," says Capps. "We start fishing in January and fish this winter method until late March."

Terrain surrounding Reelfoot Lake is flat and exposes anglers to cold, harsh winds. Because of the wind, Capps only fishes on calm days. "Crappie are also very sensitive to the temperature, which is something I'm always mindful of," notes Capps. "By around noon or one o'clock, the fish move up—not in toward the bank—but up vertically. They suspend 4 to 5 feet in the same area. I've caught crappie only a few feet deep when the lake was calm and the water temperature barely above freezing."

Good winter places to catch crappie are near Caney Island and around nearby Green Island, says Capps. "Spain's Point off of Green Island is always a good place," he adds. "Wherever I fish, I work vertically and keep the boat moving. I always cover new water."

Spring

When water temperature reaches the mid-50s, usually by late March or early April, crappie move closer to the shoreline, but not right on it—and sometimes not even really close to it. "I won't catch a 1½-pound crappie in the bushes on Reelfoot, like I sometimes do on Kentucky Lake," notes Capps. "I might catch small crappie, but I never fish Lower Blue Basin any shallower than 5 feet deep."

Capps and Coleman are often 500 to 600 yards away from the shoreline when they find distinct drops in the lake bottom that range from 5 to 7½ feet in a short distance. "I know a few places with hard sand bottoms that must warm up more quickly than other places because fish move to them first in early spring," says Capps.

Many crappie never migrate out of Reelfoot's deep water, notes Capps, but move vertically to spawn on stumps a few feet beneath the surface. "I won two Reelfoot tournaments in 1996 fishing 6 feet deep but in 15 feet of water," recalls Capps.

Swan Basin and Grooms Pocket are among the Lower Blue Basin sites that Capps touts as good areas for spring crappie. Although shallower and clearer, Upper Blue Basin and Buck Basin also have numerous crappie.

"I shorten my rig when fishing the shallow basins," notes Capps, who says that the average large black crappie for him weighs about 1 pound and the average white crappie is between 1¼ and 1¾ pounds. "Lots of white crappie are taken from Upper Blue, but mostly black crappie come out of Buck Basin."

Summer

Fishing activity slows down after the spawn, especially as air and water temperatures rise and oxygen problems occur. "Thermocline can get pretty bad on Reelfoot and the lake turns over quite a bit," explains Capps. "I fish either at sunrise or at sunset in the summer. I fish shallow over deep water. This time of year I sometimes have fish hit my top hook, and as soon as they do, they'll come out of the water because they're suspending very shallow. They also suspend so close to cover that I occasionally get snagged when I try to set the hook." Capps always fishes the shady sides of cover.

Fall

Between late September and mid-October—around the first frost—thousands of gizzard shad become visible near the shoreline, says Capps. "Shad move toward the bank, and we begin catching crappie in fairly shallow water," he says. "This movement by crappie is similar to the one they make in the spring, but the crappie are moving for a different reason. They're looking for food and warm water rather than for nesting sites. This is when we have our best fishing in terms of numbers."

Fall crappie are minus their heavy spawning sacks and are lighter than spring fish, but many still weigh at least a pound, says Capps. Keystone Pocket and Champney Pocket are excellent places to catch fall crappie in Lower Blue Basin. "We call this area 'the bar' because it has a long stretch that is a consistent 6 feet deep," explains Capps. Swan Basin, east of Keystone and Champney Pockets, also attracts concentrations of shad in water 5 to 7½ feet deep, he says.

Capps drops his Reelfoot rig to the bottom and gives it two or three cranks. "I fish around the biggest bunch of shad I can find because I know crappie are underneath them," he says. "Fish don't jerk the pole out of my hands in the fall, but I catch a bunch of them, and it's a lot of fun."

Reelfoot lily pads are among the good bluegill habitat during certain times of the year. When searching for Reelfoot's large bluegill, look for bubbles to help find beds. Once located, use crickets, worms, or tiny lures (such as the Grizzly jig) to catch them.

BLUEGILL

Guide Billy Blakley lives to catch largemouth bass, but he is among numerous anglers who always find time to catch Reelfoot's hard-fighting bluegill, which the lake is famous for having in large sizes and numbers.

Spring

Blakley begins catching bluegill in mid-March by fishing alongside Reelfoot Lake's "old bonnet stems," which are roots from the previous year's lily pads. "These are scattered all over the lake," he says.

A tiny feather lure is his favorite artificial bait. "It's called a Grizzly Jig," says Blakley, whose favorite colors include a pink leadhead jig with black and blue feathers and a white leadhead jig with black feathers. "If there is a bluegill anywhere around, I guarantee it will hit this lure."

Blakley fishes a ⅟₈₀-ounce Grizzly Jig on a 9-foot fly rod that is sensitive and helps him quickly feel strikes. He uses a small spinning reel and spools it with 4-pound-test monofilament. He places one BB-sized splitshot 3 inches above the lure and tightlines about 2 feet deep around lily roots, only moving his bait occasionally with a subtle shake. "I fish this way in March, April, and May until the bluegill begin to bed," notes Blakley.

Blakley also fishes beside cypress on calm days in early spring, using his trolling motor or paddle to move around them. "This is a way to pick up a few fish, maybe even as many as a dozen from a good tree," says the guide.

Bluegill have usually moved to their nesting sites by mid-May and bed "from 6 inches to 6 feet deep," says Blakley. "Using a long rod becomes real necessary if they're bedding shallow," notes the guide. "If I get too close to a bed with my boat, I know I'll spook the fish."

Blakley makes a couple of changes in his technique when he fishes deep. "I use crickets on No. 6 wire hooks instead of jigs, and I sometimes use a real small quill float," he explains. "When there's no wind, bluegill have a light bite and a small float helps with detection."

Beds vary in size, but Blakley locates many of them under logs or alongside hollow stumps. He moves often to find beds in this cover-rich lake. "Some of the logs I fish are in the same places year after year," he notes. "I've caught as many as 280 bluegill off a bed, but I usually leave long before I catch that many fish."

Blakley catches numerous bluegill between 10 and 14 ounces that are 8 to 9 inches long. The largest bluegill he ever caught weighed 1 pound 10 ounces. He loses quite a few hooks. "If I find a bed, I don't mess it up to save a hook," he says. "I bend my hooks several times before I start fishing so that they come out of snags a little easier, but I still lose hooks."

Bluegill inhabit all of Reelfoot Lake, but Blakley notes that Lower Blue Basin—because it's the deepest basin—frequently gets overlooked, especially by out-of-town anglers. "That's probably the most overlooked end of the lake," he says. "A bunch of beds are in that basin but they're harder to find."

Blakley locates many beds by scouting for them. Males sometimes advertise their beds by creating bubbles while they construct nests. "I find beds by watching for surface bubbles," says Blakley. "I ride around on calm days and look for them. Most of the time the bubbles cover an area about the size of a bathtub. I mark these with a stick and go back the next day."

Bluegill often bed through June. Blakley quits fishing for bedding fish by July 4. Spring is by far the best time to catch Reelfoot's bluegill, he says.

Summer and Fall

When the spawn is over, Blakley returns to live cypress and fishes a ⅟₈₀-ounce Grizzly Jig around them. He also fishes the edges of large moss patches that "are about the size of a living room."

"I work my jig the same way I do in the spring, just shaking the tip of my fly rod every now and then," says Blakley. "I fish this way all summer and into late September or early October when I quit fishing to go hunting."

CHAPTER 2

Kentucky Lake

(NORTHERN SECTION)

A Reservoir with Millions of Hungry Fish

One of America's longest running sportsman's programs—*The Tennessee Outdoorsmen*—filmed an extraordinary crappie episode on Kentucky Lake in June 1997. While the camera rolled, four anglers, fishing from two boats, fought one crappie after another. Many anglers don't realize that June is excellent for catching Kentucky Lake crappie, but as this segment of the *Outdoorsmen* proved, it's an ideal crappie-catching month. Had that particular *Outdoorsmen* been taped another time, the result likely would have been the same. While April is the best month to catch crappie around stumps, bushes, brush, limbs, and other visible shallow cover, it's just 1 month out of 12 when these fish bite.

Kentucky Lake is famous for crappie, but it's also known for largemouth, catfish, bluegill, shellcracker, and white bass. Smallmouth fishing is also good.

Great fishing lakes attract great anglers, and Kentucky Lake has its share of greatness. Among the experts are its fishing guides, a few of whom even have national fame. All of these men enjoy discussing their techniques developed by decades of angling experience.

GAME FISH RATINGS

Largemouth Bass	🐟 🐟 🐟 🐟
Smallmouth Bass	🐟 🐟 🐟
Crappie	🐟 🐟 🐟 🐟 🐟
Stripe (White Bass)	🐟 🐟 🐟
Shellcracker (Redear)	🐟 🐟 🐟 🐟
Sauger	🐟 🐟 🐟
Catfish	🐟 🐟 🐟 🐟
Bluegill	🐟 🐟 🐟 🐟

LARGEMOUTH BASS

Like most Kentucky Lake guides, Glen Stubblefield is a good crappie fisherman. He is better known, however, for his largemouth bass, smallmouth bass, and even catfish abilities. Stubblefield is a Kentucky Lake fishing dean. He has fished this run-of-the-river lake for nearly half a decade and has guided for the better part of that time.

Winter

When water temperature reaches 45°, usually in late February or early March, Stubblefield begins his fishing year. Although he doesn't catch numerous

KENTUCKY LAKE (NORTHERN SECTION) AT A GLANCE

Location:	Stewart, Benton, Humphreys, and Houston Counties
Size:	108,277 acres (entire reservoir)
Length:	157.6 miles (entire reservoir)
Shoreline:	1,970 miles (entire reservoir)
Summer pool:	375 feet
Winter pool:	354 feet
Impounded:	1944
Featured species:	Largemouth Bass, Smallmouth Bass, Crappie, Stripe (White Bass), Sauger, Catfish, Shellcracker (Redear), Bluegill
Other species:	Yellow Bass, Spotted (Kentucky) Bass, Striper, Hybrid (Cherokee Bass)
Description:	Run-of-the-river lake with clay and gravel on much of the river bottom. The lake widens in its northern half where the Big Sandy River has a large presence. The backs of bays and inlets on the west side and in the Big Sandy River have muck bottoms from years of silty runoff. Limestone and chert are also present in parts of the lake. The east side is fed by cool, clear streams and has rocky banks. Tree stumps are present in parts of the reservoir.
Main tributaries:	Tennessee River, Big Sandy River, West Sandy Creek, Eagle Creek, Little Eagle Creek, Swamp Creek, Lost Creek, Standing Rock Creek, Leatherwood Creek, Hurricane Creek, Cane Creek, Whiteoak Creek, Turkey Creek, Big Richland Creek, Trace Creek, Beaverdam Creek
Landmarks:	Kentucky Lake runs almost the entire vertical length of Tennessee from Pickwick Dam, near the Alabama state line, north beyond the Kentucky border. Cities near the lake's northern section include Camden, Waverly, Erin, and Dover. Nearby state routes include 76, 232, 147, 20, and 50. The closest interstates are I-40 and I-24.
Operated by:	Tennessee Valley Authority

See Appendix C for map information

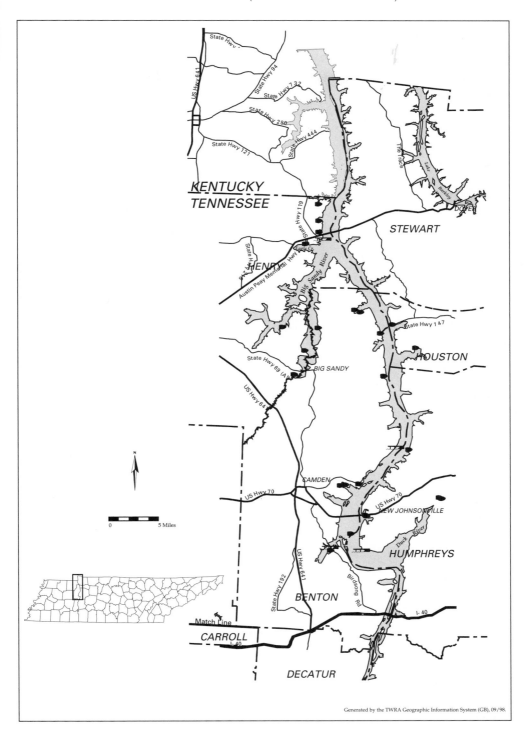

winter bass, Stubblefield does land his biggest largemouth when it's cold outside. Perhaps surprisingly, he catches most bass in shallow water with crankbaits. "The best lure that I use for big fish is a No. 8 Shad Rap which I pull across gravel humps or high spots where there isn't cover," says Stubblefield. "I catch fish that are only 3 or 4 feet deep."

Main lake points near the mouths of creeks are where Stubblefield primarily fishes in winter. Because water levels are low this time of year, these points are shallow. Topography maps reveal some humps or rises, but only time spent fishing will reveal the majority of them.

An 18-mile stretch between the US 79 bridge (Ned McWherter Bridge) in Tennessee and the US 68 bridge in Kentucky is where Stubblefield spends winter. Lost, Piney, Hughes, Byrd, Tischel, and Clay are among the creeks he fishes. "Every one of these will have at least some of the humps or high spots that I like to fish," he says.

Stubblefield casts crankbaits on a 7½-foot spinning rod using 8-pound-test monofilament. "When my lure hits the bottom, I'll pull it 3 or 4 feet by moving the rod tip," explains the guide. "Then I'll take up the slack so that I can feel what's going on. I call this hand-feeding them."

Stubblefield tosses pearl- or shad-colored crankbaits, but he especially likes lures with silver sides and black backs. Shad Raps are his favorite winter plugs, but he also throws Poes 300 series or Fat Free Shads in the Excalibur series. Finding humps or high spots is more important in late winter than actually locating shad, notes Stubblefield.

"Most of the bass I catch are between 4 and 9 pounds," he says. "Some people insist on throwing jigs this time of year, but I'll catch five bass to their one by using crankbaits."

Spring

When water temperature warms to the mid-50s, largemouth begin migrating toward bays to spawn. "I follow them into the bays and eventually all the way to the back of them," says Stubblefield, who fishes secondary points in early spring with plastic worms and spinnerbaits.

His favorite lure becomes a ⅜-ounce tandem spinnerbait with a small Colorado blade above a large willowleaf blade. He throws copper blades on cloudy days and silver blades in sunshine. "There are only two spinnerbait colors as far as I'm concerned, and they are chartreuse and white, and solid white," says Stubblefield.

When largemouth reach their spawning sites, Stubblefield switches baits. "It takes them about two weeks to get back to where they spawn," he notes. "Once they get there, I move real slow so that I don't spook them."

Stubblefield flips or pitches around structure with plastic lizards or jig and pig combinations. Sometimes he entices strikes with a topwater lure. "The best topwater bait I use for bedding bass is a No. 11 gold Rapala," says the guide, who uses a baitcasting reel spooled with 10-pound-test monofilament when tossing light lures. Because bass are shallow, he often sees them before casting. "I lob the lure lightly and then start twitching it," says Stubblefield.

Inexperienced anglers often situate their boats over suspending bass when Kentucky Lake rises. Many anglers mistakenly think bass move closer to the new shoreline, says Stubblefield. "I have some of my best days when the water is high," says the guide. "I have caught 30 and 40 fish when the water was in the trees, but I was fishing the same places that I always fish because the bass didn't move."

Kentucky Lake largemouth don't stay around bedding sites long. Stubblefield has an advantage over other anglers who don't realize this. "Most fishermen keep fishing in the backs of bays about two weeks longer than they should," he explains. "Once the fish spawn, most of them move back out to the main channel points where they spent the winter. That's where I go, too."

Smaller bass continue hitting around shorelines, but when big fish quit biting, Stubblefield leaves the banks. "It takes big bass about two weeks to get to spawning sites, but it only takes them about two days to work back out to the humps and high spots."

When largemouth suspend around humps, usually by early May, Stubblefield either fishes a Carolina rig with a plastic lizard or tosses deep-diving crankbaits. He slowly retrieves the Carolina rig with a 7-foot rod and a baitcasting reel spooled with 14-pound-test monofilament. He places a ¾-ounce weight 30 inches above a 3/0 hook with an offset bend in it.

Numerous good plastic lizards exist in the angling market, but Stubblefield prefers Zoom lizards. Watermelon, pumpkin, chartreuse, and junebug are his favorite colors.

Water levels are normally higher in late spring than in winter. Stubblefield fishes the same areas where he catches winter bass, but fishes several feet deeper. "It's still not necessary to locate baitfish, but the bass are feeding," he says. "This is a fun time to fish because largemouth gather on these high places, and I catch 10 or 15 of them off one spot."

Crankbaits work well on main points pulled across gravel. Stubblefield throws DB3s, Fat Free Shads, and Poes 400 series lures. His favorite color consists of chartreuse in combination with blue and black, but he also likes lures with gray sides and blue or green backs.

"What I'm doing is imitating shad that have grown 2 or 3 inches since they hatched," he says. When tossing crankbaits this time of year, Stubblefield uses a 7½-foot rod and a baitcasting reel with a 4:1 gear ratio. This allows him to wind quickly, but still retrieve his bait at a moderate pace. He doesn't have to worry about cranking speed. "I catch 90% of my largemouth right off the top of humps this time of year," says Stubblefield.

Summer

Humps hold fish in summer, but these humps are out in the channel and a long way from the creek mouths where Stubblefield has success earlier in the year. He continues fishing the 18-mile stretch of river between US 79 in Tennessee and US 68 in Kentucky. Stubblefield prefers this area because he finds more gravel there. He notes, however, that humps are few and far between.

Stubblefield begins looking for largemouth 10 feet deep and throws crankbaits capable of probing 12 to 14 feet. He also uses a Texas rig to fish 12-inch worms. "My favorite worm colors are tequila sunrise and red shad," says Stubblefield. "The fishing is slow, and I may fish all day for only two or three strikes, but the bass weigh from 3 pounds up." His Texas rig consists of ⅜-ounce sinkers and 5/0 Gamakatsu hooks. Stubblefield fishes "real slow" around cover or structure.

Occasionally Stubblefield travels into Big Sandy River; however, he spends most of his time fishing the Tennessee River, where he believes the biggest and most numerous largemouth reside. Whether bass, catfish, or crappie, Stubblefield patterns the fish's movements. "About the only time I fish for largemouth around a bank is that brief period in spring during the spawning run," he notes.

Fall

As water temperature cools, Stubblefield looks for surface activity. Largemouth sometimes feed aggressively in shallow water. Locating baitfish is important, whether on the surface or not far below it. "Fish under shad," he says. "I mostly fish the mouths of creeks and in the main lake, but I'm looking for drop-offs and cover in fairly shallow water. The drop-offs might only step down 3 or 4 feet."

Spinnerbaits, topwater baits, and plastic lizards are among lures that catch fall bass. Stubblefield stays north of US 79 this time of year. Stumps line the Tennessee River here, especially on its west side. They become visible when the water falls, and Stubblefield catches many bass around them until his fishing year ends in October. "That's when I start hunting," he explains.

SMALLMOUTH BASS

Largemouth are the most predominant bass in Kentucky Lake, but good populations of smallmouth inhabit the reservoir, too, especially along the lake's east bank and in bays where cool streams enter it. Glen Stubblefield is an excellent smallmouth bass angler, and, although known best for catching crappie, guide Steve McCadams is, too.

Winter

Smallmouth bite year-round, and winter sometimes provides great fishing for patient anglers. Live bait—either shiners or tuffy minnows—attract smallmouth hits in creeks. Chunk rock, old shoals, ledges, gravel bars, and other deep cover hold fish. "Casting light tackle with small grubs or spinners fished slowly along main channel points also works well," notes McCadams. "A slow retrieve is always best in winter."

Spring

In March and early April, smallmouth stage near rocky secondary points inside bays, notes McCadams. Riprap, shallow gravel points, and large chunk provide good habitat. "I would say that 95% or more of smallmouth caught in Kentucky Lake are taken from its east side," he says. Whiteoak, Hurricane, Leatherwood, Standing Rock, Panther, Hughes, and Byrd are among creeks that feed Kentucky Lake with cool water suitable for smallmouth.

Glenn Stubblefield knows that the northern half of Kentucky Lake holds many smallmouth, and he has learned when and where to catch them with spinnerbaits.

"I start a day by fishing deep bars next to creek channels, with twister-tail grubs on light leadhead jigs," says McCadams. "I parallel the ledge of a channel or secondary channel and try to cover a lot of water by fan casting. I make four or five casts on top of the ledge, four or five casts on the break, and four or five casts on its deep side. Then I move 30 yards and start over, watching my depth finder to make sure I stay parallel to the ledge. I cover a lot of water to find smallmouth either in their pre- or postspawn modes, but once I catch one fish there are usually others with it."

Smallmouth anglers should search for humps or any other irregular structure, says McCadams, who stresses the importance of sonar and an ability to read topographic maps. Crawfish-colored crankbaits are good spring lures. So are 3- and 4-inch plastic grubs and worms. Rebel Crawfish and Charlie Brewer Slider worms are among the artificial baits that catch smallmouth.

Smallmouth don't go far after the spawn. Anglers should continue fishing the same creeks and bays around old shoals and rocks. "I work the upper ends of feeder creeks, especially when lake levels are high," says McCadams.

Summer and Fall

Creeks and bays on the lake's east side are always the best place to catch day-time smallmouth, either early in the morning or late in the evening, once summer arrives. Guide Glen Stubblefield fishes the east bank, but for him the best smallmouth action occurs after sunset.

"Once other fishermen figure out how to catch them, they'll know Kentucky Lake is full of smallmouth," he says. "They're hard to catch during the day, but at night I can usually call the shots on where I'll get strikes. I catch smallmouth and spotted bass in the day, but I'm usually fishing for largemouth. At night I fish for smallmouth because I've patterned their movements."

Stubblefield fishes for nocturnal smallies from mid-June through mid-October. Smallmouth move shallow after dark and feed around chunk rock. Stubblefield mainly works rocky shorelines and points near creek mouths. "I'll see the rock that attracts fish," he says. "It's fairly big and spills from the bank into the lake. I roll a spinnerbait over the rocks slow enough to touch the bottom."

Smallmouth are usually feeding 2 to 3 feet deep, says Stubblefield, who situates his boat in water about 10 feet deep and throws to the shoreline. "I use 6½-foot rods and baitcasting reels," he says. "I usually tie on two different spinnerbaits. I'll put a short-armed spinnerbait on one rod and a long-armed spinnerbait on the other. When the fish are a little finicky, I catch them better with the longer arm."

Stubblefield tosses ⅜-ounce spinnerbaits with red and black skirts and single No. 5 Colorado blades. He attaches No. 11 pork rind to it. Black marabou flies with rind also catch smallmouth, he notes.

Good fishing begins immediately after dark. Stubblefield often stays out until sunrise, ending his trip where be began. "I catch lots of fish doing this," he says. "We [Stubblefield and a partner] hung 32 bass on our best night in 1997 and 7 on our worst night. I have caught quite a few 5- and 6-pound smallmouth."

Some anglers disdain a full moon. Stubblefield welcomes it. "I think it actually helps increase my success," he says.

CRAPPIE

Who better to ask about Kentucky Lake crappie fishing than two anglers who have guided there for decades and who, as a team, were crowned the world's best crappie fishermen in 1996 when they won the Crappiethon Classic, the championship event of the Crappiethon Tournament Trail?

Steve McCadams and Jim Perry already had national reputations as top-notch anglers before they won their impressive title, but they heightened that reputation shortly after their victory by joining with other anglers to purchase the very tournament trail from which they won their championship.

Kentucky Lake crappie bite year-round provided you know how and where to catch them. Guides and championship anglers Jim Perry (left) and Steve McCadams (far right and inset) know exactly where they are.

Now the owners of Crappie USA and American Crappie Association (formerly Crappiethon), McCadams and Perry spend many hours educating anglers about crappie fishing, including readers of this book.

Winter

Crappie fishing is excellent all over Kentucky Lake, but McCadams and Perry usually fish within a 5-mile radius of Paris Landing State Park near the confluence of the Big Sandy and Tennessee Rivers. Catching crappie—lots of them at anytime of the year—is a matter of learning their favored habitats, both anglers say.

"A crappie's metabolism is different from that of a bass," explains McCadams. "A largemouth is hard to catch when the water temperature gets cold, but crappie hit when it's 33° and there's ice on your rod tips. They eat aggressively year-round."

McCadams and Perry fish deep in winter—at least deep for Kentucky Lake. From December through February, they catch many crappie between 18 and 25 feet in main river channels. Drop-offs, bars, humps, stumps, or other irregular features attract fish.

"We fish in places where crappie have the best of all worlds, where they can move but still have cover to suit their needs," explains McCadams. "We look for baitfish. A sandbar where the top is 10 feet deep and the bottom drops to 25 feet is ideal. Crappie suspend in the deep water because that's where baitfish school in winter."

McCadams and Perry use an old and famous jigging technique for catching winter crappie. Called the Kentucky Lake Double-Hook Bottom Bumping rig (Kentucky rig for short), this technique once helped anglers feel and identify structure that they could not see (see Appendix A). It consists of two hooks baited with minnows (or leadhead jigs with plastic tubes or grubs) tied 12 to 18 inches apart, with the lower hook tied 12 to 16 inches above a ¾- to 1-ounce sinker. The heavy weight, knocking against the bottom, is what helps anglers identify structure. The two hooks increase bait coverage.

Casting plastic baits on leadhead jigs also catches winter crappie. McCadams and Perry toss ⅛- to ¼-ounce jigs when fishing deep. Any number of small plastic baits catch crappie, including plastic grubs and tubes. Tackle boxes should have a variety of lure colors, including chartreuse combinations, says Perry, who retrieves his lure slowly in cold water.

Winter is an ideal time to distribute manmade crappie beds. McCadams and Perry have dropped scores of them at various depths, which helps them catch crappie moving from deep to shallow water and then back out again.

"Not all crappie move at the same time, and a lot of them will never even see a shoreline in spring," explains Perry. "They'll stay right out in the river and spawn on top of bars when the temperature gets right. In the last several years Steve and I have put quite a few beds out in fairly deep water, and we begin fishing these in March."

Crappie beds dropped on bars 12 to 15 feet deep attract migrating fish. "You can never have too many beds because of various factors, such as the wind, that impact fishing," notes Perry.

Stakebeds make good Kentucky Lake cover, adds Perry, who—as a former mussel diver—has inspected the reservoir's silty bottom. "I've seen brush piles that were covered with silt about a year after they were put out." Silt clings more to brush than to stakes, especially brush with leaves left intact.

Spring

As water temperature rises to the mid-50s, many crappie continue migrating toward shore, but McCadams and Perry don't wait for this movement. By this time they have caught numerous crappie from deep beds and natural cover. The first third of bays often have suspending fish in them when the water temperature hits the mid-50s, notes McCadams, who moves with the crappie as they stair-step to spawning sites.

"Crappie don't have an idea of what the date is," says McCadams. "Water temperature and water color are important to their movements. When water reaches the low 60s, usually in early April, fish start dropping eggs. When it gets between 62° and 66°, Kentucky Lake has a full-fledged spawn."

Water color often determines how close crappie get to banks. Kentucky Lake's bays and creeks—Big Sandy River, West Sandy River, and Eagle Creek among these—always have stain, but some years they are more turbid than others. "Crappie spawn shallow if the reservoir is dingy," says McCadams. Dingy water interferes with light penetration, which crappie need for egg incubation. If the reservoir is clear, crappie spawn a little deeper, he explains.

Crappie are caught on both the west and east banks of Kentucky Lake, but the west side is usually more stained and quicker to warm. "The average depth of Big Sandy River (on the lake's west side) is only 7 or 8 feet," says McCadams. Stumps and manmade crappie beds line Big Sandy and its tributaries.

Kentucky Lake was once known for its great buck bush fishing. Occasionally crappie still spawn in bushes, but not as often as decades ago. Many of the deeper bushes have rotted away, and the water doesn't often reach existing shoreline bushes before the major spawn. Manmade beds fill a void in areas once occupied by buck bushes, says Perry. While fishing guides and other crappie anglers don't advertise their beds, the state's wildlife agency has marked many fish attractors throughout Kentucky Lake.

Minnows fished below bobbers or on tightlines (a small sinker and a No. 1 or No. 2 hook is adequate for tightlining) catch countless bedding crappie, as do small plastic grubs or tubes. Among McCadams's favorite lure colors in dingy water are chartreuse and red or chartreuse and pink. Anglers should always include many different "live" or fluorescent colors in their tackle, he notes. Purple, motor oil, and other muted colors catch fish in clear water.

Light leadhead jigs—usually $\frac{1}{16}$-ounce—are ample weight for fishing shallow water unless the wind is strong. "I always maintain control of feel," explains Perry. "More weight helps me with feel when the water is rough."

Gravel banks and points are excellent places to catch males when water temperature increases and male crappie move ahead of females to spawning sites, notes Perry. "Fishing gravel bottoms or points is an especially good way to catch fish when the water is clear and crappie are easily spooked," he says.

McCadams and Perry often catch crappie fishing vertically. Perry chooses rods based on water clarity. The clearer it is, the longer the rod he uses to avoid sitting directly over holes and frightening crappie. His rod sizes range from 7 to 12 feet.

Perry lets the natural shake in his hands move his jig or minnow, while McCadams occasionally twitches his bait. Both anglers advise against excessive jigging. "That's a no-no in crappie fishing," says Perry. "I don't put my bait on a trampoline because it doesn't look like anything natural."

Rigging a jigging pole is simple. "When I use the Kentucky rig, I might have on any number of different line strengths, but when I use jigging poles, I normally have on 8-pound-test monofilament," notes Perry. "I always tie my jigs directly to the line with no swivels or snaps, and I fish as vertically as possible."

Summer

The first few days after most fish have spawned—usually by late April or early May—is the only time when Kentucky Lake crappie fishing is difficult for McCadams and Perry. They know that crappie migrate to deeper water, but the fish don't relate to structure, explains McCadams. By June, however, they are suspending alongside manmade structure, ledges, humps, stumps, and other lake-bottom features.

Fishing vertically over ledges 18 to 20 feet deep is a good way to catch fish by July, note the guides. Threadfin shad school at this depth. "Crappie like ledges in summer because there's a lot of food and deep water above and below them," says Perry, who fishes with McCadams on the down-current side of ledges. Crappie ambush baitfish and other food that washes past them.

Fall

Fall continues to be the most underrated time of year for catching crappie, says McCadams. Weather patterns are stable and water temperatures cool, which helps create comfortable and predictable angling. Many crappie move into bays as the water temperature cools. "Crappie follow baitfish into shallower water and stay close to cover," says McCadams. "Brush piles, stakebeds, or stumps are places where we find them."

Crappie usually inhabit Kentucky Lake's bays and creeks until November or December, when falling water temperature forces shad back to deep holes in main channels. Crappie follow the baitfish, and fishermen should, too.

STRIPE (WHITE BASS)

Guide Kenneth Bennett has fished Kentucky Lake since the early 1970s. Like so many other Kentucky Lake guides, he is a jack-of-all-angling-trades. One of his favorite species is white bass. Aggressive and strong, "stripe" often attack anything that remotely resembles baitfish. Other times, however, they are as selective as any Kentucky Lake fish. Weighing up to 2½ pounds, local anglers refer to big white bass as "blue tailers" because of the blue hue present in their tail fins.

Winter and Spring

Crankbaits, spoons, spinners, and plastic grubs—especially white or chartreuse—are excellent white bass baits fished below dams in cold weather. A Kentucky license is required, but fishermen who desire winter white bass action will find it near boils and the fast water just below Kentucky Dam.

For Bennett, good stripe fishing begins between late April and early May. "A short spawning run occurs about this time when stripe move into Big Sandy River," says Bennett. "If I get lucky and catch this run, it's extremely fun, and I catch big fish." Unfortunately, the run is short and unpredictable. "It's a day-to-day thing, sort of like fishing for crappie when they get into buck bushes," explains Bennett. "It happens, but it doesn't last long, and you have to be ready on short notice."

White bass often indicate their whereabouts by attacking shad on the surface. Occasionally, seagulls draw attention to stripe by diving for the same shad that the fish are chasing. White Rooster Tails, silver and blue Rat-L-Traps, and Pop-Rs are among the popular baits that white bass strike quickly. Matching the size of shad is important, Bennett notes.

Topwater fishing is especially fun, as Bennett learned a few years ago. "I was fishing a crankbait and got it hung up," he recalls. "I had a rod with a Pop-R already tied on, and I thought 'What the heck, I'll give it a

Schooling and surfacing white bass create great action on Kentucky Lake. Guide Kenneth Bennett especially likes catching "blue tailers."

try.' The stripe tore it up. I could let it sit there without any movement and get hits, but if I twitched it just a little bit, fish went crazy."

White Rooster Tails tantalize stripe. Bennett tosses ³⁄₁₆-ounce Rooster Tails in spring when shad are small. He increases the lure size as baitfish grow. Medium- or light-action rods and spinning reels spooled with 6- to 10-pound-test monofilament are ideal for white bass fishing.

Bennett often locates postspawn stripe around drop-offs in the main channel of the Tennessee River, especially when current is strong. He also finds them suspending over sandbars in Big Sandy River and in the mouths of Kentucky Lake's many creeks. "Where the creeks originally hit the Tennessee River before the lake was impounded is where I catch white bass," he says.

Bennett tosses crankbaits or spoons when stripe suspend deep. He often throws No. 9 Shad Raps and sometimes No. 7s. He also likes jigging spoons. His favorite jigging lure is a 1-ounce Hopkin's Spoon.

Even white bass are occasionally finicky. Bennett forgets about shad size at such moments and uses small baits. Sometimes he tosses clear lures. "A Tiny Torpedo is made in a clear color and is one of the topwater lures that I've had luck with," he says.

If white bass are difficult to find, Bennett starts riding and looking until he sees surface activity or locates fish with his sonar. "Every now and then I venture back into a creek when I can't find them in the usual places," he says.

Summer and Fall

Summer is the best time to catch Kentucky Lake's white bass, particularly July and August, says Bennett. White bass are abundant in or near the river channel close to US 79. They are extremely aggressive, says the guide, who fishes drop-offs and points where he finds schooling shad with his sonar. "July and August are when fishermen can plan a trip to Kentucky Lake knowing that they'll catch stripe," says Bennett.

White bass often surface, but not for long. "It takes practice, but I've learned to fish a Hopkin's Spoon on the surface," says Bennett. "If the fish come up while I'm jigging, I'll throw it instead. I also have several rods with other lures tied on to catch them while they're up." Short surface-feeding sprees are common, he notes.

Good white bass fishing sometimes extends into September. After that, stripe are more difficult to locate and usually smaller. Bennett believes anglers have removed many large fish by that time of year.

SAUGER

The northern section of Kentucky Lake may not be worth a long trip specifically for sauger, but they do inhabit the area. Tennessee resident Sherman Hale has spent many days since 1973 trolling this area for them. He has witnessed good sauger years and bad ones.

Through the Seasons

Sauger are found below many dams in winter, including Kentucky Dam. They are also caught on various jigs and plastic baits in main river channels, on drop-offs, and in the mouths of creeks. Consult chapters on Kentucky, Barkley, Cheatham, Ft. Loudon/Tellico, and Douglas Lakes for winter sauger techniques.

Beginning in May, Hale catches sauger near the confluence of the Tennessee and Big Sandy Rivers. He catches most of them while trolling near US 79 and Paris Landing State Park. "Years ago I started catching sauger in the spring, and people would tell me I'd better enjoy it while I could because sauger disappear when summer arrives, but I have always caught them in summer and fall."

Trolling for sauger is a leisurely pursuit that Hale begins in May. He spends the first part of a day fishing for other species, pursuing whatever is biting best. He spends the second half of a trip trolling over flats or around the old banks of the Tennessee River before the impoundment submerged them. Any number of deep-diving crankbaits catch sauger, but Hale mentions Wiggle Warts and Rapalas as good choices. He is not particular about color.

In the summer, he trolls around the main river channel, making sure to pull his lures near ledges and other drop-offs. Hale trolls upriver, downriver, and even "crossways."

CATFISH

Guide Glen Stubblefield patterns the movements of all his targeted fish, including catfish. Although he catches a few channels and an occasional flathead, blue catfish are his predominant catch. Many of his catfish top 10 pounds.

While numerous catfish anglers use cut bait, chicken liver, stink baits, or worms for bait, Stubblefield primarily relies on tuffy minnows to attract big cats,

A good time to catch large Kentucky Lake catfish is the middle of the summer. Guide Glenn Stubblefield uses a tuffy minnow on a simple rig to attract big cats on hot, sizzling days.

including a 61-pound blue catfish that he caught a few years ago.

Spring, Summer, and Fall

Late spring to early summer is when catfish become easy to pattern and when Stubblefield begins fishing for them. Before then, they are scattered on flats—in areas that were crop fields before the TVA impounded Kentucky Lake. The fishing is slow, but cats can be caught in the flats by patient anglers fishing the bottom.

When the surface temperature reaches 80° to 85°, catfish move off flats into cooler, deeper water around the Tennessee River's original banks. By July they are usually 30 to 35 feet deep. "When they go to the river bank, I can catch 30 or 40 pounds of fish from one hole," says Stubblefield.

Bottom structure is crucial for catfish success. "A lot of people don't realize how structure-oriented catfish can be," says Stubblefield. "They like to hang around stumps and other structure that was in the river before TVA impounded it."

Stubblefield often fishes creeks where a tributary originally entered the river. He works the north side of these mouths, where the current is strongest. He also fishes around sunken islands. "I'll find catfish from one end of the river to the other in these type of places," he says.

Stubblefield's angling style is simple. He fishes vertically, jigging with either a tuffy minnow or a Catawba worm. "About 90% of the time, I'll use minnows that most people buy for crappie fishing," says Stubblefield. "When I can get them, I'll also use Catawba worms. They make great catfish bait, but unfortunately are only around in July and August."

Stubblefield secures one minnow or Catawba worm on a sharp 1/0 hook with a twisted shank. He smashes the minnow's head before using it to create a blood flow that helps attract catfish.

Stubblefield's gear consists of a strong 5½-foot rod and a baitcasting reel spooled with 20-pound-test monofilament. He ties a leader (with 30-pound test) to a barrel swivel and a 1-ounce sinker 6 inches above his hook. This allows Stubblefield to keep his bait a few inches off the bottom and in strike zones.

Even when current is stronger than he prefers, Stubblefield fishes the same technique. "I always use a 1-ounce bell sinker no matter how fast the water moves," he says. "I'll use my trolling motor in swift water to keep my line vertical."

A strong, sharp hook is important because catfish have hard mouths. Dull hooks cause many missed fish. "I'll buy 100 hooks at a time, and while I'm watching television, sharpen every one of them with a whetrock," says Stubblefield. "I'll get them razor sharp."

Sometimes catfish are so active they strike Stubblefield's bait before it reaches the bottom. "A lot of days I have a 58-quart cooler full by 10:30 in the morning and have to go back to the ramp to empty it." Most of Stubblefield's catfish are caught after 9 A.M. His best success is during daylight hours. "They just don't seem to hit well on Kentucky Lake at night, at least not for me," he notes.

Stubblefield primarily fishes Kentucky Lake's west bank. He particularly likes hot, sunny days. "The hotter, the better," he says. "Overcast and cool days are the worst days for catching catfish. I don't know why, but they are."

Eagle, Shannon, and Swan Creeks are among tributaries that feed Kentucky Lake. He pursues catfish until late September or early October. When the water begins to cool, catfish scatter and become difficult to pattern.

SHELLCRACKER AND BLUEGILL

Many Tennessee lakes offer good shellcracker and bluegill fishing. Kentucky Lake is an excellent reservoir for catching lots of these fish in good sizes. Guide Garry Mason is yet another of the talented anglers on Kentucky Lake who catches whatever the customer orders, including panfish.

Spring and Summer

Spring is the best time to catch pre-spawn bluegill and redear—better known by anglers as shellcracker. Shortly after crappie quit spawning, these fish begin hitting aggressively as they prepare to bed. Ultralight rods and spinning gear with 4- to 6-pound-test monofilament are ideal for panfish angling.

While bluegill and shellcracker inhabit many bays, Mason primarily fishes the Big Sandy River watershed. He has particular respect for shellcracker. "Bluegill fight pretty hard, but if shellcracker got up to 3 pounds on a regular basis no one would fish for bass," says Mason.

Shellcracker fishing requires patience. "They are extremely shy, and I'm very careful when approaching them," says Mason. "When I locate a bed, I back away from it 20 or 30 feet."

Guide Garry Mason uses his "Mason Method" (see Appendix A) to catch Kentucky Lake's scrappy bluegill and shellcrackers.

Bushes, stumps, fallen trees, and aquatic grasses are among the cover often found near shellcracker beds. "If I go searching for a new shellcracker site, I head for a bay or cove and look for buck bushes or grass near drop-offs where fish can swim quickly to deep water to feed but still be close to their bed," says Mason. "I always look in shallow water for areas that have been dug out because that is a telltale sign bluegill are bedding," he adds. "I'm looking for shellcracker, but bluegill always seem to bed near a shellcracker nest and are easy to see."

Once a shellcracker bed is discovered, it often assures good fishing for seasons to come. "Experience has shown me that shellcracker return to the same beds year after year," explains Mason.

Crickets, red wiggler worms, and night crawlers are among the good panfish baits, says Mason, who fishes them on a ¹⁄₁₆-ounce leadhead jig tied below a small cork float. Mason believes that a sinker crimped on his line reduces sensitivity, so he uses a tiny jig instead.

Unlike bluegill that grab the bait and run, shellcracker strikes are sometimes difficult to detect because they inhale the bait and don't always run with it. "If redear are hitting, I don't wait for a bobber to go under because I'll lose a bunch of swallowed hooks," says Mason.

Mason also tosses artificial baits for shellcracker, including Bees Wax Moths. Small grubs and other plastic panfish baits also catch fish. Mason's favorite plastic colors are black, chartreuse, and blaze orange. "I throw dark colors on bright days and bright colors when it's overcast," he says.

Occasionally Mason works a bed with artificial bait slowly retrieved beneath a bobber. Sometimes the float isn't necessary. "Shellcracker like moving bait and feed a lot off the bottom," explains Mason. "If the water is high, I'll let my jig sink and then reel it slowly."

Shellcracker beds are sometimes no larger than a coffee table, and many anglers overlook them. "I once saw three guys sitting in a boat, and the guy in the middle was catching shellcracker while the other two were catching bluegill. I've seen fishermen catch shellcracker and keep moving down the bank, not knowing what they had just found."

Bluegill fishing is even easier than shellcracker fishing in spring. They are more numerous than shellcracker and their beds are easier to find. Crickets, red wiggler worms, and night crawlers are good live baits, as are many small plastic baits or bug imitations.

Many anglers plan Kentucky Lake bluegill trips in late July or early August because of the huge mayfly hatch there. Fish gorge on mayflies, which float on the surface. Popping bugs, dry flies, and nymphs are fun artificial lures cast with fly rods. Small white Rooster Tails are among small spinners popular with spincasting anglers.

CHAPTER 3

Kentucky Lake

(SOUTHERN SECTION)

A Reservoir with Millions of Hungry Fish

The upper end of Kentucky Lake is riverine, and the lake doesn't broaden until it reaches the mouth of the Duck River just south of New Johnsonville. It broadens again at the Big Sandy junction.

All game fish species are present in Kentucky Lake and its tributaries except trout. Largemouth bass, crappie, smallmouth bass, stripe, sauger, and bream are the most sought-after species. And there are many guides who work this lake from Pickwick Dam to the Kentucky border (see Appendix B) to provide you with fishing instructions and put you on fish. You have to decide which part of this 158-mile lake you want to fish. The following suggestions should help.

LARGEMOUTH BASS

Camden guide Bob Latrendresse fishes up- and downstream from New Johnsonville. Boat launching in the New Johnsonville area is on US 70 at the western foot of the bridge. Birdsong Creek is notable for its marina and fishing. Billy Hurt Jr. from Spring Creek fishes mostly around the Cuba Landing area. Both of these guides talk here about bass fishing on Kentucky Lake.

TWRA fisheries biologist Tim Broadbent says, "Most of the fishing pressure is from Big Sandy to

GAME FISH RATINGS

Largemouth Bass	🐟 🐟 🐟 🐟
Smallmouth Bass	🐟 🐟 🐟
Crappie	🐟 🐟 🐟 🐟 🐟
Sauger	🐟 🐟 🐟
Stripe (White Bass)	🐟 🐟 🐟 🐟

the state line. But our studies show the best largemouth bass fishing is from Big Sandy down to New Johnsonville. Their populations have improved steadily over the last five years."

KENTUCKY LAKE (SOUTHERN SECTION) AT A GLANCE

Location:	Stewart, Benton, Humphreys, Decatur, Perry, and Hardin Counties
Size:	108,277 acres (entire reservoir)
Length:	157.6 miles (entire reservoir)
Shoreline:	1,970 miles (entire reservoir)
Summer pool:	375 feet
Winter pool:	354 feet
Impounded:	1944
Featured species:	Largemouth Bass, Smallmouth Bass, Crappie, Sauger, Stripe (White Bass)
Other species:	Yellow Bass, Spotted (Kentucky) Bass, Striper (Rockfish), Hybrid (Cherokee Bass), Catfish, Bluegill, Shellcracker
Description:	From New Johnsonville south to the headwaters below Pickwick Dam, Kentucky Lake is a flatland, riverine reservoir with many tributaries. There are also about 15 large islands in this 100-mile stretch.
Main tributaries:	Trace Creek, Beaverdam Creek, Indian Creek, Duck River, Birdsong Creek, Eagle Creek, Blue Creek, Crooked Creek, Toms Creek, Lick Creek, Cub Creek, Cypress Creek, Marsh Creek, Beech River, Cedar Creek, Whites Creek, Short Creek, Beech Creek, Roach Creek, Hardin Creek, Stewman Creek, Doe Creek, White Oak Creek, Horse Creek, Beason Creek, Mud Creek, Snake Creek, Chambers Creek, Robinson Creek
Landmarks:	Nearby cities on major east-west routes include New Johnsonville on US 70, Blue Creek (Cuba Landing) on I-40, Perryville on US 412, Savannah on US 64, and Pickwick Dam on TN 128. Nearby north-south routes on the lake's eastern side include TN 13 from Waverly to south of Linden, and TN 128 from south of Linden to Clifton, Savannah, and Pickwick Dam. North-south routes on the lake's western side include TN 69 from Camden south to Parsons, Decaturville, Saltillo, and Crump; TN 22 from Crump to Shiloh; and TN 142 from Shiloh to Southside.
Operated by:	Tennessee Valley Authority

See Appendix C for map information

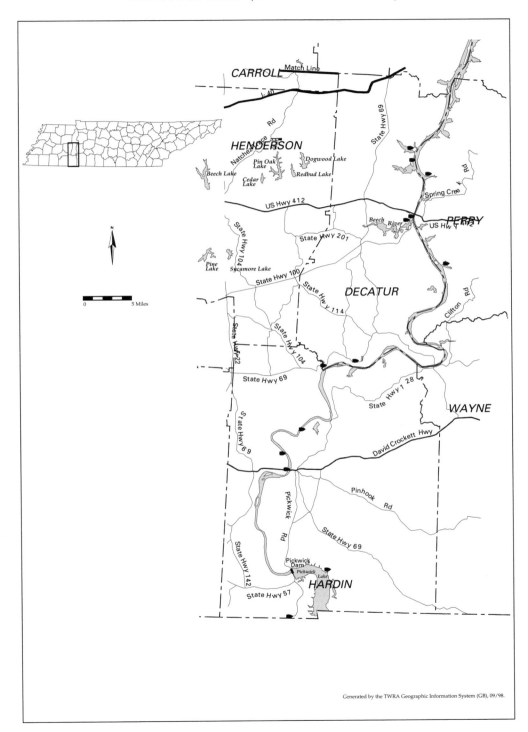

Generated by the TWRA Geographic Information System (GB), 09/98.

Cathy Summerlin's weighty largemouth bass came from one of Bob Latrendresse's favorite creeks near New Johnsonville.

Winter

Bob Latrendresse says, "I concentrate on the 5-mile stretch from Morgan Creek (river-mile 119) to Toms Creek (river-mile 124). The lake isn't wide open like farther downstream at New Johnsonville or Paris Landing; it's rather confined. The mouths of the creeks look like what they are, narrow creek mouths about 15 to 20 yards wide, but farther down you have to look for the creek mouth drop-offs with your sonar. These are easy to find."

A Little George weighing ½ ounce and silver spoons weighing ⅜ ounce are his top two baits for February bass. "I want something that imitates a shad," he says. "You've got to fish slow this time of year because the bass aren't real aggressive. They'll be a little more aggressive in warmer water, but you've got to find a spring to have warm water."

Latrendresse looks for bass among deepwater stumps and downed trees. "I find that bass are on stumps in the creeks, mostly near the mouth. I also find them on steep slopes. I don't know why, but it may be that baitfish hang around because of some underwater eddies you can't see. When I'm diving [Latrendresse also dives for mussels], I find places that break real quick into a bluff or steep bank, then come back out, and eddies form there that hold food for bass.

"But my main spots to fish are the creek mouths. They have both gentle slopes and steep drop-offs, and have a lot of trees that settled in the mouth. I approach the mouth real slow. I turn off my motor about 50 yards away and use my trolling motor to get in position, and I turn my sonars off. I've been over the area with my sonar many times and know where the cover and drops are. I don't want to make any sounds that would alarm the bass. I use my trolling motor very little; I'll drift from the upper side of the mouth downstream."

Latrendresse approaches each creek mouth differently because the cover and shape of the bottoms are diverse. He has no fast rule about casting parallel or perpendicular. He casts to cover and fishes the area thoroughly. As he puts it, "I try everything."

He catches more bass at creek mouths and doesn't fish the main channel banks. And he only goes up a creek if he knows there's a spring in it. There aren't many rocky banks in this area, but he doesn't pass them up on sunny days. The rocks absorb and hold the heat that attracts baitfish and bass. Most of the shad are deep and holding at the creek mouths, and of course, that's where the predator bass feed. His favorite creeks are Morgan, Crooked, Roan, Toms, and Marsh.

In the New Johnsonville area the river is wider, and there are more creeks and backwater. Latrendresse says, "The river is usually muddy, cold, and high. And I'll tell you right now, if I wanted to catch bass in winter, I would head for the steam plant harbor. They discharge warm water, between 60° and 70°."

The harbor is downstream (north) of New Johnsonville. Go north of the US 70 Bridge and turn right into the second canal. This leads to the harbor and discharge area.

"There are big rocks in this area, and crankbait and spinnerbait work real well," he says. "You've got to work the bait really slow. You need to hit what I call 100% of the bank; you do that by casting parallel. Jigs work real well, as do minnows. You'll catch smallmouth and spotted bass in there, too."

Billy Hurt Jr. from Spring Creek guides out of Cuba Landing on Kentucky Lake. Hurt says, "Fishing is good from Pickwick Dam to Paris Landing in January, but I concentrate more around the Perryville area to Cuba Landing. There is about a 20-mile stretch that has small feeder creeks that enter the Tennessee River. Up the creeks there are some straight banks, and it doesn't take much for bass to move up the bank and be shallow."

This is important because after a few warm sunny days, the bass move into those areas. On winter days you can get a lot of heat on the rocky gravel banks. The fish move up close to the surface and can be caught with small crankbaits. Bass seem to prefer steep banks in winter.

"Depending on the weather pattern, they move up and down," Hurt says. "The longer we have good weather, the shallower the fish are going to be. A rock or slate bank holds fish real well. You can work the main river channel, but you generally don't catch as many largemouth there. They tend to be inside the creek mouth.

He says, "My favorite way to locate fish is to use a spinnerbait. I start with a ½-ounce spinnerbait and put small willowleaf blades on it. Instead of using

***Stan Warren catches largemouth bass
on upper Kentucky Lake at night with
spinnerbaits.*** *(Photo by Stan Warren.)*

the normal steady retrieve, I yo-yo it down the steep bank.

"When you pick it up after a fall, it'll feel kind of spongy, and you'll want to shake it off or pull it free from a snag, but that's the way bass feel in the wintertime. Set your hook. A lot of times they don't swim off with it, they just hold it."

When the water temperature drops below 40° the fish slow down, as do the baitfish—everything is slower. Anglers must take this hint and slow their baits, too. If not, you're not imitating the forage. Hurt says bass won't bite something that's out of the ordinary.

"Many largemouth are near the creek mouths. I believe they have come from the backs of creeks. Bass don't usually move very far. They stay at the mouth because it's a little warmer, and they will move back up the creeks when the water warms up. And this is the closest place they are going to find a deep channel where they can lay on the ledges and wait for food to come by."

There are a few crawfish available, but bass forage mainly on shad. Shad go deep once the water gets cold and their food is not near the surface. Bass follow them. The baitfish are down and slow, and the bass find them an easy meal because they don't have to work as hard.

Shad school near the mouths of the creeks because the water is warmer, especially in a hard winter when the backs of the creeks freeze. They'll hold near the front of the creeks, and you can locate the bass with a spinnerbait or small crankbait.

"Once you get them pinpointed," says Hurt, "you can get right over the top of them and use a ¾-ounce jigging spoon. You can catch them one after the other, cast after cast."

"The schools vary in number, and [bass] school by size. If you catch 4-pound-class fish, that's about the only size fish in that school. The same is true if you're catching 2-pound fish. A lot of times you can go down a bank and find a school of fish one size and move another 20 feet and find a school of another size. If you locate a school of 12- to 14-inch fish, you can't sit there and expect to catch any 16- to 18-inch fish. The best thing to do if you get on a pattern of smaller fish is move. The bigger ones are there, you just have to locate them."

Hurt says another hot spot is along the bluffs. "If there is current, the fish will find a break in a bluff wall and hold there. They are waiting for schools of baitfish to drift around these breaks. The bass are sluggish, and they aren't going to work hard either at holding in the current or chasing baitfish.

"Some of the walls around the Perryville area are deceiving. They are gravel, which works well because it heats up well in the sun, but it comes out shallow for a few feet and then it will drop. Sometimes the wall changes from what you initially see as a flat area of about 4 feet deep to a drop-off of about 10 or 15 feet. That's a good spot to fish."

The fish are usually from 7 to 25 feet deep. The first thing you have to establish is what depth these fish are. The harsher the weather the deeper they will be. If you have a week of below freezing weather, the big fish are going to be deeper. If you have a week with some 60° weather and the surface water and rocks are heating up, you'll find fish shallow.

"When I start, I'm looking for how deep they are. I cast almost parallel to the wall. The bluffs fall off fairly rapidly. This angle gives me a longer time with my bait in the water, and I'm able to keep up with what depth the bait is. If I catch a fish at a certain depth and I'm holding at 25 feet and fishing almost parallel, I know that particular fish was in deep water. Then I pull up closer to the wall and fish closer. I'm able to tell what depth I'm in and pinpoint the fish. After I know how deep they are, I can pull off the wall and work that depth. But the best way is to get right over the top of them with a jigging spoon."

"I had an experience three years ago in January where I was catching them on buzzbaits," says Hurt. "It was just one day, and the only time I've ever done it. My father and I watched a baitfish run, and we noticed a swirl behind it. I pulled out a buzzbait and he laughed at me. After the second largemouth I put in the boat, I noticed he was throwing one, too. We caught 20 bass that day on buzzbaits. The weather had been sunny all week; that made the difference."

To fish a creek mouth, Hurt positions his boat out from the mouth and casts a Carolina rig with a small bait, either a Zoom centipede or a Gitzit on a No. 2 wire hook. Usually he uses a 4-foot leader.

You need to know where the edge of the deep channel runs. Cast shallow and bring your bait so that it falls off the side into deeper water.

"Generally, I cast to the upriver side of the channel," he says, "so the bait washes down, just like a baitfish would be traveling. You always pull your bait with the current and down the slope. The downriver side of the mouth doesn't seem to work as well because the bait doesn't wash up the slope. Fishing is much better when there is current."

Without current, instead of trying to find breaks in the wall, Hurt fishes horizontal ledges that have a cutback for a good ambush point. The baitfish won't be moving down the wall without current, so bass hold at the depth of the baitfish and hide under the ledge. This is the time to cast perpendicular to the wall rather than parallel.

Hurt concludes with this advice, "Early morning is not the best time to fish in the winter. The fish are more active midmorning or after. Take plenty of warm clothes to meet any weather situation. It's easy to take clothes off to be comfortable, but you don't want the weather to turn and you not have enough clothing to keep fishing."

Spring

"In April I start at Camden Bottoms using lizards and Poe's crankbaits," says Bob Latrendresse. "TVA harbor is another good largemouth spot in spring. Spotted bass are active, too, especially at Morgan Creek.

"I've seen big largemouth spawn in 10 feet of water; I think there is too much pressure for them in the shallows. I use a very slow retrieve with a spinnerbait, so I can feel the Colorado blade go thump, thump, thump. I'll feel that blade stop, and then it feels like a fish is on, but I don't set the hook—I let the fish set the hook. The slow retrieve is better until after midspring." (Latrendresse wouldn't tell us his secret color.)

Crappie beds are a great place to fish in April and May for bass. "I still use the spinnerbait," he says. "The back of Eagle Creek where there are a lot of downed trees is a hot spot, too.

"Flipping a spinnerbait with a big splash has worked well for me. A 6-inch Culprit jerkbait does a good job, too. I concentrate on the riverbanks near the channel around Cuba Landing. There aren't many islands there, but there are more upstream, and those are good for flipping."

A lot of fishermen miss the best bass places by not fishing the riverbanks where the bank stair steps into deep water.

He says, "The fishing is better when there is current. The bass get behind stumps and trees or whatever cover's down there. The jerkbait and spinnerbait are my favorites. The only thing bad about a jerkbait is that you tend to jerk the bait away from the fish when you see it start to take it. I do it all the time. That's exciting! I still catch a lot of big fish.

"I'll tell you one of my secrets; I sort of hate to tell it because a lot of people are going to read this, but the bass at New Johnsonville get so much pressure. Down here at Cuba Landing it's another story. You need to find a creek with a no-wake zone. Where boats go slow are the perfect places for bass fishing. Look for the drop-off at the mouth of the creek, put a worm or lizard on a Carolina rig, and fish it in June. I'll guarantee you'll catch some big fish."

Latrendresse says in July and August bass fishing slows down on the lake. "It's like my crappie fishing—it's too hot. That's when I start my guide service

Billy Hurt Jr. pulled this bass off the river-channel bank at Mousetail Landing the day after a cold front passed through.

for smallmouth bass on the Buffalo River. Last year I started fly fishing for smallmouth. I know that's another story, but that's where I go when it's too hot to fish on the lake."

In summer, you can fish the willowfly hatches. Many anglers like to use a fly rod with a popping bug. You can catch a lot of 2-pound bass and as many bream as you want. The hatches start in July and last into September in some years. Latrendresse thinks the Duck River area has the best hatches.

Summer

Billy Hurt Jr. says Cuba Landing gets moderate fishing pressure, and there are a lot of bass in that area over 5 pounds. Cuba Landing is on the west side of the Tennessee River just north of I-40.

"The success anglers have in this area depends a lot on the water level," says Hurt. Two dams, Pickwick Dam upstream and Kentucky Dam downstream, control Kentucky Lake. If we have excess spring rains, then the water will be 358 to 359 feet above sea level, which means there will be water in the bushes. Some years water is in the bushes in the first part of July. Some years it isn't. But even if we don't get high water, there are other places you can go to catch big bass."

The bushes are the first places to hit when the water is up. There are almost always some big fish in the shallows. Hurt casts a jig and a topwater bait among the bushes.

"I like a small Pop-R or sometimes a Tiny Torpedo. These usually bring some nice fish to the surface," he says. "The secret to knowing which bushes to fish is knowing where the nearby deep water is."

All bushes are in shallow water, but bass, especially big bass, will have an easy escape route to deep water. This can be the channel in a good-sized creek or the main river channel.

"If the water is falling, this brings the fish to the outside of the bush where your topwater baits work well. Here's another secret (this works even better if you locate a bush line that you can cast parallel to): By retrieving your bait close along the front of the bushes you keep your bait in the strike zone longer.

"When the water is up but not moving, that is, not rising or falling, the bass move deep into the bushes. You've got to use baits you can fish in heavy cover. You can fish back among the bushes and not be productive; sometimes it takes putting your bait right at the base of a bush or in a treetop. You'd be surprised how tight a bass will hold on cover.

"A lot of times it'll look like you can't even get a bait in the cover, then you may notice a small hole to put your bait in. The bass will grab it. It'll amaze you that a big fish can even get in such tight places," says Hurt.

He uses a Springer jig to fish the bushes. Tomato color is his favorite because it looks like a crawfish. Hurt chooses the Springer jig because of its bullet-shaped head. He says the head doesn't hang up inside the fish's mouth like a bulkier head does. The head slides out of the mouth so the hook gets better penetration.

"A bass has a powerful jaw. It can close down on your bait, and when you set the hook, it won't move. I've fought bass to the boat, then it opened its mouth, and the jig came right out. The line stretch prevents all your hook-set from reaching your bait."

Later in July the water level will drop and anglers need to look for other places to fish.

"When the water is normal or low, many anglers fish the secondary points in the bigger creeks that have a fairly steep drop-off. Crappie anglers have put out a lot of brush piles, and these often hold bass. You can see stumps on the edge of channels, and these hold bass, too."

Morgan and Eagle Creeks are the best ones in the Cuba Landing Area. Morgan is upstream and Eagle is downstream and both are across the river from Cuba Landing.

"Fishing the larger creeks is a key to catching fish when the weather gets hot. Morgan and Eagle have feeder creeks that help keep the temperature down," Hurt says.

"Of course fishing along the main river bank is good. A lot of people ignore this structure except to throw a spinnerbait. Early morning is the time to fish these banks with topwater baits. As the sun gets higher the fish slip off into deeper water, then you need to go to a Carolina rig to fish the drops and points."

Hurt uses a lizard and centipede on his Carolina rig. He uses the centipede in the hottest weather because bass like smaller baits then. He says bass see a lot of large baits, and the change-up puts more fish in his live well. Four-inch baits in pumpkin and chartreuse, and watermelon seed are his top choices.

"Sunny days the watermelon seed excels, and cloudy days the green pumpkin is better. Light-colored baits prevail on sunny days and darker ones on low-light days. I like using the earthy colors most; they blend in. A natural-looking bait to a bass is more effective. Bass locate food by movement and then sees it when he starts after it," concludes Hurt.

Fall

"Points and shallow water on muddy flats are two places I find bass in the fall," says Bob Latrendresse. "I use a fly rod on the points, and I cast a Little George over the flats. The most productive way to find bass is to look for them working on the top."

Bass leave the shallows usually in November. "It depends on the weather," he says. "Cold, windy, rainy days, the bass are going to be stubborn. But on a sunny day they'll be back in the shallows. You know we've always heard that bass hate the sunlight, but it's not true. They like the shadows because they can hide in the dark and ambush food. I've seen bass floating just inches under the surface like they were getting a suntan."

He adds, "You know the lake is changing. Twenty years ago when I started diving, I saw lots of stumps. Now they've about all gone. Places like Birdsong and Trace Creek are filling in. There is a deep cut upstream near the creek, but where the water widens, it's shallow. I've found bass on these flats out in the middle of nothing.

"In the fall I prefer using a fly rod, but for rod and reels, I like using top-water baits and jerkbaits on top of bars and river islands," Latrendresse says.

SMALLMOUTH BASS

The smallmouth bass population in Kentucky Lake is improving in the mid-section, but it has always been excellent in the headwaters—from Perryville to Pickwick Dam. Mussel divers below Pickwick Dam say it is unbelievable how many smallmouth are there.

April is said to be the best month for smallies below the dam. That's when they move on the gravel bars, but you can scare up some smallmouth action during all seasons of the year. And live bait ranks as the top catcher.

Winter

"Most smallmouth fishing in February is done below Pickwick Dam within 3 miles of the dam. It's better fishing than on Pickwick Lake," says Pickwick guide David Harbin. "Naturally, conditions vary depending on rainfall. When

Bob Pingel hefts a keeper smallmouth caught in Kentucky Lake's headwaters. *(Photo by Stan Warren.)*

the dam gates are open, it's tougher fishing, but you want a little current. The water temperature is around the upper 40s to lower 50s, depending on how cold the winter is. Water clarity is good if there hasn't been a lot of rain. The extra demand for heating in the winter means they generate a good bit of the time, providing good water flow. Too much current, however, makes you move too fast for proper bait presentation."

Harbin says there's a good shad forage base that stays upriver year-round. Most anglers are sauger fishing, and you don't have competition for bass. In winter you have a good chance of catching bigger fish, but not the numbers you would later in the year. Four- to six-pound fish are usual during February.

"You need a slower presentation in cold water. The channel depth is about 24 feet. I fish the banks between 12 to 15 feet deep depending on the current and where the bass are holding. They hold in the eddy areas. The riprap runs from the dam downstream a good ways. The riprap goes from the bank down to the channel."

Between the boat ramp and the dam there are some cottonwood and sycamore trees near an eddy. This is a good location for smallies. Harbin says it's hangy but the fish are there.

"Live bait is your best bait," he says. "Anglers will probably have better luck with creek minnows, and it's best if you catch your own. You can buy shiners locally if you can't get creek minnows. It's hard to catch shad because they are in deeper water.

"The slipfloat is a good way to fish live bait. You set the stop on your line to fish the depth where the fish are. I use about ⅛-ounce splitshot, or enough to keep the minnow from swimming up. I place the weight between 8 and 12 inches above a 1/0 gold Tru Turn hook."

Harbin recommends casting upstream while drifting with the current, using the trolling motor to keep the bow pointed upstream. Use your motor to slow your drift and stay the desired distance from the bank or rock piles.

He uses a 6-foot, one-piece spinning rod for extra sensitivity and suggests a spinning reel with a 5:1 ratio or higher. He uses 8-pound-test Magna Thin line.

The chartreuse grub 2½ to 3 inches long on a ⅛-ounce jighead is the best artificial bait. Smoke glitter is also a good color. "Use as light a jighead as you can. In stiff current you may need a heavier jig to get to the bottom. It's best to use 8-pound-test line in the river. As the jig moves with the current along the bottom, tick the rocks, keep your rod tip up, and use a slow retrieve."

Late February when the water starts warming up, he casts a deep-diving crankbait like a Shad Rap or Model A Bomber that runs 6 to 10 feet deep and works the riprap.

"The southwest bank has some eddies, creek mouths, and an area called the narrows," Harbin says. "It's a rock pile that forms a narrow area of water that starts across from Bellis Botel and runs down 2 miles to where the power lines cross the river. This area is about the best fishing on the river. It takes more than an hour to fish this stretch. When I finish, I go back and start again."

He says live bait under the slipfloat is the best technique at the narrows. "This is the most productive way for fishing, letting the bait drift along the rocks."

Spring

Stan Warren, an outdoor writer and veteran angler from Bethel Springs, says, "Smallmouth bass are becoming more prominent in the creel surveys on Kentucky Lake. I don't think people appreciate the population of smallmouth that exists away from the Pickwick Dam area. If they would spend more time casting something compatible with both largemouth and smallmouth, which could be a Carolina rig or crankbait, on the channel drop-offs, channel edges, and farther out than the shoreline-angler usually fishes, they'd find that whole stretch from the dam downstream to New Johnsonville has a lot of smallmouth bass.

"As you move farther up the river from New Johnsonville into a more riverine environment where the current is more pronounced, both shoreline breaks and offshore breaks will hold smallies. The upper end of Kentucky Lake is considered the more traditional smallmouth area. But from New Johnsonville upstream, there are a lot of old channels coming into the lake, a lot of breaks, and a lot of offshore cover—more than people might realize—such as standing timber. These are good places to pick up smallmouth."

Warren says the best places to fish for springtime smallies are from Pickwick Dam to Wolf Island. From the Bellis Botel down to the second set of power lines crossing the river is probably the best section within that stretch.

"Most anglers fish the western shoreline," says Warren. "The Narrows, a sheltered body of water on the west side created by a big rocky bank, is still a good place, too. But there is beginning to be more and more known about the other side of the lake. There has been a lot of new riprap put in, and there is a bar below the Botel. Both have been overlooked. It's 8 feet deep and stays at that depth a good way from the shoreline. The bottom has chunk rock and is a good place to prospect for smallies. Instead of fishing the traditional springtime baits such as the jig, you can cast a medium-running crankbait that will dive to 8 feet. You can fish 60 yards away from shore and still be in good smallmouth country. You'll want to watch your depth finder for big rocks or clumps of rocks. Any of the visible current breaks along either side of the river can be good smallie holding places."

Warren suggests anglers drift and cast with crankbaits, using different action baits and different colors. You'll feel the crankbait ticking the gravel and rocks and you'll know you're in smallmouth country. Warren has had success with the medium-running Bandit in bone color with an orange belly. He says this is a good color for the river and the lake in spring and fall. Shad patterns are also good.

"These fish live in a river environment and live by ambush," he says. "I don't believe the color is as critical as in a clear lake. They don't have much time to make up their mind to eat whatever bounces off the rock they are hiding behind. But it is critical that you have confidence in what you are throwing."

Smallmouth usually spawn in April and largemouth spawn in May in the upper end of Kentucky Lake.

Summer

"The transition from spring to summer patterns occurs in mid-May," says Stan Warren. "The fish move deeper and orient a little more tightly to cover. In the spring smallmouth orient more to current flow than the time of day. In the summer there is heavier flow because of more demand for electricity, and the fish stick closer to cover and breaks.

"The west bank is more vertical and the fish are close to the rocks. You'll need a heavier jighead to get a more vertical fall. Once you reach 3 feet deep, your lure is away from cover. If you cast a crankbait, I suggest you cast one that will stand on its head and get deep in a hurry. Storm's Lightening Shad in the small size and Bill Norman's Deep-Little-N in the Tennessee Shad color are traditionally good. The angler shouldn't be too far from shore and make the cast quarter the current, either upstream or downstream—cast tight and keep the bait in the strike zone as long as possible.

"On the east bank, I think the crawfish color has the edge in the summertime. You'll also catch a lot of spotted bass, too. Make long casts over the shallow area. The water will be a little deeper because more water is flowing through the dam in summer."

Topwater action is good early and late in the day if the flow is sufficient. The bass will range up to 3 pounds and are usually plentiful. Cast a Pop-R or a propeller-type bait. You don't need heavy tackle according to Warren because most of the cover is rock. He suggests using 10-pound test or lighter.

"The traditional bait for night fishing downstream from the dam is the spinnerbait," says Warren. "I like a bulky jig, one with a big profile that is light and will still sink in the current. I may start with a ⅜-ounce jig and drop to a ¼-ounce jig when the current is reduced. You want the jig to fall as slowly as possible along the rock banks. This technique will wipe the fish out!

"Night is a great time to fish live bait. A threadfin shad or 5-inch shiner hooked behind the dorsal fin so their head is facing up, pitched to the bank and drifted, will load the boat, too. I like to use a No. 1 or 1/0 Eagle Claw salmon-egg hook. I don't use any weight—just the hook. And you need a trolling motor to keep you off the bank while you drift. That's a pleasant way to fish."

Warren warns first-time night anglers that the water level usually drops in the evening or at night, and there may be rocks shallow enough to harm a prop, lower unit, or boat that would be safe in deep water. Stay between the channel buoys until you learn the river.

Fall

Warren says, "The fall pattern is a little trickier to call because of the weather. The transition may come in September or as late as early November, but if I had to name a time, I'd say late September. Usually when you see the yellow Sulfur butterflies migrating through, you should look for the smallmouth and spotted bass running shad minnows on top along the rocky banks.

"Last year during the fall pattern, I had a smallmouth and a largemouth, both weighing more than 7 pounds, that I caught on the same plug. Both of them were chasing shad.

"You can catch a lot of fish on a crankbait, buzzbait, or spinnerbait. But the clear Crazy Shad propeller plug and the clear Zara Puppy have become the baits of choice for the fall pattern in the tailrace and on Pickwick Lake. Some days they want it moving fast and other days you have to finesse them. The way you gauge that is, if you see fish chasing minnows, throw right in the middle of the fray and make some noise. When the fish go down, you can either switch to a crankbait or keep working your topwater plug slower, giving it a little more tempting demeanor," he says.

Also, soft-plastic jerkbaits provide excitement. Warren says that the Zoom Fluke and Mann's Shadow are about the best. He prefers the thin Fluke because it looks more like a shad, but his fishing buddy prefers the Fluke with the hook pocket, which is a thicker and heavier bait. These baits work very well when the fish go down after feeding on the surface. A "kick-kick-kick-drop" type of retrieve is awesome, says Warren.

"One trick I'll pass along is when you're using a smoke, shad, white, or clear glitter bait that looks like a shad, dip its tail in some of that chartreuse dye that comes in a bottle. The threadfin shad has some yellow in its tail. That little difference in color has caught me more fish than any modification I've made," Warren says.

The areas that Warren says are good in the fall, farther downstream, are the Wolf Island area, the Diamond Island area, the current break at Shiloh, and any of the creek mouths. The best spot in his opinion is under the second set of power lines from the dam. He also says to look for major current breaks—these have the potential for yielding a big smallmouth bass. The lower end of the Narrows has also been a big-fish producer. Warren has caught a few smallies over 8 pounds and more than a few over 7 pounds. "All but one are still swimming," he says. That *one* must have been a wall-hanger!

CRAPPIE

The majority of crappie anglers wet their lines only during the spring. Most crappie are caught then, but is it the best time to catch this member of the sunfish family? Many guides say that catching crappie in January can be better than in the spring. Crappie schools are much larger in winter than at other times of the year, and once you locate them, you are likely to catch your limit quickly. The trick is locating them.

Winter

Guide John Hunt of Waverly says, "You need to fish from 10 to 25 feet deep along the creek channels. The tightline rig or slipfloat rig are about the only two ways to catch them (see Appendix A). I suggest you use a small tuffy minnow this time of year."

Hunt says you can locate these large schools of crappie in old creek channels. "Use your depth finder to locate where an 8-foot deep ledge drops off to 20 or 25 feet. Crappie don't require cover this time of year. They will hold on a steep drop out of the current, and they will school real tight. Once you locate them you can catch a lot of crappie."

The important factor is current. Crappie won't expend more energy than necessary, especially in cold water, where it takes longer for them to digest food for needed energy.

"Most crappie are going to be out of the current off the main river," says Hunt. "There is a good bit of current this time of year, so they will be deep, holding behind some structure or cover in the creek channel in the large embayments." Hunt recommends creeks with deep water for wintertime fishing on Kentucky Lake.

"A lot more people fish in winter than they used to," concludes Hunt. "Some days you'd think it was spring with so many people out there."

Bob Latendresse says, "I fish from the New Johnsonville area upstream to near Perryville. Around Perryville the river is narrow, not as wide as it is at

New Johnsonville. You can see where a creek enters, rather than having a wide area that looks like a bay. These are good places for crappie to hold. You don't need a sonar to find the creek channel.

"In the winter the crappie will be in the bay water, but they will be deep on the creek channel drops. There's a spot in Birdsong where the water is 12 feet deep in winter and the crappie seem to hold there. My dad and I caught about 120 crappie in about two hours there. To catch crappie during the cold months, fish the deep drops in bays and the riverbanks. Just downstream of the Duck River mouth is another one of my wintertime crappie holes," says Latrendresse.

"Crappie go to what I call their feeding grounds in the winter. The baitfish go deep where the water is warmer, and the crappie are there, too."

Bob Latrendresse grew up on Kentucky Lake and knows more good crappie holes than he can fish in a year. This is a sample of a springtime catch.

Latrendresse uses minnows and jigs side by side. He says "But I catch more fish with minnows in winter than with jigs. I know people will argue about it, but I've been fishing here a long time on this river, and that's what I've found works for me. I use the tightline rig [see Appendix A], but I use only one hook. You can catch just as many fish with one hook as two, and you won't lose near as many minnows. I hook the minnow behind the dorsal fin, being sure to miss the spinal cord."

He uses the 12-foot ultralight crappie pole. In deep water he switches to a spinning rod. But he claims the light pole is easier when fishing all day.

He adds that the crappie fishery is better now than he has seen in some years. "I used to dive for mussels, and on one of my last dives in 1997, I looked at a stump that had thousands and thousands of little crappie around it. We've got good reproduction, the best I've seen in 20 years of diving."

Spring

Bob Latrendresse says, "Crappie start gradually moving shallow about mid-February. They move at different times in different creeks. Birdsong will warm up faster than Beaverdam, maybe because Birdsong has a lot of feeder creeks. But I've seen that change from year to year. It might have to do with the water level, too.

"At the end of February, the first of March, they'll spread out. You can find some in the New Johnsonville area in the harbor where the discharge warms the water. Crappie will spawn there in February."

Camden Bottoms is a good spot when they are pumping out the bottoms. You'll catch all kinds of fish, including stripers there, but crappie and stripe are most abundant. "I mean, you'll load the boat in a couple of hours," he says. "But you have to catch it at the right time and get there early. There is only room for about five boats to fish a spot about twice the size of a kitchen table."

Latrendresse says that Birdsong, Eagle, and Beaverdam Creeks are the places he likes to fish in the first half of March. Trace Creek and some of the other streams on the east side of the lake are cooler, and crappie spawn there later. There you can catch late-April crappie.

"After they spawn, that's one of the hardest times to find them. I do find them along the riverbank, but it's tough to find them," he says.

Think of crappie as companies of soldiers. They form tight units, well back of the action on the front lines where they spawn. Next they move together from their base camps to the mouths of creeks and then into shallow water nearer their objective—their spawning grounds. In stages, they move closer until they are ready to attack their seasonal ritual. Just before their assault, they fan out and invade the shallows.

In the spawning grounds they're attacked by jigs, minnows, and small crankbaits, but they suffer a small percentage of casualties. The survivors spawn, care for their fry for a while, then retreat. They are no longer organized but form loose units as they make their way back to their base camps. This retreat takes two to four weeks.

John Hunt fishes close to the I-40 bridge near New Johnsonville for postspawn crappie. He says, "From here to the state line are the best places for crappie in the whole river." He names Bird Song, Cypress, Cane, Leatherwood, and Harmon Creeks as top places to fish because they have deep water channels where crappie can spend most of the time out of the river's current.

"After they spawn I use a Charlie Brewer's Slider," says Hunt. "I also use jigs and minnows but usually they'll take that Slider."

Hunt is logical about locating postspawn crappie. "They are on their way back to deeper water, so I fish between where they spawn and the deep water where they are heading. They usually go to the first visible cover they see after spawning in shallow water. I cast to stumps and brush in about 6 feet of water on gravel banks. Then I work out to deeper water."

Hunt, as well as other crappie guides, have fished Kentucky Lake for many years, and they agree jigs and minnows are baits of choice. If you combine the spider rig (see Appendix A) with Hunt's logic for fishing the areas between the spawning grounds and the main river channel, you shouldn't have much trouble catching postspawn crappie.

Summer and Fall

I don't fish for crappie in the summer," says Latrendresse, "because the flesh gets mushy. As a guide, I've found that people don't want to fish for crappie in the heat of June, July, and August. But you can catch them along the riverbanks in anywhere from 10 to 20 feet of water, and you can find them in deep creeks."

Latrendresse resumes crappie fishing in September and October around Birdsong, the intake at the TVA harbor, stakebeds along the riverbank, and along the river bars. In October crappie begin moving into the shallows following the baitfish.

"You'll catch a lot of small crappie this time of year," he says. "By December they move out deep again and form schools."

SAUGER

Most of our state's sauger populations are in the Tennessee River system, but there is good fishing in the Cumberland River system, too. Jeff Smith of Nashville has made a study of sauger on the Tennessee and Cumberland Rivers and found something that should interest sauger anglers.

Winter

Jigging the shallow river bars in broad daylight is not a common practice—most of us tend to fish the deep holes—but Smith has discovered sunlight is no deterrent to sauger. Dr. Woodson Carter of Lewisburg and Jeff Smith share their jigging techniques, but first Smith talks about river bars and a surprising sauger forage species.

Smith says the best conditions on Tennessee rivers occur after a heavy rain has raised the water level, made it muddy, and created a strong current. As the water level falls and clears, the fish are ready to bite.

"Mussel beds and gravel bars are the two best structures on the rivers," he says. There are two mussel bars below the mouth of the Duck River. Live mussels, mussel shells, and gravel make the hard bottom that sauger prefer.

The bars are within the channel markers and one is about a mile long. Watch your sonar for the bottom to come up from 40 feet to 25 feet then drop to 40 again for the short bar. The longer one gradually goes up to 16 feet then gradually drops back to 40 feet. It isn't level on top and it tapers on two sides.

There are several drift patterns you can run on the long bar. Use your sonar to stay on either side, in the middle, on one of the two ends, or in one of the troughs on the uneven top. There is a drop between the two bars that holds sauger, too. Keep in mind that the fish will be in different places when conditions change.

Bob Latrendresse also guides for bluegill and shellcracker. This hunk of a shellcracker came from near New Johnsonville.

Smith recommends fishing the shallow water on top, then down the sides. "Sauger like these bars because of the hard bottom and, before the shad die off, they are there feeding on drum."

Drum are bottom feeders. They dine on snails, mussels, and other mollusks. These mussel bars attract the drum, and the sauger move in to feed on them. "I usually find drum 2 to 4 inches long in the sauger's stomachs," says Smith.

"I first discovered this some years ago. I had several 3-pound sauger in my live well. When I looked in there later, I saw regurgitated drum. That was my first clue. Since then, when I clean fish, I check to see what they have been eating. Before the shad kill, about 70% of the fish will have drum in their stomachs."

His experience has proved this is true for both the Tennessee and Cumberland River systems. "Sauger aren't eating these fish by mistake. I thought it was unusual at first, but after so many years of seeing it, the drum have to be a main part of the sauger's diet."

Shad is part of the sauger's forage, but there is one period when that's about all they eat. Threadfin shad are susceptible to disease during cold weather. When the water temperature drops to around 39°, they begin to die. During this die-off, sauger are taking advantage of the opportunity to eat their fill.

You have probably heard that sauger and walleye bite best on a cloudy day. No doubt that is a good fishing condition, but sauger have been caught too often under a cloudless sky at midday in less than 20 feet of water, even 2 feet of water, to conclude that sunlight turns them off.

Light does not hurt their eyes. Fish shy away from light because they can be easily seen and they feel vulnerable. Sauger move to the shallow water bars, points, and shorelines to feed no matter how bright the sun, as long as there is some wind or current to break up the light and make them feel safe.

Jigging for sauger is as traditional as evergreen trees at Christmas. The standard rig is a football-shaped jighead. This design gives the rig lateral stability in swift water and the 1- to 1¼-ounce weight gets it to the bottom. A stinger hook is also traditional on these jigs.

Doc Carter fishes the Tennessee River from Pickwick Dam to Savannah. He uses a 1¼-ounce rounded jighead with a 3- or 4-inch Sassy Shad. Doc likes the blue-, gray-, and green-colored Sassy Shad on a red jighead. He also uses a stinger hook.

The stinger is 3 inches of 4-pound-test line tied to the jig's eye with a No. 1 treble hook on the other end. "I don't impale the plastic shad with the stinger hook," he says. "I've tried it both ways and leaving it free works better."

Smith uses a 3-inch Mister Twister tail on a 1-ounce jig with a short stinger. "The stinger is just long enough to cover the tail. I don't use a minnow either. I've been using the plastic grub for years with good success in water that is around 50°. It isn't as effective in cold water. You are better off using a minnow when the water is less than 50°."

The 12-inch lift of the rod is a common jigging method. With the jig resting on bottom, reel in your slack line so your rod tip is close to the surface. As you drift over sauger structure, lift your rod tip about a foot and ease it back down. Sauger feed right along the bottom and this movement attracts them.

Some anglers use a swift upward sweep with the idea that snagging a sauger is as good as getting one to bite. Sonars are employed this way, also. There are times they work better than jigs or minnows. When sauger quit hitting, switching to a Sonar can revive their interest in feeding.

You can cast Sonars from the bank and bump them along the bottom. Set the hook when you feel resistance. Sauger do not smash a bait. They take hold of it in their toothy mouth, turn it head first, and swallow. They grab a bait in their jaws rather than suck it in like a bass does. If it doesn't like the feel of your bait, it will release it immediately. A quick hook-set is important to landing sauger and walleye.

Another technique Smith uses on vertical walls, bluffs, and casting below dams is a ¾-ounce jig with two hooks tied up the line. Place one hook 8 inches above the jig and the other hook 12 inches higher. The jig and hooks should be baited with minnows. Let the jig hit bottom and rest there. After a minute, move it a little and pause again.

Smith makes the 1-ounce Erie-style jig from a Do It Company mold. This style's hook stands up at a 45° angle from the bottom. This makes it easier for the sauger to get it in its mouth.

He hand-colors the leadheads with a durable vinyl jig paint. He used to leave them natural but has discovered that colors can make a big difference in the number of hits he gets. On sunny days, fishing in 20 to 25 feet of water, Smith says orange, yellow, and pink are the best colors. A red or pink head and a pink hair skirt outperforms chartreuse five to one. He adds that on some days it doesn't matter what color you use, they'll hit anything. The yellow- and orange-colored jigs work well in muddy water, too.

On dark cloudy days he has found that a blue color works best. Red is a good second choice.

There are many diverse sauger hot spots on the Cumberland and Tennessee Rivers. The key to locating fish is finding where they eat. Gravel and mussel bars are two such places. Putting your bait where drum feed seems to be a factor many anglers haven't discovered yet. These bars are shallow and reports are indicating that sauger spend more time in shallow water than once thought.

Bob Latrendresse says, "I find sauger start hitting in December around the mouth of the Duck River, Birdsong, Camden Landing, and the mouths of the big creeks. They like debris, such as logs and rocks, especially gravel and mussel bars. Fishing improves in January. I know some guys who fish the mouth of the Duck River every day and catch their limit of sauger. Fishing seems to taper off in February."

Spring and Summer

"The TVA harbor is a good spot to fish for sauger in March and April," says Latrendresse. "In the summer I troll for them along the river bars. Lashlee's Crossing and Camden Landing have good bars. Use a chartreuse or red crankbait that runs about 15 feet deep and has a rattle in it. You have to go slow with 50 yards or more of line out. You want to zigzag from the bar to deep water and back. Your lure has got to bump bottom. You catch most of your sauger between 5 and 10 feet of water. You've got to do this the first three hours, and last few hours of daylight, or if it's cloudy, you can do it all day. This works from June into the early fall. You'll catch bass, stripe, drum, catfish—all kinds of fish. Set your drag light so the fish won't break your line. Also, you need one of those things that gets your lure off a snag, or you'll lose a fair number of baits trolling this way. Stumps are about 15 feet deep in summer."

STRIPE (WHITE BASS)

In winter stripe concentrate below Pickwick Dam. One- to three-pound fish are common. Stripe are known as hard fighters, and while most species are lethargic during winter, this cool-water species is hardy and bites aggressively from the dam to Pittsburg Landing.

White, chartreuse, or green, 2- or 4-inch grubs, on ⅛- or ¼-ounce leadheads get the job done. Fish the primary river points, creek channel mouths, laydowns, and rocky areas. The eddies below structure and cover, such as stumps and rocks, are likely to be your best spots. Also, let the current wash your bait under the laydowns. This is risky, but fish often hit your bait before a limb gets it. Cast upriver and bring the lure into the eddy. Stripe, as all fish, face the current so they can see food heading their way. You should fish grubs close to or on the bottom, with a slow retrieve. Live minnows fished on a Carolina rig also catch stripe.

CHAPTER 4

Pickwick Lake

Tennessee's Bronzeback Bounty

Pickwick Lake cannot be beat for smallmouth bass angling. Dale Hollow Lake is its nearest rival, but Pickwick has produced large numbers of trophy smallies longer than Dale Hollow has.

Only the lower 8 miles of the 53-mile lake are in Tennessee. State Line Island on the east and the mouth of Yellow Creek on the west mark the boundary with Alabama and Mississippi, but your Tennessee license is valid upstream to the mouth of Bear Creek at river-mile 225. This gives you another 10 miles of Pickwick to fish. Your Tennessee license is not valid beyond the mouth of Bear Creek, either upstream on the Tennessee River or in Bear Creek. Nor is it valid upstream in Yellow Creek beyond the MS 25 bridge. But within these 18 miles are all the fish any Tennessee angler could want.

SMALLMOUTH BASS

Lou Williams from Henderson has been guiding for about 15 years. The last 10 years have been on Pickwick Lake. He says the best months on Pickwick are October, November, and December because there is less traffic on the lake. Outdoor writer and expert angler Stan Warren likes those months, also. Williams will talk about spring and summer, and Warren will tell us about fall and winter.

GAME FISH RATINGS

Smallmouth Bass	🐟🐟🐟🐟🐟
Striper	🐟🐟🐟
Sauger	🐟🐟🐟

Spring

"In the springtime the fish start migrating to the flats with stumps on them," says Lou Williams. "You've got two situations because all the fish in the lake don't go to the flats. The fish that live in deep water, adjacent to the spawning flat, will move to those areas. There are fish that live along the channel, on humps and shell mounds, and those fish spawn there—they don't go to the flats. It's like you've got city folks and country folks; they like different things. Those that live along the channel may never go to the bank."

In March when the smallmouth start migrating, you may have to follow them up a creek or ditch and get on the flats. "Those flats may be 14 feet deep or shallower," he says. "It depends on the water clarity as to how deep they spawn. The hardest time to catch fish is during this transition period, the time they leave the deepwater area and go to their spawning flats, because they are scattered. When they start staging, that's when they gather on a point on the bank, on a channel point, on a point off a flat or hump, or at one or both ends of an island.

PICKWICK AT A GLANCE

Location:	Hardin County Tennessee and northwest Alabama
Size:	6,163 acres in Tennessee
Length:	8.4 miles in Tennessee
Shoreline:	42 miles in Tennessee
Summer pool:	418 feet
Winter pool:	408 feet
Impounded:	1938
Featured species:	Smallmouth Bass, Largemouth Bass, Sauger
Other species:	Catfish, Bream, Crappie, Stripe (White Bass)
Description:	A flatland, run-of-the-river reservoir with many islands in the 8-mile run to Alabama. The lake is just over a mile wide near the dam and narrows to a little less than a mile where it leaves Tennessee. It has a silt and gravel bottom, sandbars, humps, stump fields, mud flats, and deep, creek bays. The lake is rich in nutrients and has good water quality.
Main tributaries:	Slate Rock Creek, Yellow Creek, Whetstone Branch, Indian Creek, Beech Branch, Panther Creek, Dry Creek, Pompey Branch, Burton Branch, Upper Anderson Branch, Boyer Branch
Landmarks:	TN 128 crosses Pickwick Dam; TN 69 runs parallel on the northeast side; TN 57 runs on the south side near the dam. Other access points are Pickwick Landing Sate Park, Burton Branch Recreation Area on Burton Branch Road, and J. P. Coleman State Park in Mississippi.
Operated by:	Tennessee Valley Authority

See Appendix C for map information

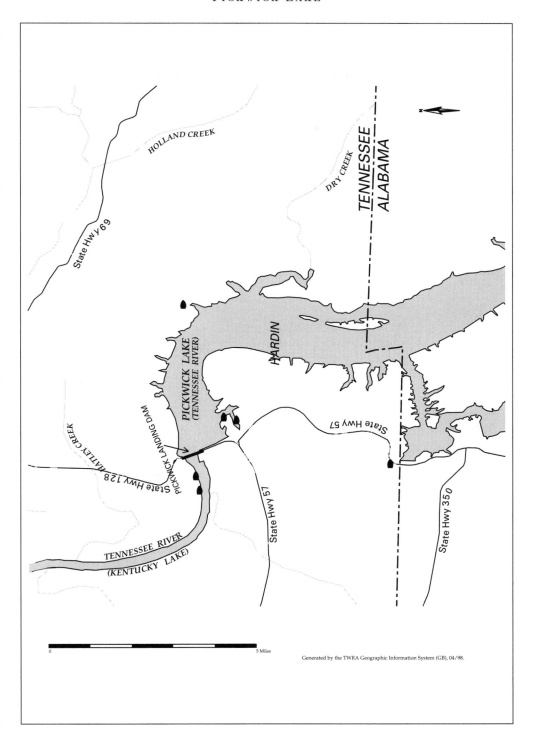

Generated by the TWRA Geographic Information System (GB), 04/98.

Ben Norman from south Alabama travels to Pickwick to sample the smallmouth action.

"The fish are moving all the time and are difficult to stay with. They may stay on a staging area for a week to 10 days before they start spreading out. You can really rack up some numbers when you find them staging. They'll stage 18 to 12 feet deep. It depends on their habitat. If they're on the river channel, they'll stage deeper than if they are on a point. All fish are not going to do the same thing at the same time, just like not everybody gets up to eat at the same time."

Once they reach the spawning flats, and the water gets up a foot over summer pool, the fish go straight to the bank. They will be right on the bank and will start feeding there, Williams says.

"In the spring I use ¾-ounce Rat-L-Traps, spinnerbaits, a Sassy Shad–type bait, and Bandit crankbaits. Depending on water clarity, you'll want to use chartreuse or a dark color. If it's clear, use a white or translucent bait. For the most part, I use a fast retrieve, but it can vary from day to day. Once they become active, a fast retrieve works until you get a front. After a front, you have to slow down and back off to fish deeper water. That's when your suspending jerkbaits come in.

"A jerkbait pays off when you can't get the other bite. Let's say you're in 14 feet of water; a crankbait that runs about 7 feet will pick up the suspended fish. I've noticed that the fish will suspend halfway from the bottom unless the water is real deep. Now there's a different angle to that, and I don't want to mislead anyone—let's say the top of a ledge is at 14 feet but the bottom is 50 feet. The fish will suspend straight out from the top of that ledge at 14 feet."

Pickwick has rock, gravel, chunk rock, bluff rock, clay, stumps, brush piles, drops with steps, and flats. "Let's say the flat is 12 feet, and you come across an area that is 12½ to 13 feet deep, the bass will get in those depressions," adds Williams.

"Everybody can see a point come off the bank and tell how it's running, but if you'll get along a gravel bank, move about 50 feet or more off the bank, and start going parallel, you'll find some humps. Those are key areas that a lot of anglers overlook. It just takes time on the water finding them; it's boring but it'll pay off."

Bear, Yellow, Dry, and Indian Creeks are good places to find smallmouth. "I don't catch them in the smaller tributaries. In March when they're gorging before the spawn, you'll find 7-pound smallmouth in 6 inches to a foot of water.

"About 90% of the time, the fish will be in shallow water adjacent to deep water—that's the sweet spot. For example, if you're on the river channel in 50 feet of water and you've got the top of the drop at 10 feet with a couple of step-downs to the 50-foot depth, you've got a sweet spot."

If you find a spot close by that is only 20 feet deep over that 50-foot depth, the fish won't be there. They'll be on the spot where it's the highest over the deepest water. Although you'll find smallmouth about anywhere, those places where it's the shallowest and the deepest are the places they use most. That's true except when they spawn. These sweet spots are the first place they come to when they start to migrate for the spawn.

He says, "It depends on Mother Nature, but they'll spawn in April and May in Pickwick. I've seen them spawn earlier and later, too. I've found the best months to catch smallmouth bass will be different every year. I've had my best month in August some years.

"Another thing, smallmouth take longer than largemouth to regain their weight because they spend more energy catching food. A largemouth will ambush prey; a smallmouth will chase it."

Summer

"The summer pattern will be humps and ledges," says Lou Williams. "They'll feed in the shallowest water in the area. If it's a hump, they'll feed on top of the hump. Smallmouth don't feed in 20 or 30 feet of water, but they can be caught there. They eliminate a lot of the water where shad can go when they are in the shallows. The shad are hard to catch in deep water because they can go up and down. In shallow water, the space is limited, and the prey is easily caught. Smallmouth will chase bait a long way, much farther than a largemouth.

"The time of day they feed depends on the current. If there is current, then the odds go up for feeding in the middle part of the day, from 11 to 2 o'clock. That's what brings the big boys out. If there is no current, the best time will be early and late in the day. My best days are when the skies are high, with an 8- to 10-mile-per-hour south wind, and current. If I can find those conditions, I'm going to catch some fish! You may have to hit the sweet spots several times during the day. In the summer, they'll feed more often, but for not as long. They may feed 30 or 40 minutes and then they're gone."

He uses a jig and curlytail, Bootlegger jig, or Hugh Harville's Sassy Shad–type bait in summer.

Williams concludes by saying, "It takes time on the water. I could tell you there is a hump right over there where I catch a lot of fish, but you may never get a bite. Time on the water means a lot, and you need to be by yourself. If you're with a fishing buddy, you'll fish rather than take the time to explore. The most important thing I can tell you is that you need a mental picture of where you're fishing. A topo map and sonar will help. Let's say you catch a 5-pound smallmouth in the area. Once you get through fishing, you need to survey the whole area. You need to know where this little dip goes, where that drops, where the highest spot is, and get a complete mental picture."

Fall and Winter

Longtime outdoor writer and expert angler Stan Warren from Bethel Springs says, "*Fall* is a glorious word, especially for a bass fisherman. The jet skis and pleasure boats are long gone, many fishermen have put away their fishing tackle in favor of firearms, and the bass of Pickwick Lake are more accessible than they have been since spring. At least, they are when the weather co-operates.

"Although much of the lake's fame is based on its production of heavy-weight smallmouth bass, there are largemouth and spotted bass in excellent numbers, as well. On a decent day, it is not uncommon to take all three varieties, often in the same location and on the same lure."

Warren remembers a misty day during the first week of November: "I eased into the bay nearest Pickwick Dam. Dropping a chrome and black A. C. Shiner into the submerged limbs of a tree, which had succumbed to erosion, I gave it four or five soft twitches, then spun the reel handles as fast as they could be turned. A smallmouth of just less than 5 pounds smashed it, but the real surprise was the trio of bass that arrived too late to play. Two of them were bigger than the one on the line. This twitch-and-go technique has proven to be a killer, not only here but on lakes like Dale Hollow and Percy Priest, as well."

He adds, "If it had not been cold, you would expect to find bass in the backs of the bays with stumps, timber, and other cover. Cast to the sunken trees and work the primary and secondary points. Also pay attention to what may be going on behind you—offshore. Pickwick has plenty of large flats where, under moderate weather conditions, schools of shad may congregate. White bass often make something of a commotion plowing into the schools, but do not be fooled. Brown bass are generally found underneath.

"While it's true you may connect with a topwater or spinnerbait, your odds go up if you drop something on the order of a Hopkins Shorty, or similar spoon, or a Cicada or Silver Buddy vibrating bait, smack down through the shad. One such situation yielded four bass, three smallmouth, and a 6-pound largemouth, on consecutive casts," he says.

"Okay, here is the worst-case scenario: a succession of storm fronts has rolled through, water temperatures are below 50°, and fish are not holding in shallow cover. A problem? Not really. What you need to do is slow down. Jigs are great, especially hair jigs or other designs that have plenty of motion even when barely moving. Deep-running crankbaits will also take their share of fish. So will a spinnerbait that is slow-rolled past bass, especially those holding under shad schools.

"Thanks in large part to Pickwick's wintertime smallmouth, there are hair jigs available suited to the task of sticking and holding something bigger than a bank-runner. One example is the Shadow Jig from Sportsman's World. This lure in ¼- and ⅜-ounce sizes carries either a premium-quality 3/0 or 4/0 hook—a sticker with enough room in the bend to handle the job."

Regardless of your jig, concentrate on main-lake points. Other "must-hit" locations, according to Warren, are those with drop-offs that resemble over-sized stair-steps or shelves. Good examples are found around Wynn Springs, Pompey Creek, Dry Creek, and the 209-mile navigational marker.

"Now comes the part where you may want to suggest I be fitted for a tight-fitting jacket with sleeves that tie in the back," he says. "The lake has numerous steep, limestone banks. Some have broken rock or gravel at the base. These may save your trip. Using jigs (I like hair jigs or a 3-inch, chartreuse, metal-flake grub), work tight to the rocks, letting your lures fall until you are sure that no strike is going to be forthcoming. Then let it fall some more. Have patience."

Since you may want to avoid the wind at this time of year, you might be able to concentrate on the rock faces that catch the most sunshine. Check the surface temperature near the bluffs and those in midlake. You may find a difference of 4° to 6°, enough to make bass active in one area and sluggish in another.

On the Tennessee side of Pickwick Lake, the rock faces on the southern edge of Dry Creek and those above and below the 209-mile navigational marker can be good for all resident, black bass species. To sweeten the pot, you will often encounter spotted bass practically stacked to the rafters. These football-shaped fish may not be heavyweights, but they are a lot of fun.

"When you look at the angling opportunities available in late fall and early winter, it is pretty easy to see that while the calendar year may be coming to an end, the fishing year, especially for trophy bass, is just getting started. You probably won't even mind the lack of competition. Of course, I may get to the best spots first," says Warren.

SAUGER

David Hancock, from Pickwick Dam, guides for striper, sauger, catfish, and smallmouth bass below Pickwick Dam. He says some sauger stay in the tailwaters year-round, but they don't school until fall and then they migrate upstream. When they get to the dam, they concentrate, and the fishing is better. Sauger spawn in March and early April here.

Steve Hacker is an Alabama smallmouth guide on Pickwick Lake who frequently catches sauger. Although he doesn't guide for sauger, he and his clients enjoy catching this tasty fish. Hacker's techniques work for smallmouth, but also work well for sauger, and his river methods are effective on the Cumberland River lakes as well as those on the Tennessee River.

Winter

"I don't usually start fishing for sauger until after deer season," says Hancock, "but I fish for them until March. There are people fishing below the dam, beginning in the fall, along the lock wall, dragging a minnow along the bottom and using a No. 5 splitshot for weight. Later in the fall or early winter, the fish begin to concentrate, and that's when I use a jig and minnow. I like the red-head jig with a green-fiber skirt tied with a stinger hook. I use a darker color when it's cloudy. I tip the jig with a minnow, but when the sauger are biting good, I don't use the minnow. I'll tip the jig with a grub or a Sassy Shad."

Hancock uses jigs weighing between ¾ and 1¼ ounces. He prefers using the lightest jig he can, depending on the depth of the water and the current. The deeper and swifter the water, the more weight it takes to maintain a vertical presentation.

"I fish from the dam down to Hardin Creek," he says. "I fish the creek mouths, downstream ends of islands, and sandbars. They are usually from 25 to 35 feet deep. Diamond Island has a sandbar at the downstream end that drops off into a deeper hole; that's a good spot. All you've got to do to find fish is put your boat in the water, start down the river, and look for boats. It's community-type fishing here. You may see a dozen boats fishing the same sandbar. You just get in line and drift like they do."

Hancock uses spinning gear in winter because it is easier to handle with gloves than baitcasting tackle. He uses 8- to 10-pound-test braided line for its sensitivity. It helps you feel the light bite of the sauger.

"I've never done any good fishing in that real swift water in front of the dam, but I fish what they call the short wall near the turbines," he says. "You can pick up sauger along the rocks across from the ramp. In fact, you can start fishing just about anywhere below the dam and catch sauger. Just be prepared to lose some jigs. Downstream at Horse Creek, Blind Bend, and Shiloh are also good places.

"I catch them trolling 12 feet deep with a Model A Bomber or a Bandit over the sandbars down the river in early April. That's where they feed after the spawn. That's one of the easiest ways to catch them," he says.

Spring, Summer, and Fall

"Pickwick Lake is a good smallmouth and sauger lake because it is a river-run reservoir with current," says Hacker. "The best sauger fishing in Tennessee is below Pickwick Dam, but I fish in Alabama mostly. The best places on Pickwick for anglers to look for sauger are in the main part of the lake and in the midlake region. They aren't in the tailraces this time of the year. They are fairly well spread out through the reservoir.

"You can find pockets of them in the main lake. I pull up on a hump or shell mound and catch four or five, even a dozen, sauger. They are scattered along these offshore features."

The intersection of the river with creek channels that have stumps are particularly good places to fish. Hacker fishes places like that on Kentucky Lake (Leatherwood Creek, for example) and catches a lot of sauger.

Sauger are pursued more in winter than during other seasons because they concentrate in winter for their spawning runs.

He says you can find sauger where two creek channels come together by looking for underwater points with stumps on them.

"Sauger are probably on these spots because the shad are foraging around those shell mounds, or it might be because the sauger are relating to structure like a bass does," he says. "It seems like sauger hold on structure like bass, at least on Pickwick they do. I guess they also suspend out in open water like walleye, but the ones I catch are related to structure some how or another—structure that is significant and different. We catch most of them 12 to 14 feet deep. Sometimes they will be as deep as 18 feet."

Hacker says he catches most of the sauger accidentally while smallmouth fishing. "We will be throwing hair jigs, bucktail jigs, Sassy Shad, and 4-inch plastic grubs on ¼-ounce leadheads. Sauger like those baits. We also catch them on Carolina rigs and crankbaits. I would say the hair jig, plastic grub, and Sassy Shad are the predominant baits that catch sauger on Pickwick.

"Some days crankbaits wear sauger out! You need one that gets down and kicks up the bottom. The sunken points on the main channel are good places for these baits. Another thing—you may think a sauger is a slow fish but they can catch a crankbait with no problem."

Hacker adds that the plainest, ugliest thing you can find that looks like a worm is what he uses on the Carolina rig. "It looks like a French fry. Zoom's Centipede is an example. It has no legs or tail or anything. It looks like a stick with ripples, but that's what the fish have been hitting, both bass and sauger. Cotton candy, pumpkinseed, and watermelon seed have been the best colors. Every time I take somebody out, we wonder what it is that makes these baits attractive to fish. It's the ugliest thing you could put on a pole but the fish will hit them."

The standard size sauger runs between ¾ and 1¼ pounds, but he catches some weighing more than 3 pounds.

"To fish sunken points, I put my boat in deep water and cast shallow," he says. "I'm more comfortable stair-stepping baits down a ledge than bringing them up. A lot of hits come when the bait is falling off a lip. I do catch fish casting from shallower to deeper water but not nearly as much as the other way. I try to keep it in contact with the bottom."

Hacker thinks sauger are pretty much homebodies. When the water cools a little, the schools of bait start to migrate and the sauger move, too. As reported on most other lakes, anglers have trouble locating them until they settle down in the late fall.

A good water condition for sauger is when the water is clear. Any mud or stain tends to turn them off. Hacker says he likes current but sometimes he catches a lot of sauger when there is none.

The day they caught so many, there was no current and the fish were in a loose school where two channels connect. They were off the point and he caught them jigging vertically. They were about a foot off the bottom.

Hacker says, "We catch sauger incidental to bass, but when we catch them, and my clients want to catch some more, we look for them in the same kind of places.

Hacker uses baitcasting rods when casting crankbaits or Carolina rigs, but jigs are cast on spinning gear. "If I had to choose one bait, it would be a 4-inch grub in a cool-ice color," he concludes.

STRIPER

Guide David Hancock says the striper fishery below Pickwick Dam is present from spring until early winter. The fish average 3 to 5 pounds with a rare 30-pounder taking someone's bait.

Spring, Summer, and Fall

"I used to guide for stripers just in the fall," says Hancock, "but the demand has increased so much that I fish for stripers from spring to early winter. My technique is pretty simple because I'm just fishing about 300 yards of water below the dam."

Live bait works best for the stripers, he says. "I use a three-way swivel, a 2-foot leader for a Kahle hook, and a 3-foot leader for the sinker. The sinker depends on the current and runs between 1 and 4 ounces. I use a 1/0 hook for the yellowtail and shiners and switch to a 3/0 or 4/0 hook when I use skipjack.

"I use a Piscator rig to catch small skipjack. I only catch about a dozen skipjack because they don't live long in the live well or on the hook. The yellowtail shad is another good bait, but big shiners and bluegills work, too. Stripers hit the yellowtail and bluegill for a short period and then stop. Stripers prefer skipjack that are about 4 inches long.

"I pull up into the boils, drop the bait to the bottom, and bump the bottom for about 300 yards. Then I crank up, go back upstream, and do it again—pretty simple."

Stan Warren fights a striper below Pickwick Dam while Doug Markham prepares to lip the fish into the boat.

He cautions anglers to call for the generation schedule because the stripers don't bite unless the turbines are generating. No flow, no fish, he warns.

"The majority of the stripers' weight varies from year to year," says Hancock. "Some years the majority will weigh 3 or 4 pounds and some years they are heavier. The largest I know caught below the dam was about 37 pounds. Every year there are some 20- to 24-pounders caught, but more commonly, 18-pounders are caught."

Stripers can be caught with topwater baits in the spring and fall. They hit best early and late in the day.

The stripers leave the area in late fall or early winter and return in the spring. Hancock says he doesn't know where they go, but "they'll be back."

PART II
Middle Tennessee

CHAPTER 5

Lake Barkley

The Last Pearl on the
Cumberland River String

Lake Barkley is indeed a pearl. It is the pet reservoir of TWRA fisheries biologist Tim Broadbent. His electrofishing studies show that more largemouth are shocked up per hour on Barkley than on Kentucky Lake. If that doesn't make you want to wet a line, then read what longtime guide Jim Moyer says. Lake Barkley's catfish have been under Moyer's microscope for more than 20 years. In that time he has developed a simple technique that will put "dinks," "deck slammers," and "ease-me-downs" in your boat. He takes you through each month and tells you where to fish and which baits work best. After reading Moyer's year-round plan, you'll be catching plenty of fish.

LARGEMOUTH BASS

There are plenty of largemouth in this reservoir, and bass fishing is good all year long. The northern Tennessee portion of the lake from about Bumpus Mills to Cumberland City has the best bass water—although good bassing can also be found in the river channel and the creeks.

GAME FISH RATINGS

Largemouth Bass	🐟 🐟 🐟 🐟 🐟
Crappie	🐟 🐟 🐟 🐟 🐟
Catfish	🐟 🐟 🐟 🐟 🐟
Stripe (White Bass)	🐟 🐟 🐟
Sauger	🐟 🐟 🐟

Winter

"Largemouth bass don't quit eating in the wintertime," says guide Jim Moyer of Clarksville. "They just slow down and may eat once every five to seven days, depending on water temperature. I think you need to slow your retrieve, go to smaller baits, and cast to sunny banks in the afternoon hours. Rock banks seem to be the best to fish in winter because [bass] get more heat and food there."

Barkley is a great fishery throughout the winter, especially for smallmouth. November and December are good months for catching smallies in the upper end of the lake near Cheatham Dam.

"December has better afternoon fishing," says Moyer. "Some of the largest largemouth bass of the year are caught in winter. Shad Raps and ⅛- or

BARKLEY AT A GLANCE

Location:	Stewart, Montgomery, Cheatham, and Dickson Counties
Size:	15,902 acres in Tennessee (57,920 acres total)
Length:	74 miles in Tennessee (118 miles total)
Shoreline:	466 miles in Tennessee (1,004 miles total)
Summer pool:	375 feet
Winter pool:	354 feet
Impounded:	1966
Featured species:	Largemouth Bass, Crappie, Catfish, Stripe (White Bass), Sauger
Other species:	Striper (Rockfish), Smallmouth Bass, Bream
Description:	This flatland run-of-the-river reservoir contains many islands, beginning between Cumberland City and Dover and extending to the Kentucky border. Bluffs are less pronounced, but Lake Barkley has many flats and a wider floodplain than the other Cumberland River impounds upstream. The reservoir is very narrow from Cheatham Dam downstream for about 50 miles. Below Cumberland City there is more backwater in the creeks. After the Cumberland crosses into Kentucky near Saline Creek, the reservoir widens slightly, but is still riverine. The bottom has some rock but is mostly mud and silt. There are many shallow areas and stumps and considerable wood along the shoreline. Lake Barkley also boasts numerous coves and creeks.
Main tributaries:	Half-Pone Creek, Barton Creek, Rocky Ford Creek, Red River, Long Creek, Lick Creek, Budds Creek, Blooming Grove Creek, Yellow Creek, Ball Pasture Creek, Cub Creek, Dyers Creek, Indian Creek, Hickman Creek, Blue Creek, Bear Creek, Burton Spring Branch, Elk Creek, North and South Cross Creeks, Saline Creek, Acree Creek, Shelby Creek, and Crockett Creek
Landmarks:	Lake Barkley begins west of Ashland City and extends into Kentucky. Clarksville, Cumberland City, and Dover are situated on the lake.
Operated by:	Corps of Engineers

See Appendix C for map information

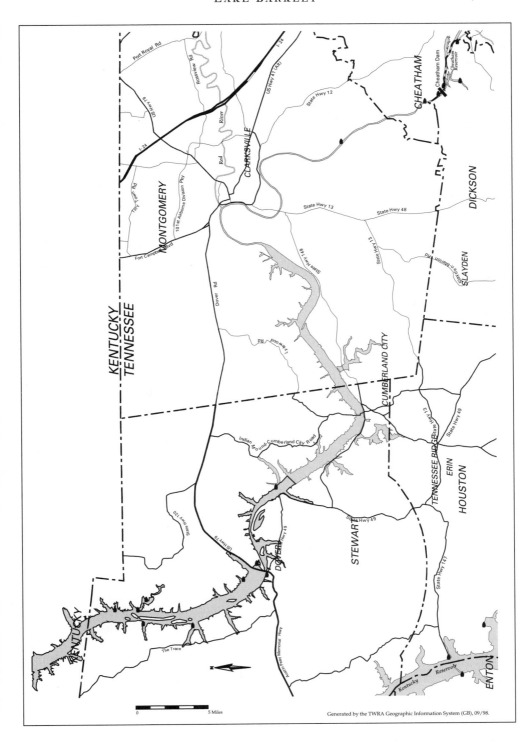

Generated by the TWRA Geographic Information System (GB), 09/98.

¼-ounce leadheads with 2- to 4-inch Power Grubs are good baits to fish over rocky points and banks. Flat baits, those like the Shad Rap and Rat-L-Trap that have a tight wiggle, are better wintertime baits," says Moyer.

In his experience, baits that run no more than 4 feet deep are good for catching bass on Lake Barkley: the Minus-1 and spinnerbaits. Live bait is not as good as artificial bait until spring. The trick is to fish slowly. "When you think you're fishing slow, slow down two more notches," he advises.

"A lot of 6- to 8-pound bass are caught all up and down the river in winter, except near Cheatham Dam because of the swift current. Also, it's a bit colder near the dam than it is in the main lake. The area around Bumpus Mills is very good.

"February is probably the slowest month of the year. At the end of February, be prepared to catch tremendous numbers of drums. They are one of the first fish to start migrating to the banks. A 15- or 20-pound drum will make you think you've got a whopper bass."

Moyer recommends translucent grubs, such as smoke, cotton candy, clear, and pumpkinseed for winter fishing. The last week of February is the beginning of jig and pig time. Black and blue combinations are very good. If the water is below 55°, use a pork trailer bait, but above 55°, plastic trailers are easier to handle; they don't dry out and get hard when not in the water.

Spring

Moyer says, "March is a great spinnerbait month for fishing around cover close to deep water. They're getting the urge to spawn when the water hits the high 50s. I concentrate on areas with shallow flats with stumps on it but close to deep water.

"We get a lot of fronts in March. One day the bass will be on the flats heading for the bushes. The next day you can go to the same place and not find a fish. When that happens, move off to deep water and cast a jig and pig but work it slowly. The bass will move up and down 20 feet depending on the severity of the front. You've got to fish slowly and be a line-watcher. If you feel anything that isn't normal, swing your rod. It doesn't cost you anything to set the hook. The bass may pick your bait up and just hold it in its mouth, and you'll have no idea a bass has your bait. Watch your line for a twitch, or if your line feels spongy, set the hook."

When the bass are on the flats during the sunny part of the day, he likes to fish from 10 A.M. until about 2 P.M. Toward the end of March, Moyer casts a red Rat-L-Trap.

"The key things to look for in March," he says, "are sunshine and water temperature. When the water reaches 55°, start throwing the buzzbait. It works better than topwater plugs. White and chartreuse are my favorite colors. When they start hitting buzzbaits, that's also the time they'll hit the suspending Rattlin' Rogue. Black and silver, black and gold, and firetiger are the best colors. Cast the Rogue on the flats, in front of the bushes and submerged stumps in shallow water, during the heat of the day."

In April we start getting consistent weather, and that's the time to start flipping spinnerbaits in the bushes. Moyer prefers the Indiana blade and chartreuse this time of year. The brighter the skirt the better. He says you'll start catching buck bass first because they move in before the females. If you're catching buck bass, he suggests you turn around and start casting in the open water, where you are sure to catch the much larger females.

He casts Mann's white Minus-1 crankbait in April, too. Bomber also makes a good white and gray body with a clear belly that's a deadly bait on the flats in the spring. The 200 series Bandit is another bait he recommends.

"Where you see scattered bushes, cast crankbaits and spinnerbaits into them," he says. "You can get the spinnerbaits in and out of the bushes better than crankbaits. If you aren't bumping limbs, you aren't fishing your bait right. Your cast can be short 10 feet to no more than 20 feet."

Bass fishing in April is very good from the Kentucky border upstream to Yellow Creek at Cumberland City. The hot spots are the bushes, the flats with creek channels next to them, and the outside bends of the creeks.

By the middle of April the backwater temperatures run in the upper 50s. When the water at 5 feet reaches 63°, the bass start spawning. Pitching a finesse bait into the beds will catch you a lot of fish. Topwater baits don't work well during the spawn.

"I don't fish deeper than 5 feet during the whole month of May," says Moyer. "I stay with the flats and bushes. Fish are going in to spawn, and others are coming out. The ones coming out are hard to catch, but the ones going in to spawn are easy to catch. May is a great month for bass fishing."

If you find the river muddy, try the backs of bays and creeks. Usually the water is clearer and warmer there. A lot of times you can see clear water in the mud line in the river. Bass will hold at the edge of the mud, or just under the mud that's on the surface, and use those places as ambush points."

Summer

After May, bass start moving to their deepwater haunts: the main lake points, the open water humps, bars on the edge of the river channel, creek channels, and bends in the creek channels. "This is when you switch to deep-diving crankbaits and Carolina rigs," says Moyer.

In June the water hits the mid- to high 70s and gets hotter as summer progresses. You'll need a sonar to find the deepwater structures that bass hold on. Bass stay in this pattern until the water begins to cool in September. Because Barkley is a run-of-the-river reservoir it cools faster than tributary lakes like Percy Priest.

Pro angler and co-star of TV's *On the Line,* Fredda Lee of Old Hickory says, "Bass move back into deep water in summer after they spawn along the channels and drop-offs. After bass recuperate from the spawn, they begin feeding with gusto. This is a prime time for catching lots of bass."

She says in summer, anglers fish creek mouths and the river channel. You can see schools of minnows orbiting the creek mouths and the bass are nearby. There is usually current in the Cumberland, and the water is cooler than in the creeks—just what bass like. Another benefit of this cool water is that bass hang around the shallows all summer.

"Buzz the logs, stumps, and floating cover with buzzbaits or topwater lures, such as the Tiny Torpedo or Devil Horse," Lee says. "Once you've tried the top, bump the cover with crankbaits. Shad Raps, Wee-Rs or similar baits probe the mid-depths. Fish a worm or jig to cover the bottom. If you believe bass should be there, cast each bait 15 to 20 times. You can fish for hours and not take a bass, then limit out in minutes. Be patient and be persistent."

Fall

Lee says, "Bass repeat their spring movements in the fall. They move back into the bays and creeks, stopping first at primary points, then secondary points. Then they move back into deep water for the winter."

Jim Moyer says, "In September you'll see the shad on the flats and the small bass hitting on the flats. Topwater plugs, small to medium crankbaits, and Rat-L-Traps will give you a great time catching these small bass.

"October is the time to fish plastic grubs along the edges of the flats. The small bass, up to a pound or so, will still be in the jumps, but the bigger bass are under them when they are in water about 10 feet deep. Run your crankbait about 7 feet deep to catch the quality bass."

September through October is when the fishing is hot and heavy. They are really feeding then. Middle Tennessee gets its first frost about the middle of October and the water starts to cool even more. Until the water temperature drops into the lower 50s, the fishing is about as good as it gets. It's part of their fall feeding frenzy. After the water hits the lower 50s and the fish start heading back deep, you should start using winter techniques again.

CRAPPIE

You don't hear much talk about the crappie fishing in Lake Barkley. It's safe to assume that the local anglers are trying to keep it a secret because this reservoir has a crappie fishery that rivals Barkley's big sister, Kentucky Lake. Crappie reign on Barkley and nearby Kentucky Lake.

TWRA creel and netting reports show a very strong crappie population. There is about a 50-50 mix of black and white crappie in the lake, but most anglers catch white crappie because black crappie prefer clear and deeper water, while anglers prefer fishing in shallow water. White crappie like murky water and stay in the shallows longer.

Once you leave the crappie fishing below Cheatham Dam, the best crappie fishing is between Cumberland City and the Kentucky line. This area includes Guices, North and South Cross, Lick, Hickman, Dyers, and Saline Creeks.

The midsection of the lake has many stumps providing abundant crappie habitat. This 35-mile stretch of the Cumberland has 13 boat launches. There are two near Cumberland City, then a 10-mile run downstream before you reach the next one. From the Dover area to Saline Creek, you can choose from 11 ramps. Poking into the bays and around the islands at Dover are among the best crappie fishing areas along Tennessee's lower Cumberland River.

Ron Tuberville holds a crappie caught on his slipfloat rig (described in the text). He and Terry Sherfield employ the bush-bumping method when crappie move among the bushes to spawn.

The following are some hot spots loaded with stumps that attract crappie; Denumbers Bay, Davenport Bay, Mammoth Furnace Bay, McNabb Creek, Cravens Bay, Fulton Bay, Honkers Bay, North Cross Creek, and Wells Creek, as well as the major creeks mentioned in the bass sections.

Spring and early winter are the two peak times for catching this delicious table fare.

Winter

Guide Jim Moyer says, "November is a great crappie month on the river. They're in 5 to 10 feet of water along the bank. Minnows seem to work best. The smallest tuffy minnow is what most of the anglers prefer. Some like shiners, but if you check with a bait shop, I bet you'll see 20 pounds of tuffies sold for every pound of shiners. Tightline is what I see used most on the river."

Most of the crappie anglers work the river channel; they don't concentrate in the creeks unless it's deep. Moyer adds, "The crappie stay along the banks until mid-December in the area around Bumpus Mills. As it gets colder they go deeper. In January we catch them at 25 to 30 feet."

As the water warms, they start moving back up, and by the time they move into the bushes in spring, they seem to hit the jigs better than minnows.

Cumberland City to the Bumpus Mills area is where he sees most of the wintertime crappie anglers.

"One thing I have noticed is that the longer a tree has been in the water, the better the fishing is," he says. "You don't catch many crappie in a fallen tree that still has leaves on it. I'll tell you one other thing—I think oak trees are better than others are. People have called me crazy for this, but it's what I have seen to be true. I catch more fish from oak trees than poplar, sycamore, elm, or any other tree that falls in the water. I won't even stop to fish a sycamore for bass. That's just one of those personal things that people come up with that make a difference."

Spring

Buck Simmons, president of B 'n' M Crappie Poles, says he prefers to jig for crappie in the bushes. "I tightline a 1/32-ounce jig on a graphite jig pole. The technique is called dabbling. You can put the pole exactly where you want it in the bushes, drop the jig by a limb, and just move the jig a little. It's deadly on crappie."

There is a great advantage to using his method of bush bumping. "With a little practice you can quickly learn to thread your pole among the bushes, drop a jig in a small space, and discern what your jig is bumping against," he says. "You can feel your way around the limbs and roots, and work various depths in the thick cover, covering a much larger area than a casting angler can.

"With a deft hand you can also get away with using light line, 6-pound test or less. The feel of your jig is not dampened by heavy line and transmits more sensitively. Another advantage to the jig method is not having to worry about having enough minnows and keeping them alive."

Two Tennesseans, Ron Tuberville of Dover and Terry Sherfield of Clarksville, fish among the buck bushes on backwater islands near Dover.

Tuberville says, "Start at the mouth of a cove within an island, or the spawning area in a lake, and keep on the move until you fish all the bushes. Dunk a minnow at the base of the bushes in front first and then those farther back. When you catch a fish, stop and give the area a thorough going-over. It seems crappie like to be close to one another, so where you catch one, you should catch others.

"The hard part is sticking your poles in the bushes without knocking your minnow off or snagging on a limb. This is where the slip bobber method becomes important. You keep your minnow, hook, weight, and bobber very close together as a single unit on your line, stick your pole through the bushes, and release your line so the minnow and bobber fall on target."

To make this unit, place your bobber stop at the depth you want to fish. Six to twelve inches is usually deep enough, but it depends on how flooded the bushes are. You have to make that decision based on the conditions. You can use a small piece of a rubber band or heavy monofilament as a stop.

"Once the stop is tied in place, slide on the plastic line guide that wedges into your bobber, then your bobber. Push the wedge into your bobber securely. Next put on your slip sinker—I like the ⅛-ounce conical slip sinker. Crimp a splitshot about 3 inches above your hook. The splitshot keeps the slip sinker off your hook."

It's a good idea to use light hooks for fishing the bushes because eventually you are going to snag. A light hook will bend before it breaks your line, provided your line is 8-pound test or stronger. A No. 2 to a 2/0 hook are popular sizes. Smaller hooks may afford you a little advantage among the bushes.

Now you have a slip bobber resting against the slip sinker against a splitshot and your baited hook all in the space of a few inches. This compact unit is easier to thread through the limbs without snagging. When you release your line, the unit drops to the water and separates with your minnow swimming on a short leash among the roots of the bushes. Crappie rarely refuse such an offering.

You can put your bait where most anglers wouldn't consider trying to reach with other methods. If there is no bite within 10 seconds, keep your pole stationary and reel in your line, then move your tip to drop the minnow by another bush. Working from front to back, this is methodical, rapid-fire fishing, even among the tangle of limbs.

"With this method you may find the largest crappie seem to be in the back of the bushes, the hardest to reach places," says Tuberville. "When you are working the bushes in the back or have threaded your pole among the limbs, you soon discover you can't set your hook in the usual jerk-and-lift. There is usually very little room to lift your pole. Of course it's a natural reflex to lift the rod, but that can get you in trouble. The remedy for this is setting your hook while leaving your pole in position and quickly reeling in, or you can pull the line in front of the reel with your free hand to set the hook. Sometimes getting the hooked crappie out of the bush can be difficult, especially if you have reached way back to a nearly inaccessible spot. But this is a nice problem to have.

Sherfield says, "You need to lift the crappie straight up, trying not to spook any crappie that might be close by because several fish will usually be around the same bush. Casting means retrieving the fish through the water and causing a commotion. This is another advantage of using a pole."

"This poking among the branches is the major reason you will need so many minnows," says Tuberville. "They frequently get knocked off going in or coming out."

Tuberville uses a 12-foot crappie pole with a Zebco Bullet 38 reel and 17- to 20-pound test. Sherfield uses a 12-foot telescoping pole with a Zebco 33 and heavy line. In most of the bushy places they fish, you would need at least a 10-foot rod to reach the back areas.

"Not all the crappie are in the thick bushes," says Sherfield, "so don't ignore stakebeds and laydowns and deadfalls in the backwater coves."

For a change of pace you may want the feel of casting and retrieving for a while. A 5-foot ultralight rod to cast $\frac{1}{32}$-ounce jigs under a pencil bobber works well, with or without a minnow.

For fishing the bushes or open-water stakebeds and deadfalls, try different baits, and fish the cover from all directions, not just from one side. After a frontal passage, crappie tend to move among the limbs, and you must place the bait in their reduced strike zone. The slip bobber rig is just the ticket to put your bait on target in tight places.

Barkley's best time for white crappie is in April and May. The weather and water level determine which weeks are the best. Stable conditions—that is, when the reservoir's water level isn't yo-yoing with heavy rains—is the ideal time for crappie fishing.

During the spring spawns, the black crappie come in earlier, around the third and fourth week of March, then depart for deeper water. White crappie will spawn later and remain in the shallows longer. In fact, the medium-size white crappie will stay year-round in about 8 feet of water.

Summer

David Woodward of Nashville, who has fished Cheatham for more than 20 years, says, "When I'm river fishing for crappie in summer, I'm more successful using jigs, minnows, or a combination of both. Locating cover is the key to catching crappie.

"I recommend new comers to the lake use a spider rig (see Appendix A). A spider rig consists of poles spread out to cover about a 10- to 18-foot swath. It's good to have a buddy onboard to help handle all the poles. The more poles the better because you can try different colored jigs or fish at different depths and fish a wider swath. This is the best crappie technique for locating fish," he says.

"Summer crappie are ready to bite if you put your bait in the right place. The right place is along the drop-offs on the river, sandbars, creek mouths, and creek channels. Creek mouths are always good spots to try first during hot weather. I like to anchor on the drop at the creek mouth and fan-cast jigs to cover the shallow and deep water. While I'm casting, I have a line or two out with a minnow. I let one minnow drift under a float in the shallower water, and the other minnow is on a tightline rig near the bottom of the drop. After I've cast the jig awhile, I'll move the minnows.

"I don't stop to fish any place if I don't mark fish with my sonar."

Fall

"When the water cools in fall," says Woodward, "the crappie move to the shallows again, chasing threadfin shad and hanging around bushes, stumps, and logs, or whatever cover is available. They don't go into the bushes like they did in the spring. I like that because it's easier fishing. They'll hold in water about 5 feet deep in fall. I like fishing along the river banks this time of year because there isn't much current and I can drift without having to fight the trolling motor to stay in good position."

CATFISH

Catfish had been neglected in Barkley by most sport anglers until Jim Moyer of Clarksville began guiding for them. Within a few years Moyer's reputation grew from a local angler to one of national status. You can take Moyer's techniques and apply them in most run-of-the-river reservoirs.

Moyer is one of only a few catfish guides in Tennessee. His clients can bring whatever gear they want, but often those rods go home in splinters, even the stoutest ones.

Moyer began guiding for cats "because there are plenty of them and they get big. People just don't know how many are here. I've taken people out who have fished here all their lives, and their idea of a big catfish is a 5- or 6-pounder. They didn't realize they could be catching 30-, 40-, or 60-pounders. It's taken me almost 20 years to get my system down to where I want it."

Winter

Catfishing is best during winter. Most of us think of catfishing as a summertime sport. That ain't necessarily so! In fact, Jim Moyer says you can't beat the winter for catching big cats. It's his most productive time of year.

He says, "I fish ledges and drops. I'm convinced beyond a shadow of a doubt that catfish are more oriented to drop-offs than any other fish. I look for a drop on a soft muddy bank that is as close to the bank as possible. If you fish a ledge that stair-steps its way down, it's pretty good at certain times of the year. But the ledge that is 5 to 10 feet offshore and drops to 30 or 40 feet is the best year-round ledge there is.

"The big fish don't move up and down much. They only move far enough to find food. When they find it, they may stay there four to six days. There is one bank I fish that is about 400 yards long, and during the course of an 8- or 10-hour day, I can't fish the whole length. I'll fish, then move 50 yards, then

Jim Moyer hefts a medium-size, Cumberland River blue catfish caught using skipjack chunks. Rods line the back of his boat and clients lift the rods to fight the catfish after the fish hooks itself.

move again, and move again, and not cover the bank. You have to go to these big fish, they won't come to you."

Moyer considers anything over 30 pounds to be a big catfish. Although blue catfish are his main target, he catches a few channels and flatheads, and he also catches striper and bass.

Moyer says, "I catch skipjack and fillet them for bait. I dice up the fillet, make a big ball, and put it on a 5/0 to 8/0 Kahle hook.

"I put the bait on a Carolina rig like people use to fish for bass. I use anywhere from 1 to 6 ounces of lead, depending on the current. I use a 1/0 swivel with 2 to 5 feet of leader, also depending on the current. The more current, the more leader I use. I want the bait to float and move with the current.

"I tightline the rig, and I can tell from the way they bite what size the fish is. One- to three-pounders, dinks, will peck the rod to death. Your 5- to 20-pound fish, what I call a deck slammer, will peck once or twice, then all of a sudden they'll try to take the rod out of the boat. The rod can jump over the seat and take off—you've got to be fast to catch it. Then you've got your big fish, the ease-me-downs, that ever so gently start to bend the rod, take it down, and keep right on going. I let it bend the rod tip about 2 to 4 inches, then sit down on him hard.

"Not only do I fish with skipjack fillets but I use the 12- to 16-inch skeletons in winter. There's a harness I rig up to fish the skeleton, and when the fish hits it, I let it run 50 to 75 feet using the Baitrunner. You've got a decent fish when you have one swallow one of those skeletons.

"I got the idea from the stinger hook on a spinnerbait. I use 30-pound test and Kahle hooks. I tie a series of hooks with about a 3-inch leader each, depending on the length of the skeleton. I've found that if the skeleton goes in the water all bunched up, fish ignore it. If the skeleton is straight, they pick it up pretty easily."

It depends on the length of the skeleton as to how many hooks Moyer uses. Usually he puts a hook in the eyes, one at the base of the head, one in the dorsal fin, and another in the tail, and that keeps it straight in the water.

"The fish are right on the ledge, and I cast downstream to put bait on several portions of the ledge, from top to bottom. I use a 30-pound anchor or more, depending on the current, and let out 50 to 100 feet of anchor rope so it will hold me on the ledge in the current.

Moyer fishes from Cheatham Dam to Bumpus Mills but never fishes right at the dam. He starts about a mile and a half downstream. "Too much rock and riprap at the dam for the kind of fishing I do, and the big ones aren't there for long," he explains. "The bigger fish hold in the deeper water downriver.

"It's been my experience that I can plot their movements week by week, starting in September at Bumpus Mills. Through the winter they move toward Clarksville and keep right on going until they get to Cheatham Dam in the spring. They spend a few days at the dam feeding, then they migrate a mile or two downstream to the eddies, ledges, and current breaks, where they will spawn. Then they go back to the river channel and start moving down to Bumpus Mills again. From one day to the next, you can just about tell where the fish will be.

"It's taken me 20 years to chase these fish up and down the river and learn their habits. I fish from four to seven days a week, and once I get on them, it's easy to stay on them. A sudden influx of water or something like that will change their pattern."

Clarity of the water doesn't make any difference. Moyer has caught them when the water was clear and when it was double-muddy. He says, "The big secret is the bait. It's the aroma of the skipjack."

Spring

David Woodward of Nashville has spent years experimenting and learning where game fish species abide during each season on the Cumberland River. It was during one of his experiments that he learned catfish could be easily caught when the water is still cold.

Woodward says, "In cold water they hold on the edges of the main channel and can be easily located with a depth finder. You'll see them holding on the last drop before the deepest part of the river channel."

Using his depth finder, he locates the edge of the channel and anchors. The midchannel depth is about 30 feet, and he parks on top of the drop at

20 feet. The water temperature in March is usually in the upper 40s. Even if you think you would be wasting time waiting for sluggish catfish to sniff your chicken liver, it usually takes less than 10 minutes to put the first cat in the boat.

Woodward says, "Most of the time the catfish hit lightly. My technique is to cast the bait toward midchannel so the current carries it from deep water up the edge of the channel. Active fish tend to be on the upper edge of a drop."

After the cast is made and the line becomes tight, he sets his rods down. Tip watching is his next technique. "Watch the tip, and when it bobs up and down, put your hand close to the rod for a quick hook-set, but don't touch the rod," he says. "If you move the rod, the catfish will feel it and leave your bait alone.

"Wait until the tip makes a **U** before you grab your rod. If it's a big fish, be sure you grab your rod before it leaves the boat," he says. "If it's a small fish, set your hook when you see a constant rhythm of bobbing in your tip."

As with most species, hooking the small fish is more difficult. The way Woodward deals with small catfish is to leave the area. "There are too many good spots on this river to waste time fooling with those little fish."

To find a good March catfish hole off the river bank, look for steep bluffs and cast out as Woodward describes. Boat anglers can locate the drops with a depth finder. His technique is simple, and since the catfish are everywhere in the river, you can all have catfish for supper in early spring.

Summer and Fall

During the summer the blue catfish are along the deep channels, except at night when they move to shallow flats next to the channels. Look for them below the first sharp bend in the river, below the dam where there are eddies, rocks, current breaks, and ledges. They will hold between 30 and 40 feet, and there are 60 to 65 spots between Lock B and Clarksville that are deep enough.

Moyer says, "In summer the cats will be on the deepest ledges they can find, and in the fall they start moving back downstream.

"One year I was on them until the middle of July and caught them at night when the dam was generating. If they aren't generating, go home. You're wasting your time fishing calm water.

"They don't bite in calm water," he says, "I don't know why but I can guarantee you it's true. I've spent many, many hours trying to get a bite in calm water. It hasn't happened yet. When they start the river again, you'll catch fish."

Moyer says, "In the fall look for catfish along the ledges downstream from the old Lock B. The big catfish will be moving downstream then."

Moyer and Woodward agree that it doesn't take long for catfish to locate your bait. If you don't get a bite within 20 minutes, it's time to move.

STRIPE (WHITE BASS)

These fish rank high among those considered to be the hardest fighters. If they have a drawback, it's their flavor. To remove the objectionable taste, remove the red meat that runs laterally before cooking.

Winter and Spring

Wintertime in the upper end of the lake is bonanza time. The other hot spots during cold weather are the creeks. Stripe move upstream and around the mouths of creeks. The creek water is usually warmer than the main channel's water. Some of the best stripe fishing, however, is just off the banks of the Cumberland.

David Woodward, longtime angler of the Cumberland River says, "Casting a white, yellow, or chartreuse jig, ⅛- to ¼-ounce, at a 45° angle from your boat, upstream to the bank,

David Woodward raises an upper–Lake Barkley stripe caught with a shallow-running crankbait.

then letting it fall following the drop-offs will fill your boat. Stripe on Barkley like the steep sandy-clay banks on the outside of a bend. Anytime you can cast a jig so that it washes under a logjam, be ready for a stripe strike."

Woodward has a saying for catching stripe in the spring: "They've got to eat, and I've got the meat." He works tuffy minnows along the bottom where current meets slack water. "Stripe are active in the headwaters of Lake Barkley and in the larger tributaries until May. Then they move downstream or out into the main channel for the summer."

Summer and Fall

Woodward says, "Summertime stripe angling is done by watching for the jumps. When the shad are being hit from below, you can cast small spoons, spinners, imitation minnows, and jigs into the fray and expect to catch several stripe before the action moves on. Trolling over sand and gravel bars, humps, and around creek junctions with small deep-diving crankbaits works good, too."

When the water cools in the fall, stripe begin to move upstream. You may locate them with your sonar, but they will be scattered. "The other seasons are better than fall," says Woodward.

SAUGER

Walleye used to be plentiful in the Cumberland River, but now they are rare, so concentrate on sauger in Lake Barkley. December through April is the easiest time to find and catch them.

"Sauger begin moving upstream when fall puts a chill in the water," says John Conder, retired fisheries biologist for the Tennessee Wildlife Resources Agency. "They leave their summer gravel bars in the main channel and start upstream to the dams. They stay in depressions in the deep water so they don't have to fight the current. Then they go into the shallows adjacent to the deep water to spawn."

The spawn won't take place until early spring, but the long prespawn period that begins in November concentrates thousands of sauger below the dams. During the rest of the year, from June until November, trolling the deepwater points, humps, and bars with crankbaits or a spinner rig (see Appendix A) with a night crawler catches fish. Troll points at creek mouths that are steep on one side with a more gradual slope on the other and cast or jig the inside pockets of these points.

Winter

Sauger begin arriving at their spawning areas in December, but better fishing occurs January through April. Spawning areas may be at the creek mouths of major tributaries or the dam. They need current, a gravel or rocky bottom, and food, which dams and creek mouths provide.

David Woodward has fished the Cumberland River year-round since the 1970s for all game fish species. He says, "One of the many cures for not having a sauger in your boat is a heavy jig, tipped with a minnow and a stinger hook. The stinger hook is the most popular remedy for short-biting sauger. Whether the stinger hook impales the minnow is up to you; I have seen it work well both ways. The weight of the jig, which ranges from ½ to 1 ounce, lets you know when it's on bottom—you will notice slack in your line. When the bait hits the bottom, wind your line in until your rod tip is about a foot from the surface. With an upward sweep of the rod (some anglers use a jerking motion), lift the jig and let it fall back to the bottom.

"Another panacea for catching sauger is a river rig. You cast and retrieve this setup. Attach a barrel swivel to the end of your main line after you have threaded on a slip sinker. You can use an egg sinker or the conical slip sinker used when fishing a plastic worm. You want a weight heavy enough to stay on bottom. Next, tie on 12 to 18 inches of line to the barrel swivel then your No. 1 or 1/0 hook. Bring the point of your hook from under the chin of a minnow up through the lips. Cast and retrieve slowly, making several stops."

Woodward adds, "Salmon anglers modify this method by omitting the slip sinker above the barrel swivel. They tie a piece of line to the swivel with two long pieces left over, one about 6 inches long and the other 12 to 18 inches long, as in the previous method. By crimping splitshot onto the 6-inch section, they eliminate the need to replace the whole rig if the weight becomes snagged.

"If you snag bottom, you will only lose the splitshot and not a lot of time retying. The disadvantage of this method is that you can't let line slide through the sinker. The extra resistance of the weight may warn the fish something is amiss. I don't think this disadvantage plays a significant role when fishing for sauger in fast water.

"My favorite method is effective without a stinger hook. Tip a bare ⅛-ounce jig with a minnow. Cast this lightweight rig upstream into the current. As it sinks, work it into an eddy or into the slow water at the edge of the current. Then retrieve it with long pauses along the way. I rarely miss connecting with sauger using this technique," he says.

Now that you have three good techniques for nailing your target, let's look at where to put your bait.

The area below Cheatham Dam has many good spots, but the amount of water being released plays a role. It is better if there is some current.

Woodward says, "I have heard anglers complain about too little and too much flow, but if you keep trying you will locate fish. Start fishing beside a vertical wall or at the end of a wall. Anchor just out of the heavy current, leaving about 3 feet between your boat and the wall. Drop a jig in the eddy next to the wall. Move it up and down vertically and as far left and right as you can reach. After you have caught those close by, it is time to change techniques."

From the same position, cast upstream into the current and let your jig wash into the downstream slack water. Hop the jig slowly back to the boat in the water close to the current. Keep your jig bouncing the bottom and don't let it get swept away. If it does get carried downstream, move your rod tip to get it back into the slower water. On succeeding casts, work the jig farther into the slack water making parallel trips back to the boat.

Woodward suggests that you make mental notes of the places you catch fish or where they hit and you missed. Return your offering ASAP. Also note how many turbines are operating. Your productive areas will change when the addition or subtraction of a turbine alters the current.

"Sauger will hold in depressions, behind boulders, ledges, or any obstacle lessening the force of water," he says. "All fish try to conserve energy and won't move unless there is an excellent chance they will get food for their effort. Locate obstacles that break the current causing an area of restful slack water for sauger, and you have a likely spot. These obstacles can be ridges, humps, depressions, or boulders. Finding them usually requires a depth finder—forget the weight on a string, the current is too swift. Sometimes you can watch for surface boils to see where big obstacles are."

The obstructions are some distance upstream from the visible surface disturbance. "Go upstream and line up so you drift over the surface boils, "he says. "This may be your answer to finding where the sauger lie. Don't stop once you pass the place, but drift for another 50 to 100 yards. After all, there are plenty of places you can't see, where fish find refuge from the current. When you've gone far enough, go back and do it again."

Woodward also suggests that when you locate an obstacle or depression with your sonar, try to anchor above or below it. Make your casts so that your bait will be near the bottom when it passes the fish's holding area. If it's too difficult to anchor, drift-fish it.

The water temperature is normally in the mid- to upper 50s in December. At this temperature, sauger are in search of a suitable spawning area. They return to the same spawning grounds if conditions are normal. Many will stop at upstream creek mouths along the way; still more than you can catch will not stop until they butt into the dam.

As early as October, small males and immature females begin showing up below the dam. The males begin arriving en masse in November, but the ladies are waiting for cooler water. When the water temperature drops to the lower 50s, the large females will join the males.

The males will stay in the spawning grounds about a month longer than the females. Females deposit all their eggs at once, so there is no need for them to hang around. Off the ladies go downstream to recover from the ordeal. The males stay to fertilize the females that spawn later; not all ladies ripen at the same time.

To catch sauger when they are in the shallows at night, whether they are spawning or not, trolling or drifting a combination rig is an excellent technique. Attach a three-way swivel to your main line. From one eye, tie a piece of line 12 inches long with a jig dressed in a curlytail and minnow. From the remaining eye, tie a 2-foot section of line and attach a floating Rapala or a shallow-running Rattlin' Rogue. These lures should be a good-size target, at least 5 inches long.

CHAPTER 6

Cheatham Lake

Cumberland River's Sleepy Downtown Reservoir

A sleeper, that's what Cheatham Lake is. It has a much better than average largemouth bass population. It's ranked among the top five lakes in Tennessee for more largemouth over 15 inches long. Fishing pressure is light, and there are long stretches of Cheatham Lake that get almost no fishing pressure. The most fishing pressure occurs in the upper and lower ends. The best largemouth bass and crappie backwater is within 6 miles of Cheatham Dam, but the best striper and smallmouth fishing is near the Old Hickory Dam headwaters. Cheatham has yielded 40-pound stripers and 13-pound largemouth bass, and it once yielded the state bluegill record of 2 pounds 8 ounces. Although Cheatham Lake looks like a river, it is one of the pearls on the Cumberland River system—some anglers say its tailwater is the best in the state.

LARGEMOUTH BASS

Preston Hulan of Nashville, who began fishing the Cumberland River below Nashville before it became a lake, says, "It's a most challenging river; it's most unpredictable. There are no obvious changes but something is different every day." His favorite bassing spots are Johnson Creek, the submerged Lock A, Hudgens Slough, Dyson Ditch, Sycamore Creek, the Ashland City Bridge pilings, Marrowbone Creek, and Sams Creek.

Hulan makes it clear you should "cast your bait parallel to shore and

GAME FISH RATINGS

Largemouth Bass	🐟🐟🐟
Smallmouth Bass	🐟🐟◗
Crappie	🐟🐟🐟
Catfish	🐟🐟🐟🐟
Sauger	🐟🐟◗
Striper (Rockfish)	🐟🐟🐟

fish the mouths of the creeks. When you do that with a white willowleaf spinnerbait, you should be in hawg heaven. But, he added, "if they don't hit that, throw a worm in the creeks around logs and such. If that doesn't work, throw a reddish-colored Deep Wee-R."

Spring

"Spring bass," says Hulan, "will be close to the bank and at the creek mouths. Use a white spinnerbait in close and retrieve it parallel to the bank." Later, in May, bass will be moving out of the creeks back into the main river, where they will maintain their territory until fall.

Largemouth rest where the current is quiet. Bass hold next to downed trees, rock piles, depressions in the river floor, the heads and tails of islands, or where current from another stream mixes with the main current causing an irregular bottom such as humps and bars. Bass wait in these places for

CHEATHAM AT A GLANCE

Location:	Cheatham, Dickson, Davidson, and Sumner Counties
Size:	7,420 acres in Tennessee (57,920 acres total)
Length:	68 miles
Shoreline:	320 miles
Summer pool:	385 feet
Winter pool:	382 feet
Impounded:	1952
Featured species:	Largemouth Bass, Smallmouth Bass, Crappie, Catfish, Sauger, Striper (Rockfish)
Other species:	Bream
Description:	Cheatham Lake is a flatland run-of-the-river reservoir. There are several rock bluffs, and the bottom is mud and silt with some rock.
Main tributaries:	Stones River, Richland Creek, Harpeth River, Sycamore Creek, Johnson Creek, Marx Creek, Sams Creek, Brush Creek, Marrowbone Creek, Indian Creek, Overall Creek, Whites Creek, Browns Creek, and Mansker Creek
Landmarks:	Cheatham Lake runs from just west of Hendersonville southwest through downtown Nashville, then northwest through Ashland City. Nearby major routes include US 31E, TN 155, TN 251, TN 49, and TN 12. The closest interstates are I-65 and I-40.
Operated by:	Corps of Engineers

See Appendix C for map information

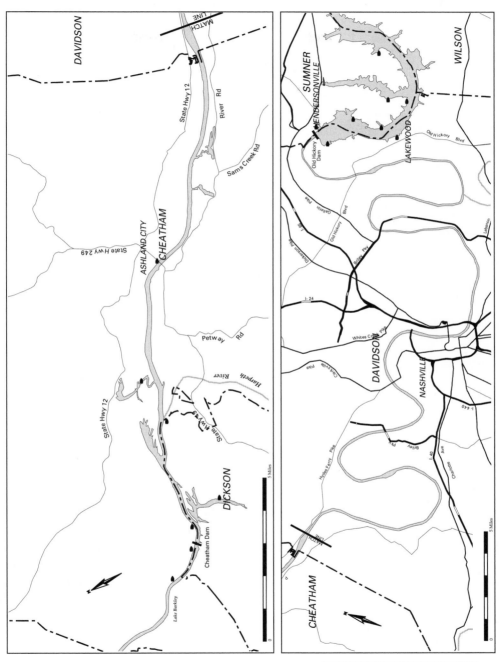

Generated by the TWRA Geographic Information System (GB), 09/98.

David Woodward fishes year-round for largemouth bass on Cheatham Lake. This female was gravid, so he released her to continue her spawn.

food to flow past, then they swim out, take the food, and return to wait for another snack.

Big fish get the best ambush spots. Remove that lunker, and another big fish will move in. Better yet, let that lunker go back to her lair once you are through playing with her. To paraphrase famous fly angler Lee Wulff, "A big bass is too valuable to be used only once."

Water temperature plays a very important role in bass behavior. Spring bass are shallow until late June. Largemouth bass find water temperature ideal between 68° and 78°. Because Cheatham Dam operates its turbines for electric power and navigational demands, the river flow varies. The water is mixed and the temperature won't vary from top to bottom. It will only change from season to season.

Hulan says, "Look closer at the lower end for good bass spots, and you will find the old submerged Lock A above the dam about a mile on the north side. It is between the shore and a green channel marker. With your depth finder, look for a standing concrete wall that will make your sonar jump from 39 feet to 4 feet. Beside this wall is a good spot to jig for bass. The current will dictate the weight of the jig you will need. One-quarter-ounce jigs perform well under normal flow.

"Johnson Creek is across the river and downstream from Lock A. You can go a mile or more up this stream for good bass angling. Upstream from Johnson Creek is the Pardue Pond Refuge and Pardue Recreation Area. This is prime bass backwater."

Dyson Ditch is the first opening upstream on the same side as Lock A. It has a small opening but enlarges into bassy backwater. Don't go rip-roaring in there, it's loaded with stumps, flats, and springtime bass.

The mouth of the Harpeth River is upstream from Pardue. Dozier's restaurant is at the mouth, and it has a dock to park your boat while you eat. It's the only place close to the river with this convenience.

Across the river and upstream a mile from Dozier's is Sycamore Creek. The launch is a couple of creek bends up from the mouth. Upstream from the launch and to the right, under the bridge and trestle, is a slough. There is a quarter-acre of fish attractors at the end of this slough. The water runs from 6 to 8 feet deep.

Sycamore Creek is about 17 feet deep from the ramp to the mouth, where it deepens to 25 feet. Then the bottom rises to 9 feet and quickly falls to 30 feet in the Cumberland River channel. These water depths are relative and the bottom shifts after heavy rains. Upstream on the main channel from Sycamore Creek is Harpeth Island. Angling is good on the island's points and the south side where the current is slack. The south side of the island is the entrance into Hudgens Slough. Use your depth finder to locate dips and holes at the mouth.

There is an unnamed cut with about 70 yards of backwater down and across from Sycamore Creek, along the southeast end of Indian Town Bluff. It is the fishiest looking place to be so small. There is a stakebed inside the first bend. You may have to use a trolling motor to get in the mouth (watch for logs), but don't pass this water without giving your jig 'n' crawfish or white spinnerbait a workout.

"All these creek mouths are good places to try, but also fish the banks on the straight parts of the Cumberland," says Hulan. "There are a lot of stumps, fallen trees, rock piles, and submerged ledges and drop-offs, especially along the bluffs, but they occur on mud banks, too. These are good ambush points for bass during the summer and winter months.

"Most of the banks have shallow shelves that extend 3 to 10 feet before they drop to another shelf at about 15 feet. The drop-off, depending on whether you're in a bend or on a straight part of the river, will slope from 45° to nearly 90°. With your depth finder you will see many irregular patterns at these drop-offs. These are frequently trees; some are covered with silt and others have their branches free. Both are good places to jig. Use spinnerbaits and crankbaits to cover the water above the drop-offs."

Another aspect of bass behavior is that bigger fish are less likely to school; they reside much deeper. Bass 12 inches or smaller will populate the shallows, taking their food from near the shoreline. They are easy targets for crankbaits and spinnerbaits. A jig and pork trailer or a plastic crawfish trailer are good baits to cast for the deeper bass.

If you are willing to travel 10 to 20 miles by boat, you can reach spots between Cleeses Ferry Ramps (one on each side of the river) and Nashville that are rarely fished. This is also true upstream from Shelby Park ramp.

Nashville angler David Woodard sums up how he fishes Cheatham: "Early morning, I start with a Tiny Torpedo or Devil Horse over points, 6- to 8-foot shelves, drop-offs from 12 to 20 feet, and eddies. As the sun gets higher, I switch to a do-nothing worm that looks like a night crawler and gets vicious hits. Later, I go to two-tone worms or lizards. Near dark, I use white and chartreuse buzzbaits with a white trailer, weedless rat, or frog."

SMALLMOUTH BASS
Through the Seasons
Cheatham's smallmouth fishery is getting better and better, especially in the headwaters. This is where guide Donny Hall of Nashville takes his clients.

Hall says, "I start fishing the rocky bank across from the Pennington Bend ramp. I usually catch some spotted bass up to 2 pounds here along with the smallmouth. When there is only one generator operating at Old Hickory Dam, the spots are active. I catch them between the surface along the shore-line down to 15 feet on top of the drop into the boating channel, about 40 feet from shore."

Smallmouth, according to Hall, become more active when two or three generators are operating at Old Hickory Dam. Cheatham Dam drawing water also increases the current and stimulates the smallies.

"Cheatham Lake is a long riverine reservoir, and the two dams at either end make or break fishing success," he says. "I don't know what the best balance of flow is between the two dams, but from years of talking with anglers who fish Cheatham and fishing the lake myself, we agree that bass don't bite unless there is some current.

Hall uses ⅛-ounce, black-haired, peanuthead jigs with a blue, plastic, frog trailer tied to 30-pound-test Spiderwire. His strong but thin line makes a big difference in saving snagged baits. Go prepared to lose a few baits among the rocks.

That upper section of the river has steep rock bluffs that hold the small-mouth. Most are caught on top of the drop at about 15 feet, although casting to the edge of the shoreline and working the bait out and along the bottom while drifting with the current picks them up, too. Hall says there are usually a few smallmouth holding close to shore, but the better fish are deeper.

He says there are very few places he can count on finding fish from one trip to the next. They move from day to day it seems.

Smallmouth are naturally strong fighters, but river fish are leaner and meaner than lake fish because they get workouts in the current.

CRAPPIE
Cheatham has a strong crappie fishery. In the spring the creeks mentioned in the largemouth section will provide you with plenty of places to fish.

Through the Seasons
David Woodward says, "Crappie will take your small jigs and minnows as they do in other waters. Your opportunities are numerous along the banks of the creeks in the lower end where you find downed trees and stumps. High water frequently resupplies the banks with crappie cover."

Summer fishing takes on another aspect. "Crappie roam the deep channel banks of the Cumberland," says Woodward. "Locating submerged trees on the channel is easy, and you are likely to find crappie there. Since the water temperature is uniform in the main channel and warmer in the creeks, creek mouths may be as far as the fish will venture during the hot summer months."

He says the crappie move shallow again in the fall and become easier to catch along the banks. "In the fall there isn't a lot of current, something crappie avoid, so I drift and cast a small crankbait, jig, or a minnow under a float. When I catch a fish, I use my trolling motor to get my boat above the fish, and anchor so they are at my back door. I'll use jigs, minnows, or a combination of both. It just depends on what they want. When they quit hitting, I fig-

David Woodward has spent years studying crappie on the Cumberland River and catches them through the seasons.

ure they are either spooked by that bait, and I give them something else, or they have moved. If I don't catch any more after trying several different baits, I pull up my anchor and start drifting again."

Crappie hold on deep river channels in winter and may prove hard to find. "I still catch plenty of crappie in winter, but I spend more time looking for them than in the fall," he says. "I fish brush and submerged trees along the outside bend of the channel with a minnow-tipped jig. I move it slowly among the branches. If I don't get a hit within a few minutes, I move to another likely spot. The channel has so many places for crappie, you need not spend much time in one area. When you find crappie, you will usually find many in one school."

CATFISH

Guide Donny Hall claims the Cumberland River has the next world-record catfish—and he may have had it on for over an hour.

Anglers are learning that cold-weather months are excellent for hanging beefy cats. This was demonstrated a few years ago by another guide from Clarksville, Jim Moyer, who has landed catfish over 80 pounds in cold weather, but finds them scarce during the summer in Lake Barkley.

Hall fishes a different section of the Cumberland—Old Hickory and upper Cheatham—to catch cats year-round. In late summer one of his clients caught a 57-pound flathead.

Doug Pelren, TWRA fisheries biologist, has been saying for years that catfish have not been pursued enough by anglers, and there are a great many "big 'uns" swimming our waters. All it takes is a little effort to catch these plentiful fish, less effort than it takes to go bass fishing. Hall proved that. He has a method for catching cats that is simple and starts off fun.

"First, you have to catch bait but without casting a net," he says. "I use a lightweight spinning outfit with a Piscator rig for catching skipjacks. It's about 3 feet long with five drop-flies along its length. These flies are much like [the ones] a fly fisherman uses. A ⅛-ounce bell sinker is attached to the bottom of the rig to add weight for casting—heavier weights can be added to go deeper or to cast into strong current."

Skipjack feed in the boils and swift current below Old Hickory Dam, so he casts his rig into and behind the boils, catching up to five skipjack per cast. "This is fun! You catch fish on nearly every cast and you can feel them hit—bang, bang, bang. You reel in a stringer of fish, not just one."

Hall catches skipjacks about 6 inches long, puts them on ice; after he catches about 30, he's ready for the big kitties. He cuts the baitfish into chunks and fills a 7/0 Kahle hook with them.

Since he had his 80-pound-test line broken by a big catfish, he has switched to 130-pound-test Spiderwire. Keep in mind you have to have a very stout rod to match that strong line.

Hall anchors on the edge of the channel drop to fish a spot where he catches mostly flathead cats. Flatheads are not like channel and blue catfish. They prefer fresh or live bait, whereas you can catch channels and blues on anything that has a strong odor, from soap to entrails.

"It doesn't take long for catfish to hit if they are in the area. If I catch cats less than 5 pounds, I move. I'm looking to catch those that weigh at least 10 or 12 pounds, and hope for 30-pounders or bigger. But any day you can catch 50 pounds of fish or more has to be a great day of fishing," he says.

Nashville angler David Woodward recommends three creeks for catfish: Sycamore, Bull Run, and Brush Creeks. He says 2- to 8-pound cats are frequently caught, but 12- to 15-pounders are common.

Summer

Woodward says he catches between 20 and 50 cats from 1 to 6 pounds with minnows, chicken livers, and night crawlers, near the tree line on Bull Creek and the creek mouth during the summer. Blue and channel cats are most often caught near the bottom.

"To catch the big flathead or yellow cats," Woodward says, "I fish the deep ledges, rocky drop-offs, and eddies, with large shiners or minnows. I fish near the 20-foot depth. I drop my anchor upstream from where they want to fish, and let the bait drift downstream into the hole because catfish are extremely spooky."

All of the Cumberland River is rich with catfish. See the Old Hickory Lake and Lake Barkley chapters for more techniques during the seasons.

SAUGER

Although walleye used to be plentiful in the Cumberland River, they are no longer because the dams created siltation that destroyed their habitat. Sauger are more prevalent than walleye in Cheatham Lake, and anglers fish for them from December through February below Old Hickory and Cheatham Dams (see the

Sauger are one of Tennessee's best-tasting fish, but most anglers only pursue them from November through February.

Lake Barkley chapter for detailed techniques). Most anglers quit fishing for sauger before their busiest spawning month, which is April according to TWRA studies, and pursue other species.

Winter and Spring

From November to March you are likely to catch sauger at the mouths of the major tributaries. Minnows or a jig dressed with a minnow, fished on the bottom, are the most effective methods. This is a good time to fish below all the dams in Tennessee.

Fisheries biologists say that once the spawn is over, around the middle of April, sauger drift downstream and stay along the main river channel and where creeks join the river channel. Fishing from sunset until dawn with topwater, imitation minnows, such as Rapala and Rebel, pays off in shallow water near the river channel. Cast downstream and "twitch" the minnow back to the boat. Shallows inside of the river's bend, shallows just above or below a creek junction, and humps, ridges, or bars in the river are the likely night spots.

David Woodward vertically fishes the lock and its walls below Old Hickory Dam. "I jig a minnow on a ¼-ounce jig or use a Carolina rig with a floating jig to get the minnow off the bottom some. One of my most productive rigs is that double-hooked, bottom-bouncing, crappie rig. I have two drop-lines about a foot-and-a-half a part. I put more lead on this rig because I use it where there is more current. I've found that sauger don't always stay in swift current, but you'd think so by looking at where most sauger fishermen are fishing. I catch a lot of sauger just to the slow side of the seam where there is fast current mixing with slow current. And I can almost always catch them in eddies below the lock walls. One thing I have noticed: If I stay in one good place, a school will swim by, and I'll catch three or four in a few minutes, and then they'll leave. They either come back or another school comes by before long. So I anchor in a spot that I'm sure they'll come by because I like to wait for them to come to me. And I usually catch more than the fishermen drifting and fighting the current do."

Summer and Fall

"Not many anglers fish for sauger after March, but they can be caught trolling a night crawler rig (see Appendix A) with spinners or an imitation minnow crankbait," says Woodward. "These are the most productive methods for catching these fish during the summer and early fall. Troll the deep water on the outside of the Cumberland River bends, along the bluff ledges of the main channel, and deep pockets at creek junctions. Sauger are going to be in the middle portion and lower ends of the lake in the summer. They'll stay there until they start feeling the urge to spawn again and swim back upstream toward the dam."

STRIPER (ROCKFISH)

Cliff Duckworth, owner of Nort's, a popular bait and tackle store in Nashville, is a former guide and has developed a simple technique for catching stripers below river dams. Keep in mind that when he talks about certain river features below Old Hickory Dam—the headwaters of Cheatham Lake—there are usually corresponding ones below other dams. The fishing below all the Cumberland River dams is similar.

Summer

Duckworth says, "The first thing you need is bait. You can catch it around the dam or at the Hendersonville discharge a couple of miles downstream. Gizzard shad stay there until the water gets cold in November, and then they scatter."

He recommends using a 7-foot-diameter cast net. Because his favorite fishing places are close by, he doesn't need to use a shad tank. He starts with about a dozen shad in the live well. When he runs out, it's easy to catch more. Duckworth says, "That way I have great bait, always fresh."

He fishes with what has become known as a Carolina rig. He says, "The water isn't very deep here, and I fish with one rod between 10 and 12 feet deep and another at about 6 feet.

"You need a 1-ounce or heavier egg sinker to keep your line vertical. I place it over a sturdy barrel swivel. A 2-foot leader is next and I use a 5/0 Gamakatsu hook because of the size of the bait. That hook is so sharp I don't have to set it. The fish does it for me.

"I run one balloon line. It's basically a free line with 10 feet of line below the balloon that I run close to the shore. I tie the balloon to the line and not the line to the balloon. That keeps from having a knot in the line. I keep the balloon close to shore. It's just a question of boat maneuvering. If the shad gets frisky and swims toward deeper water, I move the boat closer to shore. They usually stay in place. I try to keep the boat in about 12 feet of water and that's about 20 feet from shore in this part of the river."

It's part of keeping things simple. He says, "I sit here with bow pointed upstream, maneuvering with the trolling motor, and looking back at the rods and the balloon. I love this easy method."

In the upper part of Cheatham Lake, just below Old Hickory Dam, the stripers Duckworth catches weigh between 15 and 25 pounds with the size bait he uses. He says, "There are no world-record stripers in here but it's pretty easy fishing."

Because the channel was dredged leaving a lot of humps and hollows, the fish are hiding in the depressions, staying out of the current, and waiting for bait to come over the top so they can pop up and snatch one. Duckworth isn't looking for structure, but he drifts over the holes waiting for a striper to nail his bait.

"Striper rarely school in these depressions," he says. "Usually individual fish hold in a spot. It seems like they have certain territories they work. It's very rare to catch two fish in the same place at the same time. There are certain holes where fish will be, but that depends on the current."

River fishing is much different than lake fishing. In a lake, fish have more water and room. In the river, they can swim under trees, rocks, and other cover quickly. And the river striper are stronger than their lake counterparts. In the river, Duckworth doesn't use any line less than 20-pound test and goes up to 40- or 50-pound. "You have got to control the fish when there is a lot of cover, and you need heavier line to do that."

On fishing the tailwater he says, "It's not my favorite. Basically, I'm a lazy person and I just don't want to fight the boils. I fish away from the dam, still in current of course, and let the bait do the work. I can sit and daydream."

Duckworth has found the fishing is better when there are only two generators operating in Old Hickory Dam. He prefers the current moving at what would be a brisk walking pace on land. With three generators operating the fishing is slower.

He drifts the entire bank. He knows certain holes where he has caught fish. But there are places he catches fish unexpectedly. He says, "I believe as the water level or current changes they move to other places. With two generators and stable conditions, I have a higher success rate at guessing where they will be."

Striper keep the same pattern pretty much all year, but the river is more stable from July through November. Duckworth doesn't change his river method, but when the river is too high or swift, he fishes a lake.

Striper sometimes hit on the surface. He's seen them in the jumps in the upper part of the river around Rome, but never seen them jump below Old Hickory Dam. It may be because there aren't big schools of shad there as in Old Hickory Lake. Shad prefer to move in slower water.

"The difference between the threadfin and gizzard shad is that threadfin are smaller," he says. "Some people call them yellowtails because they have a yellow tint. A full-grown threadfin is about 4 inches long. It's a great bait for hybrids, but gizzard shad are better for striper because they are stronger."

As for bream as bait, Duckworth says, "Bream have a tendency to swim along and not get too active, but a shad will try to escape when a striper is near. That extra distressed activity attracts the striper. When I see a rod tip jump up and down, I know to get ready—the shad is in danger. Sometimes the shad will try to climb on top of the balloon to get out of the way."

He also uses skipjack. "You can catch all the skipjack you want by casting a small, white, crappie jig. But the stripers in the upper end of Cheatham Lake are smaller fish. Skipjack are better suited for big stripers. You would want to use a 2-pound skipjack in Melton Hill where you can catch a 50- to 60-pound striper. Skipjacks are too big for the 15- to 20-pound fish below Old Hickory Dam," he says.

Duckworth concludes by saying, "I like to fish simply. Shad fit my fishing style. There are people who have to be casting. People should fish the way that is comfortable. I drift, letting the current and shad do the work. I save myself for the big fight of getting the striper in the boat."

David Woodward offers another slant on the striper. He says, "Shiners and goldfish are legal bait on Cheatham. They are the best live bait to use for rockfish. The next best bait is a white, ¼-ounce jig with a Sassy Shad. Drift these baits below schools of minnows you detect with your sonar.

"I tie a 2/0 or 3/0 steel hook about 8 inches above a 1- or 2-ounce sinker, depending on the current. With the minnow hooked through the lips, I put it just below the school of baitfish. I look at my graph to see that there are big fish below the school. If I don't see big fish, I don't fish that school. I move around until I find what I want.

"Sometimes those big fish under the baitfish are catfish or largemouth bass, I can't tell until I catch one to know for sure. But whatever it is, it's big enough to be fun."

Woodward says rockfish are usually found in 25 to 30 feet of water and occasionally near 50 feet. Below the dams are top-notch places to fish for striper year-round.

Some anglers cast cut shad from the bank into the swift water below the dam. They use several ounces of lead to keep the bait on bottom. Other anglers, using live or cut shad, run their boat into the swift water then drift their bait on bottom and downstream for 100 yards. Both techniques are effective. Ten- to thirty-pound striper are common in Cheatham, with some reaching 40 pounds.

CHAPTER 7

J. Percy Priest Lake

The Astonishing Music City Reservoir

Nashville residents know that J. Percy Priest Lake is an excellent fishing reservoir, but visitors from outside the midstate speeding by on Interstate 40, fighting to change lanes in the ever-increasing traffic, should probably be told that the Music City's congestion and development hasn't hurt the lake's game fish population. Anglers must always monitor Tennessee's reservoirs and streams to assure no one abuses them, but Percy Priest is an example of how humans can prosper without destroying things in nature.

Furthermore, don't think that Percy Priest is an average lake because it sits in the shadow of a metropolitan city, and don't be mislead by congestion. Abundant populations of game fish inhabit this lake and will strike the right presentation, even when skiers, swimmers, and personal watercraft shatter the tranquillity.

LARGEMOUTH BASS

Smyrna resident Larry Shaffer has fished Percy Priest for more than two decades and considers it a "phenomenal" largemouth bass lake. He is a part-time guide, a tournament competitor, and an angler who spends thousands of hours each year pursuing bass.

GAME FISH RATINGS

Largemouth Bass	🐟 🐟 🐟 🐟
Smallmouth Bass	🐟 🐟 🐟
Crappie	🐟 🐟 🐟 🐟
Hybrid (Cherokee Bass)	🐟 🐟 🐟 🐟
Striper (Rockfish)	🐟 🐟 🐟

Winter

Percy Priest's bluffs should be among an angler's first winter stops, says Shaffer. The colder the water gets, the steeper the bluffs should be. "I feel comfortable that I can catch fish from Priest anytime of the year," says Shaffer who has occasionally pulled largemouth through skims of ice.

Shaffer's favorite method for catching sluggish largemouth is flipping pig and jig combinations. "Flipping is similar to casting a fly rod, only it's done upside down with a baitcasting reel," he explains. "I can put bait in places that are impossible to cast and do it repeatedly. I can also make a lot of tosses quickly in a short amount of time because I'm only fishing a few feet away from my boat."

Shaffer flips against bluffs that have cover beneath them. Tree tops and chunk rock harbor baitfish and attract hungry largemouth. He flips ⅜- to ½-ounce jigs with a 7½-foot rod and a baitcasting reel spooled with 20-pound-test monofilament. The colder the water, the slower he works his jig.

J. PERCY PRIEST AT A GLANCE

Location:	Davidson, Wilson, and Rutherford Counties
Size:	14,200 acres
Length:	46.4 miles
Shoreline:	213 miles
Summer pool:	504.5 feet
Winter pool:	480 feet
Impounded:	1968
Featured species:	Largemouth Bass, Smallmouth Bass, Crappie, Hybrid (Cherokee Bass), Striper (Rockfish)
Other species:	Saugeye, Catfish, Bluegill
Description:	The lake's upper section near the headwaters is narrow. The reservoir widens in the midsection and becomes deep and wide near the dam. Percy Priest has steep bluffs, many drop-offs, sharp points, humps, islands, and long channels. Rocky banks and bluffs are common, as are mud banks.
Main tributaries:	East Fork of the Stones River, West Fork of the Stones River, Stones River, Fall Creek, Spring Creek, Stewart Creek, Hurricane Creek, Suggs Creek, Hamilton Creek
Landmarks:	The lake's lower end is within sight of downtown Nashville. Other cities near the reservoir include Smyrna, LaVergne, and Murfreesboro. Nearby highways include US 41/70S and TN 171. The closest interstates are I-40, I-840, and I-24.
Operated by:	Corps of Engineers

See Appendix C for map information

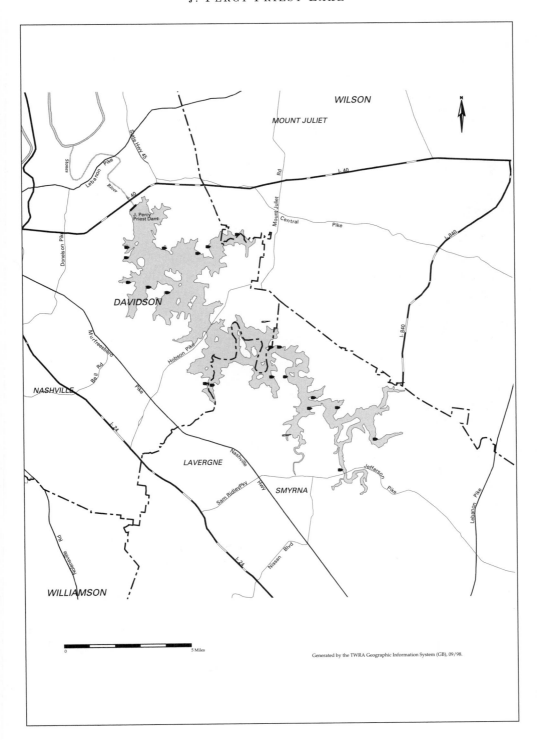

Generated by the TWRA Geographic Information System (GB), 09/98.

Fishing steep bluffs does not necessarily mean fishing deep. "If I hang fish that are down 10 feet, I'm catching bass that I consider deep," notes Shaffer. "Most of the fish I catch are only a few feet below the surface and suspending around cover."

Many jigs are available on the angling market, but Shaffer favors Rattlin' Bootlegger jigs. Pork helps slow his presentation. A Bo-Hawg Frog is his favorite trailing piece. Shaffer varies the size of his jig and pig until he finds a combination that the fish prefer.

His surroundings dictate Shaffer's color selection. "If the water is dingy or the day overcast, I try something like black and chartreuse," says the guide. "If it's sunny and the water is clear, I'll try black and blue. I want to use a bait that has a natural profile, but that is seen by the fish."

Tournament professional Larry Shaffer fishes Percy Priest year-round, catching largemouth through skims of ice in winter or in deep water on the hottest days of the year. Spinnerbaits and buzzbaits should be in every fisherman's arsenal. Each has a time during the year when bass can't resist them.

When mid- or late-winter warm fronts move through Middle Tennessee, Shaffer searches for hungry bass in shallow water. "If we get a couple of warm days in January or February, fishing can be fabulous," says Shaffer. "Back-to-back-to-back 65° days can change the surface temperature from 40° to 60°." During these rare fronts, bass find heat in shallow water and gorge, he explains.

Locating baitfish is key to catching bass anywhere. Percy Priest is full of shad, which often suspend in creek channels. When not working bluffs or shallow water, Shaffer bounces ¾-ounce spoons off river- or creek-channel ledges under schooling shad. The warmer the water, the higher he bounces his spoon and the quicker he snaps it; the colder it is, the slower he works it.

While strikes are sometimes rare in winter, largemouth frequently weigh between 3 and 5 pounds, says Shaffer.

Spring

As water temperature begins rising, Shaffer throws crankbaits that imitate Priest's shad. He retrieves them slowly with spinning gear and 8-pound-test monofilament. Among his favorite early spring lures are No. 5 and No. 7 Shad Raps, Deep Wee-Rs, and Deep Baby Ns. He catches most of his late winter–early spring bass between 7 and 10 feet deep.

Many bass are working their way toward spawning sites by March, stopping to stage and feed. "Finding bass in spring is just like in the winter, or anytime for that matter—look for shad first," says Shaffer. "Fish are moving into pockets, into creeks, and onto flats. They hold in areas near baitfish. A map can help locate these areas."

Once fish start bedding, Shaffer returns to baitcasting gear and flips jig and pig combinations or throws spinnerbaits. He always uses a stinger hook on spinnerbaits to catch tentative bass. Plastic lizards, crawfish, or worms worked on a Carolina rig also catch fish once largemouth move into coves, creeks, or onto flats. Among Shaffer's favorite plastic colors are pumpkin-chartreuse, junebug, and smoke. He uses ¾- to 1-ounce sinkers to stir the lake bottom and attract attention. He also uses jerkbaits to coax strikes.

"Spring is when I catch my biggest largemouth on Percy Priest," says Shaffer, "but summer is when I catch the greatest number of them."

Summer

After the spawn, Shaffer often fishes secondary creeks and the outer ends of coves and creek pockets. Although some bass still inhabit shorelines, many large fish move near main points and creek channels. Shaffer locates them 5 to 15 feet deep alongside drop-offs next to channels.

Avoid the sizzling summer heat by fishing early or late, but if heat isn't a problem, Percy Priest bass hit all day, even during the hottest hours, assures Shaffer. Slow rolling spinnerbaits and slowly working Carolina rigs are good ways to catch channel dwellers, but Shaffer prefers throwing large crankbaits such as DD-22s or Fat Free Shads.

Fall

When water temperature starts falling, big largemouth become active and are stimulated by buzzbaits, says guide Gene Austin. When surface temperature has hit the mid-60s, usually around mid-October, he has had memorable buzzbait days. "Once the water temperature gets about 65°, Priest has its best topwater fishing all year," says Austin. "Buzzbaits are great fun, but so are propbaits like Tiny Torpedoes."

Austin looks for shallow pockets near shorelines, but makes sure these pockets have "an old creek channel coming out of the surrounding woods." He tosses buzzbaits over water 1 to 5 feet deep. Bass stage close to stumps, lining the high side of creek beds. "They isolate on these stumps or move toward the creek mouth," says Austin. "They hang tight to the stumps until they're ready to feed. Once they get hungry, they move into the creeks."

Most of Austin's buzzbait fishing occurs near Seven Points Recreation Area or just below Hobson Pike Bridge. "Places I fish are full of big largemouth," says Austin. "I have caught limits in October with nobody else around."

Because heavy topwater lures frighten fish in shallow water, Austin tosses ⅛-ounce buzzbaits. White is his favorite color, but a number of shades should work during this aggressive period. A No. 9 Countdown Minnow is among the excellent hard-plastic topwater lures, he notes.

SMALLMOUTH BASS

Guide Gene Austin is a good largemouth bass angler and an expert smallmouth fisherman. He began bass fishing Percy Priest Lake shortly after the Corps of Engineers impounded it. For him, being attentive is the biggest key to successful smallmouth angling.

"Wind, water color, and water temperature—they're the important elements I notice anytime I fish," says Austin. A frequent mistake made by anglers is avoiding uncomfortable windy banks. "Fish gather in these areas, and anglers should, too," says Austin.

Bass hang around windy banks to eat baitfish pushed into these areas by choppy water or to gorge on crawfish scurrying for cover. Stain also attracts bass, as do a few degrees difference in water temperature during certain times of the year.

Winter

Smallmouth action is often slow in January and February, but Austin's fish usually measure 15 inches or longer. "To have a good day of winter fishing, I must slow down my bait presentation," notes the guide.

When the day is cold but the fish aren't really deep, Austin tosses dark-colored crankbaits that have lots of wobble. Shad Raps and Fat Raps are among his favorite Percy Priest crankbaits, especially if they include his favorite winter colors: combinations of brown and orange or blue and black.

Much of Austin's winter is spent near Bryant's Grove, Hong Kong Island, and the Boy Scout Youth Camp, all of which are above the easily found Hobson Pike Bridge. While crankbaits catch fish, Austin's favorite cold-water lure is a ¹⁄₁₆-ounce, brown and orange hair fly, fished "naked, just like it comes out of the package." He notes, "This fly is deadly on rocky shorelines and beneath bluffs. I don't want my fly falling like a spark plug. That's why I throw a light lure on 6-pound monofilament."

Live bait is also good. Austin sometimes fishes with 3- to 4-inch shiners—unless it's really cold—and then he uses 6- to 7-inch shiners to attract big bass that eat sporadically in winter and seem to prefer large baitfish.

Spring

Water temperature begins increasing in late winter and Austin searches for the warmest holes, even if those holes provide only a few degrees of extra heat. Crankbaits catch many fish for this guide, who varies his lure speed until he finds the right action. "Sometimes smallmouth move into water only 2 or 3 feet deep, especially in stained, slightly warmer areas," he notes.

Priest smallmouth are in their prespawn mode by March and this is when Austin throws his favorite lure. "March and April are great times to catch Percy Priest bass," he says. "Smallmouth are shallow. I can't name all the excellent baits for catching them in spring, but personally I think ⅟₁₆-ounce hair flies—either in a green and orange or brown and orange combination—are the best lures anybody can throw."

Smallmouth love crawfish, and using imitations of these crustaceans is an excellent way to catch them. Guide Gene Austin throws crankbaits with "lots of wobble" in late winter and early spring.

Fishing a fly is easy. "Just let it drop naturally, and after it hits the bottom, flick it and let it suspend and fall back to the bottom," says the guide. "Hair bunches toward the front and the tail flares like it's really something alive. The key to fishing this lure is not to overwork it. During this time of year, a 9-pound bass will hit as lightly as a 9-ounce bass."

Crankbaits or spinnerbaits catch smallmouth after the spawn. Shad colors are good but always have chartreuse lures. "The fish have not moved far from where they spawned," says Austin. "They're still in shallow water."

Summer

Plastic 4½-inch worms catch smallmouth in June and July as Priest grows warm. Sometimes Austin tosses 6-inch lizards in areas he knows holds more largemouth than smallies. He spends much of his time working rocky banks or gravel points. "Fishing continues to be excellent," he notes. Water color is much clearer in summer. Gourd-green, cotton-candy, pumpkin-pepper, and pumpkin-chartreuse are light colors that are among Austin's favorite early summer shades.

Austin works more deeply around the same banks and points that hold fish during earlier months. Stump fields or other fairly deep structure—12 to 15 feet—often attract fish, he notes. Tuffy minnows are also excellent summer bait. A No. 6 hook and small splitshot is all that is needed to fish tuffies. "Believe it or not, minnows are deadly on big bass around rocky shorelines," says Austin.

Many Percy Priest anglers become nocturnal in summer, including well-known guide Jack Christian. He favors hair jigs and short-armed spinnerbaits, both with pork-chunk trailers, when he pursues Percy Priest's nighttime bass. In June 1998, he discussed his techniques in a column published by *Southern Outdoors* magazine.

"Examples of places I fish are long sloping points, humps, creek and river channel drop-offs, etc.," he wrote. "In Percy Priest, the depth of these spots ranges from 6 to 18 feet on top of the structure, falling to water as deep as 50 feet. Typically, I'll hold my boat over water at least 20 feet deep, and I'll cast up onto shallow structure."

Christian favors ¼- or ⅜-ounce jigs with No. 11, black or brown pork-chunk trailers. He often throws ½- to ¾-ounce Aggravator spinnerbaits with a single No. 5 or No. 6 Colorado blade. "I'll alternate using these two lures on the same spots," says Christian. "Sometimes the bass will take the jig better; other times they want the spinnerbait. . . . I fish the jig with either of two retrieves, depending on how good the bite is. If bass are feeding actively, I'll reel the jig just fast enough to barely keep it off the bottom. Every once in a while, I'll let it touch just to know it's close to the structure."

If that technique fails, Christian changes his retrieve to a "lift/drop," working his lure across the bottom with short hops. He lets the jig rest up to five seconds between hops. Many fish hit during this pause, he explains.

Spinnerbaits also catch bass near the bottom, according to Christian, who uses a "yo-yoing" motion to attract strikes. Stair-stepping spinnerbaits down channel drops also catches fish, as does working points "shallow to deep."

"I'll usually start in around 6 feet of water on the inside of the point, position the boat over deep water, and cast up on the structure," he explains. "Then I'll work toward the end of the point." Christian fishes humps just the opposite of points, retrieving from "deep to shallow." He casts in the deeper water first and then works progressively higher on the hump.

Fall

Austin repeats his spring smallmouth techniques in the fall, but also includes buzzbaits in his arsenal, especially in October. Hair flies and spinnerbaits catch smallmouth as they move shallow to feed on crawfish and shad. Boat traffic has decreased enormously by fall, making Percy Priest even more attractive to serious anglers.

CRAPPIE

Guide Harold Morgan was an accomplished steel-guitar player before he quit the entertainment profession to become a full-time fishing guide. During more than three decades of guiding, Morgan has learned to play crappie as well as he played music, especially on Percy Priest.

One of his favorite fishing methods, however, gets its name from a famous crappie lake elsewhere in the Volunteer State.

"I like fishing a technique known as the Kentucky rig [also called the Kentucky Lake Double-Hook Bottom Bumping rig]," says Morgan. "Before there were electronics, fishermen on Kentucky Lake used this method to help them locate structure and drop-offs. I still use it to catch fish. One great thing about the rig is that I can fish in thick structure without staying constantly hung up."

The Kentucky rig—as tied by Morgan—includes 8- to 10-pound-test monofilament spooled on a spincasting or a closed-face reel, two monofilament leaders, two monofilament droplines, two hooks, and a three-way swivel.

Morgan ties the top ring of his swivel to the main line, then attaches two 36-inch monofilament pieces on the other rings. On one line he ties two droplines—about 8 inches each—and attaches 1/0 hooks to them. He ties the first dropline 8 inches below the swivel and the second 18 inches below the top hook. He then ties a 1-ounce bell sinker to the tag end of the other leader.

"One reason that I use two hooks is because crappie often rise in the water column, especially after the sun gets up," explains Morgan. "This method helps find fish that have moved into areas more comfortable for them. Sometimes I get lucky and catch two fish at a time."

The heavy sinker actually helps prevent lost tackle. A gentle jigging motion combined with the sinker's weight often pulls snagged hooks free. Morgan primarily uses minnows on the Kentucky rig, but small plastic tubes also catch fish for him.

Winter

When water temperature cools, crappie suspend around channel drop-offs and ledges. Minnows fished deep beneath bobbers are excellent winter baits. Morgan spends the coldest winter months setting out fish attractors, usually dead hardwood trees that he anchors with bricks to the lake bottom. His more than 300 beds at varying depths are the reason Morgan is a successful crappie guide.

Spring

Crappie are moving by late March toward shallow spawning grounds in the upper end of Percy Priest, where the water is always quickest to warm. Morgan stays above Hobson Pike Bridge in early spring, catching crappie over stumps and in coves that are close to river or creek channels.

The Kentucky Lake rig is an old method still used to locate and catch crappie. Guide Harold Morgan uses it and is one of Middle Tennessee's most successful crappie anglers.

The Kentucky rig catches many deepwater fish, but in April—or whenever the fish move into shallow water—Morgan switches to lighter tackle. "That's when I like to tie on a small leadhead jig and a plastic grub, or put a minnow below a float and sinker," explains Morgan. "I cast near the bank and let my float sit for 30 to 45 seconds. Then I start retrieving it slowly until I get a hit."

Morgan prefers small plastic tubes when fishing vertically, but works shorelines with curlytail grubs. His favorite leadhead color is red and his favorite grub color is chartreuse. "I have experimented to see if there is a difference in the number of hits I get when I use a red leadhead jig versus when I don't use it," says Morgan. "I know that the red head pays off. I believe crappie recognize it as a minnow's gill."

Summer

Crappie scatter after the spawn and are difficult to locate for much of May, says Morgan. Once they school again—usually by June—fishing is excellent. This is when sonar and planted cover benefits Morgan the most.

"Crappie hit every day between June and September," says the guide. "I may not get the limit every time out, but I can find good schools of hungry fish."

In summer Morgan fishes near Seven Points Recreation Area and Cook's Recreation Area on the deeper and cooler end of Priest. Some anglers catch crappie by trolling small crankbaits or spoons in or near channels, but Morgan fishes with his Kentucky rig over cover, with minnows or plastic baits.

"Crappie fishing really gets great in September regardless of air or water temperature," says Morgan. "It just doesn't matter how hot it is. The fish are in deep water, but they hit like crazy."

Fall

As the water temperature cools in October and November, crappie move back into shallow water. Morgan follows this migration and catches many fish 6 and 7 feet deep with the Kentucky rig and by casting plastic grubs or tubes beneath bobbers.

"Most people quit fishing for crappie after April or May because they think the fish have put their coats on and left the lake, but crappie bite most of the year, maybe even better at times other than spring," says Morgan.

HYBRID AND STRIPER

Guide Gene Austin spends many days pursuing black bass, but also spends hundreds of hours chasing Percy Priest's Cherokee bass and stripers. While a world record may never come from Percy Priest, its hybrids and stripers are healthy and fun.

Winter

From December through much of February, tightlined shiners catch numerous hybrids and stripers, says Austin. Finding shad is essential to successful fishing. Once found, he lowers shiners to the same depth as schooling baitfish. Most of the fish he catches this time of year are in the lake's lower section between Hobson Pike Bridge and the dam.

"I hook my shiners two ways," says the guide. "I lip hook one. The other I hook below its dorsal fin or the top of its tail. I get a struggling appearance from the lip-hooked shiner and a more natural look from the other. I stay with the presentation that attracts strikes."

Percy Priest sometimes experiences shad die-offs in winter, which can be good or bad. Good because it activates hungry fish, but bad because an abundance of struggling baitfish sometimes makes getting attention for live bait more difficult. If shiners don't work, Austin ties on spoons, white grubs, or other flashy lures.

Austin uses small sinkers to fish shiners, unless the lake is choppy and the bait won't stay stationary without larger weights. Between 6- and 10-pound-test monofilament, depending on choppiness, is strong enough to catch big fish in deep, snag-free water.

Spring

Bank fishermen often reveal when striper and Cherokee bass are hitting. Many anglers gather on shorelines close to the dam or even behind the dam in late winter and early spring. Red Fins, Little Macs, and white bucktail jigs are among hot striper and hybrid lures that bank anglers throw.

Austin always fishes from his boat and notes that wind plays a major role in his success. He crafts strategy to counter shifting breezes. "I don't start fishing right after I locate a school of hybrids or stripers," he explains. "I toss out a buoy marker and try to locate a second school. I do this because wind sometimes moves shad and the fish disappear with them. The second school gives me somewhere else to fish quickly."

Austin changes baits until he determines what the fish want. Spoons in different shapes and sizes are among the artificial baits that he carries on each trip along with live bait.

Fish are usually moving up-lake by sometime in April, often staging around Burnt Island (the first island above the dam) a few weeks before heading to summer holes near Cook's Recreation Area, Seven Points Recreation Area, and Hamilton Creek Park.

"Several baits catch them at this time," says the guide. "Two are live baits and two are artificial. If we have hot temperatures in early spring, small bluegill seem to attract more strikes than shad. If spring temperatures are normal, I have more luck with live shad." A 6-inch, salt-and-pepper Slug-go and a 4-inch, trout-colored Fin-S Fish are Austin's two favorite artificial baits in June and July. "I don't put any weight on the Slug-gos. Sometimes I work them topwater, other times I let them sink until I find active fish. I like to fish the Fin-S Fish with a leadhead jig."

Summer

From July through September, stripers and hybrids usually school under baitfish in Suggs and Viverett Creeks, both near Seven Points Recreation Area. Fish also stage near the Hobson Pike Bridge just below mile marker four and mile marker five, notes Austin. Summer is when he catches many Cherokee bass over deep water.

Hybrids and stripers often surface early. Soft jerkbaits are good lures, but so are Pencil Poppers, Zara Spooks, Jumpin' Minnows, and other hard-plastic topwater baits capable of being thrown a long way.

Sometimes Austin catches hybrids shallow. "July and August are excellent months to catch hybrids trolling mud flats," says Austin. "If it's a typical July or August day—bright with little wind—a Deep Wee-R in a shad color, silver and black, or silver and blue, is excellent. So is a DD-22 or other crankbait that digs into the mud. I use a lure that imitates a big baitfish because shad have gotten large."

Fishing early is vital to success during summer's dog days. Hybrids often hit viciously until around 10 A.M., and "then they are finished for the morning," says Austin, "except for one brief unpredictable period during July or

Percy Priest is among Tennessee's top Cherokee bass reservoirs. Anglers catch them with a variety of baits and tactics. Guide Gene Austin has much luck in summer with a Fin-S Fish.

August when, for reasons I don't know, they hit like crazy for about 45 minutes, starting around 11:30 in the morning."

Always be aware of thermocline in summer, and keep bait either in or above it. Usually the thermocline is no deeper than 18 to 20 feet, according to Austin.

Jeff Hudson, a Cherokee bass and striper guide, has late-summer success with live bait. "In early September the water in Priest is still hot," says Hudson. "Hybrids and stripers are in open water in the main body of the lake. They relate to humps, flats on the river channel, and points along the channel. Later in the month, if the lake has cooled down, they migrate to shallower water."

A hump is a mound of dirt, rock pile, sunken island, or any feature that rises from the lake bottom and is "about the size of two automobiles," says Hudson. Humps and the bends of major channels are the most productive for big fish, he notes.

"Most of the time water temperature is in the upper 80s in reservoir-type lakes such as Percy Priest," he explains. "This factor determines where fish will be. For instance, Suggs Creek on Percy Priest has a horseshoe bend in its channel, and I can almost always find fish in that bend."

There is another key to locating hybrids and stripers that most anglers don't consider. "Plankton is at the beginning of the food chain," says Hudson. "This is a microscopic plant that minnows and shad eat. Shad also eat small minnows, but their main forage is plankton. Since hybrids and stripers eat shad, they are usually near these schooling baitfish, which are normally close to blankets of plankton."

Plankton often forms a black band on sonar equipment and is easy to identify, says Hudson. "Most fishermen don't know what that band is, but it's plankton. It can be so dense that on a graph it's a solid mass."

Fall

October and November pose the toughest striper and hybrid challenge for guide Gene Austin. As the water cools and the thermocline disappears, hybrids and stripers scatter. Austin suggests fishing shorelines at night for aggressive feeders. Tributaries also provide good angling in the lake's headwaters.

Spring Creek, Fall Creek, and the forks of Stones River occasionally have impressive runs of hungry fish. White plastic grubs are among good baits when runs occur.

CHAPTER 8
Old Hickory Lake

One Hundred Miles of
Great Freshwater Fishing

A student at Tennessee Technological University completed a study on the movements of Old Hickory Lake's striper in the early 1990s. Results indicated that rockfish, known for their mammoth appetites, are wide-ranging travelers moving up and down the long Cumberland River reservoir.

Had the student implanted a camera in the fish instead of a transmitter, their journeys would have made fantastic television. With numerous tributaries feeding the lake for almost 100 miles between Cordell Hull and Old Hickory Dams, these large fish would have revealed hiding places for crappie, sauger, walleye, largemouth, smallmouth, white bass, and various species of catfish. Instead, anglers wanting to learn the secrets of Old Hickory's fish must either search for them or find a fishing guide who knows their whereabouts.

Fortunately, some of Old Hickory's guides don't mind talking about their techniques, which isn't quite as good as being in the boat with them, but does help shrink the lake's huge size. Many fish inhabit Old Hickory, from heavy largemouth bass to possibly world-record rockfish.

GAME FISH RATINGS

Largemouth Bass	
Smallmouth Bass	
Crappie	
Striper (Rockfish)	
Stripe (White Bass)	
Sauger	
Walleye	
Catfish	

LARGEMOUTH BASS

Old Hickory Guide Dayton Blair didn't play sports while growing up because they would have interfered with his fishing. "You've got to understand, I didn't do things that most kids do. I didn't play baseball, football, or basketball—I fished. That's all I've ever done, that's all I know, and I wouldn't trade that for a million dollars," says Blair.

Winter

Old Hickory is the site of many largemouth bass tournaments, including some with national presence and huge prize money. For Blair, it's a lake on which he has had many memorable days and nights. "It's loaded with fish," says the guide. "Old Hickory produces many, many largemouth bass, especially for the pressure it gets."

OLD HICKORY AT A GLANCE

Location:	Smith, Trousdale, Wilson, Sumner, and Davidson Counties
Size:	22,500 acres
Length:	97.3 miles
Shoreline:	440 miles
Summer pool:	445 feet
Winter pool:	442 feet
Impounded:	1957
Featured species:	Largemouth Bass, Smallmouth Bass, Crappie, Striper (Rockfish), Stripe (White Bass), Sauger, Walleye, Catfish
Other species:	Bluegill, Shellcracker
Description:	This run-of-the-river lake is narrow for miles below Cordell Hull Dam and widens as the river approaches Old Hickory Dam. Shallow in many areas, the reservoir has considerable wood and numerous sandbars, gravel bars, and drop-offs. Bluffs line many banks, and there are many creeks, coves, and pockets. The Gallatin Steam Plant is an excellent place to fish during cold months.
Main tributaries:	Cumberland River, Cedar Creek, Rocky Creek, Spring Creek, Brunley Branch, Bartons Creek, Bledsoe Creek, Bulls Creek, East Camp Creek, Station Camp Creek, Spencer Creek, Little Creek, Shutes Branch, Drakes Creek
Landmarks:	Old Hickory is close to Nashville and even closer to Carthage, Hartsville, Lebanon, Hendersonville, Gallatin, and Mt. Juliet. Nearby routes include TN 10, TN 25, TN 109, TN 6, and TN 45. The nearest Interstate is I-40.
Operated by:	Corps of Engineers

See Appendix C for map information

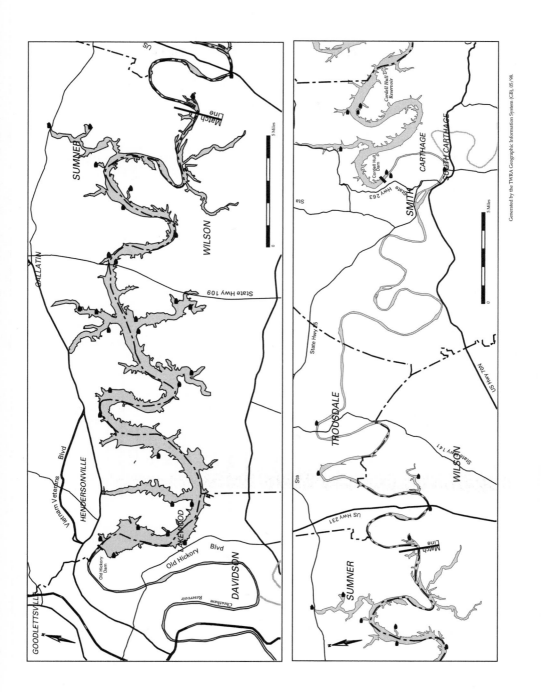

Generated by the TWRA Geographic Information System (GIS), 05/98.

Much of Blair's winter is spent fishing Old Hickory's tributaries. Among these are East Camp, Station Camp, Spencer, and Drakes Creeks. Because Old Hickory has lots of shallow water, Blair catches numerous largemouth in shallow areas.

"I fish the edges of channels, especially in bends where they sweep banks," says Blair, who attracts many strikes by flipping lures around fallen trees, bushes, or other cover in water 1 to 6 feet deep. His favorite flipping bait is a ½-ounce jig and pig with rattles. Junebug and solid black are his best colors.

Many Old Hickory largemouth begin prespawn searches for nesting sites in late winter. "A lot of people don't seem to understand or believe it, but this is the time of year when I can see largemouth in 1 foot of water," says Blair. "I can see most of the 6- and 7-pound fish I catch."

Largemouth are shallow when water temperature reaches the mid-50s, says Blair, who often tosses spinnerbaits or Rat-L-Traps around shoreline cover in early spring. "Sometimes I'll actually flip a Rat-L-Trap. When my Rat-L-Trap hits the water, I give it a quick pull and then let it sink. This is when they nail it. I pull the lure with a ripping action. I'll move the tip of my rod about 3 inches, which makes the plug move about 1 foot." Blair's favorite lure colors are combinations of blue and silver or black and silver.

Blair determines the size of baitfish that bass are eating before he selects his spinnerbait. He uses spinnerbaits with small willowleaf blades early in spring but increases blade size as baitfish mature. "The spinnerbait I use the most is made by Hoppy's," says Blair. "It has a long shaft that I like because I fish around cover a lot, and trailer hooks keep me hung up." Chartreuse and a combination of chartreuse and white are among some excellent spinnerbait colors.

As water temperature rises and bass prepare to spawn, Blair flips jig and pig combinations, plastic lizards, worms, or crawfish around bedding bass. He catches numerous largemouth with Carolina- or Texas-rigged baits. In the spring of 1996, Blair caught two largemouth that both weighed more than 9 pounds.

Summer

Largemouth inhabit Old Hickory's creeks year-round, but in summer Blair catches numerous bass around ledges, drop-offs, or humps in the lake's main channel. "When I fish the channel, I work plastic baits on a Carolina rig, or I throw deep-running crankbaits that imitate shad," explains Blair. Fat As, DB3s, and Fat Raps are among his favorite lures.

Largemouth react to the frequent water discharges that slightly raise Old Hickory Lake, says Blair. "They have a tendency to feed an hour before generation occurs, during generation some, and then real well again about an hour after it ceases," notes Blair. "Between 9 A.M. and noon is a good time to get on Old Hickory because the Corps of Engineers normally generates somewhere between midmorning to midday."

Blair searches for holes where rocks or other submerged structure diverts water flow and creates ambush areas where bass suspend out of the lake's strong current. He always waits for the lake to settle after generation ceases. "I think bass have to adjust for a little while to the changing water," says Blair. "This may not be what is happening, but most of the time they start hitting again about an hour after the generation ends."

It's difficult for Blair to catch fish when generation doesn't occur, unless he locates milfoil. Some years Old Hickory has more milfoil than others, depending on eradication efforts. "If I find milfoil, I can catch largemouth most anytime," says Blair. Plastic worms, jerkbaits, plastic frogs, and plastic mice, dragged across this vegetation, catch bass, says Blair. Spinnerbaits, buzzbaits, or jig and pig combinations work great, fished around its edges.

Fall

As good as milfoil is in summer, it produces even more fish in fall. "I like to use plastic mouse or frog imitations," says Blair. "The number and size of bass I catch with these lures is unbelievable. Some days I bet I catch 40 largemouth in just an evening and a bunch of the fish are 3-, 4-, and 5-pounders."

White, chartreuse, black, and green are among Blair's favorite lure colors. He prefers that his mice or frogs have plastic skirts rather than plastic legs or tails. The skirt is more durable, according to Blair. "I fish these baits just like I would a Zara Spook or other topwater lure," he says. "I just ease them slowly over the milfoil."

SMALLMOUTH BASS

Dayton Blair is an excellent largemouth angler, but he also has years of smallmouth experience. Smallies inhabit the main body of Old Hickory Lake, but Blair catches most smallmouth in the cooler river sections near Cordell Hull Dam.

Winter

Shiners or shad make great smallmouth bait in winter, says Blair, who tight-lines live bait in the eddies created by chunk rock or other river-bottom structure. "When there is generation, smallmouth wait in these eddies for bait to come to them," says the guide.

Blair places a ¼-ounce sinker 12 to 14 inches above a 3/0 hook and baits this with a 4- to 5-inch shiner. Sometimes he substitutes store-bought shiners with shad, which he catches with a cast net in the warm canal waters next to Gallatin Steam Plant several miles down-lake from the dam.

"When fishing for smallmouth, I find fairly deep banks with eddies and throw against them," says Blair. "When the sinker hits the bottom, I start reeling the shiner back slowly. This is similar to floating a minnow close to the bottom. Live bait works great in winter. Smallmouth just can't pass it up."

Blair catches most fish from 9 to 20 feet deep, depending on water temperature. Smallmouth suspend around humps, drop-offs, indentions, or other river-bottom changes. "When I find a spot that has a smallmouth, it seems like there is usually at least one more fish nearby," he says.

Because of tough winter conditions and the size of the bass he catches, Blair uses 15-pound-test monofilament spooled on a baitcasting reel. "Little fish don't seem to hit much in winter," he says. "I've caught a lot of smallmouth in winter and most of them have weighed from 2 pounds up."

Spring

Blair turns to artificial baits in spring and stays with them until the next winter. "When the water starts warming up, I use crawfish imitations in combination with tube jigs," he says. "I stick the crawfish inside a tube, but not too far back on the hook. I want its pinchers to extend beyond the hook so that the bass identify the lure as a crawdad."

Blair's favorite crawfish color is amber embedded with green flakes. He tosses crawfish on ⅛- to ¼-ounce leadhead jigs. He also occasionally throws 4-inch worms. Buzzbaits also have their days. "When I throw a buzzbait, I position my boat about 1 foot from the bank and cast parallel to it," notes Blair. "I fish over gravel and chunk rock when I use buzzbaits."

Summer and Fall

Guide Donny Hall searches for smallmouth with a technique different from most Old Hickory anglers. "I drift over old rapids below the dam," he explains. "You can find where these are by going to the state archive in Nashville. It has old maps that were once used for navigation purposes."

Hall casts upstream while drifting the shoals and tosses a ¼-ounce hair jig with a plastic trailer. He believes this jig resembles a crawfish and bounces it slowly across the river bottom. A black hair fly with a sapphire-blue pork or plastic trailer is his favorite color combination.

Hall motors back upstream and moves a few feet to the left or right after each drift, thoroughly covering a shoal. If smallmouth aren't biting, or the current is too strong for drifting, he works around broken or chunk rock along the bank.

CRAPPIE

Donny Hall and Dayton Blair advertise themselves as jacks-of-all-fishing-trades. Both fish year-round in pursuit of a variety of fish, including crappie. Harold

Morgan, a well-known, full-time crappie guide, has also spent many days catching Old Hickory fish. Their expertise should help anyone who pursues crappie.

Winter

Winter crappie often suspend 18 to 20 feet deep around drop-offs on river or creek channels, notes Hall, who spends the coldest months setting out brush piles in preparation for spring fishing. Locate old brush piles and drop a minnow straight down, he suggests. Also fish around fallen trees in the lake's many creeks. Crappie often move near shoreline cover during the day, notes Hall. When they do this, he uses live minnows to catch them around submerged limbs about 15 feet down.

Spring

Both Hall and Blair begin catching prespawn crappie in late winter. Hall begins fishing in late February, Blair a few weeks later. "By the time redbud trees bloom, crappie fishing is great on Old Hickory," says Blair. "Anybody can catch them."

Hall fishes minnows below bobbers on telescopic graphite rods. These long poles let him get tight to cover without worrying about perfect casts. He catches numerous shoreline crappie between late February and late April. Blair often tosses marabou jigs, especially if minnows fail him. "I like the subtle movement of a feather jig," he explains. "Sometimes I get hits on a jig when I can't get them on anything else."

Chartreuse or white, ⅛-ounce, marabou jigs are good Old Hickory colors, says Blair. So are white- or clear-plastic tubes, notes Hall, who tosses artificial bait during the waning days of spring. Old Hickory's many creeks harbor countless crappie.

"Early in spring, I catch crappie in Spencer Creek, Station Camp Creek, Drakes Creek, Shutes Branch, or just wherever there are creeks with drop-offs in them," says Blair. "I find fish holding to natural structure, such as stumps, rock piles, and log jams. As it gets warmer, a lot of crappie move under bushes or around stumps that are 3 or 4 feet deep on flats."

Sonar helps track moving fish. Hall has watched crappie move from 10 to 2 feet of water during spring days. "I catch fish right off the bank as late as early June," notes Hall. "I use 10-pound test in spring because this is also the time of year when catfish run the banks. Sometimes I catch as many catfish on minnows as I do crappie."

Summer and Fall

Harold Morgan spends more time on Percy Priest Reservoir than on Old Hickory, but has still spent thousands of hours catching Old Hickory crappie. He advises summer anglers to fish deep with minnows or with small plastic baits.

"I fish sandbars near the main river channel," says Morgan. "If I look on an electronic graph, these sandbars resemble fingers. They're not usually very big. A friend of mine, John Ed Garrett, told me about them."

Crappie suspend around sandbars throughout the year. When fish aren't near shorelines, bars provide easily located structure. "Some of these sandbars are 25 feet deep," says Morgan. "I catch most of my fish off the sides of them, not off the top. I've seen some bars rise to where they are only 6 or 7 feet under the surface, but then drop all the way back down to 20 feet deep. They'll rise and fall like this several times."

Sandbars sometimes shift because of the river's strong current, meaning Morgan occasionally must relocate them. Many sandbars are found near the main river channel. Several are within sight of Old Hickory Dam, says the guide.

As water temperature cools, many fish move shallow. Morgan continues fishing sandbars, or he heads to creeks and to cover near channel drop-offs.

STRIPER (ROCKFISH)

In the summer of 1997, guide Ralph Dallas landed a 62-pound striper, which at the time broke Tennessee's state record. It was the largest rockfish ever landed by him, but not the biggest he had ever hooked. Dallas believes world-record rockfish inhabit Old Hickory, and he is as likely as anyone to eventually break that record. Even if he doesn't, the veteran angler—recognized as one of the best striper fishermen in America—often catches 30- and 40-pound fish.

"Old Hickory has ideal habitat for large stripers," says Dallas. "Cold water discharged from below Center Hill and Cordell Hull Dams makes this possible, along with the stocking program established by the Tennessee Wildlife Resources Agency. Old Hickory is nationally famous for its rockfish. Millions of large gizzard shad give stripers something to eat at almost any time, and fish grow fast and big as a result."

Winter

Ralph Dallas has guided on Old Hickory Lake since 1975, but began competing in national striper tournaments in the late 1960s. He knows much about following stripers up and down Old Hickory's run-of-the-river lake. Stripers bite year-round, even in the coldest months. In fact, Dallas catches winter stripers in "good sizes and numbers."

Gallatin Steam Plant is an excellent site to look first for winter rockfish because it discharges warm water into a canal connected to Old Hickory. Many baitfish inhabit this area because of its warmth. These baitfish—primarily gizzard shad, threadfin shad, and skipjack—attract hungry game fish.

Bank access is good at Gallatin Steam Plant, but boat access from the lake is also easy. Skipjack often school in the canal and are caught for bait with

Guide Ralph Dallas holds a former state record striper that he caught and mounted himself. Strong hooks with live bait and large sinkers are important for catching these big fish.

small artificial grubs or tiny spinners. Large crankbaits or plastic shad imitations also catch stripers. Among Dallas's favorite lures are 7-inch Red Fins and 9-inch, shad-colored, Fin-S Fish.

Winter rockfish frequently inhabit the river for another 10 miles downstream from the Gallatin Steam Plant. A common hangout is Drakes Creek, a large tributary of Old Hickory that flows past Hendersonville. After using electronics to locate baitfish in creeks or coves, Dallas trolls with live shad.

His rockfish setup includes four to five baitcasting combinations, strong 7/0 hooks, rod holders, and two small balloons. He feeds line from two reels at least 100 feet behind his boat. He ties small balloons to both lines. "I also trail two lines a shorter distance directly behind the boat without balloons," notes Dallas. "It takes big reels to do this." He places all poles in rod holders mounted around his boat's gunnel.

Dallas controls bait depth with softball-size balloons that he attaches to his lines with rubber bands. He often relies on barometric pressure to help him determine appropriate depth. Cold fronts and high pressures push baitfish down, according to the guide. Low pressure pulls them up. Rockfish stay beneath fluctuating baitfish, and Dallas adjusts his balloons accordingly.

"During some cold fronts (with high pressure), I may fish as much as 100 feet between the balloon and bait, which makes my bait go deeper," explains Dallas. "On low-pressure days I might use as little as 20 feet in order to fish as shallow as possible, especially if I see surfacing rockfish."

Boat speed is also instrumental to controlling bait depth. "I'm always trolling when I freeline," notes Dallas. "It takes experience to understand which speed works best, but never stop moving."

Dallas often freelines behind side planer boards, which spread out his bait presentation. "In fact, I'm most effective when I use side planer boards because I cover twice as much water," says Dallas. When using boards, Dallas trolls an extra line between them and increases his number of rigs to five.

While stripers consume small shad on many other impoundments, Old Hickory fish prefer large baitfish, says Dallas. Locating shad is vital to catching stripers. Dallas expects lots of action when he finds shad schooled in coves.

"Years ago I learned an important lesson on Tims Ford Reservoir," recalls Dallas. "I could go down there in winter and find coves full of big schools of shad, but not draw rockfish on a graph. I learned to free-swim my line through the baitfish and I caught stripers in great numbers, even though I hadn't seen them. All I had to do was find the bait and then match their size."

Because they are strong, Dallas uses 7/0 Eagle Claw hooks (style 84). Other gear includes Abu Garcia 6500 reels, spooled with 80-pound-test braided line, and 7-foot, heavy-action Fenwick rods that he considers just right for stripers. Despite this heavy gear, Dallas had his line broken three times in 1996.

Don't ignore an area that doesn't produce on a given day, says Dallas. Striper are wayfaring fish and venture into many places.

Occasionally, Dallas abandons his boat to stand on the bank when he locates stripers that are easily reached with shoreline casts. Seven-inch Red Fins and red 5½-inch Little Macs catch many stripers, including fish in the warm canal alongside Gallatin Steam Plant.

Generators in operation below Cordell Hull Dam do affect striper fishing, notes Dallas. More than two generators makes fishing tough. If the water is rolling, Dallas heads to the back of large creeks where current is weaker.

Spring

Rockfish are spread out in Old Hickory as spring begins warming the lake. Dallas often tosses artificial bait this time of year. Red Fins twitched on the surface and plastic Fin-S Fish are among his favorite lures. "In the spring of 1996, we [Dallas and his friends/customers] caught several 50-pound fish with the shad-colored, 9-inch, Fin-S Fish, and I became a big user of that lure," says the guide.

Dallas threads his Fin-S Fish with a 7/0 hook, but to attain more holding power, he attaches an extra-strong 6/0 saltwater treble hook to it. He keeps it stationary by sliding a torn piece of plastic worm between the point of the threaded hook and the shaft of the treble hook. He works the Fin-S Fish across the surface.

Striper occasionally break the surface. Dallas considers this a bonus. He never launches his boat planning to find breaking fish, but always has a Red Fin or Fin-S Fish tied on and ready to cast toward breaking schools.

Summer

Striper move upriver in summer where the water is much cooler, says Dallas. He catches many fish from the Cordell Hull Dam downriver about 10 miles. Nearby Caney Fork River, loaded with shad and small trout, also provides cool water and excellent summertime angling.

Dallas alters his fishing technique in summer. "I bottom fish a lot in hot weather with cut bait," he explains. "Skipjack is the best cut bait there is when it's available, but gizzard shad works almost as well." Gizzard shad are easy to catch with cast nets from many sites, while skipjack can sometimes be caught below dams with small plastic grubs or hair flies.

Dallas also uses 7/0 Eagle Claw hooks when fishing with cut shad. He keeps his bait stationary with flat sinkers (also known as dollar sinkers). Current flows over these weights without disturbing them. "Stay in eddies near the shoreline when bottom fishing," says Dallas. "Cut bait makes an easy meal for rockfish, but it is extremely important that it's kept fresh. I change it every 15 to 20 minutes. If I don't, I'll end up catching more catfish than stripers. Sometimes I change bait every 10 minutes."

Stay away from creeks, warns Dallas. Thermocline forms in summer, and temperatures comfortable to striper are often in oxygen-depleted depths below this layer. Striper leave creeks when thermocline forms, says the guide.

"Rockfish continue hitting below Cordell Hull Dam in fall, but many fish move downriver, particularly between Highway 231 and Misty Cove (about 7 miles downstream from Highway 231). "I'll find a lot of big fish in this area in both the spring and the fall," notes Dallas.

Be fishing by daybreak, says Dallas. The Corps of Engineers frequently has generators operating by midmorning and strong current makes main-river fishing difficult later in the day. Dallas catches many stripers in river bends—some of these sweep near shorelines and others don't.

Regardless of distance to the bank, Dallas always situates his boat in water about 20 feet deep. He trolls freelines parallel to the shoreline, almost duplicating his winter fishing style. "The only difference is I don't use balloons and I only release about 50 feet of line instead of 100 feet," he explains.

Large rockfish suspend in bends. "Big stripers love to lay around trees this time of year," says Dallas. "Strikes usually occur when bait is pulled past a tree." Expect to lose many hooks to these trees and perhaps a few to fighting fish. "Stripers around these trees are monsters," says the guide.

Large gizzard shad works best as bait in fall, notes Dallas, who uses cast nets to catch his shad in the backs of creeks. Some of his shad reach 15 inches.

He hooks his baitfish twice—once through the nostrils and once between the dorsal fin and tail. He attaches the back stinger hook to the front 7/0 hook with a strong piece of monofilament. "We catch many stripers in the 30- and 40-pound range on the stinger," says Dallas. "Rockfish are notorious in the fall for grabbing a shad by the middle of its body and running with it."

Trolling motor speed is vital to finding strike zones. Zigzagging is one way to control bait depth. "Move the motor left and the bait on the right side rises," says Dallas. "Move it right and the left bait comes up. I'm covering the whole ball game by doing this. It's a very effective way to cover a lot of water."

Keep shad alive and fresh, says Dallas. Dead shad work poorly, unless used as cut bait. Aerated holding tanks are essential for striper fishing. Chemicals are available that keep baitfish lively if mixed correctly with well-oxygenated water. Dallas always makes sure to match the temperature of his aerated storage water with the temperature of the water from which he removes his baitfish.

STRIPE (WHITE BASS)

Old Hickory is one of Middle Tennessee's best white bass lakes. It is so good that a stretch of it near Hendersonville has long been nicknamed "Stripe Alley." Just like its larger rockfish cousin, white bass are channel dwellers that follow baitfish. And just like striper, they school and feed aggressively.

Through the Seasons

Matching baitfish size is vital to catching stripe. White bass often pursue small shad in the spring, sometimes breaking the surface as they attack. Any number of small crankbaits catches them when they surface, including flashy Rat-L-Traps.

Guide Dayton Blair catches many white bass with "eyes the size of nickels" and weighing "2 to 2½ pounds." He favors white or pearl-colored plastic grubs when he locates schools suspending near the river bottom. Spoons are excellent when stripe hug the bottom.

White bass often stay deep during summer's hottest daytime hours but surface frequently in early mornings or late evenings. Guide Harold Morgan catches them on the surface throughout the year by fishing late. "I launch my boat a few hours before dark and watch for them in the jumps," says Morgan. "Stripe especially seem to like white and yellow colors. A good place to catch them is near the dam, in Drakes Creek, Station Camp Creek, Barton's Creek, or in Stripe Alley."

Stripe Alley begins below the home of country music star Johnny Cash, who lives on a bluff near Avondale Recreation Area. Trolling is an excellent way to catch suspending white bass. In-line spinners such as ABUs, Rooster Tails, or Mepps catch numerous fish.

"I start trolling near Johnny Cash's home and work upriver near the old river channel," says Morgan. "I troll 10 to 15 feet deep just off the main channel. When I get to the river bend at Avondale, I make a right turn and work on either side of the river. The left side is better because the right side eventually hits a bluff. I work to the mouth of Cedar Creek. That stretch is Stripe Alley. I load up through there."

A method that Blair favors for surfacing stripe, regardless of the month, requires a weighted float. "I can cast weighted floats a long way," he says. "When I reel this float, it makes a constant bubbling noise, and it doesn't matter if the fish are on the surface or not because that noise drives them crazy and they attack the fly from wherever they are."

Blair ties floating flies 1 to 2 feet behind the bobber. His favorite fly

Old Hickory Lake is famous for Stripe Alley, located near the home of country music star Johnny Cash, but large "nickel-eyed" white bass also school below dams.

color is a silver and white combination. "I've tried replacing the fly with a jig and it doesn't work as well," he notes. Blair often trolls until he locates suspending schools. He favors in-line spinners for trolling or small crankbaits such as Wee-Rs or Deep Wee-Rs.

Anglers should also fish around creek mouths, which are common hangouts for predatory fish, including white bass. Morgan jigs vertically with a Hopkin's Spoon when working creek mouths. "If I find one white bass, I'll find a bunch of them," he notes.

Guide Donny Hall catches large stripe in the summer below Old Hickory Dam by using small skipjack, which school by the thousands there. He catches 3- to 4-inch bait in the swift water below the dam by tossing tiny white jigs. Using a Carolina rig with a ⅜-ounce egg sinker and a 1/0 hook (he uses a heavier weight if current is strong), Hall hooks his skipjack near the tail and throws downstream alongside eddying water. He catches white bass with as many as three generators operating. (Remember, always wear life jackets below dams, and never anchor over turbines.)

SAUGER AND WALLEYE

Although sauger populations have dwindled in some Tennessee waters, a healthy population inhabits the Cumberland River, including the waters below Cordell Hull Dam. Walleye are also found in Old Hickory Lake, although they aren't as numerous as sauger.

Winter, Spring, and Summer

Winter is an excellent time to catch sauger on spawning runs. Walleye are also caught in winter, but are pursued more commonly in early spring when they also school to spawn.

Old Hickory guide Jim Duckworth prefers to sauger fish when most other humans are comfortable in warm buildings. "The greatest condition I hope for is snow," says the guide. "The colder it gets outside the better the fishing is, unless the generation below Cordell Hull Dam is cut off and there is no current. If that happens, I go home because sauger won't be very active."

Overcast skies are also excellent for sauger fishing, while blue skies are Duckworth's least favorite condition. Duckworth spends much of his time on the upper portion of Old Hickory Lake, from Highway 231 to Carthage.

Some of what Duckworth knows about sauger he learned as a diver for the U.S. Fish and Wildlife Service. He has observed sauger while swimming right alongside them. "I have seen how sauger like to get under logs that sit parallel in the river about a foot or so off the bottom," says Duckworth. "If I can locate these logs (with sonar equipment), I bounce a jig on top of them and then let it roll off."

Many logs (and other cover) are found in deep holes below bluffs. Gravel bars also provide good sauger habitat, notes Duckworth, who drifts over bars and works his bait vertically. Heavy leadhead jigs tipped with minnows are common sauger lures. "I use a 1-ounce jig made in Lebanon that's called a Roly Poly," says Duckworth. "I put a 2- to 3-inch minnow on the jig and . . . a stinger hook (tied to the main hook) near the tail, but not in it. I place it parallel to the backbone. This gives me two hooks."

Sauger start "getting the idea to spawn" when the water temperature drops into the mid-50s, says Duckworth. As the temperature continues falling, sauger become more active. When it dips into the mid-40s, they enter a prespawn feeding frenzy. If there is a "magic number" for Cumberland River sauger, "it's 44° to 46°," says Duckworth.

Guide Dayton Blair catches sauger below Cordell Hull Dam beginning in November, but notes that many of the fish are small migrating males. He favors ⅛- to ¼-ounce leadhead jigs with 3-inch white or pearl plastic grubs. Green apple is also a good color.

"I catch sauger and walleye from the bank by casting upstream about 15 yards and then reeling slowly," explains Blair. "A lot of people don't understand how easy this kind of fishing can be, but it is."

Blair also vertically jigs the river bottom. "One of the best ways for me to catch sauger is to start drifting at the dam and to keep floating until I catch fish," he says. "By that, I mean I start at the boils and float down the river for 5 miles if necessary."

Guide Donny Hall catches sauger around old locks, especially Lock Four near Station Camp Creek. He also fishes in creek mouths. "The creeks don't have to be big," notes Hall, who vertically jigs a 1-ounce leadhead tipped with a minnow.

"When I fish around locks I get in the eddies and drift in circles," says Hall. "I keep my eyes on my depth finder to see what is below me. I use my trolling motor to stay on top of a school. I don't give up on holes if I know they have been good before because sauger move a lot. These old concrete locks attract baitfish, which is the reason sauger are also there."

Walleye also hang around locks, below dams, in deeper holes of the main river channel, and in the canal alongside Gallatin Steam Plant, according to Dayton Blair, who uses the same plastic grubs to catch walleye as he tosses for sauger. When casting for walleye below dams, Blair stands on the riprap and throws upstream at about 11 o'clock and then lets his jig fall for a few seconds before retrieving it slowly. Many hits occur near the bank, he notes.

Late evenings are excellent times to catch walleye, says Blair. Few anglers venture out when it's cold, but fishing gets better as temperatures fall. One to two operating generators are best for stimulating walleye, says Blair.

Many anglers also catch walleye below Center Hill Dam in the Caney Fork River. Crankbaits, spoons, grubs, and in-line spinners are good walleye baits. So are night crawlers. (See Center Hill and other chapters for more information on walleye techniques in Middle Tennessee.)

CATFISH

Donny Hall is outfitted as well as anyone who specializes in Old Hickory catfish angling. He has year-round knowledge on how to land cats, from small, tasty channel catfish to huge blue and yellow cats.

Winter

Few anglers consider fishing for catfish in winter, but that is Hall's favorite time to catch big fish. "Catfish have migrated out of the creeks and congregated in the main river channel by winter," says the guide. "Big blue cats especially seem to love January and February."

Catfish thrive in run-of-the-river reservoirs and are attracted to the strong scent of cutbait that inhabit these waters, especially skipjack shad.

Trial and error is required to find good fishing spots, but anglers should start by locating sharp edges in channels, says Hall. "I make sure to have a long anchor rope and a good anchor, but I don't drop it in the middle of the channel. I always situate myself to the side of it. A good depth finder is essential to this kind of fishing."

Much of Hall's catfish action occurs below Old Hickory Dam, except in the winter, when abundant generation makes the river too swift for comfortable angling. When water temperature hits the 50s, Hall catches catfish between 25 and 50 feet deep, many of which exceed 20 pounds. Much bigger catfish inhabit Old Hickory, especially in the waters around submerged locks where Hall has hooked these huge fish.

Cut bait, particularly skipjack (also known as river herring), is Hall's favorite bait. He also likes gizzard shad, which at times is easier to obtain than skipjack. Both species have oily flesh that saturates the water with a catfish-attracting smell. Many anglers catch skipjack by tossing small white or chartreuse jigs, spinners, or spoons below dams. Cast nets or dip nets work well for gizzard shad near the wing walls below dams.

Hall's gear and tackle is easy to use, but it's larger than normal gear. "I like fishing Carolina rigs," says Hall. "I use heavy slip or egg sinkers for my weight and tie them above barrel swivels. I tie on 12- to 18-inch leaders below the swivels and attach the leaders with 7/0 to 10/0 hooks. I'll use 1- to 5-ounce sinkers, depending on current strength."

Hall has two primary rod and reel combinations. His smaller gear consists of 7-foot graphite rods with 80-pound-test braided line, spooled on Ambassadeur 6500 baitcasting reels. His rods are custom built with saltwater blanks and stainless steel guides. His largest gear, for when he pursues huge cats, has 130-pound-test braided line spooled on Ambassadeur 7000 baitcasters.

Once on the lake, Hall casts downstream and uses two to three shad chunks on each hook. Rod holders are essential to keeping his poles stationary and allowing him to use three or four rods simultaneously.

Spring

Hall's winter technique should work on most run-of-the-river lakes year-round; however, he also catches Old Hickory catfish in spring around shoreline cover or structure. "I'm actually fishing for crappie in spring, but I catch a lot of catfish, too," says Hall.

Most shoreline catfish are from 1 to 6 pounds, notes the guide, who catches them with minnows fished beneath bobbers. "I catch catfish this way from April to June," he says. "I have caught up to 25 cats from one hole while crappie fishing."

Many catfish are caught around

A Piscator rig is a series of small flies that anglers can use to catch skipjack. These baitfish—used live or cut—make irresistible bait.

riprap, trees, or rocky points. Sometimes Hall catches them in small creeks after a rain. "They like to get into shallow water after a good rain and feed on minnows," he explains.

Summer

Hall prefers fishing below Old Hickory Dam in summer because boat traffic isn't as heavy. He returns to his winter technique but sometimes uses shrimp for bait rather than shad. Hall searches for catfish habitat and then anchors.

"Look for fallen trees in water 20 feet deep or so," he explains. "This is usually good, especially if a small spring or creek is nearby. Chunk rock on bluffs with downfalls around them attracts baitfish and hungry cats. A lot people think mud bottoms are good. There may be a few catfish on them but not as many as around rocks."

Fall

Hall continues fishing below dams to catch migrating catfish in fall. He changes location frequently because catfish move around a lot. If he hasn't caught any cats after 30 minutes, Hall moves to another spot.

Guide Dayton Blair jigs for catfish below Cordell Hull and Old Hickory Dams. "My brother, dad, and I have gone below those dams and caught 60 or 70 catfish in a few hours, but none of them more than 6 pounds," says Blair. "From 2 to 6 pounds, though, I can catch catfish all day throughout the year."

Chicken livers cut into bite-size chunks make great bait. Sauté them in blood-fish scent before a trip. "I catch catfish up and down the river but have the best luck close to dams," says Blair.

Blair uses a three-way swivel for his catfish rig that he jigs vertically. He ties a ¼- to ½-ounce sinker on one of the swivel rings that is 6 to 8 inches long. On the other, he ties a 2/0 or 3/0 hook that is an inch or two shorter than the sinker line. He increases sinker size when current is strong. "There is no shortage of catfish below the dams," says Blair. "None at all."

CHAPTER 9

Cordell Hull Lake

The First Pearl on the
Cumberland River String

Cordell Hull Lake looks much like the Cumberland River did before Cordell Hull Dam was built near Carthage, with the exception of being wider and deeper near the dam. The lower end differs also by having a little warmer water and a larger population of largemouth bass.

Dale Hollow Lake has a great influence on the water temperature of Cordell Hull Lake. While Dale Hollow Dam is discharging its 47° water from the bottom of the lake, it can lower Cordell Hull Lake's temperature by 6° to 8° overnight. Although this affects the main channel's temperature, there is little or no effect on the water temperature in the tributaries. That's where most anglers find their warm-water, game-fish action.

Although stripers are not one of the predominant species on Cordell Hull, 60-pound stripers are caught below the dam. They run up to 40 pounds in the lake. The larger ones stay in the lower end near Defeated Creek and the smaller ones move farther upstream near Whites Bend. Because Cordell Hull has cool water in the main channel, the stripers aren't stressed by summer water temperatures and are active near the surface during the summer. Apply the same techniques and strategies described in the Old Hickory chapter on this lake.

GAME FISH RATINGS

Largemouth Bass	🐟🐟🐟
Smallmouth Bass	🐟🐟◀
Crappie	🐟🐟◀
Sauger	🐟🐟🐟◀

Buffalo Bluffs (near Buffalo Creek) is a good spot to fish with a Little Mac.

And to make the fishing even better, Eurasian milfoil has taken hold in parts of the lake. Anglers praise this aquatic plant because it provides shelter for young fish and also attracts game fish that prey on the small fish that stray from cover.

LARGEMOUTH BASS

"Cordell Hull Lake is the best lake in Region III for big largemouth bass," says Anders Myhr, fisheries biologist with Tennessee Wildlife Resources Agency. "It doesn't have a big population, but what it has is nice."

Winter

Guide Jim Duckworth fishes natural springs in winter. "There are some springs in Indian Creek and in Roaring River at the ramp. There is also a big, shallow, flat area that's real good. Shad stay in there and that keeps the bass

CORDELL HULL AT A GLANCE

Location:	Smith, Jackson, Putnam, and Clay Counties
Size:	11,690 acres
Length:	72 miles
Shoreline:	381 miles
Summer pool:	508 feet
Winter pool:	499 feet
Impounded:	1973
Featured species:	Largemouth Bass, Smallmouth Bass, Crappie, Sauger
Other species:	Stripe (White Bass), Striper, Bream, Catfish
Description:	The Cumberland River originates in Kentucky, and the head-waters of Cordell Hull Lake are in that state below Lake Cumberland. This run-of-the-river reservoir is riverine its entire length, with many tributaries, islands, and bends. It has rocky bluffs and flatland, usually opposite the bluffs, offering anglers both steep and gently sloping banks—rocks associated with the former, and wood with the latter. Milfoil grows from the dam upstream to Granville. Much of the Cumberland River carves into the western edge of the Cumberland Plateau. The lake has only two marinas: one at Defeated Creek near Carthage and the other at Granville.
Main tributaries:	Defeated Creek, Buffalo Creek, Indian Creek, Martin (also called Martins) Creek, Salt Lick Creek, Flynns Lick Creek, Wartrace Creek, Little Indian Creek, Jennings Creek, Roaring River, Sugar Creek, Brimstone Creek, Dry Fork Creek, Mill Creek, Obey River
Landmarks:	Cordell Hull Lake is northeast of Carthage. Granville is on the lake, and the lake runs west and north of Gainesboro. Celina is on the lake to the east and just south of the Obey River.
Operated by:	Corps of Engineers

See Appendix C for map information

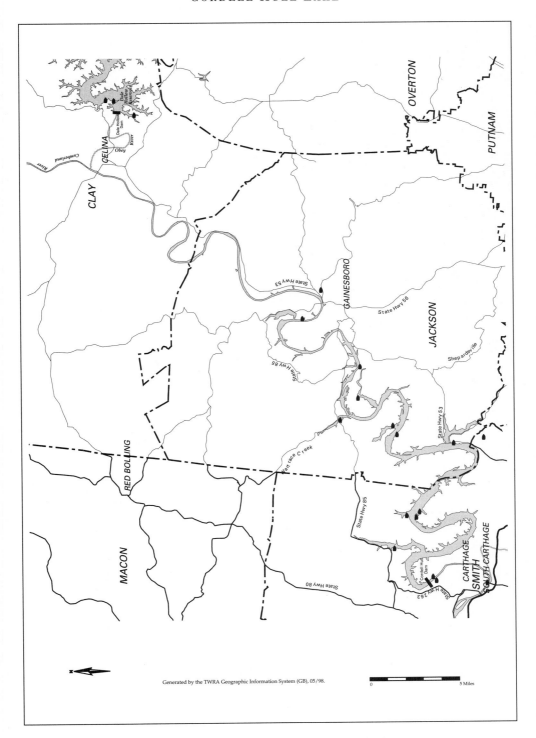

Generated by the TWRA Geographic Information System (GB), 05/98.

0   5 Miles

This largemouth bass, caught by Jim Duckworth, represents the good population of larger-than-usual bass in Cordell Hull Lake.

around. The springs are a few degrees warmer than the river and that's why the fish are there. I use jigs, slow-roll a spinnerbait across the bottom, or cast a red-shad plastic worm. Most of the shad have grown bigger than bass like to eat, so they are looking for something else." Buffalo Creek, at the lower end of the lake, is another good creek for bass in winter.

"I think evening is the best time to fish during the winter," says Duckworth. "If there is sun shining during the day, it will warm the water a little and the fish are a little more active. I fish more on the rocks than on the dirt or wood. If I can find wood on the rocks, then I use a purple Charlie Brewer Whirly Bee."

Spring

"When the water temperature hits about 53°, bass begin to move into shallow water," says Duckworth. "That's typically two or three weeks after Percy Priest hits that mark. Keep in mind that largemouth bass have been in the creeks all winter, and in the spring they move to the edge of the flats on these creek channels. They spawn on these creek flats."

Spinnerbaits are Duckworth's first choice for springtime bass. "I prefer white and white with chartreuse in the early spring, either a ½- or ⅜-ounce, with a Colorado blade on the front, and a willowleaf blade behind it."

The largemouth bass spawn around 63°, according to Duckworth's observations.

"I fish the wood in the shallows and the northeast corners of the lake that get more sunlight. I cast a ¼-ounce, chrome and blue, or chrome and black, Rat-L-Trap in clear water, and a firetiger color if there is any stain," he says.

"Martin, Indian, and Defeated Creeks are the three largest creeks, and they warm faster. Salt Lick and Wartrace Creeks have fish in them, but not as many because the conditions aren't that good for largemouth. The best fishing is from Granville downstream," says Duckworth.

He adds that by late spring when the water reaches 70°, the bass move to the main-channel points, and he fishes the drops beyond the flats. Natural-colored Power Craws and Salt Craws are his baits of choice.

Summer

"In the summer," says Jim Duckworth, "I fish the humps and points on the main channel with Carolina rigs and lizards. The lake points that are steeper and have the current flowing into them are the best ones. The humps I like are from 5 to 12 feet deep. Again, I fish from Granville to the dam for large-mouth bass. The area around Buffalo Creek is a hot area—not only the creek but the bluffs."

Duckworth suggests casting a spinnerbait around the edges of the milfoil and casting live shad into the pockets and around the edges. He says, "Be sure to tell your readers that the grass comes and goes in Cordell Hull. We had it several years ago, then it disappeared only to return again. When it's there, I start fishing it in July and fish it until sometime in October."

Fall

"The bass start moving into the creeks again in the fall," says Duckworth. "I start on the primary points just to check if they are there, and then hit the secondary ones. I keep moving while casting a spinnerbait or a Rat-L-Trap. I'm looking for shad being worked over by the bass. When I find that action, I stop to cast a Pop-R, Spit-N Image, or slow-roll a spinnerbait."

SMALLMOUTH BASS

Jim Duckworth says smallies are what make this lake interesting to him, and the fishing around Granville is awesome. Smallmouth make up about 20% of the black bass population along the main channel, he says. The same names keep coming up for the best fishing areas: Martin, Indian, and Buffalo Creeks. But he says, "The bluffs near the dam is one place not often mentioned when talking about smallmouth bass, but it is a very good area."

Winter

Duckworth says, "There are some anglers who fish the cracks in the bluffs with long fly rods. They flip creek minnows to the cracks. I fish the long bluffs and the main lake points with the float and fly method. The Whirly Bee works real well on spinning gear, with 6-pound test, around wood on the bluffs, too. I let the Whirly Bee drop about 7 feet before I start moving it.

"I'll say 10% of the logs larger than 6 inches in diameter angling into the water will yield a big smallmouth. Stay on the rocks with deep water beside it," he says.

Spring

"Jig and pig, and a plastic craw, fished on main-channel gravel points with deep water next to it, is the best springtime strategy," says Duckworth. "It's rare to catch smallmouth more than 200 yards from the river. I've found the

The best smallmouth habitats on Cordell Hull Lake are around the Granville area, according to Jim Duckworth.

white Whirly Bee to be a good bait, but a heavy fish can straighten the hook because it's designed as a crappie bait, not a bass bait. But it works."

Smallmouth bass begin to spawn around 58° on gravel flats in about 8 feet of water, he says.

"Shad-colored jerkbaits work well on smallmouth and largemouth in the spring. I fish the points where the smallies stage before heading to the spawning areas," he says.

Summer

"I fish for summer smallies the very same way I fish in winter," says Duckworth. "I fish faster in summer, of course. I'll also cast a spinnerbait and deep-running crankbaits on the main lake points. The fish will be about 15 feet deep most of the day.

"Nighttime is the best time to fish for smallies in hot weather. I use a black light, fluorescent line, and ⅛- to ⅜-ounce jigs with a Power Craw, or I'll slow-roll a dark-blue or black spinnerbait with a gold or silver Colorado blade. I use dark colors for contrast because the fish can't see color at night. When they look up at the bait, the dark color stands out against the lighter sky. The fish see the silhouette. Some anglers will use contrasting-colored blades on their spinnerbaits, too."

Duckworth fishes from the edge of the bank down to 25 feet at night with the Power Craw. "I can't say enough about the Power Baits. Berkley's testing showed that a smallmouth bass will hold a Power Bait for an average of 5 seconds, while the salt-impregnated craw is held less than 1 second. That extra time helps a lot with your hook-setting ratio."

He says the points that receive current are more productive than others. "Probably the single best spot for summer smallmouth of all the places I've talked about are the bluffs on the north side of the river near the dam."

Fall

"During the day," says Duckworth, "I'll cast crankbaits that run 5 to 7 feet deep. I cast the No. 5 and No. 7 Shad Raps in the Tennessee Shad color because the lake is usually clear in the fall. If there's a stain in the water, I'll go to a firetiger color. I'll also cast a spinnerbait. But the key is to fish the rocks. Fish from the main-channel points up the creeks as long as there are rocks and the water is deeper than 5 feet. Keep looking for shad being worked over, too, so you can cast to the jumps."

CRAPPIE

For years, this sleeper reservoir has only leaked information about its good crappie fishery. John Kruzan, who lives on the lake, says he catches slabs in the creeks in the lower end. Sometimes it takes extra looking to locate crappie because the water is cooler than most Middle Tennessee lakes. In May, Cordell Hull's surface temperature can run 10° below that of Center Hill Lake, thereby lengthening the spawning season.

Fall and Winter

Darryl York from Carthage says, "My favorite species to fish for is crappie. I fish Defeated Creek near the dam, and Martin and Indian Creeks at Granville. I also fish some sloughs, but mostly I fish the three creeks."

York says he catches crappie from around trees. "I fish trees that stick above the water, and limbs and bushes. Milfoil is good in the spring, but in the winter I fish mostly trees in about 30 feet of water. I cast ⅟₃₂-ounce jigs on 2- or 4-pound test, with a 6½-foot, ultralight spinning rod. I use chartreuse jigs for crappie year-round."

He says there's no hurry to get on the lake early in winter. "I get started around 9 A.M. and I'll fish about 30 trees a day. I'll catch two or three fish from a tree and that's about it. They seem to spook real easy in winter. I may come back to a tree later if I catch some off it.

"If I don't catch a fish within 10 or 15 casts, I move to another tree. I back-off from the tree about 30 feet and cast into it, letting the jig settle to the bottom with the bail open, and then reel it back real, real slow. Sometimes they hit it on the fall, but 9 times out of 10, they hit when I come up through them. They are in a neutral stage, nonaggressive, and that jig has to be right in front of them before they'll bite it. They won't chase it."

York sometimes uses minnows on a hook with a little splitshot for weight and fishes it the same way as his jig technique. Sometimes he adds a slipfloat and fishes down to 20 feet. "The trees are in 30 feet of water and the fish usually are between 12 and 20 feet. I've found that I have my best luck using the smallest minnows I can find."

Crappie move, he says, from the trees out to the channel, following shad, but at some time during the day, they will be around the trees. "Mostly, it's being at the right spot at the right time during the winter. They won't be on the main channel because it's colder. The crappie stay in the creeks, and the bass do, too."

He fishes the same technique and the same places from fall through winter. And he notes that the best depth for crappie is 30 feet, except in the spring, when they move shallow to spawn.

Spring

"In March crappie start moving up," says Darryl York. "When the water reaches the lower 50s, they start moving shallow, and 66 is the magic number. That's when they spawn. From 58° to 64° is when you can really get a hold of them because they are in about 2 feet of water." York fishes the same three creeks mentioned earlier year-round.

"In the spring I fish with a 10-foot fly rod using a jig under a float. I stay with 4-pound test and pop that little jig around the shallow trees and bushes. I use ⅟₄₈- and ⅟₃₂-ounce jigs. I don't fish with any jig over ⅟₃₂ ounce. The jig I make, called Crappie Critters, works good, so does the Slider and several others. Zebco and Daiwa make little reels with a trigger handle, and that's what I use on the fly rod."

York says to look for shallow, sandy banks with trees close to deep water. "They'll come into 2 feet of water or less to spawn, but they've got to have deep water—about 8 feet—nearby so they can escape when spooked," he says.

"Some days they like live bait and some days it's jigs. I found that when they aren't biting too good, they prefer live bait, but when they are aggressive, I can catch them better on jigs. And you can catch more, faster, on a jig. After a front comes through, they prefer live bait because it swims in front of them. They can't leave them alone. You always want to keep your bait above the crappie because they feed upward."

Summer

"Starting in the middle of June through August is when I fish at night for crappie," says York. "I'm fishing the same three creeks, Defeated, Indian, and Martin. I fish the bluff areas and along the creek channels in summer.

"I put the boat in about 30 feet of water, tie a rope to the bank, back off, drop an anchor, and pull the ropes tight so I stay in one place. I put my lights out and wait about an hour for the shad to find the lights. My lights are tube lights about 12 inches long and are submergible. I put them down about 12 to 16 inches. When they're on, it looks like a car underwater. They operate off a 12-volt marine battery."

York says he catches stripe, sauger, and a lot of other different fish at night.

SAUGER

Darryl York says the lake is full of sauger. "TWRA shocked them not long ago, and they said you could catch sauger about anywhere you fish. [Cordell Hull] has probably one of the highest concentrations of sauger in the state. A lot of the fishermen catch sauger casting for bass."

Guide Jim Duckworth says, "Cordell Hull is my favorite sauger lake." Both anglers agree that the best time to catch sauger is in the winter.

Winter

Most Tennessee anglers concentrate on catching sauger during the cold-weather months. Sauger begin to school and move toward their spawning area in late fall and are close to the spawning grounds by December. The spawn may last into April, but by March many anglers are casting for other species, ignoring some prime sauger-fishing time. In the winter, anglers find vertical jigging to be most efficient.

Jim Duckworth fishes the deep holes. "I fish in water 45 feet or deeper with a gravel bank preceding it. I drift and bounce the bottom with

Doug Markham (front), with guide Jim Duckworth, lands a Cumberland River sauger using a jig and Sassy Shad with a stinger hook.

a 6-inch lift. The second I touch the bottom, I lift it and then ease it back down.

"I use both live and artificial baits. For artificials, I like the Fin-S or a Long John on a ¾-ounce red or pink jig if the flow is moderate, but if the flow is strong, I'll use a 1¼-ounce jig. I tip the jig with a minnow when the action is slow.

"I always use FireLine because it has no stretch, and because the sauger bite so light, I can feel it better through this line. I've learned to set the drag at about 5 pounds of pressure. If I don't, my wrist, elbow, reel, and the fish's jaw will all be damaged. I've found that anglers setting the hook with no-stretch line, like the fused or braided lines, will rip the hook from the fish's mouth, more often than not, if the drag is not set properly."

Duckworth uses a weight stabilizer on the end of his spinning rod handles. "The balancing point is at the front of the spinning reel. I think it increases my catch by about 30% because it is more sensitive. It also reduces fatigue from lifting a jig all day long," he says.

In November, Duckworth fishes Defeated and Buffalo Creeks. In December, he moves to the mouths of Hurricane and Martin Creeks and fishes the deep holes in front of the Granville area bluffs.

Darryl York says, "I use a 1-ounce leadhead jig with a good-size tuffy minnow, shiner, or creek minnow in the winter. I use a No. 4 treble hook for a stinger. I vertical fish jigs in January and February—that's the best time to fish that way around Gainesboro. Any place that has sand or gravel bars is a good place to fish. The sauger hold there before they spawn and they spawn on these bars."

He jigs for sauger in 35 to 40 feet of water. "I fish right in the middle of the river channel. They are usually on the flat part of the channel. Where the bottom is flat with sand or gravel, they are going to be there."

Spring, Summer, and Fall

"I start trolling sandy points and gravel bars in the spring," says York. "The sand and dirt warms up faster in the spring, and the fish tend to hold on those points and bars on the main channel. I troll around the dam area.

"I troll the crankbaits from spring until winter. The Series 300 Bandit, No. 5 and No. 7 Bomber, and Excaliburs are all good baits. I like the shad pattern, but it doesn't matter if it's green, blue, black, or red—the color doesn't matter as long as it has the body like a shad." York trolls 15 or 20 feet deep using 8-pound test.

The tailwaters of Cordell Hull Dam is another place York likes to troll in the spring and early summer. "I troll crankbaits for walleye and sauger below the dam. Fishing is good until around mid-June. I'll fish all the way down to Hartsville the same way I fish up on the lake," says York.

Jim Duckworth says you'll catch sauger year-round using deep-running crankbaits and soft-plastic baits on the main points and bluffs of the river. "Stealth is most important when fishing gravel bars or deep holes. Use only your trolling motor," he cautions. "When you need your big motor to get back upstream to drift an area again, get far away from your fishing zone.

"Trolling also works. The sauger are going to be about 20 feet deep," concludes Duckworth.

CHAPTER 10

Dale Hollow Lake

A Cut above the Rest

Whether you believe that D. L. Hayes caught the world-record smallmouth in 1955, or that the record belongs to someone else, the fact remains that the largest smallmouth ever caught anywhere in the world came from Dale Hollow Lake near Celina. Hayes's fish has been verified by a thorough study of data by TWRA.

And, if you believe the comments of anglers who spend a lot of time fishing Dale Hollow, the next world record will come from there, too.

Dale Hollow is inarguably the best smallmouth lake in the state—a cut above the rest. The deep, cool reservoir, renowned for its clear water, is also home to good populations of largemouth bass, spotted (Kentucky) bass, walleye, muskie, and rainbow trout. In the last year or two, increasing numbers of crappie have been caught, but at this writing they do not make a significant fishery, especially when compared to the species just mentioned.

No other lake in Tennessee has excellent warm-water, cool-water, and cold-water species. If Tennessee's Cumberland River system of lakes were strung together on a necklace, Dale Hollow Lake would be a diamond surrounded by pearls.

GAME FISH RATINGS

Smallmouth Bass	🐟 🐟 🐟 🐟
Largemouth Bass	🐟 🐟 🐟
Rainbow Trout	🐟 🐟 🐟 🐟
Muskellunge	🐟 🐟 🐟
Walleye	🐟 🐟 🐟

SMALLMOUTH BASS

Dale Hollow's darling bass is the bronzeback. Dale Hollow gave up an 11-pound, 15-ounce smallmouth to D. L. Hayes on July 13, 1955. This state record stands today and is larger than the recognized world record of 10 pounds 4 ounces.

Gene Austin of Corporate Guide Service is sure he saw a buddy loose a smallie pushing the 15-pound mark. After watching that fish jump and throw the bait, Austin camped out in his boat for three days trying to coax another

DALE HOLLOW AT A GLANCE

Location:	Clay, Pickett, Fentress, and Overton Counties
Size:	27,700 acres
Length:	51 miles
Shoreline:	620 miles
Summer pool:	663 feet
Winter pool:	661 feet
Impounded:	1943
Featured species:	Smallmouth Bass, Largemouth Bass, Rainbow Trout, Muskellunge, Walleye
Other species:	Spotted Bass, Crappie, Bream, Catfish, Stripe (White Bass)
Description:	A highland reservoir, Dale Hollow offers flooded hollows and creeks. The lake is riverine from the upper end, where the East and West Forks of the Obey join near East Port Dock, to Sunset Dock. Downstream from there, the lake begins to widen. The reservoir has steep bluffs as well as long shallow points that follow the rolling contour of the area's farmland. The Wolf and Obey Rivers supply most of the impoundment's water, and after the two rivers join, Dale Hollow takes on a lake's proportions. The lower end is wide and very deep and boasts steep banks, a few tapering points, and high rock bluffs. The Corps of Engineers and TWRA continue to ensure water quality as well as good fishing through their stocking programs.
Main tributaries:	Illwill Creek, Fannys Creek, and Sulphur Creek are Kentucky's major tributaries. Tennessee's tributaries are Obey River, Wolf River, Horse Creek, Indian Creek, Long Branch, Lick Run, Mitchell Creek, Carter Creek, Irons Creek, Colson Creek, Holly Creek, Poor Branch, Natty Branch, Pusley Branch, Ashburn Creek, Lanear Creek, Jouett Creek, Jolly Creek, Cove Creek, Eagle Creek
Landmarks:	Dale Hollow Lake is located on the Kentucky border halfway between Nashville and Knoxville. Nearby communities include Byrdstown, Love Lady, Celina, Free Hills, and Timothy. Nearby routes include TN 52, TN 53, TN 111, and TN 294. The closest interstate is I-40.
Operated by:	Corps of Engineers

See Appendix C for map information

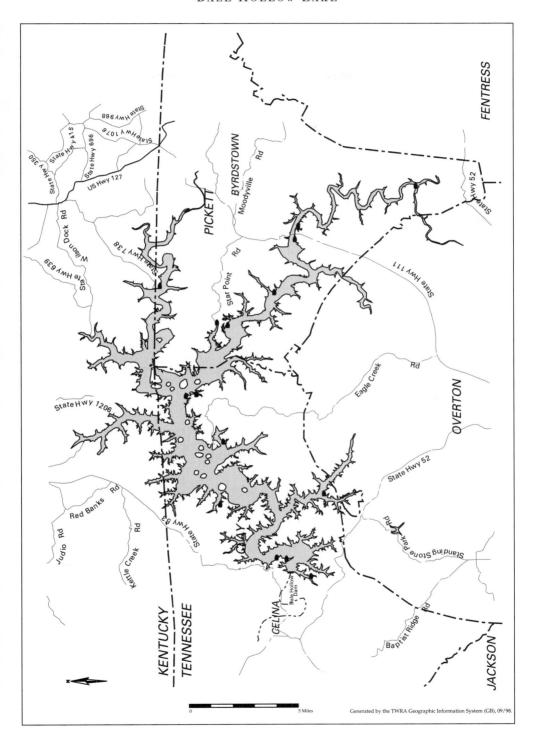

Generated by the TWRA Geographic Information System (GB), 09/98.

D. L. Hayes holds the mount of his 11-pound, 15-ounce, Dale Hollow smallmouth bass caught in 1955. It is Tennessee's state record, as well as the largest smallie ever recorded in the world.

strike. He believes the new world record is still swimming in Dale Hollow Lake—just where, he won't say.

Another angler, who knows Dale Hollow extremely well, grew up fishing with his daddy when the lake began backing up from the new Dale Hollow Dam more than 50 years ago. He is Billy "Mr. Smallmouth" Westmorland. Today, Westmorland produces the weekly TV program *Fishing Diary* on the Outdoor Channel and is a famous smallmouth angler. He, along with other anglers and guides, helps give us a complete picture of the lake's smallmouth angling.

Winter

"Call it D. H., Dale, or Dale Hollow, it's a big lake," says smallmouth guide John Cates of Kingston Springs, "and it has big smallmouth bass. In addition to the world's largest smallmouth, D. H. has another reputation—it's a tough lake to catch fish in. You have both sides of the coin, Dale Hollow has big fish and it's hard to fish."

Cates has beaten Dale Hollow's stingy reputation by adopting the minnow method. He isn't sure who showed him the technique, but thinks it was a nephew who lives on the lake.

The method: "I use the minnow method from December through March," Cates says, "the only months I guide on the lake. This is so simple to rig; I use 6-pound-test line on an ultralight rod and reel, then I tie on a gold 1/0 Aberdeen hook. That's it—except for the minnow—a 4- to 5-inch shiner.

"Smallmouth can see well in the clear water, so you don't have to sink your bait to the bottom. They can pick out the silhouette of an injured baitfish against the sky from 30 feet below."

Cates fishes from Willow Grove down-lake to a mile beyond First Island (the first island above the dam). He casts to points or bluffs, then lets the shiner do the work.

"I keep the boat 30 to 40 feet from shore and cast the minnow close to the point or bluff," says Cates. "I watch my line for a tick that indicates a pick-up or I watch to see it moving at a speed too fast for it to be just the shiner. I give the bass a count of three, reel in the slack, and set the hook. This method couldn't be more simple."

Gene Austin grew up guiding on Dale Hollow and he says, "From January to the second week of March is the major transition period on Dale Hollow Lake. It's the best time of year for trophy smallmouth bass."

Austin is a jig fisherman. As a rule he uses a ⅛-ounce leadhead with a 4-inch chartreuse, smoke, or pearl grub. His jigging varies according to the weather.

"If it's a bright sunny day," he says, "I start at 15 feet deep and fish out to about 25 feet. I fish two or three of my best places at this depth. If I don't catch anything, I go back to fish those same spots again, but a lot deeper."

Austin tries to find a pattern early. That means catching three fish at the same depth on the same structure. "If I can get three fish on mud, gravel, little shelves, or the side of a channel point, I know I can go similar places and catch fish."

On overcast days smallies move up the water column, and Austin starts fishing at 6 feet and fishes down to 18 feet.

"Cloudy and windy days are the best on Dale," says Austin. "Cloud cover and wind cut down on the smallie's vision. The windy banks are best because of the wave action. The water becomes dingy, dislodges food, and if the wind blows long enough, baitfish go to these banks. This creates good conditions for picking up smallmouth in shallow water."

He adds that you need to give the smallies the slowest presentation you can. "Cast your jig, watch your line, and be patient until it hits the bottom. The key to fishing in winter is to fish as slowly as you think you can, and then slow down even more.

"It's hard to fish slowly in the wind, but it's the best time. Fish the main channel points and the secondary points, the long tapering points that gradually go from 2 feet to 50 feet deep. I like positioning my boat in about 30 feet of water and fishing the point at about the 10-foot depth."

Austin also fishes little gravel banks that have a drop. There are a lot of these located between the main channel point and the secondary points in Kyle Branch, Indian Creek, Horse Creek, Long Branch, Lick Run, and up Mitchell Creek. Many of these banks have shelves [locate them with your

Guide John Cates's "Minnow Method" is simple to use and catches plenty of smallmouth bass from December through March near bluffs and pockets in coves.

sonar] at about 18 or 20 feet deep. Some will have three or more shelves that stair-step. If bass want to feed, all they have to do is swim up from 30 or 40 feet. It's a very short distance from that depth to a shallow gravel flat where food is found," says the guide.

Spring

Billy "Mr. Smallmouth" Westmorland of Celina is a national celebrity angler and probably has more fishing experience on Dale Hollow than anyone. He says, "I would urge anyone who fishes Dale Hollow to use small lures and light line and fish 15 feet deep or deeper. Cloudy, windy days would be best because of the clear water. Concentrate on points, all points, for smallmouth.

"From mid-March until Memorial Day," he continues, "use deep-diving crankbaits, small grubs, and small jigs with pork. During prespawn you need to look for small rock, or pebble bottoms—almost like sand—with some clay. Smallmouth like a little bit of clay. They seem to prefer the black shale gravel, and those are the things I look for on sloping banks. Smallmouth spawn in 10 to 12 feet of water, but they'll be 15 to 20 feet deep just before that happens. You can catch them on crankbaits—that's about the only time to catch any decent fish on a crankbait. I like to fish a crankbait occasionally, but little grubs will work when everything else fails.

Smallmouth stay on these structures until they complete their spawn, which usually begins in April, but sometimes lasts into May. The water temperature on the upper end of the lake is about a month ahead of the lower end. Smallmouth usually spawn in April, five days before the full moon, if the water temperature is right. Sometimes they'll spawn in March in the upper end, in the Wolf and Obey Rivers.

"I start fishing in the upper end and move down the lake," he says. "After they spawn, they don't hit very much for two or three weeks."

Austin also grew up on Dale Hollow and has guided there since high school. He says, "Look for pea gravel mixed with mud or red clay—that's a smallmouth place. In the spring, you should fish in front of willow bushes and on the secondary points in creeks."

The float and fly technique (see Appendix A) has become popular on Dale Hollow. It was developed in East Tennessee's clear-water lakes, but as with most successful fishing tools, it didn't remain a secret for long.

Summer

Westmorland says, "After Memorial Day, fish at night with pork on spinner-baits and jigs. Vertical and sloping points with underwater humps and steep breaks and drop-offs are the best structures. You can't go wrong fishing points.

"I think points are the best structures because smallmouth can find any depth of water they desire pretty quick on the sides of the points, and it seems like points are where baitfish like to stay. It was the first thing I looked for when I was fishing tournaments," says Westmorland.

"Night fishing is good through the fall, and if you can handle the cold, it is better than day fishing during winter."

Fall

"Mid-October is a good time for surface lures, then until mid-November when the fish begin moving from deep water to creek channel banks and drop-offs," says Westmorland.

His favorite time to catch smallies is November until January, with jigs and a lure called the Silver Buddy.

Trophy hunters concentrate on the midsection of Dale, from Mitchell Creek to the junction of the Wolf and Obey Rivers. This is a lot of water, but to help you focus, look for the structures and bank conditions discussed by Westmorland and Austin: shale points that extend out 20 to 30 feet from the bank and are close to deepwater drop-offs. Look for weeds and fish from 15 feet down.

Rather than trying to cover a lot of water and running out of gas in the process, get a map of the lake and choose five to seven creeks to fish. Focus on fishing a few places thoroughly. It will save you frustration as well as gas.

Do your homework before you fish Dale Hollow for the first time. Call a dock in the area you plan to fish, and get their report. Get a map (see Appendix C), pick a few areas, and fish them thoroughly. Dale Hollow has plenty of smallies all over the lake; you need to fish deep and stay at it to be successful.

LARGEMOUTH BASS

Yes, Dale Hollow has largemouth. Some big ones, but you don't hear much about them because most anglers would rather catch a 5-pound smallmouth than a largemouth of equal weight.

Winter and Spring

Largemouth bass like water warmer than their small-mouthed cousins and are frequently found in the backs of creeks. There is little fishing pressure on largemouth bass during winter.

Gene Austin says, "March to June are the months for daytime fishing. Look for areas with a gentle slope and deep water nearby. The largemouth responds to plastic worms or crawfish cast parallel to the shoreline. Perhaps the best areas are the upper end of Wolf River and the lower end of the lake, from Cedar Hill Dock up to Willow Grove Dock in the mouth of Irons Creek. In the spring look for bedding largemouth in the backs of coves and creeks among Sycamore and Cottonwood roots. Angle for these fish with a topwater Rapala or floating red worm."

Westmorland says, "Largemouth usually spawn in March before the smallmouth do because the water near the surface is warmer. You can find the largemouth back in the willows. It's a lot of fun to use a floating worm without a weight."

Summer and Fall

Westmorland says, "Worm fishing is the best technique for largemouth bass in summer. The backs of the coves are where I fish early in the year, but by summer the bass usually move out to the first deep water close to those coves.

"But it's night fishing in the summer that is best for using a worm or spinnerbait. Largemouth bass prefer a worm more often than anything else does. Weed beds or underwater grass are the places to fish at night."

When the water temperature drops, get out your topwater baits. From October until the water temperature drops below 50°, largemouth bass are feeding heavily and topwater action is good in the backs of coves and along feeder creek banks.

Gene Austin says, "Fish for largemouth just like it was springtime. Bass are moving close to the surface looking for shad. I suggest throwing leadheads with shad-colored grubs, spinnerbaits, and, of course, topwater baits.

"Night fishing continues to be good. I'd get in the creeks and cast the secondary points on to the back of them," he says.

RAINBOW TROUT

There are no bad months for catching rainbows. They are near the surface in early spring and late fall because the water temperature is comfortable then. The remainder of the year, you need to fish deep. Rainbows are larger in the lake than below the dam, according to U.S. Fish and Wildlife Service officers assigned to the Dale Hollow Hatchery.

Corn and night crawlers have been the perennial favorite baits. One-sixth-ounce Crippled Herring spoons and small Mepps or Rooster Tail spinners are

Dale Hollow is known for smallmouth bass, but it has a strong population of spotted and largemouth bass, too. Jeff Samsel shows us a sample of this fishery.

good artificial favorites. Power Eggs, however, have taken the place of most baits with a great many anglers. Open the jar, put one to three eggs on a hook, and cast—clean and easy. The built-in scent works better than real salmon eggs.

Summer

Fishing at night at the dam during the summer is a ritual for many house-boaters, but successful trout fishing is not limited to summer. Anglers pick their spots early in the afternoon and tie to the dam. When dark falls, they place lighted lanterns around the boat decks, sit in comfortable chairs, and drop baited hooks over the side.

Any boater can fish at the dam. Guide Ernie Paquette of Kingston Springs says, "The dam is a popular fishing site for anglers wanting to catch trout at night. There are lights along the dam, but it is better if you take a lantern or battery-powered light. I use a submergible light, lowered about 20 feet, to attract baitfish and trout. The underwater light proves more effective because the trout are deep and surface lights attract baitfish close to the surface. Trout will come up to feed, but they are usually smaller ones, less than 3 pounds."

Ultra- or light-spinning tackle is ideally suited for trout fishing. Lines between 4- and 8-pound-test are good choices. Dale Hollow's water is clear, and the more invisible your line, the better.

"A depth finder is very helpful," says Paquette, "not to find the bottom, but to locate the depth the fish are cruising. If you don't have sonar, you can count off about 50 feet of line. That's the depth the trout prefer in the summer."

Paquette uses whole kernel corn for chum and notes that cottage cheese is also a good trout-attracting chum.

Tackle is simple: hook, line, and sinker. A sharp, No. 8 to No. 4 hook is better for corn and Power Eggs. A No. 2 hook is better for minnows and night crawlers. You don't need much weight; one or two pieces of small splitshot will do.

Paquette says, "Tie to the dam or drift in front of it, both methods work. A light in or over the water is not necessary to attract trout, but some extra light seems to help by concentrating baitfish near it.

You can legally use several rods, so try setting a few out at different depths—30, 40, and 50 feet. When you catch fish you can adjust to the productive depth."

Paquette prefers night crawlers. "After the bait is in position, cast a handful of corn over your line. You can see the small yellow kernels fall for a long way. Then wait for the strike. If you are using several rods, try different baits, too."

You may want to use your trolling motor to move slowly away from the dam and along the walls if you aren't catching fish close to the spillways. If you have been using lights without results, turn them off. Trout behavior is not predictable, and lights occasionally have a negative effect.

"If nothing is working for you, ask the people who are catching fish. I have always found other anglers willing to share successful techniques while fishing in front of Dale Hollow's dam," says Paquette.

Trout fishing is good year-round below Dale Hollow Dam. The Obey River is fairly small and you can cast across it. It is stocked regularly from the hatchery located on the Obey River's north bank.

MUSKELLUNGE

Although not a primary species here, Dale Hollow has some of the best muskie fishing of all the state's reservoirs.

The best months for hanging a muskie are December to April. Most knowledgeable muskie anglers cast their lures between Mitchell Creek and Jouett Creek, and those that know a little more have narrowed the area further, focusing on Irons Creek to Ashburn Creek.

Muskies hit large lures, up to 12 inches long, the same ones you would cast for stripers. Bucktail spinners and spoons are also good baits (see the Great Falls Lake chapter).

Ambushing from the weeds is a vital part of muskie behavior, earning them the nickname "Water Wolf." Trolling the points is more efficient than casting. Large baitfish weighing close to a pound, or about a foot long, are appropriate for still fishing.

WALLEYE

Anders Myhr, a TWRA fisheries biologist, says, "The competition for food between the alewife and the walleye fry proved to be the trouble—alewife out-compete young walleye. This means stocking is necessary to maintain a walleye population.

"We learned from tagging studies that there are two distinct spawning walleye populations in Dale Hollow. Before the river was impounded, there was the native, southern strain of walleye, but after the impounding, coal mining upstream hurt those fish. To repopulate the lake, some walleye from New York were brought in, as well as walleye from other states. These new fish stayed in the lower half of the lake, and the indigenous fish stayed in the upper portion of the lake. Even in the summertime, these two populations don't overlap much."

Since 1964, Myhr has noticed the upper population of walleye to be twice the size of the lower lake walleye. That goes back to the theory that the southern strain was larger. Arkansas has some of that strain, and TWRA imports some of them.

Myhr adds, "The bass population has increased dramatically over the last 17 years that the alewife have been in the lake. The alewife fits a specific niche. They only come to the surface to spawn in late April and early May. Alewife stay at the thermocline and will be 40 feet deep all summer. The walleye utilizes the alewife because they are oriented to that depth in the summer. The rainbow trout orients below the thermocline and works on the alewife, too. The smallmouth also utilizes them. But spotted and largemouth bass utilize the threadfin shad more."

Winter

Famous angler Billy Westmorland says, "The best time to catch walleye is during February when the fish run upstream to spawn in the headwaters. You can catch them before the run and during it. After the spawn, the fish scatter and are more difficult to find."

Westmorland notes that walleye scatter after they spawn in late winter, and again in early winter. He thinks that in November they are moving toward the headwaters. So the best catching periods are prespawn, during the spawn, and in summer.

"The best bait to use in late winter and early spring when you can find walleye is a small crankbait. You can troll the banks or cast it. On rough, windy days, you can catch them casting. Once they get up the river, the 3-inch

Guide Gene Austin grew up on Dale Hollow and fishes for smallmouth and largemouth bass, specializing in smallies like this one in early spring.

twister grub on a ⅛- or ¼-ounce leadhead is the best bait I've found. White, chartreuse, or green are the colors that work best for me."

Spring
In late spring, Westmorland recommends trolling a deep-diving, Bagley's, imitation-minnow crankbait or any of a dozen similar baits. "Troll real slow," he says, "and get down 20 feet or more. When the fish are deeper, I use a spinner–night crawler rig. That gets down to about 30 feet."

Summer
Westmorland says, "All the summer months are really good for catching walleye, all the way into November." He trolls the spinner–night crawler rig during the summer at a depth of about 30 feet. This brings up the question of stratification: where is the thermocline? Westmorland says that the thermocline runs about 32 to 34 feet once the lake stratifies. There is enough dissolved oxygen for fish in the thermocline, below that in the hypolimnion, the oxygen becomes depleted as the summer gets hotter.

Fall
Walleye fishing is stable until November according to Westmorland. The fish often move up the water column as the lake cools but still bite the above-mentioned baits when presented to them. In November, the fish begin to move—leaving anglers to scratch their heads, wondering where they went.

John Conder, retired TWRA fisheries biologist, says sauger do the same thing. "Come November, walleye and sauger slowly head for their spawning grounds. The fish don't quit eating, they just don't stay put long enough for an angler to find them day after day. You may be better off fishing for a different species until they arrive at their spawning area."

The best time to catch walleye is debatable. The Corps of Engineers' "Fishing Guide" states that December through March are the best months. Guides and dock managers say June through August are best. Both are probably correct because of the two walleye populations. One spawns in the midlake area and the other up the river arms.

After they spawn, they spread throughout the lake. Their pattern is stable again for the summer months, following the large schools of alewife. Once you locate the baitfish, jig with curlytail jigs or live minnows below the baitfish. From sunset to dawn is the best time of day to catch walleye.

CHAPTER 11

Center Hill Lake

The Rare and Replete Reservoir

Every Tennessee lake has at least one abundant game fish willing to strike or bite an angler's presentation. That particular fish is among species that attract countless wide-eyed fishermen to it. Some reservoirs have at least two such fish, others have three, some even have four, but a rare few have five or more. This chapter is among the longest in *The Compleat Tennessee Angler* because Center Hill Lake belongs in that "rare" category.

Smallmouth, largemouth, spotted (Kentucky) bass, black-nosed crappie, walleye, bluegill, and white bass are among fish that inhabit this Middle Tennessee reservoir in such abundance that a month rarely passes on Center Hill when something isn't biting.

Among featured anglers are William Emerton, a walleye and bass angler better known by his friends as "Wild" Bill; longtime *Tennessee Outdoorsmen* host Jimmy Holt, who cut his teeth catching Center Hill smallmouth; TWRA wildlife officer Ben Franklin, who spends much of his off-time pursuing bluegill, smallmouth, and huge black-nosed crappie; and Tim Staley, a Center Hill guide and successful tournament angler with decades of largemouth experience.

GAME FISH RATINGS

Largemouth Bass	🐟🐟🐟🐟
Spotted (Kentucky) Bass	🐟🐟🐟🐟🐟🐟
Smallmouth Bass	🐟🐟🐟🐟🐟
Crappie (Blacknose)	🐟🐟🐟🐟
Walleye	🐟🐟🐟🐟🐟
Bluegill	🐟🐟🐟🐟
Stripe (White Bass)	🐟🐟🐟

LARGEMOUTH AND SPOTTED (KENTUCKY) BASS

Though known more for smallmouth, Center Hill is a good largemouth and spotted (Kentucky) bass lake. Guide Tim Staley has landed countless numbers of both species since he began fishing Center Hill more than three decades ago, including, according to him, "thousands of Kentuckies over 4 pounds."

On a given day, any of the three bass species hit Staley's artificial presentations, although his target fish is usually largemouth.

Winter

When surface temperature is between 48° and 52°—usually December to February—Smith catches bass on slowly retrieved crankbaits. "I can catch fish all over the lake as long as the temperature is close to 50°, but I stay in the lower section because it's slower to get cold," he notes.

CENTER HILL AT A GLANCE

Location:	De Kalb, Putnam, White, and Warren Counties
Size:	18,220 acres
Length:	64 miles
Shoreline:	342 miles
Summer pool:	685 feet
Winter pool:	618 feet
Impounded:	1948
Featured species:	Largemouth Bass, Spotted (Kentucky) Bass, Smallmouth Bass, Crappie (Blacknose), Walleye, Bluegill, Stripe
Other species:	Catfish, Stripe (White Bass), Rainbow and Brown Trout (in the tailwater below Center Hill Dam)
Description:	The reservoir is very narrow at its headwaters and widens as it moves toward the dam. Rocky shorelines, gravel points, and bluff-lined banks are common. There are numerous narrow ridges and rolling hills around the shoreline and much limestone in the lake.
Main tributaries:	Caney Fork River, Indian Creek, Holmes Creek, Big Hurricane Creek, Little Hurricane Creek, Second Creek, Mine Lick Creek, Falling Water River, Fall Creek, Pine Creek, Sink Creek, Collins River
Landmarks:	Cities near Center Hill include Smithville, Sparta, McMinnville, and Cookeville. Nearby routes include US 70, TN 56, and TN 96. The closest interstate is I-40.
Operated by:	Corps of Engineers

See Appendix C for map information

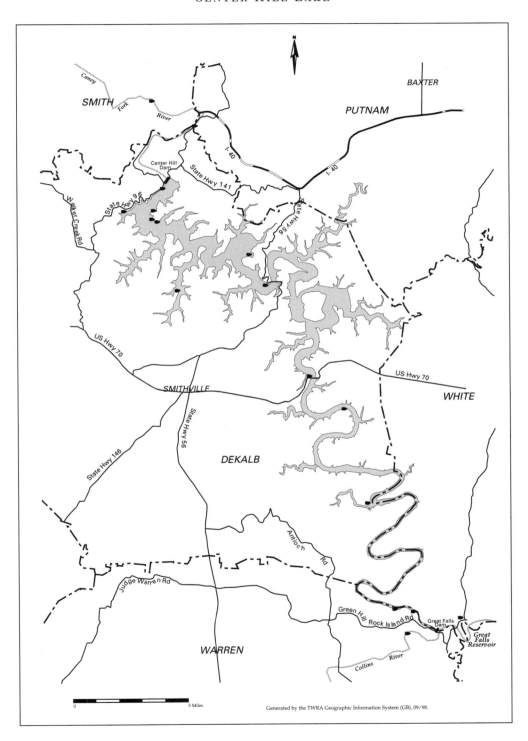

Staley fishes creeks this time of year about one-half to three-quarters back. He searches for chunk rock banks "where a break (a drop-off or ledge) goes from deep to shallow water." Falling Water and Mine Lick Creeks are among excellent bass areas. Because winter fish often suspend deep, Staley casts parallel to shorelines so that he can keep his lure in strike zones for most of his retrieve.

Staley's favorite winter lure is a deep-diving Bandit crankbait. In clear water his favorite colors are shad or a blue and silver combination. If Center Hill is "slightly stained," he tosses crawfish or perch colors, while chartreuse, deep red, or bright orange crankbaits attract strikes in muddy water. Staley tosses a Hot Lips when bass are suspending beyond a Bandit's reach.

"Crank the Bandit quickly down to about 8 feet and then slow the lure way down," says Staley. "I bump stumps, trees, or whatever is at that depth. I don't catch many largemouth if I crank too fast, but I catch more spots and smallmouth. Once I bump something, I stop cranking and let the lure rise just a little. A lot of times I attract attention when I start reeling again."

Staley tosses crankbaits with spinning reels on 7-foot rods, with medium to medium-heavy action and "fast tips" that increase his casting distance. Flexible tips also prevent many crankbaits from being ripped from a fish's mouth. Light 6- to 8-pound-test monofilament spooled on spinning reels keeps his lures deep. "I go to 6-pound test if I want to keep using the Bandit and need to get it a foot or so deeper than usual," he explains.

When water temperature increases a few degrees, normally by late February or March, largemouth, spots, and even smallmouth congregate in the heads of creeks. "This is usually when we get floods and high water," notes Staley. "Most people don't do this, but if they'll go back in creeks or pockets where there is water running in, especially if there has been warm rain, they can catch big fish.

"It's fairly common for Staley to go into Sink Creek or Pine Creek and catch 20 to 30 bass from holes 3 to 6 feet deep. I catch lots of spots between 2 and 4 pounds, a bunch of largemouth between 3 and 5 pounds, and occasionally even 6- and 7-pounders," he says.

Warm water attracts bass, but so do crawfish, worms, and other food washed into the lake. A 4-inch plastic crawl, fished on a Texas rig, or a crawfish crankbait, worked barely beneath the surface, catches fish. Tuffy minnows are also good. "I tear bass up fishing minnows on 4-pound test with BB splitshot and No. 4 hooks," says the guide.

Pumpkin with chartreuse dyed into its pinchers is Staley's favorite plastic crawl color. He uses a crawl on a ³⁄₁₆-ounce jig. Sometimes he actually fishes the water pouring into the creek. "That's when I use a ¼-ounce jig," he says, noting that bass get into the swifter water when feeding aggressively.

Spring

When water temperature reaches the high 50s, usually late March or early April, bass scatter and search for beds, says Staley. Smallmouth bed before largemouth. Staley often fishes the lake's upper section first and then works down-lake as water temperature rises. By doing this, he extends the bedding period.

"Spinnerbaits are good when fish start looking for beds," says Staley. "I throw around the base of trees when surface temperature is between 58° and 62°." Males are usually preparing beds at this time, while females lay farther away from the shoreline around trees and out of sight.

A chartreuse and white Aggravator with two big blades (the larger one a willowleaf, the smaller one a Colorado) is Staley's favorite spinnerbait. One blade is always silver, the other always gold.

Just before largemouth bed, Staley catches them around shorelines by flipping Booza Bugs. This is also a particularly good time to catch spotted bass hiding between chunk rocks, he notes. Staley's favorite fly is a 5/16- or 9/16-ounce bug, trailed with black, or black and blue, 2-inch pork rind.

When bass couple, Staley's favorite lure is a floating worm. "I would rather float a worm as eat," he says. "Actually, I skip it over the top of the bass and let it hit the bank. This gets their attention. When they look to see what happened, I pull the worm off the bank. Sometimes they come out of water 6 or 7 feet deep, and I just see a flash. I have never had more success with any other lure. I'll catch 30 to 50 bass on a good day."

Water temperature is usually between 62° and 65° when largemouth are "loving each other," says Staley. Worm colors are important. Red sparkle works well on bright days, black grape on cloudy days, and white if it's cloudy or if Staley just wants to see the worm better. His favorite 8-inch worm is a Seeker, while Stan Sloan makes his favorite 9-inch worm, known by locals as the "Center Hill Worm."

Jerkbaits are also excellent lures for bedding bass and for postspawn fish. A Fluke and Rattlin' Rogue are Staley's favorite baits. If bass aren't hitting topwater, Staley crimps a small splitshot above his Fluke and fishes it 6 or 7 feet deep.

"I catch largemouth, spots, and smallmouth doing this," he says. His favorite Rattlin' Rogue—when it's overcast—is black and silver with an orange belly. On sunny days, he prefers a blue back with silver sides. A pearl-colored Fluke with a gray back is his favorite soft jerkbait.

Summer

Staley throws deep-running crankbaits when the water gets warm. His favorite summer lure is a DD-22. Because fish suspend deep, Staley parallels the shoreline—just like in winter—to keep his crankbait in the strike zone for as long as possible. "I catch some of my biggest fish of the year doing this," he says. "I catch bass all day in June and July, at about 12 to 18 feet, by fishing in the same creeks where the bass spawned or by fishing main lake points. I especially like to fish where mud has been stirred up by boat traffic."

Staley uses baitcasting reels spooled with 10-pound-test monofilament for tossing big lures. He retrieves fast to get his crankbait deep and then he slows down once he reaches the appropriate depth. "My best DD-22—at any time—has a blue back, green sides, and an orange belly," he says.

Because he is a tournament angler and because fishing is good after sunset, Staley night fishes beginning in June. Six- and eight-inch plastic worms fished on a Texas rig and weighted with a ⅛-ounce bullet sinker make an excellent night presentation, he says. Water temperature is still comfortable in June, and most bass don't suspend lower than 10 to 12 feet, he notes.

As temperature increases, however, Staley moves out on channels and bluffs and catches bass 15 to 20 feet deep. Brush and rock piles hold many bass, he says. For those who disdain night fishing, the best daytime activity occurs during early mornings or late evenings.

As the water gets its warmest, Staley primarily works drop-offs, which are abundant in Center Hill, especially on the lake's lower end, he notes. Many drop-offs are around points that jut from bluffs "where they come up shallow on the inside and drop 60 to 70 feet on the outside."

Bass stack around drop-offs in July, August, and September because they feed on nearby flats and can quickly swim back to cool water. "I can sit around and pick fish off as they come up to feed," says Staley, whose favorite bait this time of year is a purple 9-inch worm fished Texas-style and weighted with a ³⁄₁₆- to ⁵⁄₁₆-ounce bullet sinker. He likes the catching power of No. 4 offset Gamakatsu hooks.

As water temperature starts dropping in late September, bass "begin following baitfish into creeks," says Staley. "This time of year is real fun to catch them while they are chasing shad. They hem shad up in the backs of creeks, and it's like watching a lawn mower go through them."

Sidewinders and Rat-L-Traps pulled through schooling shad catch many fish, says Staley, who especially enjoys throwing blade baits this time of year. "I'll cast a Sidewinder past the shad and then bring it back to the school," he explains. "Once there, I let it fall 3 or 4 feet before I pull it again. Bass eventually knock the fire out of it. I'll catch largemouth, spots, and smallmouth."

Staley catches bass this way until water temperature falls into the 50s and shad go deep. "What I do after the surface temperature drops is go back in a creek and use my depth finder to locate shad near the bottom," notes Staley. "Usually they are between 10 and 35 feet. I use a flasher to find them. If I see them in a cone shape, that indicates to me that bass are feeding and have spooked the baitfish."

Sidewinders and the Hopkin's Spoon are good lures at this time. "When water temperature drops below 50°, I jig spoons 35 to 60 feet deep," he says. "Some days I'll catch 20 to 60 bass."

SMALLMOUTH BASS

Jimmy Holt has caught thousands of fish in front of hundreds of thousands of viewers, as host of the long-running show *Tennessee Outdoorsmen.* He has caught many more with no one watching, especially in his youth when his favorite lake was Center Hill, and smallmouth bass were a great love of his.

Holt gives much credit for his angling success to his older brother Jack, who took Jimmy fishing as a young man and even bought his first outboard motor. Jimmy learned much from Jack, but he also learned a lot from his private experiences and diaries, which he kept during many seasons on Center Hill.

Center Hill is best known for smallmouth, but local bass anglers know it has a good population of largemouth and spotted bass, too. Tennessee Outdoorsmen host Jimmy Holt's favorite Center Hill smallmouth bait is a hair fly. As a youngster, he used flies to catch countless smallmouth around submerged rock fences.

Holt used an assortment of crankbaits to catch mainly largemouth in the 1960s, when, he says, they were more numerous than smallmouth. Eventually Center Hill became known more for its smallmouth, and in time Holt discovered a lure that became his favorite artificial bait. After watching how successful Jack had become with a Doll fly, and having had little success with it himself, Holt made a decision.

"One day I asked Jack to give me some of his Doll Flies and pork rind," recalls Holt. "I gave him my tackle box and told him to keep it. I decided I was going to fish that fly until I knew how to use it. I started fishing it, and I'm telling you, until this day, I've have never used a better lure than a ¹⁄₁₆-, ⅛-, or ¼-ounce fly for smallmouth, spots, or largemouth. I fish it shallow, deep, or in between."

Although Doll Flies are no longer manufactured, artificial flies are still among Holt's favorite lures. "I pour my own heads and I buy synthetic hair from craft stores to tie my own flies," he says. Any number of store-bought flies and plastic or pork trailers catch fish, provided anglers fish them correctly.

"I never work a fly by picking it up and dropping it or bouncing it off the bottom," notes Holt. "As soon as it hits the water, I raise my rod tip and start cranking and watching my line. Watching the line is the most important part of fishing a fly. When I start reeling, I have a slight bow in the line. If it goes slack, I know I'm on the bottom and need to reel faster. I'm swimming the jig, keeping it moving. Sometimes a strike is just a flick in the line. Sometimes it's a thump. If I haven't had a strike, I stop the fly at the boat and drop my rod tip. I've caught a lot of good fish by letting the fly fall right by the boat."

Holt tosses flies with 6-pound-test monofilament on a medium-action, 5½-foot rod. He uses a Mitchell 308 reel because its 3:1 cranking ratio helps slow lure presentation. "More modern and faster reels work, but I'm hooked on Mitchells," says Holt.

Winter

He doesn't fish Center Hill as regularly as he used to, but Holt would still practice the same routine that brought him much success. "I had a route like a milkman," he recalls. "When I fished in winter, I would start at Cove Hollow Marina and stop at every rock fence all the way to Mine Lick Creek. I caught lots of 2½- and 3½-pound smallmouth from around these submerged walls."

Lay out from walls and work flies over their deep ends. "Sometimes I would let the fly actually bump the fence, but most of the time I swam it slowly over the rocks," says Holt. "There were times when I left Cove Hollow and hit four or five fences and caught four or five fish."

Submerged trees, chunk rock, and gravel points also hold fish. "Don't pass them by," says Holt. "Some are better than others, but it takes experience to figure that out." Rocky banks also provide good smallmouth habitat but require long casts, especially when Center Hill is "super clear," he notes.

White, or a combination of brown and orange, are Holt's favorite fly colors. He favors ⅛-ounce leadhead jigs. While he uses synthetic hair, many kinds of hair catch fish. Holt once had a neighbor who fished with pet hair. "He had a dog that got to where it wouldn't come near him because he clipped all the hair off its tail to make flies," he recalls.

Many anglers catch smallmouth by flipping jigs or tossing spinnerbaits around shoreline bushes when the lake is high. December was Holt's favorite winter month, followed by January and then February.

Spring

While February provided Holt his slowest small-mouth action, March brought new life to Center Hill. "That's when smallmouth really got active again," he says. "I would catch smallmouth using the fly and working the same areas as winter. When I started catching a lot of little smallmouth, I knew it was time to change locations and fish topwater."

While smallmouth fishing is good in the middle and lower sections of Center Hill, angler "Wild" Bill Emerton catches smallies using live bait in the lake's headwaters.

Raccoon Hollow, Little Hurricane Creek, Big Hurricane Creek, and Indian Creek were among areas where bedding smallmouth attacked topwater lures. "I looked for shallow areas around long, chunk rock banks where there weren't any big drop-offs," recalls Holt. "Topwater action only lasted about a week, but this was the greatest fishing ever. Most smallmouth weighed between 2 and 3 pounds."

Holt's favorite lure was a 4-inch Topper, which is no longer made. Rattlin' Rogues or any number of topwater baits should get excellent results. Lure color didn't seem to matter much during these aggressive few days, but Holt's most-used Topper was yellow with a tint of green. "I could see them following it," he reminisces.

Angler William "Wild Bill" Emerton has been featured on Holt's *Tennessee Outdoorsmen.* Emerton is known best by local anglers for his walleye expertise, but he also catches many smallmouth in Center Hill's headwaters below Great Falls Dam. April is a good time to start catching smallies, including females that weigh up to 5 pounds.

Using live shad or live crawdads, Emerton fishes below bluffs between the Sandbar Ramp in Rock Island State Park upstream to the famous Blue Hole. "If I start out catching small males, it won't be long before larger females show up," he assures. "They'll be there sometime during the week."

Emerton catches shad with a cast net in the swift water above the Blue Hole. He locates them by watching hungry shorebirds. "They might be schooling on the left side of the river, the right side, or even the middle," he says. "They're hard to see in fast water, but wherever there is a heron standing around is where the shad will be."

Emerton favors shad about 3 inches long. He hooks them through the lips and places a small splitshot several inches above the bait. Smallmouth usually suspend 5 to 10 feet deep. "I cast and let the current take my shad about 15 feet down the side of a bluff," he explains. "I'm winding in slack all the time and never hitting bottom."

Keeping shad lively is vital to successful fishing. Emerton only catches enough bait for two to three hours and stores his shad in his live well or in an oxygenated cooler. One to two cups of rock salt helps keep his bait fresh.

Emerton's gear consists of a 6-foot, medium-heavy-action rod and a spinning reel spooled with 12-pound-test monofilament, which withstands sharp ledges and most hard-fighting fish. "Sometimes I'll hang something, and I won't even be able to turn it before my line breaks, but it could be anything from a bass to a big drum or catfish," he says.

April is the best month for headwater smallmouth fishing, says Emerton, but he also catches bedding smallies in May. A number of plastic baits, including flies, worms, and lizards, catch spring smallmouth, but Emerton believes live bait works best.

Summer

By June, "smallmouth are coming off the bed," says Emerton. The best headwater fishing begins at daylight and often ends shortly after sunrise. "Be on the water at daylight because sometimes they quit hitting by 5:30 A.M.," he notes. "Other days they may hit until 6:30 A.M., and I've even seen them hit up to 10 o'clock, but the earlier I get there, the better I do, most of the time."

Emerton continues fishing live bait in summer, but artificial bait—worms, lizards, and other plastic imitations—also catch fish. Shad are more difficult to locate in summer, which is why Emerton sometimes uses crawfish.

In the lake's mid- and lower section, smallmouth fishing is excellent just before sunset and any time after dark, according to Ben Franklin, a Center Hill angler since the mid-1970s. Franklin lives close to the lake and has fished it thousands of times. "The best time to night fish is when one-quarter to three-quarters of the moon is visible as it's phasing toward a full moon," says Franklin. He believes Center Hill is "one of the top three smallmouth lakes in America."

Franklin primarily catches smallmouth with artificial baits. Black lights are vital to night fishing, he notes. In May, June, and the first part of July, he fishes the lake's lower end, from Sligo Marina to the dam. After that, he works from Sligo upriver, where there is less boat traffic. He spends much time fishing points and "little rounds" on bluffs. "Little rounds stick out from the bluffs to make small points and have sharp ledges," he explains.

Franklin's favorite May bait is a 4-inch, plastic Original Ringworm fished on a ¹⁄₁₆-ounce leadhead jig. "I use a light head because in May smallmouth feed shallow at night, from 6 inches to 8 feet deep," says Franklin, who throws light-colored worms on bright nights and dark-colored worms on black nights. His favorite shades are brown with an orange tail, and June bug with either a chartreuse or red tail.

Franklin often catches bass during the last hour before nightfall. The Original Ringworm catches smallmouth before sunset, but so does a Hootin' Nanny, a twin-tailed grub that has a rubber skirt. Franklin's favorite grub colors are clear with black and silver flakes, or pumpkin with brown and red flakes.

In June, Franklin fishes at night with a ⅛-ounce fly and rind. "I like a Booza Fly," he notes. He also tosses a Ninny Fly with a 2-inch crawl, which is a popular Center Hill bait. A motor oil fly, with a brown crawl that has orange pinchers, and a blue fly, with a junebug crawl and chartreuse pinchers, are his favorite "light of the moon" colors. On dark nights he tosses a black-and-blue fly and junebug crawl with chartreuse pinchers.

When fishing worms or flies, Franklin uses 8-pound-test monofilament and a spinning reel. "I let the fly fall, pick it up, and then let fall again around shallow points and bluffs," he says.

As water temperature rises, Franklin increases his lure weight to reach smallmouth suspending in cooler, deeper water. A ⅝-ounce spinnerbait catches smallmouth and largemouth. Bubblegum is Franklin's best color for spinnerbaits on bright nights, while tequila, with combinations of black, blue, and bubblegum, is his favorite bait on dark nights.

Bubblegum or green pork rind catches fish on light-colored lures, black and white rind works well trailing darker lures. Franklin uses baitcasting gear spooled with 15-pound-test monofilament when tossing heavier baits.

"In July and August smallmouth sometimes suspend 20 feet deep," he notes. "I fish below bluffs when they're deep. I also toss a fly and rind combination this time of year, but I switch from ⅛-ounce flies to ³⁄₁₆-ounce flies—mostly solid blue flies, or black and green ones. A 101 Original Pork Frog is important to Franklin's success. "I trim the fat off all rinds because it gives them better action," he notes.

A plastic Gitzit also catches summer fish, notes Franklin, whose favorite colors are brown, smoke, or brown with red flakes. "I fish a Gitzit on a ³⁄₁₆- or ¼-ounce leadhead jig with a weed-guard," he notes. "I work it slow, just like I do a fly and rind or a Ninny Fly and crawl. Basically, this is the way I fish all summer long, and I catch as many smallmouth as anyone."

Fall

Day action has picked up again by late September or early October. "I always headed back to Center Hill about the time the World Series started," recalls television host Jimmy Holt. Rock walls and points—where he caught many smallmouth in winter and early spring—provided pleasant angling moments for Holt. Hair flies and topwater baits are among the lures that he recommends.

Although he doesn't use them, Holt also notes that many anglers catch fall smallmouth with creek minnows or shiners on gravel points. William Emerton agrees. "I see people fishing from Sligo Marina down-lake," he says. "They fish on the bottom and catch nice smallmouth that weigh 3 pounds and up."

CRAPPIE

Few fish have generated more angling interest than black-nosed crappie, which the state's wildlife agency (TWRA) originally stocked in Center Hill for research reasons, but because they became so popular, the agency continues releasing them yearly. "Blacknose made a big change in the crappie fishing on Center Hill and in people's perspective of crappie fishing here," says Ben Franklin, a TWRA wildlife officer and crappie angler.

A blacknose has a stripe that stretches from its nose to the top of its head, but biologically it is categorized as a normal black crappie. In an effort to learn how successful stocked crappie would be in a reservoir Center Hill's size, the TWRA stocked thousands of them in the lake. Blacknose are easy for biologists to identify in scientific surveys because of the stripe.

Although considered a simple black crappie, Franklin believes blacknose are special. "They're unbelievable," he says. "To me they seem to fight stronger than our native crappie, and I've even seen them jump like a bass."

Franklin locates crappie by finding submerged cover. Brush piles, tree tops, and boat docks attract them. "Fishermen who don't find cover here will have a disappointing trip," says Franklin, but he adds that brush piles are easy to locate with sonar. Franklin has helped place many brush piles in Center Hill. "Some of the piles stretch as long as a house," he says.

Winter

Fishermen catch stripeless black crappie and sometimes even white crappie in Center Hill, but blacknose is the main species caught. November is the best month to catch big fish, according to Franklin. His angling method early in the month is different from the one he uses only a few weeks later.

"For some reason, and I don't know why, blacknose hit minnows in September, October, and the first part of November, but usually quit hitting them toward the end of the month," he explains. "I can still catch a few fish with minnows, but they hit jigs better from late November until March or April. Most people don't realize how good crappie fishing is in November, but I doubt there is another lake any better than this one at that time. I catch big fish. I'm talking crappie 14, 15, and 16 inches long."

Because he fishes brush piles, Franklin uses weed-guards on $\frac{1}{16}$-ounce marabou jigs or plastic tubes. His favorite marabou color is hot yellow, but white also catches many fish. His favorite tube colors have yellow bodies with chartreuse tails, red bodies with white tails, orange bodies with chartreuse tails, dark green bodies with chartreuse tails, and salt-and-pepper bodies.

His gear includes medium-action, 5½-foot graphite rods and spinning reels spooled with 4-pound-test monofilament. Franklin casts beyond cover in winter and lets his jig lightly drift back into the brush. "About 90% of the time, I get strikes as I pull my jig through the brush and it falls off a limb," says Franklin. Crappie usually start hitting jigs first in the lake's lower end, including Holmes Creek and Indian Creek. Both creeks have numerous coves and pockets with brush.

Pine and Sink Creeks usually become good crappie areas early in January, notes Franklin. "I use the same jigs in January, February, and March," he says. "By late January, many crappie are found anywhere from 1 to 30 feet deep, but most are suspending at about 10 feet deep."

Center Hill fisherman Ben Franklin usually catches black-nosed crappie around brush piles, but in spring says they are easily found near shorelines and caught with minnows beneath bobbers.

Many fish are caught around docks. "People fish off slips with minnows and jigs and catch a bunch of blacknose," says Franklin.

Spring

Crappie are nearing the shoreline by late March or early April, says Franklin. The roots of cottonwood and sycamore trees provide excellent crappie cover. Minnows fished below bobbers on wire hooks is as good a way to catch shoreline fish as any. "I fish 3 or 4 feet deep around the banks," says Franklin. "I keep moving until I find crappie." Franklin catches shallow crappie from late March through early May.

Summer and Fall

Crappie return to deep cover and around boat docks after they spawn. Summer months provide the slowest action for Franklin, but patient anglers can catch fish with plastic baits or minnows. Crappie hit more aggressively when water temperature starts falling in mid- to late September. Many anglers catch fish around TWRA fish attractors, especially the one in Holmes Creek, notes Franklin.

Franklin casts beyond cover—just like in winter—and lets his lure slowly fall into brush. His only difference in presentation is that he tosses minnows rather than lures. "I still use a ¹⁄₁₆-ounce leadhead jig on 4-pound test, but the fish favor minnows," he says. November is Center Hill's best crappie month, but September and October are also good, says Franklin.

STRIPE (WHITE BASS)

There was a time when 1½- to 3-pound white bass inundated Center Hill's headwaters, and fishing was incredible. While stripe aren't as numerous as years ago, they have shown improvement in the 1990s, according to avid Center Hill angler William "Wild Bill" Emerton. "We had one of the best years we have had in a long time in 1997, but the stripe weren't real big," he says.

Winter and Spring

Emerton begins catching white bass near Great Falls Dam in January, but they become more prevalent in February and March. "Early in the year I throw the lightest thing I've got, like a ⅛-ounce Twister Tail, a hair jig, or any little lure with a spinner on it," notes Emerton. Chartreuse, green, or white are good lure colors. Emerton does most of his white bass fishing between Warren County Park Dock, in Rock Island State Park, upriver to the Blue Hole, if Center Hill's water level has risen enough to float his boat.

Stripe feed aggressively during their spring spawning run. Sometimes Emerton catches them while he jigs vertically for walleye, but often he catches them casting in shallow water. "There is an island just upriver from the Sandbar Ramp with a lot of willow trees, bushes, and rocks around it," says Emerton. "I get within casting distance of it and catch lots of stripe."

Bank fishing in late winter and early spring is the best way to catch white bass, notes Emerton. Stripe frequently feed on shad near the Corps of Engineers' hydroelectric plant in the shoals. "Fishermen in boats need to cast toward the bank," he says. "Bank fishermen need to throw downstream around the edge of the fast water."

Summer and Fall

After the spawn, Emerton locates baitfish to help find white bass. Stripe stay in the headwaters near Great Falls Dam in summer and chase minnows all day, he says. Shad swim in the shoals early, and white bass follow them.

Emerton suggests looking for commotion in the fall. White bass often attack schooling shad on the surface, but so do smallmouth, largemouth, and spotted bass, he notes. Night fishing is also good. Minnows, shad, or spoons, fished below a lamp or floating light, catches fish that gather to gorge on schooling shad.

WALLEYE

William Emerton drives an 18-wheel truck for a living but would be an excellent Center Hill fishing guide if he grew tired of the road. For more than 20 years, Emerton has fished the ribbon of Center Hill Lake near Rock Island State Park, catching countless limits of walleye from its headwaters.

Winter and Spring

Walleye feed aggressively before they begin their spawning run. Emerton catches walleye in late February and early March, but works slowly in cold water to solicit strikes. His favorite winter bait is a ¼- to ½-ounce hair jig tipped with a tuffy minnow. "I occasionally use a ⅛-ounce fly if the wind is still, but most of the time I use a ¼-ounce jig," he says. Chartreuse is Emerton's favorite hair color, but yellow, red, and orange also attract walleye.

The headwaters of Center Hill Lake is one of the state's most popular walleye holes. "Wild" Bill Emerton has caught thousands of fish in the spring using blade baits.

Emerton hopes for wind in early winter because it helps move his boat gently over walleye holes. Later in the winter, when Center Hill starts rising, current from nearby Great Falls Dam replaces wind as his main boat propellant.

"Fish real slow in early winter," says Emerton. "I drop my line to the bottom, crank it just a little, and then barely flick the fly. Just enough to make it move." Emerton fishes the main channel and uses his trolling motor for control. He locates numerous walleye between the Sandbar Ramp in Rock Island State Park and the mouth of Sink Creek near Pate Ford's Marina.

"Fish are all over the lake, but I can eliminate a lot of boat travel and searching by fishing in that area," says Emerton. "I can catch walleye in bigger water, but it might take a couple of days to find them. I know they are in this stretch of the lake and that's where I go. Sometimes I catch three or four keepers at daylight and then don't pick up another fish until the afternoon. The key to catching walleye is being on the water when they decide to bite."

Emerton's "perfect" walleye gear consists of a medium-heavy, 6-foot rod and a spinning reel spooled with 8-pound-test monofilament. Marking baitfish or identifying bottom structure is not important; dressing warmly is. "I've been on the river when I was concerned about whether I could get my boat on the water because of ice on the ramps," he explains.

As Center Hill rises, Emerton migrates closer to the lake's thinnest segment. Two generators below a Corps of Engineers' hydroelectric plant create a strong current there. The higher the lake rises, the further upriver Emerton moves. When it's strong enough to replace wind as his main boat propellant, Emerton switches "to the heavy stuff."

"I know I have to stay in touch with the bottom, and that's difficult when current is strong," says Emerton. "That's why I start using a ½- to ⅝-ounce Sonar. Water level can change quickly. I might be fishing in 10 feet one second and 20 feet the next."

Emerton's favorite lure is a Sonar that he ties through its center hole (it has three), but many other baits catch walleye, including jigs tipped with minnows, spoons, or hair flies. Emerton fishes as close as possible to the powerhouse, but is careful around shallow rocks. He jigs vertically in the fast current and works holes repeatedly where he gets strikes. As Center Hill rises, he often fishes close to shorelines. Large rocks and boulders provide excellent walleye habitat.

Beginning 100 yards upriver of the Sandbar Ramp and extending to the hydroelectric plant, only lures with single hooks are legal from January 1 through April 30, notes Emerton. Tennessee's wildlife agency prohibits the use of multiple hooks because biologists believe numerous walleye get snagged by them.

Walleye longer than 16 inches are common once females enter Center Hill's headwaters, says Emerton. "I even hear of 5-, 6-, and 7-pounders being caught, and occasionally a 10-pounder, but most of the time I catch smaller fish than that," he says.

Bank fishing is good, close to the hydroelectric plant, notes Emerton. Because water is swift and shallow there, bank anglers toss lighter baits to minimize the amount of lost lures. A ¼-ounce leadhead jig fished with a chartreuse Twister Tail is a popular bank lure, says Emerton.

Most walleye have spawned by mid-April, and daylight fishing for casting anglers is good only until about 7:30 A.M. "Right around daylight is the best day fishing after the spawn ends," says Emerton. Walleye are caught, however, by some anglers who troll crankbaits from Blue Hole to Sandbar. For Emerton, walleye fishing is best at night after the spawning run ends.

Summer and Fall

After the sun sets, Emerton throws crankbaits in shallow water between Rock Island State Park and the Corps of Engineers' hydroelectric plant. His favorite summer lures are black and silver No. 7 Shad Raps and No. 9 Countdown Rapalas.

"I usually throw downstream and work my lure as close to the bottom as possible," says Emerton. "I even bounce them off rocks. A lot of fishermen don't seem to know that walleye can be caught this way, but they hit crankbaits at night all summer long and into fall."

Emerton often anchors in water 20 to 30 feet deep and casts into water 10 feet deep or shallower. Sometimes he works his bait across the surface. "I'll let it sit a few seconds and then give it a twitch or jerk," he says. "Fish tear my lure up if they are anywhere close."

Moonlight is important. "Fishing is good all night if the moon is near full, but if it's in a dark phase, I fish until about 9 or 10 o'clock, quit awhile, and then come back from 3 to 5 in the morning, which is a super-good time to catch walleye," explains Emerton.

When crankbaits fail during dark moon phases, Emerton heads downriver a half-mile or so, pulls out a floating light, and waits about an hour for shad to collect under its glow. "I don't have to be in the current when I'm fishing this way," he says. "Walleye come to me." Emerton uses a cast net to catch schooling shad for bait, or he works a spoon or Sonar beneath gathered baitfish. A No. 1 or No. 2 hook and a small splitshot is all that is needed to fish live bait.

From early summer to fall, daytime anglers catch walleye by trolling deep-diving crankbaits (Shad Raps, Bang-O-Lures, Bombers, Hot 'n' Tots, Hellbenders, etc.) in channels, beneath bluffs, and over gravel bars. Many anglers fish near Sligo Marina, Johnson Chapel, or Ragland Bottom Recreation Area where Center Hill widens, says Emerton.

Spinner rigs, such as a Hot 'n' Tot Pygmy, are also good artificial baits when fished with a trailing night crawler or minnow.

For avid angler Dan Ward, Center Hill's summer walleye fishing is excellent, especially after the lake's thermocline forms. "When it gets real hot and the lake develops a strong thermocline, I tear walleye up," he says. "Walleye tend to feed every 12 hours for about 30 minutes. If I'm on the water when they're ready to feed, I usually have a great time. Experience has shown me that walleye are going to be in one of two places, either over gravel bars or near bluffs."

When fishing gravel bars, drag a Hot 'n' Tot (the crankbait, not the spinner) in the gravel "and really let it dig the bottom," urges Ward. "Most people use a spinner rig and troll real slow, but I don't like fishing this way. I would rather use a crankbait and troll faster."

Many of Ward's successful trips occur when it's sunny. "Before I started fishing Center Hill, I heard that clear water makes fishing tough in the sunshine, but I catch walleye in the middle of the day under bright skies," he says. "Most of my better fish have come at night and just before daylight, but I catch plenty of fish in daylight."

Ward has caught walleye between Sligo Marina to Center Hill Dam. "Straight out of Cove Hollow Marina are three or four points that hold walleye, and there are always at least a few fish hanging around the dam's riprap," he says. An area near Davies Island is also a walleye hangout. "I troll with a Hot 'n' Tot or Hellbender in a place known as the Narrows."

Ward always looks for shad. "Walleye relate to baitfish more than structure," says Ward. "Sometimes they suspend 60 feet in water that is 110 feet deep, but they're inactive at this time. When they decide to feed, they swim beneath baitfish."

BLUEGILL

While he is a competitive bass angler and also spends many days catching black-nosed crappie, angler Ben Franklin always makes time for Center Hill's bluegill. "I have fished every Tennessee lake from Nashville east, but I've never seen a bluegill lake as good as Center Hill," says Franklin. "I catch them all year, and most of them will be about the size of my hand."

Winter, Summer, and Fall

While few winter anglers fish for them, Franklin knows that bluegill bite in cold water. "Use a cricket and cast parallel to a bluff," he says, noting that he once caught bluegill 70 feet deep while jigging a 4-inch spoon for bass. "Let the bait fall until it reaches a school."

Bluegill suspend shallower in summer and fall along bluffs and hit crickets, worms, or any number of small artificial baits. Some anglers use heavy sinkers to speed bait past smaller sunfish and reach larger bluegill, notes Franklin.

Center Hill Dam also provides incredible bluegill fun. "Starting after the spawn, I can go to the dam—and I mean get right against the concrete—and throw a cricket parallel with the wall," says Franklin. "I'm not kidding; one summer several tractor-trailers couldn't have hauled out all the bluegill caught there."

Spring

Finding Center Hill's bedding bluegill is simple, and once located, anglers can catch "100 fish in no time," says Franklin. Gravel bars and willow trees are key to finding fish. Anglers who locate these together should find bluegill beds.

"Get two tubes of crickets and you'll load your boat," says Franklin. "There are not that many gravel bars on Center Hill, so finding these is easy."

Franklin catches most bluegill about 8 feet deep using crickets and casting a small hook and small sinker on 4-pound-test monofilament. He uses a hook with a long shank to prevent aggressive bluegill from swallowing it. While Franklin primarily catches bluegill in May, panfish anglers should try fishing the same areas in June and July for rebedding fish.

CHAPTER 12

Great Falls Lake

The Muskie Old Reservoir

Old, sleepy, and nearly forgotten, Great Falls Lake has been around longer than most Tennesseans. And most Tennesseans probably have never heard of this reservoir, built for hydroelectric power by the Tennessee Power Company back in 1916. It gets its name from the Great Falls of the Caney Fork River. Those who visit Rock Island State Park are familiar with the lake.

The Caney Fork and Rocky Rivers join 2 miles above Great Falls Dam, and the Collins River joins them just above the dam. These rivers form Great Falls Lake above the dam, and just below the dam is Center Hill Lake.

MUSKELLUNGE

Also known as the "water wolf" and the "fish of 10,000 casts," the muskellunge is a cool-water species. The muskie is a predator of the highest order, but it often takes hours of fishing to entice one to take your bait. It has a mouthful of teeth, which means you must use a steel leader, and it is a sight feeder, which means night fishing is a waste of time. Muskie were once common in many of Tennessee's streams before they were dammed.

Today, their numbers are fewer, but thanks to TWRA's stocking programs augmenting their natural reproduction, anglers have the opportunity to try their luck at hooking the ferocious "water wolf." Great Falls Lake is one the best waterways in the state to fish for them.

Guide Dwayne Hickey of McMinnville has been muskie fishing for 15 years on Great Falls Lake, and the last 3 years on Center Hill Lake. He

GAME FISH RATINGS

Muskellunge	🐟 🐟 🐟
Trout	🐟 🐟 🐟

fishes year-round and offers us some instructions on where and how to catch these fierce fighters.

Winter and Spring

"I concentrate on Center Hill from winter till the end of May," says Hickey. "This is about the best fishing of the year. I fish all the creeks from Blue Hole down to Pates Ford, especially Pine Creek and Sink Creek. Muskie relate to cover like bass do, and they prefer wood like bass do. You can pattern them much like you do bass.

"I concentrate on the feeder creeks, sloughs, or any cuts, but primarily the larger creeks. I cast a large tandem spinnerbait, and I put a live shiner or creek chub on the trailer hook. I slow-roll it around wood and brush. I also cast large rattling crankbaits, such as Bill Norman's DD-22 and the Believer, a traditional muskie lure. It's a 7-inch, broken-back bait with rattles. Firetiger is the best color in winter. Hickey says it's important to fish all the baits slowly.

GREAT FALLS AT A GLANCE

Location:	White, Van Buren, and Warren Counties
Size:	2,270 acres
Length:	22 miles
Shoreline:	120 miles
Summer pool:	805 feet
Winter pool:	762 feet
Impounded:	1916
Featured species:	Muskellunge and Trout
Other species:	Crappie, Largemouth Bass, Walleye, Sauger, Smallmouth Bass, Stripe (White Bass), Bream, Catfish
Description:	A hill-land and run-of-the-river reservoir, Great Falls lies at the foot of, and is fed by streams flowing from the western Cumberland Plateau. The lake is riverine and formed by three rivers. It has rocky bluffs and moderately steep, wooded banks that become steeper farther up its tributaries.
Main tributaries:	Collins River, Caney Fork River, Rocky River, Calfkiller Creek, Laurel Creek, Cane Creek, Hickory Valley Branch
Landmarks:	Great Falls Lake is located between McMinnville and Sparta on US 70S. State routes 30 and 111 and US 70S (TN 1) form a triangle around the largest portion of the reservoir.
Operated by:	Tennessee Valley Authority

See Appendix C for map information

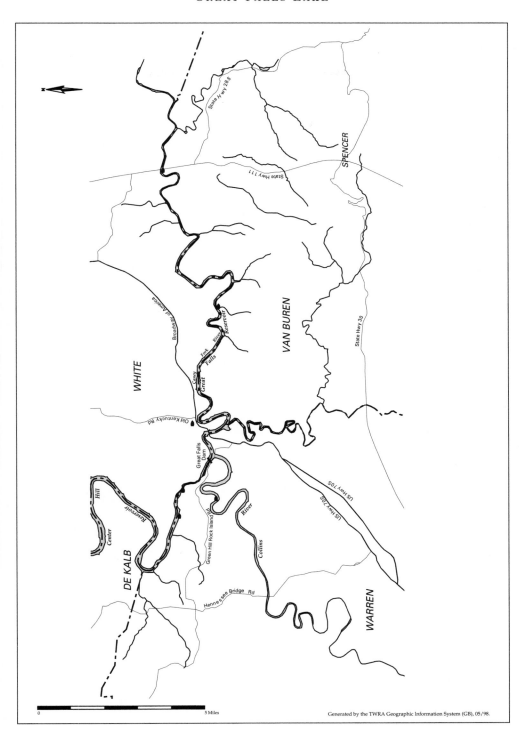

Generated by the TWRA Geographic Information System (GB), 05/98.

Dwayne Hickey catches muskie up to 35 pounds from Great Falls Lake with large tandem spinnerbaits and large-size muskie plugs.
(Photo compliments of Dwayne Hickey.)

"Muskie head upstream to spawn; that's why it's easier to catch them in winter. They usually spawn in March, maybe into April. The upper reaches of Rocky River, Collins River, Caney Fork River, and Calfkiller River on Great Falls Lake are where they are from winter through spring. Collins River is one of my favorites. I catch them on the Believer and the Pikie Minnow. Bucktail, in-line spinners work better when the water warms up."

Summer and Fall

"After they spawn," says Hickey, "some fish stay in that area, but in early summer when the rivers clear up, many of them move downstream. That's when I start spot-fishing. The river is low and you can see muskie in potholes and in the shallow water. It's something else to see a 20-pound muskie lying in 2½ feet of water."

Hickey uses polarized, yellow-lens glasses to spot the fish in the shallows. "I cast in front of the muskie and retrieve the lure with an erratic action," he says. "From spring through fall, one of my favorite ways is to use live bait: suckers, gizzard shad, and bluegill. If they won't hit an artificial bait, they'll attack live bait.

"I use the same techniques in the summer and the fall: topwater plugs, buzzbaits, Zara Spooks, and live bait. The key to muskie fishing is being on the water during cloudy and rainy weather. Days like that are the absolute best times. You get multiple strikes on those days," he says.

Anyone who fishes for muskie will see the fish follow your lure. Hickey says that's common when he casts for them, but he has a trick for the curious fish. "I have live bait on a hook hanging over in the water about 2 feet deep. I'll be casting artificial lures. In summer and fall, they may be a little sluggish, and I'll get several follows. They won't hit the lure, but they'll follow it to the boat out of curiosity. I make a figure eight at the boat with the bait and that works sometimes. But about 70% of the time they'll hit the live bait hanging over the side. I set a loose drag on the reel."

Hickey spools 17- to 20-pound-test Stren on his Abu Garcia 6500 baitcasting reel. "I can handle about any muskie with that, using a steel leader, of course. I use a 7-foot, All Pro flipping stick and a 6–6 All Pro casting rod. You've got to have rods with backbone. If your hooks are not needle-sharp, you might as well stay at the house." A steel leader is a must because the muskie's teeth can cut through 20-pound-test monofilament easily.

After mid-June until near the end of November, Hickey says to use the spot fishing technique. Muskie begin moving upstream in early winter and start back downstream about the end of April. "I didn't know they moved that much," he says. "But from talking with fishermen and from my own experience, they move like walleye. There are some that stay upstream all year, just like some walleye. The best fishing is from mid-February through April."

Muskie can live to be 30 years old and weigh more than 60 pounds. A legal muskie, one that's 30 inches long, will weigh about 6 pounds and will be about 4 years old. A 40-inch muskie will weigh about 18 pounds and a 50-incher will weigh about 30 pounds.

Trolling is the preferred technique of some anglers because you can cover more water in a shorter time.

If you are slow trolling three lines, your number one and three rods should be pointing out from your boat's transom in opposite directions. Your number two rod is in the middle of the others pointing behind your boat. The number one rod has 5 ounces of weight holding your bait 20 feet behind the boat. The number two rod had 3 ounces of weight 30 to 40 feet behind your boat. Number three has 1 ounce of weight about 60 feet back. Measure 2 feet between the weight and your bait. You will have to vary your weights and depths depending on the lake features. You can troll live and artificial baits.

TROUT

The following are tributaries with trout: Calfkiller Creek and Caney Fork River in White County; Cane Creek, Laurel Creek, and Rocky River in Van Buren County; Mountain Creek, Charles Creek, Hills Creek, Taylor Creek, North Prong of Barren Fork River, Barren Fork River, and Collins River in Warren County.

The upper Caney Fork River has two sections. It is a small stream from its origin near Campbell Junction in Cumberland County to the community of Dodson in south central White County. The section downstream from Dodson becomes a navigable river. South of Sparta under the TN 111 bridge is a launching ramp. It's about 15 miles downstream from TN 111 to Great Falls Dam with an average depth of 8 feet. Trout, smallmouth bass, largemouth bass, rock bass, catfish, bream, and muskie are the primary species found here.

Canoeing the Caney Fork makes an excellent float trip. You can put in at Dodson and take out at any of six bridges downstream. There are other take-out areas where roads come close to the Caney Fork. The river is Class I below Dodson and suitable for beginning canoeists.

Calfkiller, another trout stream, joins the Caney Fork about a mile below the TN 111 bridge. It contains the same species as the Cane Fork. Calfkiller is easily canoeable from Sparta to the Caney Fork.

The Rocky River is an excellent trout stream. The best trout action is from the mouth of Laurel Creek upstream to above White Hill. Smallies, largemouth, and crappie are prevalent near the mouth, with muskie, bream, and rock bass also found there. You can use a motorboat from the mouth of the Rocky River upstream about 5 miles to the mouth of Laurel Creek during summer pool. A canoe will serve you better farther upstream. The Rocky is 20 miles long with an average depth of 3 feet.

Laurel Creek, a 10-mile trout stream with a 3-foot depth, is fair for wading and canoeing. It joins the Rocky River due east of Spencer. There is no launching ramp on the Rocky River.

CHAPTER 13

Normandy Lake

Seventeen Miles of Bliss

Normandy is a small lake with strong populations of largemouth, small-mouth, spots, crappie, and stripes. Only 17 miles long, it doesn't take long to find enough good fishing holes to make you happy.

Doug Pelren, with TWRA's Region II, says that Normandy offers anglers some big largemouth bass fishing, but that these fish have seen most of the artificial baits. Pelren recommends using live bait to seduce the lunker bass.

TWRA and some anglers report a strong smallmouth fishery, but the anglers want to keep it a secret. Because we found no one willing to discuss the smallmouth, we suggest taking ideas from the other chapters that detail smallmouth techniques and applying them on this small lake.

LARGEMOUTH BASS

Outdoor writer and pro bass angler Tom Waynick lives on Normandy Lake. He fishes the lake several times a week, spring through the fall, for bass and crappie. He admits Normandy can be a tough lake for catching fish in the winter. Waynick says 8-pound bass are commonly the winners of the weekly tournaments held on Normandy.

Winter

"Bluffs on the main channel are where most [largemouth] are caught. I think the lower 4 miles of the lake will be your best bet. Live minnows work well, but for artificials, the 4-inch worm fished in finesse fashion is probably the best. The Creepy

GAME FISH RATINGS

Largemouth Bass	🐟 🐟 🐟 🐟 🐟
Crappie	🐟 🐟 🐟 🐟 🐟

Crawler or Spider Jig baits have been real good on Normandy, better than on other lakes in this area.

"Casting parallel to the bluffs is the way to go. Put your boat against the bluff and you'll be in 15 to 25 feet of water. Cast along the bluff and work your worm or jig along the bottom down the ledges. Those bluffs have two or three ledges, and the bass should be holding on one of them. They move up to feed in the 12- to 15-foot range and drop down when they aren't. On sunny days they'll move to about 8 feet but they stay on the same steep banks," he says.

In February the bass begin moving back into the creeks but still relate to the steep banks. "You should use the same baits and techniques, but they are beginning to move into a springtime pattern."

Spring
"In March, in their prespawn mode, you can catch largemouth bass on slow-cranking, small crankbaits, slow-rolling spinnerbaits, and by working a floating

NORMANDY AT A GLANCE

Location:	Bedford and Coffee Counties
Size:	3,200 acres
Length:	17 miles
Shoreline:	72 miles
Summer pool:	880 feet
Winter pool:	859 feet
Impounded:	1976
Featured species:	Largemouth Bass and Crappie
Other species:	Smallmouth Bass, Stripe (White Bass), Bream, Catfish, Spotted (Kentucky) Bass
Description:	This hill-land, tributary reservoir has several creeks that boast standing timber. Normandy has steep banks opposite long, sloping banks, as well as flats that drop off into the Duck River channel.
Main tributaries:	Duck River, Boyd Branch, Riley Creek, Vaughn Hollow, Davidson Branch, Carroll Creek, Bobo Creek, Crumpton Creek, Hale Creek
Landmarks:	Shelbyville and Manchester are the cities closest to Normandy. The nearest major routes are US Alt 41 and Normandy, Cat Creek, Mountain View, and Devils Backbone Roads.
Operated by:	Tennessee Valley Authority

See Appendix C for map information

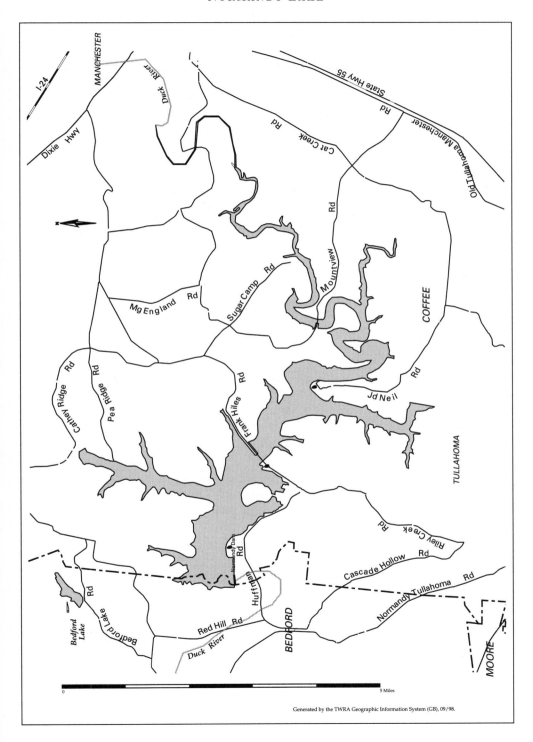

Generated by the TWRA Geographic Information System (GB), 09/98.

Tom Waynick says largemouth bass are on the deepwater points in summer, and he uses deep-diving crankbaits to catch them.

worm. Suddeth's Little Earl, Deep Wee-R, and Bandit crankbaits also work well. They prefer a crawfish pattern this time of year," Waynick says.

"There's one trick I do in early spring. I go into a creek, watching my temperature gauge. The main lake will be colder, so I go back until I see the water temperature rise, and continue until the temperature starts to fall again. I fish that stretch where the water is warmer. In that warm section I try to find where the creek channel comes closest to the bank; generally that will be in a bend. I cast a big, shad-colored crankbait for big bass. Charlie Ingram told me this trick, and the first time I tried it, I hauled in a 6-pounder."

The full moon in April is when bass get serious about spawning. The hot spots are pockets and pea-gravel flats. "I still cast small crankbaits and spinnerbaits in April," says Waynick. "They're scattered then and these baits cover a lot of water.

"If you're going down a bank and see a ditch or little ravine coming into the lake, it causes a small depth change in the structure. I noticed during the drawdown that usually there are stumps or something associated with these depressions. You need to back off the bank some to fish it. There may be bass on the shallow sides, but the big females will hold in these depressions until its time to move up on the flat to spawn. These ditches are migration routes that bass use during the rest of the year, too," he adds. Most of the bass spawn in May but may continue into June.

Summer

"There's a dead spell after the spawn," says Waynick. "The largemouth move into their summer pattern when the water hits the mid-80s. They'll hold on points in deep water and on the river- and creek-channel drops. They look for drops between 12 and 18 feet. Carolina and Texas rigs with 8-inch worms have done well in summer."

Waynick suggests anglers look for jumps at the points and mouths of the creeks. "You catch a lot of Kentuckies in the jumps. That action lasts all summer. In the fall they move farther up the creek and keep jumping."

Pete James of Lynchburg says, "Normandy produces more bass over 8 pounds than any lake in the state! I fish a lot of tournaments on Normandy, and there are a couple of anglers that tear everybody up with 8-pound bass."

James, who lives on Tims Ford Lake, has been fishing south central Tennessee for many years, producing his *Wishin' I Was Fishin'* TV program, and has uncovered a secret.

"I've discovered a neat pattern on Normandy. I had been fishing like everyone else; early morning, working the stumps, flats and points, and the creek-channel drop-offs. This new method was noticed while I was crappie fishing.

"I was working a huge ash tree catching crappie. A couple of guys behind me were trolling down the center of the river between mile 5 and mile 7. I wondered, what are these guys doing? Well, Normandy is chock-full of shad, gill to gill, and they float around in dense clouds. These guys were slowly trolling for walleye through the middle of the clouds of shad, but they were catching largemouth bass in 12 to 15 feet of water. They were using a bottom-bouncing rig with a night crawler. I thought I should try that.

"Meanwhile, I noticed that every time a school of shad came by, I would catch crappie. I started to chase the shad so I could catch crappie, but I ended up catching largemouth. I discovered that largemouth were the ones driving these schools of shad around. So I started casting a Shad Rap and Vibra Max among these shad—right out in the middle of the river in the dead of summer. Man, this is a great pattern. Now I catch a limit every time I go fishing using this method."

James says these nomadic shad run the river and don't hang around structure. If you're not having any luck with spinnerbaits, plastic worms, grubs, or crankbaits in the usual spots, move into the middle of the river and look for clouds of shad on your sonar. Then cast a bait that will get down to 15 feet.

"Don't chase the bait," he cautions. "The bait will be chased to you. What I do is use my trolling motor to head upriver against the current or against the wind, whichever is stronger, so I can control the boat. You'll see the shad boiling on the surface like an incoming tide. I cast beyond them or to the side of them. If you cast into them, you'll spook them. The bass hang with the schools. They may not be feeding on shad but they don't want to lose track of dinner."

James recommends ripping a Wiggle Wart, Shad Rap, or Vibra Max through the school. The bass will hit more out of instinct than from hunger.

Fall

Tom Waynick says bass start moving to the backs of creeks in October, following the schools of shad. Look for shad; that's where the bass will be. They use the Duck River and the big creeks: Carrol, Crumpton, and Riley. Topwater chuggers work well in the fall. He uses a clear chugger in clear water and a shad-colored one if there is any stain.

CRAPPIE

During the 1980s, crappie populations declined on most Tennessee lakes, but in the late 1990s, they have turned the corner. Normandy has moved into a good cycle. Also, the black-nosed crappie have been stocked in Normandy and some have reached the 10-inch minimum. The forecast for Normandy looks very bright.

Winter

"There's not much to say about winter fishing for crappie on Normandy," says Tom Waynick. "Minnows are best but jigs work good sometimes. I fish 22 to 35 feet deep on the channel drops in the main body of the lake and fish in the standing timber in Riley and Carroll Creeks. That's pretty simple, but that's about the best way to fish when the water is cold. About mid-February more crappie begin moving into the standing timber in the creeks. That's when the crappie fishing gets promising."

Spring

"In early spring I start fishing the standing timber," says Waynick. "If they aren't there, move to the nearest flat, and fish the deep side of it first. Keep going shallow until you find them. They will be somewhere between the trees and flats."

March and April are when crappie begin staging to enter the shallows for their spawning ritual.

"You can catch them in front of the riprap at the dam by casting shad-, chartreuse-, or chrome-colored deep-diving crankbaits like the Little Earl, Deep Wee-R, or Model A Bomber. Swimming pink leadheads with a white grub also does a good job.

"At first I start catching them about 15 feet deep up to about 10 feet. As the water warms, they move closer to the rocks. By the first of May, I'm casting at the edge of the rocks and I get hit within about two cranks. At the corner of the riprap, near the ramp and parking lot, are some fish attractors, and they will spawn in there. April and May are the best months for crappie on Normandy. It's my favorite time of year."

Waynick doesn't limit his crappie fishing to the riprap. He says the rounds (the large rounded points) in Riley Creek are other places he fishes. He uses

artificial bait in the spring, although
minnows will work. He says he finds
them faster by casting baits that cover
a lot of water in a short period of
time. Then he can concentrate on
them once he finds them.

"It's hard not to find a flat or gentle, sloping point that doesn't hold
crappie at some time during the
spring. I was fishing with Vernon
Summerlin one spring on a wind-
blown flat with jigs. We were after
crappie, and we may have caught
some, but I do remember we caught
saugeye and stripe—that surprised us.
Fishermen catch saugeye by accident,
I don't know of anyone who can fish
this lake and catch them on purpose," says Waynick, "but crappie are
a different story. They're hot in the
spring on this lake."

*Tom Waynick catches crappie, like this
black-nosed crappie, along the riprap at
the dam in early spring and in summer.*

Summer

Tom Waynick says, "Summer is my second most favorite time to fish for crappie. The key to finding fish is locating where the water changes temperature.
You can see this on your sonar screen; it forms a line or a line of fish symbols,
depending on your setup, usually 18 to 25 feet deep. Crappie may be cruising
the channel following shad or holding along a channel drop. When I find
them, I drop minnows, small jigs, or a combination of the two near the depth
I see fish."

When you drop your bait, stop a foot or two over the fish. Crappie move
up to feed, not down. You've got to watch your line because they don't hit
hard in summertime, he cautions.

"When the sun goes down, grab the lanterns and head for the nearest bridge
spanning the main channel. These areas offer the fish several appealing features. The shade of the bridges attracts them during the daytime, and then they
just hang around after the sun goes down. Bridges generally narrow a body of
water. This funneling effect produces current, and baitfish flow through as well.

"Night fishermen hang lanterns over the side, and the light attracts insects.
The insects attract small fish, and small fish attract larger predators. You have
the entire food chain of a lake right before your very eyes. Drop minnows or
small jigs with grubs down through the baitfish pod and hang on. The only

George Gregory catches crappie among Normandy's standing timber in Carroll Creek using tiny jigs on ultralight gear.

problem you may have catching crappie in this situation is keeping other species like stripe and Kentuckies off your line.

"I've seen anglers troll small, deep-running crankbaits along the old river channel. Those serious crappie anglers with the big engines also have a small kicker motor so they can troll slowly enough for the crappie to eat the lure. They let out lots of line so the bait will get down as deep as possible, and then they follow the channel," he says.

Preferred baits for trolling on Normandy are the Little Earl, Rebel Deep Wee-R, and Model A Bombers. Shad, chrome, and chartreuse colors work best according to Waynick.

Fall

George Gregory of Lynchburg is probably the best-known crappie angler in Moore County, as well as the town's most respected horticulturist. Gregory has developed a green thumb working at the Jack Daniel Distillery for the last 20 years. His specialty is cultivating roses, when he's not fishing on Normandy or Tims Ford.

"I think Normandy is the best crappie lake in the state," says Gregory. "I've fished it for a long time, and it has an abundance of crappie. For a few years we didn't have good spawns, but I think it has recovered from that. It's an excellent place to fish because it has a lot of cover.

"In the fall, the deepwater areas seem to be best because they are drawing down the reservoir. I fish bridge pillars and any tree in water 20 to 40 feet deep. Crappie are in these trees practically all the time. They aren't affected by the drawdown because they are close to the channel."

Gregory catches crappie weighing close to 3 pounds. His average big crappie is about 2½ pounds, but he knows of people who have caught 4-pounders.

"I fish the pillars around the bridge at Barton Springs, the bridge at the 6-mile marker, and any standing timber. It's best, if there is some color in the water, to fish the standing timber in Carroll and Riley Creeks. I like to find them when they are in that standing timber. You talk about having a ball; that's the ideal place to catch them."

He loves to cast the ½2-ounce jigs he makes. "I only tie hair jigs. I use all colors of craft hair. I get lots of colors and mix them. I'll use yellow or orange on a red-head jig if the water is clear, I'll use yellow and chartreuse—the brighter colors—when the water is dingy," he says.

November is one of best months of the year. "I think everybody that fishes Normandy catches crappie then. Riley and Carroll Creeks are good places, as well as the standing trees right in the center of the channel. The crappie may be as shallow as a foot on down to 6 feet—they aren't real deep.

"In October and November, crappie will usually be in the same place year after year. They may leave if the oxygen is not there or if maybe some of the cover has deteriorated, or maybe they might just move into an area close to the old spot. I fish the spot where I caught them the year before, and if they aren't there, I look in the next likely place close to it. Most times they will be close to the old spot."

In October, Gregory goes back to using 4-pound test because the water has some color; the fish aren't going to be as deep, and he usually catches larger fish. In summer with the clear water, he uses 2-pound test.

"Four-pound test lets the jig work good, and the larger-diameter line lets it fall a little slower, keeping the bait in the strike zone longer. The 4-pound test holds better in rough cover, but some of those big crappie will still break it. I used to use ⅟16-ounce jigs but they fall too fast. That's why I only use ⅟32-ounce now.

"You have to use a 6- or 6½-foot spinning rod with a slow tip to cast these jigs effectively. I cast out 20 to 30 feet, let my jig sink, and slowly reel it in, always watching my line. I fish shallow or deep the same way. I just start reeling sooner when fishing shallow.

"If someone is fishing Normandy for the first time, I'd say fish a ⅟32-ounce jig, go to the standing timber, just let your jig fall, and watch your line. The big fish will make a tick in your line; it won't jump. As the water gets colder, the fish are more aggressive. Your line will jump, and there's no doubt you got a fish, but in October they may hit lightly."

His last piece of advice is to watch the weather fronts. "They will affect fish. Before a front they will be biting wide open. Afterward, they move deeper and hold tighter to the cover. They may get right against the cover, and if you don't put your jig close, you won't catch them," concludes Gregory.

CHAPTER 14

Woods Reservoir

Middle Tennessee's Astounding Little Lake

Most Tennessee lakes were dammed for flood control or to create electricity, but Woods Reservoir near Tullahoma was impounded to strengthen national security. For decades, the U.S. Air Force has used water from the lake for military projects at Arnold Engineering Development Center. That Woods would become an excellent site for crappie and bass was unlikely in the minds of those who built it, but planned or not, the military should add fishing to its list of successes engineered at the AEDC.

Nearly 4,000 acres in size, Woods has provided decades of excellent fishing, although tens of thousands of Tennessee anglers are unaware that crappie are sometimes so abundant in Woods that biologists rank it among Tennessee's best crappie reservoirs. Bass fishing is also good, as many locals know, including television host and Woods Reservoir junkie Pete James.

"For its size, Woods is probably one of the best, big bass–producing lakes in Tennessee," says James, the host of *Wishin' I Was Fishin'*, a weekly outdoors program aired by Rifkin Cablevision in Middle Tennessee. James primarily fishes Woods for largemouth, while Clyde Hill, a Woods and Tims Ford guide, specializes in smallmouth. Both enjoy catching Woods Reservoir crappie.

Other fish species inhabit Woods, including numerous catfish. Because of PCB contamination, however, the Department of Environment and Conservation advises against eating them. Woods also has bluegill, shellcracker, and other sunfish. Although their populations are small, walleye and muskellunge inhabit the lake as well.

GAME FISH RATINGS

Largemouth Bass	🐟🐟🐟🐟🐟
Smallmouth Bass	🐟🐟🐟
Crappie	🐟🐟🐟🐟🐟

Most anglers go to Woods to catch bass and crappie, which are the species discussed in this chapter. James has made hundreds of trips to it since the early 1980s, while Hill has fished the military reservoir regularly since its 1952 impoundment.

LARGEMOUTH BASS

Winter largemouth fishing requires patience. Nearby Tims Ford Lake offers much better, cold-weather largemouth angling than does Woods, according to James. Hill primarily fishes for smallmouth in winter, but sometimes catches largemouth on hair jigs and other artificial baits that he works slowly along channels in the lake's lower half. Live bait fished around channel ledges and drop-offs, riprap, or the mouths of creeks, catches fish for patient anglers, notes James.

Spring

James's biggest Woods largemouth weighed more than 7 pounds, but he has caught many fish in excess of 5 pounds. Prespawn largemouth are usually active by March and remain so into April, he says. Numerous lures catch

WOODS AT A GLANCE

Location:	Franklin and Coffee Counties
Size:	3,980 acres
Length:	12 miles
Shoreline:	65 miles
Summer pool:	960 feet
Winter pool:	957 feet
Impounded:	1952
Featured species:	Largemouth Bass, Smallmouth Bass, Crappie
Other species:	Walleye, Muskellunge, Bluegill, Shellcracker, Catfish (There is a warning against consumption of catfish)
Description:	The lower end of the lake, from TN 127 to the dam, is wide with steep points and drop-offs in the main river channel. Above the bridge, the impoundment is narrow and shallow with large flats and shallow coves.
Main tributaries:	Elk River, Bradley Creek, Brumalow Creek, Rollins Creek
Landmarks:	Woods Reservoir is near Tullahoma and Winchester. Boat access is limited, but Morris Ferry Dock is near TN 127, which crosses the lake. The nearest interstate is I-24.
Operated by:	Arnold Engineering Development Center

See Appendix C for map information

WOODS RESERVOIR

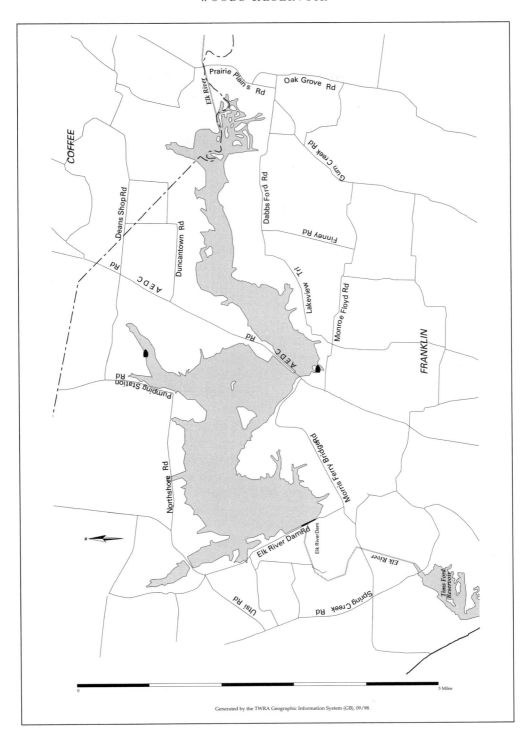

Generated by the TWRA Geographic Information System (GB), 09/98.

For its size, Woods Reservoir may be one of the best largemouth lakes in Tennessee.

prespawn largemouth, although only one is James's favorite. "It's a spinnerbait, and it's my favorite lure in the whole world," says James. "It's called a Dixie Dancer and it's awesome. A friend of mine named Andy Murdock turned me on to it. He told me that it worked on Woods. Boy, does it."

Dixie Dancers are sold locally in community bait shops. Anglers unable to obtain one can duplicate James's success with other spinnerbaits. "I fish the ⅜-ounce, all-chartreuse Dixie Dancer with a double-silver Colorado blade and a stinger hook," notes James. "Nine out of ten times the stinger hook catches my fish. I trail a curly-tailed grub off the hook and bass nip at that tail. They are more curious than hungry, so I usually catch curious bass."

White and chartreuse is also a good spinnerbait color combination, notes James. "I can wear the bass out with spinnerbaits in April," he says. "I slow-roll my spinnerbaits in the middle of the day after the water warms up, and this drives largemouth crazy." Grass and gravel banks are excellent places to fish, notes James, who uses a baitcasting reel spooled with 10-pound-test monofilament to toss spinnerbaits.

As boat traffic increases and bass see more "hardware," James tosses 4-inch Charlie Brewer Slider Worms on 6-pound-test monofilament and spinning reels. Motor oil is his favorite color.

Summer

As air and water temperatures rise, James fishes anytime between 5 P.M. and 8 A.M. the next day. From June until September, largemouth fishing is good.

Woods has many shallow stumps in its upper portion, where James catches nocturnal bass close to Jail Island.

James fishes a 6-inch plastic worm below a ¼-ounce cone sinker. Red worms with white tails catch most of his nighttime bass. James always sprays or rubs a fish attractant on his plastic. "It doesn't matter what kind I use—or who makes it—as long as I have fish scent on my worm," he explains.

James is quiet when he approaches largemouth in the lake's shallow upper end. He believes bass are wary of loud night anglers. He works slowly once situated. "I fish the shoreline some, and around duck blinds in the middle of the lake on the upper end," says James. "I also fish deep pockets and areas gouged out by river current up there. I get up on the flat side of channels away from deeper water and cast into the current. I fish slower than what normally feels right—slower than slow."

Points in the lake's lower half, or channel drop-offs in that section, are also good night-fishing spots, says James. Deep-running crankbaits and plastic worms or lizards fished on Carolina rigs are good bass baits.

Fall

Just as in spring, as the water begins to cool, spinnerbaits worked near shorelines attract many hits. So do bronze-colored Shad Raps, adds James. Although he often casts next to shorelines, James sometimes backs off and casts parallel to them in water 12 to 14 feet deep. "I catch as many crappie doing this as bass," he notes. Most of James's fall fishing occurs within sight of Morris Ferry Dock on either side of TN 127.

SMALLMOUTH BASS

Clyde Hill began fishing Woods Reservoir as a high school teenager. He has caught thousands of fish, including countless largemouth. His favorite fish, however, is the smallmouth.

Winter

Smallmouth prefer cool water, which is why Hill spends much of his time below TN 127, eliminating about half the lake. "From Highway 127 to the dam is the coolest part of the lake and is best for smallmouth," says Hill. "I catch 10 smallmouth to 1 on that side." The lower end also has many ledges or other drop-offs along the main river channel.

When water temperature is below 50°, usually December through February, Hill works his lures slowly. "It's slow fishing in winter, not like in the spring," says Hill. "I have to work pretty hard for six or seven strikes, but the fish I catch are good ones."

Woods is a good largemouth lake, but it also produces many smallmouth. Most anglers catch smallies below the TN 127 bridge in the deeper, lower end of the lake.

Hill once landed an 8-pound, 2-ounce smallmouth, but notes that smallies between 3 and 5 pounds are more common. "They're sluggish when they bite, but they come to life when they get hooked," he says.

A ⅛-ounce hair fly fished with spinning gear and 6-pound-test monofilament is Hill's best winter combination. He favors dark-colored flies, usually brown or black, but he also tosses brown and orange combinations. Regardless of season, he uses ⅛-ounce leadhead jigs.

Winter smallmouth suspend around channel ledges. "Cast the fly and let it drop," says Hill. "Smallmouth hit when the fly falls off a ledge. I catch most fish about 15 feet deep, working my fly real slow."

Spring

Smallmouth become more active as water temperature rises, especially when it gets above 50°, says Hill. Woods Reservoir has numerous flats with stumps, which provide cover and attract smallmouth. Creek ledges and other drop-offs also hold Woods Reservoir smallies.

Spinnerbaits are good spring lures. Hill throws dark-colored spinnerbaits when the lake is dingy and light colors when it's clear. Chartreuse is good regardless of lake stain, he notes. If smallmouth are feeding on bluegill, Hill uses a willowleaf blade on his spinnerbait. He prefers a Colorado blade if shad is their primary food source.

Hill also tosses shallow-running crankbaits, working them quickly through water that is beginning to warm up. "I don't retrieve slowly like some people might expect in early spring," he says. "I burn it up. This is a trick I've learned. It's something that works a lot for me."

Because it is shallow, Woods Reservoir cools and warms quickly. After a few warm days back to back, the lake's upper layer often provides a comfort zone for hungry bass. Anglers should try working shorelines when water temperature spikes.

Hill often changes his lure speed when throwing crankbaits. He stops the lure to let it momentarily suspend. "I catch most of my fish on a crankbait when I make it stop and go, stop and go," says Hill.

Summer

Using soft plastic baits—often 4-inch worms, lizards, or crawls—Hill continues catching smallmouth around channel ledges until temperatures soar. He also occasionally catches fish with shallow-running crankbaits on flats. Hill uses spinning gear to toss crankbaits and baitcasting reels to fish Carolina rigs. Smallmouth are always more prone to strike small baits, he notes.

When the summer turns hot, night fishing is best on Woods Reservoir, says Hill. He suggests that anglers fish near channels and drop-offs with worms, lizards, or other plastic baits on Carolina rigs, or that they toss spinnerbaits and slow roll them around channel ledges and drop-offs.

Fall

For Hill, fall fishing is a repeat of spring techniques. He fishes hair flies in channels around ledges and drop-offs, always staying below TN 127. Smallmouth become more active as water temperature falls—until it gets below 50°.

CRAPPIE

When Woods Reservoir has a banner stretch of successful crappie spawns, biologists for the state's wildlife agency consider it among Tennessee's best crappie lakes. But even when it doesn't, Woods Reservoir offers good crappie fishing.

Winter

Crappie inhabit Woods's shallow upper end, but angler Pete James and guide Clyde Hill catch the majority of their fish in the lake's lower half, just above the TN 127 bridge to the dam.

Both anglers fish deep water in winter. "I never fish the bank for crappie during the cold months," says James. "I fish drop-offs and river and creek channels. I find quite a few of these near the dam and in front of Morris Ferry Dock. In fact, I fish the entire river channel in front of Morris Ferry Dock. A lot of crappie also hold on sharp drop-offs right in front of Camp Arrowhead and pretty close to Elder Island."

Angler Pete James catches crappie year-round and depends heavily on the attraction of small tuffy minnows, even when he uses plastic grubs.

Small tuffy minnows make good winter bait. "I like fishing with minnows year-round, but especially in the winter. If I miss hits, crappie will usually come back for live bait," explains James. "Most of the time they won't hit a jig again."

Hill catches many crappie with plastic grubs that he threads on ⅛-ounce leadhead jigs. Chartreuse or a combination of chartreuse and white are standard grub colors, but Hill always carries an array of colors with him. Both Hill and James use spinning reels and 6-pound-test monofilament when crappie fishing.

Hill catches many winter crappie about 10 feet deep, while James frequently finds fish about 17 feet down. Locating drop-offs is a key to winter fishing. Hill prefers to cast and retrieve in channels, while James fishes vertically near the bottom.

"I start on top of a drop-off and use a ¼-ounce bell sinker to feel the bottom," says James. "My weight is below two hooks that I have looped on droplines around a leader. I look for rough parts on the ledge and lightly bounce the rig. I usually average 12 to 18 crappie during only a few hours. I could probably catch a limit if I fished all day."

Spring

Crappie fishing is easy beginning in March. "Anybody can catch crappie on Woods then," says James. "It's a matter of going out for an hour and half, catching a limit, and going home."

Spring means fishing the shoreline for James. However, Hill continues working underwater structure in river and creek channels. He also tosses plastic grubs on ⅛-ounce leadhead jigs. James prefers a lighter presentation, tying on a ¹⁄₃₂-ounce jighead with a 2-inch, chartreuse and white curly-tailed grub. The slow fall of this miniature lure attracts strikes, James says.

"I also continue to use a minnow," notes James. "I tip my hook with the smallest tuffy I can find because I believe it gets me strikes when the jig by itself sometimes won't. The minnow also slows my lure's descent."

Watch the moon for optimal crappie fishing time. "The week before the first full moon is the best time to catch crappie," says Hill. "This is just before they spawn." Crappie between 10 and 13 inches are common in Woods, says James. Hill adds that his largest Woods crappie weighed between 2 and 2½ pounds and that 1-pound fish are common.

Summer

June through August is James's favorite time to catch crappie because boat traffic decreases significantly, especially in the mornings. Most spring anglers have quit crappie fishing, but crappie don't quit biting.

"In summer, I look for isolated shrubs located on flats first thing in the morning," says James, who continues fishing for crappie below TN 127. "These shrubs are always good for slab-size crappie early, and I mean before I even see the sun. Don't pass up wood either, even single sticks because sometimes crappie hold next to them. When the sun comes up, crappie move off these flats, but they don't have to move far before they reach the channel."

One excellent flat is near the dam in front of Camp Arrowhead. James fishes the lower side of the flat early and then moves to the river channel, where he drifts minnows on his crappie rig.

If the wind cooperates, James's favorite summer technique is drifting the river channel's outside bank, then turning around, and using his trolling motor to work the channel inside. He begins fishing near Camp Arrowhead, drifts to the lake's north bank (near the AEDC's water-pumping station), and then continues to float the channel past Morris Ferry Dock. "I fish between 17 and 22 feet in summer," says James. "I can catch crappie any day of the week."

Fall

Fall fishing techniques are a repeat of spring. Hill continues to fish around channels, while James locates crappie near shoreline structure. As air and water temperatures fall, many crappie migrate toward the bank, and by October are "as shallow as they will get," says James. Just as in spring, James catches many crappie with a ⅟₃₂-ounce jig that he threads with a chartreuse and white grub.

CHAPTER 15

Tims Ford Lake

A Bass and Striper Delight

An angler visiting Tims Ford for the first time might be confused by its big creeks, numerous coves, and deep water, but like any other impoundment there are keys that open doors to successful fishing year-round on this mid-southern Tennessee lake. Two of the reservoir's most avid and best-known anglers don't mind sharing their large ring of keys, which they have collected through decades of fishing.

Crappie, walleye, and other game species inhabit Tims Ford, but most anglers who come to this reservoir pursue bass and striper because of their abundance. Examine other chapters for the methods of catching the less numerous species, keeping in mind that Tims Ford is a deep, clear lake.

Among the large creeks that feed the 10,700-acre lake are Elk River, Rock Creek, Boiling Fork Creek, Hurricane Creek, Little Hurricane Creek, and Lost Creek. Without a Tims Ford map, anglers might accidentally find several of these, but a willingness to span the 34-mile reservoir is vital to catching bass and striper.

SMALLMOUTH AND LARGEMOUTH BASS

Tims Ford has a bigger population of smallmouth bass than largemouth. Local anglers realize this and toss baits that appeal to both. Smallmouth often ignore large lures, and no one likes being ignored, including Terry Smith, a salesman for Travis Boating Center in Winchester, a guide, and a successful bass tournament competitor. "On Tims I always fish for

GAME FISH RATINGS

Smallmouth Bass	🐟 🐟 🐟 🐟 🐟
Largemouth Bass	🐟 🐟 🐟
Striper (Rockfish)	🐟 🐟 🐟 🐟 🐟

smallmouth and largemouth at the same time," says Smith. "I'll miss out on a lot of smallmouth hits if I don't downsize my bait."

Winter

Tims Ford is well known for its scrappy smallmouth, many of which are caught on the coldest days of the year. When water temperature falls below 50°, the fishing is slow and simple. Two baits help Smith catch the majority of his fish—a hair fly retrieved slowly and a tuffy minnow hooked through the lips with a tiny splitshot placed 18-inches above it.

"I catch bass in coves where baitfish have congregated," says Smith. "Baitfish are in the deepest coves in the deepest creeks, and they suspend 15 to 20 feet most of the time in winter." Smith prefers the lower end of Tims in winter, from Little Hurricane Creek to Lost Creek. "I like the lower end because it cools down slower," he explains. "I always fish where bass are the most active."

Smith primarily catches smallmouth this time of year. He gets many hits with ⅟₃₂- to ⅟₁₆-ounce hair jigs, tossing the lighter lure on "blue bird days

TIMS FORD AT A GLANCE

Location:	Moore and Franklin Counties
Size:	10,700 acres
Length:	31 miles
Shoreline:	241 miles
Summer pool:	888 feet
Winter pool:	865 feet
Impounded:	1970
Featured species:	Smallmouth Bass, Largemouth Bass, Striper (Rockfish)
Other species:	Spotted Bass, Stripe (White Bass), Walleye, Bluegill, Catfish
Description:	A reservoir with many creeks, coves, pockets, and bluffs, Tims Ford offers both rocky and muddy banks. The lake widens as it nears the dam and has numerous large creeks with long channels.
Main tributaries:	Elk River, Lost Creek, Hurricane Creek, Turkey Creek, Little Hurricane Creek, Fall Lick Creek, Kitchens Creek, Dry Creek, Wagner Creek, Boiling Fork Creek, Rock Creek, Taylor Creek
Landmarks:	Winchester, Decherd, and Estill Springs are the cities closest to the lake. The closest routes are TN 16, TN 50, and TN 130. The closest interstate is I-24.
Operated by:	Tennessee Valley Authority

See Appendix C for map information

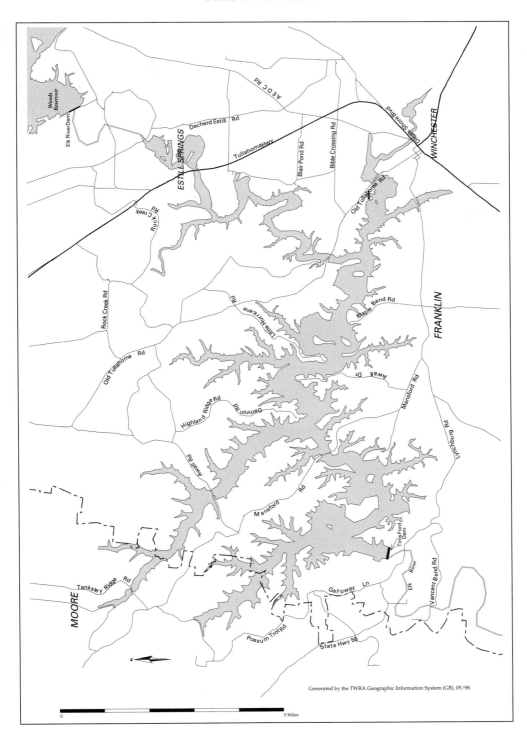

Generated by the TWRA Geographic Information System (GB), 05/98.

0   5 Miles

Tims Ford anglers know to downsize their lures in order to have their best luck. While largemouth inhabit the lake, it is predominantly a smallmouth reservoir.

when the wind isn't blowing." Green should always be included in the hair because crawfish are abundant in Tims and their pinchers have a green hue in winter, says Smith. Green and orange is his favorite color combination.

Four- to six-pound-test monofilament spooled on a spinning reel prevents flies or minnows from falling too fast, notes Smith, who "doctors" his jigs to increase natural appearance and to slow descent. "I get a small piece of plastic worm, thread it on the hook, then glue it under the hair," says Smith. "This causes the hair to flair out and makes a big difference in appearance."

Smith always fishes above schooling shad and he retrieves slowly from shoreline casts. Because his bait is light, Smith uses medium- and medium-light-action rods with spinning reels. He prefers a 4-pound monofilament over 6-pound test, especially for small flies. Most Tims Ford smallmouth weigh from 2 to 4½ pounds. The lake has a large smallmouth population, but is not known for huge fish.

Spring

When water temperature reaches 55°, usually by late March or early April, Smith tosses spinnerbaits or small crankbaits. He also travels up-lake where the reservoir is shallower and warms up quicker. Creek pockets with gravel bottoms are excellent sites to catch prespawn smallmouth. Smith searches for the warmest pockets he can find.

Smith tosses crankbaits that resemble crawdads. Among his favorite lures are Deep Little-Ns, Baby-Ns, and Wee-Rs. White and chartreuse spinnerbaits with double willowleaf blades—one gold and one silver—also catch early spring fish. Smith believes a gold blade resembles a crawdad, while silver resembles a shad. He uses spinning reels spooled with 6- to 8-pound-test monofilament to cast crankbaits, but tosses ⅛- to ¾-ounce spinnerbaits with baitcasting gear.

When surface temperature hits 60°, Rattlin' Rogues and other hard plastic jerkbaits provide great topwater action. "I'm not saying I can't catch bass on jerkbaits before the water hits 60°, or even after it passes that, but it seems like whenever it's right at 60°, jerkbaits are excellent," says Smith. "There is a big, big key to fishing them on Tims Ford. I make sure my lure has either an orange or red belly."

Smith is always prepared to vary lure size. "Some days I use a 5-inch jerkbait and some days I use a 6-inch jerkbait," he says. "I mainly fish around roadbeds and other structure."

When surface temperature hits 65°, largemouth become vulnerable to floating plastic worms around their beds. Slug-Gos, Fin-S Fish, and other soft jerkbaits catch many fish. "I throw these around brush piles that I've put in the coves and also around downed trees," says Smith. "Gravel is also important to largemouth."

Pink or white, 6- and 8-inch, floating, plastic worms entice aggressive strikes. "I've tried many different colors, but either pink or white are as good as any colors I throw," says Smith, who uses 4/0 and 5/0 Gamakatsu hooks when floating worms. He improves his success by slightly altering his hooks. "I bend them out a little to help with penetration," Smith explains.

Depending on water clarity, Smith uses baitcasting reels spooled with either clear or green monofilament (10- to 12-pound-test) to toss topwater plastic. Clear water calls for clear line. He also fishes under and alongside private boat docks.

Anglers can lengthen the excitement of spawning bass by fishing Tims' shallower upper segment first and then moving down lake as spring grows warmer. "I can get a month-and-a-half of this type fishing if I want to," says Smith. "In the case of largemouth, I just keep finding water that is the 65° on the surface, and I mean 65° in the morning, not in the afternoon when the sun has warmed up the lake."

When not catching largemouth in late April or early May, Smith searches for smallmouth with a Carolina rig. He catches many fish on 4- and 5-inch plastic lizards. "I look for a pocket where the wind is blowing in it," he says. "I strictly fish windy banks for smallmouth this time of year."

Pumpkin, watermelon, and green pumpkin are among Smith's favorite plastic-lizard colors. He places lizards 2 to 4 feet below a sinker, depending on water clarity. Clearer water requires longer leaders. Smith's main line is 17-pound-test monofilament. His leader is 12-pound test.

Summer

Topwater lures work great in summer. Pro-Rs, Tiny Torpedoes, Rattling Pro-Pops, Nip-I-Diddees, and buzzbaits are among lures that catch smallmouth and largemouth around cover early in the mornings or late in the evenings. In the heat of the day, Smith works 4- and 5-inch plastic lizards or 6- and 7-inch plastic worms, on a Carolina or Texas rig, around bushes 15 to 20 feet deep.

"If I can't find bushes, I fish the same baits on main-channel points that gradually drop to the river," says Smith. Watermelon, pumpkin, and green pumpkin are Smith's favorite colors. Locating baitfish is important and makes sonar essential. Smith always fishes above baitfish. "I usually find shad between 10 and 20 feet deep," he says.

Fall

As water temperature falls and the Tennessee Valley Authority begins dropping the lake level, smallmouth and largemouth devour crawfish stranded on shallow gravel. "Tims can drop as much as a foot during a day, and bass go into a feeding frenzy," says Smith. Small, crawfish-colored crankbaits, just like Smith tosses in spring, are deadly. So are the same white and chartreuse spinnerbaits he uses with double willowleaf blades (one gold, one silver). "I run my spinnerbait just under the surface," he says.

STRIPER (ROCKFISH)

David Patton became a full-time striper fishermen in the mid-1980s but has fished Tims Ford since the TVA impounded it in the 1970s. He is also a successful tournament angler who travels the country each year competing nationally.

Patton fishes year-round, learning much about striper from Tims Ford. While a state- or world-record rockfish isn't likely to come from Tims, the lake has a good striper population. The average catch for Patton weighs about 12 pounds, he says.

Winter

Much of Patton's winter is spent in the lake's lower half, where he trolls large tributaries such as Hurricane and Lost Creeks. Whenever water temperature is below 55°, Patton fishes Tims' lower end.

Patton finds stripers by closely watching his depth finder. He is over a good hole when his graph turns black. "I want to find as big a school of shad as possible this time of year," explains Patton. "When I say big, I mean a school hundreds of yards long and 10 feet deep. In winter, shad congregate in big creeks and stripers follow them there."

Locating shad is vital to successful angling, but shad aren't Patton's winter bait of choice. Instead, he prefers store-bought shiners. "Stripers here like smaller bait better when the water is cold," says Patton. "I've seen them absolutely inhale shiners when the water temperature was 49°. I find the top of schooling shad and then fish just above them."

A trolling motor is as essential to Patton's fishing style as sonar is. "I cover big areas," he explains. "I fish a stretch of river that is over a mile long, and then turn around and fish that same stretch back to my starting point. If I'm in a boat, I'm usually trolling."

Patton trolls six lines. He trails four of them behind his boat and tightlines the others on Carolina rigs alongside his vessel. Each Carolina rig consists of 17-pound-test monofilament, a 1½-ounce egg sinker, a two-way swivel, a strong but small hook (No. 1 style 84 Eagle Claw), and a live shiner. He ties a 3-foot leader below each swivel.

Patton flatlines two of his trailing outfits on side planer boards, which spreads his bait presentation and allows him to fish the other two flatlines between them. He adjusts each line (also 17-pound test with No. 1 hooks) to sink just above suspending shad. Sinkers aren't usually needed on the back rigs unless shad are deeper than normal. "In that case I add small splitshot," says Patton.

Speed helps keep Patton's bait in strike zones. "I move slowly and just bump the trolling motor," he says. "I'll rev it up and then ease it down. This raises and lowers my bait."

Live gizzard shad make excellent striper bait. Angler David Patton sometimes works harder finding baitfish than catching rockfish, but his hard work usually pays off.

Patton hooks a shiner under its bottom lip and through the roof of its mouth. Because Tims Ford rockfish rarely grow to trophy sizes (30 pounds or more), Patton uses Ambassadeur 5500 reels and 7-foot, medium-action rods. "I get out my big stuff when I go see my striper friend Ralph Dallas on Old Hickory Lake," he says.

Spring

As water temperature begins rising, Patton spends a brief period in early spring fishing from the bank. "I go find a red clay bank and sit on it," he says. "There's a bunch of these on Tims Ford. I don't fish around rocks because I stay hung up."

He is a sophisticated angler most of the time, but Patton enjoys bank fishing with cut bait. "It's a terrific way to catch rockfish," he says. "The fish are really traveling in early spring and often move into shallow areas and eat

Tims Ford stripers won't break any state records, but the lake has a good population of these aggressive fish, and they bite year-round.

everything in sight. "The best striper banks are on the main river channel or largest creeks," notes Patton, who usually bank fishes from about mid-March until mid-April.

Cut gizzard shad helps Patton catch many stripers. He slices his bait in half and fishes it on a Carolina rig similar to his winter tightline setup, except that he uses a 3/0 hook because his bait is larger. Water depth is not a major concern. Patton fishes several rods and reels anywhere from 4 to 24 feet, depending on the slope of a particular bank.

"I make sure my bait is fresh, but the messier the shad is, the better it is," says Patton. "Rockfish have a great sense of smell." Gizzard shad are difficult to catch in Tims Ford, so Patton catches most of his bait from nearby Normandy Reservoir with a cast net.

Unless he is sitting on a bank known to be good, Patton only stays in a nonactive area for about two hours. "I may not be having any luck, and then a school will move on a bank, and every rod I've got will go down at once," he says. Patton expects to catch at least one bank fish for each hour he fishes. "That's a pretty good average," he notes.

Although he doesn't throw crankbaits often, Patton points out that many Tims Ford anglers catch stripers early or late in the day by tossing Red Fins. He suggests that lure anglers look for stripers attacking shad near shorelines this time of year.

When surface temperature reaches the mid-60s, Patton says striper fishing is poor just about everywhere, except below Woods Reservoir Dam. "When water temperature reaches 65°, striper head to Woods Dam to spawn," explains Patton. "This is when lots of people fish for them, so it's obvious when the spawn is under way."

A number of artificial baits catch spawning stripers, including topwater lures, plastic grubs, and bucktail jigs.

Summer

As surface temperature nears 70°, usually by May, rockfish "spread out across the reservoir and can be found on any major point in the lake," notes Patton. Finding baitfish is essential this time of year, but so is marking stripers. "If I mark one fish with my depth finder, there are usually several others nearby," says Patton.

Patton trolls in summer, moving slowly with 6- to 8-inch, live gizzard shad on tightlines and flatlines. He fishes his tightlines with 1-ounce egg sinkers and 3/0 hooks. "I motor across a point with my fish finder on and my eyes watching it," says Patton. "Most of the time the fish are 20 to 30 feet deep." Many times stripers suspend near the bottom.

Occasionally, Patton fishes 15 to 20 feet, where either a creek or a spring pumps cool water into Tims Ford. If he finds schooling fish, he slowly trolls over the school with a single rod and live, tightlined shad. "I don't catch more than the limit when the water gets real warm in summer because stripers succumb to stress this time of year," says Patton. "If I troll over a big school with several rods, I could easily hang a fish on every rig."

Some striper anglers downrig this time of year, trailing bucktail jigs, rabbit-hair jigs, or deep-running crankbaits, notes Patton. Bombers and Long-As are popular Tims Ford crankbaits. White and chartreuse are good hair colors.

Many stripers congregate on the lake's lower end in late summer. "From New Mansford Bridge down is where the majority of them are," says Patton. Stripers slowly migrate to the lower end as the days grow hotter. Patton continues marking fish with his sonar and fishing points around channels.

Fall

Patton looks for early fall stripers in the main river channel's "big water" close to Tims Ford Dam. This is when stripers are the most difficult for him to catch. "Thermocline disappears, and the fish really spread out," says Patton.

By late September or early October, surface temperature is normally in the low 70s. Cool evenings draw shad to the surface and rockfish follow them. "Fishing is slow in the fall, but I can catch five or six stripers real quick when I find them," notes Patton, who looks for surface activity and keeps an eye on his depth finder this time of year.

Patton trolls with six outfits, much like in winter. He releases two lines behind side planer boards, two flatlines without boards, and two tightlines on

Carolina rigs. He also occasionally downrigs with bucktail jigs. "I like white bucktail if the water is clear, and chartreuse if it's dingy," he says.

Other downrigging anglers use rabbit-hair jigs and crankbaits. A manual downrigger with an 8-pound ball, a clip, and a depth counter works fine on Tims Ford, where rockfish below 25 feet are difficult to reach because of standing trees, explains Patton.

Rockfish have a tendency to move up-lake when the drawdown begins. Their movement resembles a spawning run, says Patton. "They work their way up the lake until about Thanksgiving," he notes. "Then they turn around and come back and head into the major creeks, where I catch them in winter."

PART III
East Tennessee

CHAPTER 16

Nickajack Lake

A Meandering Milfoil Reservoir

Anglers refer to the landscape surrounding Nickajack Lake as the Tennessee Grand Canyon. Among the inspiring sites above this run-of-the-river lake are the bluffs that line it. Although more the size of a gorge than a canyon, the encompassing beauty around Nickajack makes a trip to this reservoir a worthy endeavor, whether or not anglers catch fish. The great thing about Nickajack, however, is that game fish are abundant.

According to television angler Benny Hull, a national traveler who rates Nickajack as one of his favorite fishing holes, the lake's milfoil provides cover for baitfish and fantastic hunting grounds for bass and other predators. Reservoirs carpeted by milfoil usually have reputations for good fishing. Nickajack is no exception.

For Hull, who was fishing the southernmost portion of the Tennessee River long before the Tennessee Valley Authority impounded Nickajack Lake, largemouth, smallmouth, and white bass are among species that excel here and that he targets every year for his enjoyment and occasionally for his nationally syndicated television program, *Benny Hull's Outdoor America*. Despite an itinerary that keeps him busy, Hull finds time to fish Nickajack at least a couple of times a week throughout the year.

GAME FISH RATINGS

Largemouth Bass	🐟 🐟 🐟 🐟
Smallmouth Bass	🐟 🐟 🐟 🐟
Stripe (White Bass)	🐟 🐟 🐟 🐟

While this chapter features largemouth, smallmouth, and white bass, other fish species inhabit Nickajack, including bluegill, shellcracker, crappie, walleye, sauger, catfish, and even striper. Many techniques for catching these fish are discussed in other chapters.

LARGEMOUTH BASS

In the early 1990s, fishermen banded together to protest the TVA's eradication of Nickajack's milfoil. It was a great example of how sportsmen, when they muster forces, can change someone's way of thinking. Although an aquatic pest if not managed, milfoil provides great cover for fish and its eradication made anglers mad. While the TVA continues to control milfoil growth, it learned the public-relations benefit of leaving some of this aquatic growth for fish and fishermen.

Winter

Milfoil is dormant in early winter, but it's easy to locate and where Hull catches many largemouth bass. Hull primarily fishes Nickajack's midsection, starting from the Bennett Lake area and covering sites downriver.

NICKAJACK AT A GLANCE

Location:	Hamilton and Marion Counties
Size:	10,900 acres
Length:	47.0 miles
Shoreline:	Not available
Summer pool:	634 feet
Winter pool:	634 feet
Impounded:	1967
Featured species:	Largemouth Bass, Smallmouth Bass, White Bass
Other species:	Crappie, Striper, Spotted (Kentucky) Bass, Sauger, Walleye, Catfish, Bluegill, Shellcracker
Description:	The upper end of this run-of-the-river reservoir is typical of a meandering river, but the lower section broadens and includes shallow bays, coves, sloughs, and a submerged lake. Much of the lake is shallow and has aquatic vegetation, including mil-foil. The stretch below Chickamauga Dam to I-24 is a popular smallmouth spot because of its rocky shoreline and bottom.
Main tributaries:	Tennessee River, North Chickamauga Creek, South Chicka-mauga Creek, Citico Creek, Lookout Creek, Mountain Creek, Bennett Lake, Mullins Creek
Landmarks:	Nickajack winds through Chattanooga and near Signal Moun-tain. Nearby routes include TN 153, TN 8, TN 2, TN 27, TN 28, TN 156, and TN 156A. The nearest interstate is I-24.
Operated by:	Tennessee Valley Authority

See Appendix C for map information

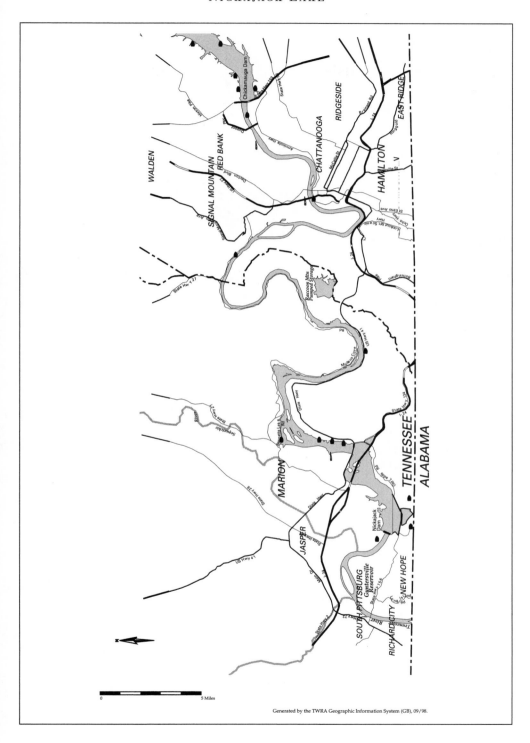

Generated by the TWRA Geographic Information System (GB), 09/98.

Television angler Benny Hull has fished Nickajack for decades and rates this reservoir as a top-notch largemouth fishery. Because milfoil is present on parts of Nickajack, plastic worms, rats, and mice are among excellent summer baits. Hull catches some of his best bass while fishing over milfoil on sizzling days.
(Photo compliments of Stump Bumper Productions.)

Hull looks for specific features starting in November, all of which attract fish, but in combination become irresistible. "Largemouth are usually under milfoil, which is one of the big keys to fishing Nickajack," says Hull. "If I can find milfoil over breaks [ledges that drop off several feet] that's even better. If I find stumps on these breaks, I have really discovered a great spot."

Hull fishes 3- and 4-inch curlytail grubs on ledges that stair-step to the river bottom. He catches many bass 5 to 6 feet deep. His favorite grub colors are smoke and glitter, chartreuse and glitter, and pearl. A spinning reel, spooled with 6- to 8-pound-test monofilament, and a 7½-foot, medium-action rod is ideal for tossing ¼-ounce leadhead jigs, he says.

"I could catch bass upriver or downriver of where I am, but to me the mid-section of Nickajack is best for largemouth in fall and winter," says Hull. "I stay 20 to 30 feet from where I decide to fish and I throw a grub on the top ledge and bounce it toward me."

Many ledges line the reservoir and milfoil patches are numerous, says Hull, who also advises anglers to fish creek mouths and ditches, especially the ones that come off flats into the river. Early winter is a good time to pursue Nickajack's largemouth because they "bunch up." "I've been out there many times and caught good fish with only a few others boats anywhere around because deer season had opened," says Hull.

Live-bait fishing is also fun. "One year on New Year's Day, I did a television show on Nickajack even though it was raining and sleeting," recalls Hall. "We caught more than 15 bass that weighed 3 pounds up, including three 7-pounders. All we were doing was using shiners under floats, which is another good way to fish Nickajack in winter."

Three- to four-inch shiners are easily found at local bait shops. Hull hooks them through the back beneath the dorsal fin because it lets them move freely. "Don't fish deep," says Hull. "Locate an area where a creek or ditch enters the river. A lot of times they lay right in the channels."

Hull fishes the same ledges where plastic grubs catch fish, particularly when grubs aren't producing. "I just pitch a shiner out and let the current take it over the top of a ledge where it's 5 to 8 feet deep and flat," says Hull.

Hull also catches bass by jigging spoons on ledges. "When I use spoons, I increase my line weight to 12- or 14-pound test," says Hull. "I'll drift 50 to 100 yards downstream and watch my depth finder. Most of the time largemouth school at a constant depth and that's where I jig."

As water temperature increases, usually by late February or early March, Hull tosses spinnerbaits, Rat-L-Traps (and other crankbaits), Gitzits, and fly and rind combinations. Crawfish colors are good for hair flies. So is solid black, says Hull, who leaves the main river in late winter to search for moving bass. Riprap emanates heat from the sun and attracts many largemouth. These are numerous in bays, coves, and sloughs, says Hull.

Spring

Hull fishes Nickajack's slack water—bays, coves, and sloughs—as bass approach their spawning period in early spring. Bennett Lake (submerged by Nickajack when the TVA impounded the reservoir), Mullins Cove, Rankin Cove, Shellmound, and the area around Nickajack Cave are among ideal places for March and April largemouth, says Hull. Bennett Lake has huge flats, ditches, and lots of milfoil, he notes. It also has submerged islands.

"I throw Rat-L-Traps this time of year as a search bait," says Hull. "This lets me cover a big area pretty fast. When I get strikes, I concentrate on a spot with other baits." Spinnerbaits and jig and pig combinations catch fish around structure. Crawfish-colored crankbaits are also good, especially worked alongside riprap close to deep water. Although milfoil hasn't reached the surface yet, it still provides good structure. "It's mostly stubble, but baitfish hang out around it and so do largemouth," explains Hull. "Once the water temperature gets around 60° or 65°, the milfoil grows pretty fast. Spinnerbaits and topwater lures work well over milfoil."

Nickajack bass are chunky. While few largemouth exceed 7 pounds, Hull catches many 3- to 5-pounders. After most largemouth spawn, he returns to the main river and throws spinnerbaits a foot or two under the surface, but over milfoil that is approaching the surface.

Buzzbaits also attract bass this time of year—or just about any time. Hull's favorite store-bought buzzbait is a Buzzer'd, made by Luhr Jensen. He also tosses Limber Neck spinnerbaits. "About 90% of the time, my buzzbaits and spinnerbaits are solid white or white mixed with chartreuse," says the television angler. "I like a combination of gold willowleaf and Colorado blades on my spinnerbaits."

Summer

Continue fishing milfoil in June and July, says Hull. Milfoil grows in shallow water, and there are many shallow areas along the main-river channel. Buzzbaits, spinnerbaits, plastic worms on Carolina or Texas rigs, floating worms, and plastic rats are all good summer lures. Hull fishes Nickajack early during the first weeks of summer, leaving the lake by 10 A.M. However, he stays longer as summer grows hotter.

"This sounds odd, but I fish all day during the hot summer months like July and August. I'll fish right in the middle of the day," says Hull. "The hotter, the better. What is happening is that milfoil is cool and has a lot of oxygen in it. Baitfish are also hiding in the milfoil. All of this makes for great fishing and bass will hit regardless of how hot it is. I've had to jump in the water three or four times during a trip to stay cool. In 1996, I caught a 10-pound bass and the temperature was 95°. I looked at my watch and it was 2 P.M."

Milfoil has gotten thick by July, and plastic rats or Johnson Spoons, with weed guards and rubber trailers, worked across the surface, tantalize many bass. Floating worms are also excellent, especially if they are pink and "about as long as a pencil," says Hull. "Don't put any weight on the worm and just let it float down through openings in the milfoil," he explains.

Nickajack doesn't have numerous docks, but Hull fishes every one he comes across. Bass seek relief in the shade provided by docks. Anglers also catch largemouth by trolling crankbaits 12 to 18 feet around submerged islands, notes Hull, whose favorite crankbait is a ¼-ounce Hot Lips Express because "it digs deep." He likes crawdad or shad colors. "Don't use line any heavier than 10-pound test and troll slowly," he advises.

Fall

Largemouth stay either beneath or around thick milfoil in early and mid-fall. Hull uses the same techniques to catch them in fall as he uses during summer. He primarily tosses buzzbaits, spinnerbaits, floating worms, plastic rats, and spoons. When water temperature begins to cool, he ties on plastic grubs and works "breaks," the ledges that hold bass in winter.

*Many anglers use live bait to catch smallmouth
below Chickamauga Dam in Chattanooga, but
Benny Hull enjoys trolling a Hot Lips Express for
fast action.*

SMALLMOUTH BASS

Nickajack doesn't have a statewide reputation for great smallmouth fishing,
but if anglers continue catching them as they have during the 1990s, it may
become a major attraction. For Benny Hull, smallmouth fishing on Nickajack
Lake is excellent, especially on the stretch of river between Chickamauga Dam
and Walnut Bridge, located inside Chattanooga's city limits.

Hull rates the shoals below Chickamauga Dam as comparable to the
famous smallmouth waters below Pickwick Dam in southwest Tennessee. "It's
blowing everybody away here," he says of Nickajack's smallmouth fishery.

Through the Seasons

Smallmouth are caught all over Nickajack, but most smallmouth anglers stay
in the ribbon of cool water between the dam and 5 miles downstream. That's
where the largest concentrations of smallies reside, says Hull.

Much of the river here is only 8 to 10 feet deep but there are 20- and 30-foot
holes. How these holes and their adjacent shoals are fished is important.
"Probably three-fourths of the smallmouth anglers on Nickajack catch fish by
bouncing live shiners off the river bottom," says Hull. "I can fish for smallmouth just about all year long, but I start around October and fish until it
gets real cold."

Anglers who tightline must keep contact with the river bottom while drifting shiners, says Hull. This requires concentration. "I might be moving over a
spot 8 feet deep and then it will drop to 20 or 30 feet. But then 50 or 100 yards

later, it's back up to 8 or 10 feet," explains Hull. "I bounce my shiner in the shallow areas, but when I hit a deep spot, I need to have an eye on my depth finder to see where the smallmouth are suspending."

Hull sometimes catches fish as deep as 30 feet where smallmouth are waiting to ambush baitfish. "I'm always ready to feed out line when I cross deep holes," says Hull. "I watch my line and keep it bouncing. I stay hung up if I don't."

Hull hooks his shiners through the mouth on No. 2 hooks and places a ¼-ounce sinker 12 to 18 inches above the hook on 6- or 8-pound-test monofilament. He lowers his bait by casting downriver and letting it fall while he drifts toward it. Other anglers increase their sinker size and drop their shiner straight down.

Live bait catches many, but Hull believes the best way to catch the greatest number of smallmouth is by trolling crankbaits, especially a Hot Lips Express. "I can catch maybe 20 smallmouth a day with shiners, but I've caught 30, 40, and even 50 smallmouth while trolling," he says.

Trolling is simple. Hull releases 30 to 40 feet of line behind the boat and trolls slowly, pulling lures through suspending fish. "I don't have to let out a lot of line," says Hull. "I catch most of my fish 8 to 12 feet deep because they usually grab it as it comes across a shoal just before that shoal drops off deep."

Sometimes Hull fishes the river's rocky banks near Chickamauga Dam, especially if he hasn't had luck with shiners or Hot Lips. Hair flies in crawfish colors are among good shoreline lures. "Smallmouth fishing is getting phenomenal here," says Hull. "For anyone who likes to catch smallmouth, Nickajack is definitely worth a trip."

STRIPE (WHITE BASS)

Nickajack Lake gets high ratings from Benny Hull for its smallmouth bass, but his praise for white bass is even greater when he compares it with other reservoirs. "I guess this lake is as good for white bass as anywhere in the country," he says. Hull estimates that Nickajack's largest white bass—he refers to these as "boat paddles" because of their shape and size—weigh between 1½ and 3 pounds.

Winter and Spring

Hull begins fishing for white bass in mid-March, when large females hold close to sandbars and eat shad. "I catch 'boat paddles' starting in March and it's a thrill," says Hull. "They don't seem to hit real well until about then." Bays, coves, sloughs, Bennett Lake, and other areas off the main channel and in the lower section of Nickajack are excellent sites for white bass, says Hull.

Minnows, plastic grubs, or hair flies, fished on sandbars, catch many stripe. Light-spinning gear is ideal for catching them. When white bass begin their spawning run, Hull follows them upriver and fishes over sandbars in the main river, or he fishes in the mouths of creeks. Chartreuse or white grubs on ¼-ounce leadhead jigs, or ¼-ounce white hair flies, are Hull's favorite baits.

Wing walls below Chickamauga Dam provide good white bass holes in April and May, notes Hull, who tosses his lures where the swift water meets the slack water. Large concentrations of white bass migrate to the dam and have voracious appetites.

Summer and Fall

As water temperatures increase, white bass spread out, but are easily found pursuing schooling shad, says Hull. "They'll bunch up in big groups and start getting into jumps usually by June," he notes. "I've seen them surfacing over areas half as big as a football field."

Toss anything that resembles a minnow to surfacing white bass. White rooster tails, white plastic grubs, hair jigs, and any number of topwater lures attract strikes. "I like to tie a leader on a topwater lure and attach a white jig to the leader,"

Benny Hull ranks Nickajack Lake as good as any for its large white bass, which he calls "boat paddles." A full stringer shown here by Doug Markham.

he says. "This gives me two presentations that resemble shad."

Surfacing white bass don't usually stay up long, but they do remain in the same area. Hull continues tossing grubs or flies, but instead of pulling them across the surface, he lets them fall until they reach the fish. "I like to yo-yo my lure back to the boat," he says.

Larger fish often suspend beneath the top layer of schooling white bass, notes Hull. "To reach them, I let my bait drop a little more before I start working it," he says. "Spoons are also great to use for bigger fish beneath schools."

Hull carries binoculars with him when he pursues white bass. If the weather is good and the water calm, the fish eventually surface. Binoculars help detect whitecaps and flashes of silver as white bass and shad tangle. He looks for activity every 5 to 10 minutes.

White bass surface all summer and into fall. As the water temperature cools, they stay on the surface longer. "I catch them on the surface up until December and then it gets pretty slow as the water starts getting cold," says Hull.

One of the best ways to find white bass in fall is to locate gulls. Gulls are great fishermen and always searching for schooling shad. Where there is shad, there is often white bass, including those 1½- to 3-pound "boat paddles," says Hull.

CHAPTER 17

Chickamauga Lake

Chattanooga's Special Reservoir

A few years ago, Tennessee crappie anglers Steve McCadams and Jim Perry finished first in the largest national crappie tournament held in America. Neither man knew much about Chickamauga Lake, but they summoned years of experience to help them locate fertile crappie water and to win a championship.

That these two Kentucky Lake fishermen won a prestigious tournament hundreds of miles from their hometown was a great honor. For the national tournament trail (known today as Crappie USA) to have chosen Chickamauga for its year-ending classic was an indication of what a special lake it is.

Crappie, obviously, are among this chapter's featured species. Largemouth, shellcracker, and catfish also attract numerous anglers to this long, run-of-the-river reservoir, especially bass anglers who catch many largemouth throughout the year.

Chickamauga has many experienced local anglers who know much about fish behavior and what entices them to strike. With their help, even newcomers to Chickamauga can utilize years of knowledge to help them succeed.

LARGEMOUTH BASS

Few anglers enjoy fishing more than Billy Joe "Baldy" Hall, who estimates he spends 250 days fishing each year. Most of his time is spent pursuing largemouth, which is why he is among the best Chickamaug bass anglers and a fierce and widely respected tournament competitor. "My best bass-tournament weight

GAME FISH RATINGS	
Largemouth Bass	🐟 🐟 🐟 🐟
Crappie	🐟 🐟 🐟 🐟
Shellcracker (Redear)	🐟 🐟 🐟 🐟 🐟
Catfish	🐟 🐟 🐟 🐟 🐟

with a 10-fish limit was 44 pounds," he says. "I've also had quite a few 30-pound-plus catches."

Hall guides when he isn't fishing in championships. He considers Chickamauga Lake an excellent largemouth reservoir. Few anglers, if any, know more about Chickamauga's bass than Baldy Hall.

Winter

Largemouth inhabit all of Chickamauga, but Hall's favorite early winter sites are between TN 60 and the Sequoyah Nuclear Plant. Starting in fall and continuing into January, largemouth attack shad in small coves alongside the

CHICKAMAUGA AT A GLANCE

Location:	Hamilton, Rhea, Meigs, Polk, and Bradley Counties
Size:	34,500 acres
Length:	58.9 miles
Shoreline:	810 miles
Summer pool:	685.4 feet
Winter pool:	682.5 feet
Impounded:	1940
Featured species:	Largemouth Bass, Crappie, Shellcracker (Redear), Catfish
Other species:	Sauger, Stripe (White Bass), Striper, Spotted (Kentucky) Bass, Smallmouth Bass, Walleye
Description:	This run-of-the-river reservoir offers numerous sloughs, creeks, submerged stumps, and bluffs. The lake bottom is mud and clay in most places. There has been considerable development on the lower end around Chattanooga. Aquatic vegetation is present, and there are many brush piles in bays, sloughs, and coves.
Main tributaries:	Hiwassee River, Wolftever Creek, Soddy Creek, Opossum Creek, Sale Creek, Gunstocker Creek, Candies Creek, South Mouse Creek, North Mouse Creek, Rogers Creek, Price Creek, Agency Creek, Richland Creek, Mud Creek, Goodfield Creek, Town Creek, Sewee Creek, Watts Creek
Landmarks:	Chickamauga's upper end flows through Chattanooga. Other nearby cities include Hixon, Soddy-Daisy, Cleveland, Graysville, and Dayton. Nearby state routes include 68, 30, 29, 58, 60, 29, 111, 153, 27, and 2. The nearest interstate is I-24.
Operated by:	Tennessee Valley Authority

See Appendix C for map information

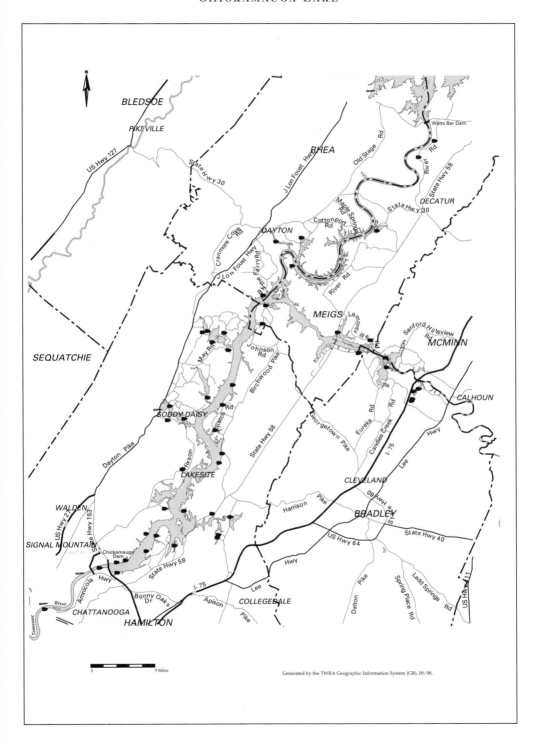

Generated by the TWRA Geographic Information System (GB), 09/98.

Anglers who learn to bird-dog their fish can increase their Chickamauga success, according to Billy Joe "Baldy" Hall, a guide and one of the best tournament anglers on the lake.

main river. "I'm not talking about big creeks or bays," says Hall. "I mean little pockets and sloughs, which I call offsets."

Chickamauga has many offsets, but one of Hall's favorites is Eldridge Slough. "All of the offsets are good," says Hall, who tosses small crankbaits this time of year. Bass are "getting fat on shad" in water that is "cool, but not cold."

A Baby N retrieved 2 to 3 feet beneath the surface is a top-notch lure, says Hall, who tosses a yellow Baby N when the lake is dingy and a white one when it's clear. "I fish this way through December and into the biggest part of January," says the guide. Hall uses baitcasting equipment "100% of the time," even when tossing small crankbaits.

Half-ounce, white spinnerbaits with a No. 5 willowleaf blade also produce many hits. "I'll buzz the spinnerbait across the surface when bass are active, but I'll slow-roll it if they're not feeding," notes Hall, who makes his own spinnerbaits.

During the coldest months—January through early March—Hall heads to bluffs in deeper water and flips ½-ounce black and blue jig and pig combinations. "The skirt is black and blue, and I like a No. 11 pork chunk," he says. "I don't work the deepest banks when fishing bluffs. I find bluffs that are 20 to 25 feet deep at the base, but this isn't where I fish. It's best to get started on the ends of the bluffs, where the water is only 5 to 10 feet deep."

Bluffs close to sloughs make ideal flipping spots. "This is where I find bass chasing shad after they leave the sloughs," says Hall, who increases his line strength to 20- or 25-pound-test monofilament. He fishes his pig and jig by lifting it "3 or 4 inches and letting it fall straight down, right into the edge of the rocks."

Chickamauga occasionally drops as much as a foot in 24 hours, which makes winter fishing tough. "Largemouth go deeper when this happens, but I have a tough time catching them when it falls that much," says Hall.

Spring

As spring approaches and water elevation rises, largemouth travel with the spreading lake into creeks and sloughs. Along the way they stop on secondary points, which Hall jokingly refers to as "sexy points" because bass couple there before moving toward the shore to spawn. Crankbaits, spinnerbaits, and plastic worms, rigged Carolina or Texas style, catch bass.

Among Hall's favorite crankbaits is a wooden Bomber. Although it is no longer manufactured (plastic imitations are numerous), he has obtained several of them, and they can still be found by determined anglers. "It runs backward," he says. His favorite Bomber colors are pearl and a combination of green and white known as "Christmas tree colors."

Because he lives in Dayton, Hall primarily fishes a stretch of river in spring that is closest to his home—TN 30 downstream to the Hiwassee River.

As water temperature increases, bass build beds around shoreline stumps and buck bushes. "When it hits 62°, largemouth go on bed," notes Hall. Chickamauga has many stumps, but few buck bushes. "If I find a buck bush, I make sure to fish it because there will always be a largemouth around it," says the guide.

Hall is successful in part because he scouts before tournaments. "I go out and ride around to find fish," he says. "Almost all the tournaments I win in April and May are because I've found most of my bass by bird-dogging them."

Most largemouth are in backwater—bays, creeks, coves, and sloughs off the main river. Once he locates bedding fish, Hall flips plastic worms on Carolina rigs, weightless Gitzits, or floating worms. "I toss just past their beds and drag my bait right to them," he says. "I'm real quiet, and I finesse my hits."

After the spawn ends, many bass move back to secondary points in the creeks and hit crankbaits or spinnerbaits. "They're starved after they get off bed, and they really feed up," notes Hall.

Knowing which points are best is a matter of fishing the lake often, but Hall mentions Moon Island—also known as Mitchell Branch—as a "red-hot" postspawn hangout. "Some points in Chickamauga are 5 feet deep and others drop off as much as 10 or 12 feet," he says. "I have success with spinnerbaits, but my favorite lure at this time is a DD-22. I can get it down and bumping the bottom real quick. I let it crawl around, and then stop it, let it crawl some more, and stop it."

Summer

Chickamauga is a shallow lake with little flow to keep it cool, which makes summer angling tough. "The deeper I fish, the better I do," says Hall, who catches many summer bass around main river points, drop-offs, and bluffs. Sometimes he fishes in sloughs if those sloughs have at least one spring that provides largemouth with relief from summer heat.

Crankbaits or plastic baits catch fish in deep holes, but when in sloughs, Hall tosses black and blue jig and pig combinations. "If I'm in backwater this time of year and not fishing a spring, I'm wasting time because this reservoir gets like dishwater," says the guide. Hall's pig and jig is a ½-ounce lure with a black and blue skirt and a No. 11 black pork chunk.

"Most of the sloughs with good springs are about 6 feet deep with rocks around them," says Hall. "That's where I like to fish, right around the rocks." Hall uses 20- to 25-pound-test monofilament when flipping jigs.

Fall

When water temperature begins to cool, usually by late September or October, Hall heads downstream—below TN 60—and fishes "offsets" again. These are the same small sloughs and coves with which he has much success in early winter. He continues using the same techniques in fall as in other seasons.

CRAPPIE

Crappie are always ready to bite. With a voracious appetite and a tolerance for cold, crappie are vulnerable to anglers throughout the year. While Chickamauga has gone through lean crappie times, it has also experienced many good crappie years.

Anglers Joe Bakes and Tim Poole don't know each other, but each has fished Chickamauga Lake hundreds of times, and each have become crappie experts, even though their fishing styles are very different.

Winter

Joe Bakes began fishing Chickamauga Lake in the late 1980s. He spends at least one day a week throughout the year catching crappie, bass, or catfish. All of his fishing is fun, but his crappie pursuit is particularly relaxing. He fishes from a pontoon boat.

Bakes begins catching winter crappie in November. He starts by finding suspended crappie, with an electronic locator, over brush piles in bays and sloughs. "Finding brush in Chickamauga is no problem," says Bakes. "Fishermen have put out hundreds of them. First, I find the edge of a creek channel. Then I look for cover. I go back and forth along a channel, up and down it, and if necessary, toward the shallows and then back. I'll stop when I see brush with crappie over it."

Bakes anchors near brush piles, situating himself so that wind and current move his bobber away from him and over suspended fish. "If the depth finder tells me that fish are suspending at 14 feet, I put my bobber at 14 feet," says Bakes, who uses slip bobbers and 8-pound-test monofilament. He hooks his tuffy minnows through the back with No. 4 gold wire hooks and gets down with No. 2 splitshot sinkers.

"For me, the best time to catch crappie from Chickamauga is in November," says Bakes. "It has always been my best month. I can pick a slough and find crappie between 9 and 18 feet deep." Brush piles produce fish for Bakes from November into March.

Many bays, sloughs, and coves have crappie, but Bakes notes Dallas Bay, a large area on Chickamauga's lower half, as "one of the best places in the world to find brush piles." Locating crappie is easy. "I catch all the fish I need close to where I launch, so I don't do much running around," says Bakes.

Black and white crappie inhabit Chickamauga and Bakes primarily catches large white crappie in winter. Regardless of how cold the water gets, Chickamauga crappie don't suspend very deep. "I almost always catch them between 9 and 18 feet," he reiterates.

Chickamauga has been the site of national crappie competition, but for Bill McConkey (left) and Joe Bakes, it's a great place to have fun while catching a bunch of fish.

Be aware of stumps during the winter drawdown, warns Bakes. Chickamauga is loaded with them. While good for fishing, they are rough on lower motor units when the reservoir recedes and the stumps stand a few inches below the surface.

Spring

As water temperature increases and triggers spawning instincts, crappie move toward stumps and other shallow structure in bays, sloughs, and coves. Anglers should do the same, especially as water rises and submerges structure. "I get back in the sloughs and set my bobbers at 3, 4, and 5 feet deep," says Bakes. "I pull into the wind and toward the shoreline as far as I can go, cut the motor, and let my boat drift. I let the wind carry me across a slough and cover as large an area as possible." If the wind is too strong, however, Bakes anchors and fishes shallow.

Tuffy minnows, slip bobbers, No. 4 wire hooks, spinning reels, 8-pound-test monofilament, and graphite fly rods make up Bakes's main gear and tackle. Occasionally, he drifts crawfish-colored jigs just for something different to do.

Crappie are usually shallow and aggressive between mid-March and mid-April, says Bakes.

After the spawn, Bakes begins night fishing. "I fish at night because I enjoy it," he says. "I find the deepest part of where a creek came into the river before TVA impounded Chickamauga and anchor right there. That's where I catch crappie all summer and even into the fall."

Bakes prefers dark nights over bright ones. "I use floating lights encased in Styrofoam and a car headlight that I've rigged into a plastic bucket," he says. "Lights attract more shad on dark nights when there isn't much illumination from the moon." Gathering shad grab the attention of numerous fish species, including crappie.

Tightlining works great at night, says Bakes, who places several lines at various depths until he finds fish. "One very important lesson that I've learned is that gold hooks do much better than hooks of other colors," says Bakes. "I catch at least five crappie to one with gold hooks, maybe even 10 to 1."

Summer

Tim Poole has fished Chickamauga all his life. Although a TWRA creel clerk on adjacent Nickajack Lake, Poole travels to Chickamauga when pursuing summer crappie. He is a devoted crappie angler who competes in national tournaments when not fishing Chickamauga.

Good crappie fishing on Chickamauga doesn't begin for him until summer. "I'll begin fishing around the first of June, but the best fishing for me begins in July when it's real hot outside," he says. "I catch more crappie in July than any other time."

Unlike Joe Bakes, who primarily uses minnows to catch crappie, Poole relies more on plastic baits and light leadhead jigs. He notes, however, that he never goes crappie fishing without taking live bait along.

Poole's fishing method requires that he slowly troll several tightlined rods over the front of his flat-bottom aluminum boat. He moves his vessel slowly forward while trolling past brush piles, stumps, and other cover or structure. "I like to fish right down the middle of creeks and sometimes down the edge of the main river channel," he says.

Twelve-foot graphite B 'n' M rods (usually four of them) and small closed-face reels, spooled with 6- to 8-pound-test monofilament, make up his favorite gear. A heavy sinker and appropriate trolling speed keep his line vertical.

Poole wraps a 1- to 1½-ounce egg sinker to the main line of each outfit (weight depends on strength of current) and then ties a swivel several inches below the line that extends from each sinker. He ties a leader to the swivel and a jig to the leader. Twelve to thirty-six inches of line between hook and swivel is adequate.

"In the summer I mostly use a technique called pushing [see Glossary]," says Poole. "I drop my line to the bottom and crank it up about a foot. The idea is to stay near the bottom. I don't fish for suspended crappie. With the heavy weight, I know exactly where my jig is. I'm not guessing at any time. It's vital that line stay as vertical as possible."

It is also important to have sonar. Poole watches his electronic fish-finder to detect lake-bottom changes and to raise and lower line accordingly. "I troll real slow, less than one mile per hour," he says. "If I go across a spot that I think should be good, but don't catch anything, I'll go back over that same area with minnows," he notes. "Every now and then, minnows work when jigs won't."

Because the heavy egg sinker provides ample weight, Poole uses light lead-head jigs, usually ¼₄ or ¹⁄₆₄ ounce. His favorite artificial baits are Hal Flies, Sure Flies, and Tom's Jigs, all of which he gets from bait shops near Alabama's Weiss Lake, a famous crappie reservoir that Poole visits each year. Hair is attached below rubber collars on all of these lures.

Crappie should hit any number of artificial baits, including plastic tubes or plastic grubs. Among Poole's favorite colors are combinations of red, green, and yellow (red head, green collar, yellow hair) and of white, blue, and white (white head, blue collar, white hair).

Fall
Crappie fall prey to Joe Bakes's spring technique or to the summer method described by Tim Poole. November is Bakes's favorite crappie month of the year. Be aware of changing water temperatures and dropping water levels when fishing Chickamauga Lake in fall.

SHELLCRACKER (REDEAR)
Anyone who has ever caught a large shellcracker knows how powerful these pan-fish are. Anyone fortunate enough to have found a bed of them is now probably an avid shellcracker angler. Also known as redear, these fish are difficult to locate in schools, outside of a few precious weeks in spring when they move shallow to spawn. Like blooming dogwood trees, shellcracker are around only for a short while, but like dogwoods, they make anglers feel good about life. Chickamauga angler Larry Bell spends many days fishing for bass and crappie, but finds a few days each spring to fight, catch, and enjoy this scrappy sunfish.

Spring
Finding spring shellcracker is easy. "We usually start fishing for them the first week or two of May," says Bell. "We don't have to search for them because we know they're always going to be in the same location every year."

Chickamauga Lake has many coves and sloughs, which are ideal habitat for bedding shellcracker and where Bell finds them. "If I find trees overhanging the water and creating a little bit of shade, I know I have a good chance of locating a shellcracker bed," notes Bell.

They are easy to find only about one month each year, but when shell-crackers bed near the shoreline they provide lots of ultralight action.

Shellcracker are aggressive. Crickets and worms fished on small hooks catch countless fish, as do tiny artificial baits. Solid black is often mentioned by shellcracker anglers as a good color for tiny plastic grubs or artificial-hair imitations. Bell uses ultralight equipment for redear. He baits his hook with either a cricket or a worm and fishes 4 to 5 feet deep under a slip bobber.

"A good 12-inch shellcracker is not difficult to catch on this lake," says Bell. "I can catch more fish than I can eat or care to clean." If action quickly ceases, don't give up on a bed. "Sometimes I sit in one spot and catch five or six fish, and all of a sudden, they quit hitting," explains Bell. "When this happens, I move to another spot with my trolling motor. After everything has gotten calm, I move back and catch more fish from the first hole."

Shellcracker are around beds for much of May. "Toward the end of the month, fishing tapers off and that's when I go back to catching crappie," says Bell.

CATFISH

Joe Bakes spends many days bass and crappie fishing, but for several weeks each year, he becomes a catfish angler. "In late September and all of October, I go catfishing," he says. Shad congregate near Sequoyah Nuclear Plant in September and October, and they come under attack by hungry cats.

Summer and Fall

Like typical run-of-the-river lakes, Chickamauga has excellent catfish populations. Read other chapters for catfishing techniques throughout the seasons,

***With the proper bait reduced to the right size, anglers can grow tired of
catching catfish around Chickamauga's Sequoyah Nuclear Plant.***

but don't miss Chickamauga's late summer and early fall action. "I use shad
for cut bait and anchor in the boils," says Bakes. "Mostly I catch blues and
channel catfish."

Bakes catches skipjack below Chickamauga Dam by tying two or three ¹/₁₆-
ounce white plastic grubs on 6-pound-test monofilament and tossing them
with light spinning gear. "Catching the bait is almost as fun as catching the
cats," he says. "All I have to do is cast upstream and reel slowly back to the
boat. I cut strips the bait about a half-inch wide and 2 inches long."

Hits occur as cut bait waffles through the boils. Strong rods, large reels,
and heavy line is what many anglers use for catfish. "The biggest catfish I've
caught weighed 30 pounds, but there are much bigger cats around," he says.
Bakes uses fly rods and spinning reels—the same gear he uses to catch crappie—but notes that he's "strictly fishing for fun." Bakes anchors his boat
above the turbulence and throws toward it. Much of his fishing is in water 60
feet deep. Wear life jackets in this dangerous water.

CHAPTER 18

Watts Bar Lake

The Lake that Has Everything

Watts Bar Lake draws a lot of attention from Knoxville and Chattanooga anglers. It is the largest of the East Tennessee reservoirs and has a large number of launching ramps along its length.

Its main body is about 25 miles west of Knoxville and 40 miles northeast of Chattanooga. The Clinch and Emory Rivers feed it from the northeast and the Tennessee River from the east. The lake is surrounded by hills rising along the main channel. There are so many bays, coves, and sloughs it would be easy to get lost. The upper end is riverine and is the most fertile section of the lake. The middle and lower end offer better fishing, except during the winter. The lower end of Watts Bar has more dissolved oxygen, less pollution, and steeper banks, but is less fertile than the upper section. Watts Bar has an advantage over many East Tennessee lakes: It's not as clear. The extra color means the fish will be higher in the water column for easier fishing. There are springs in the midlake section that add oxygen and cooler water for better fishing in the summer. These springs also attract baitfish in summer. The Kingston Steam Plant, at the mouth of the Emory River and about 3 miles above the mouth of the Clinch River, is the premier hot spot during the winter because the warm-water discharge attracts plenty of baitfish and in turn draws predators.

GAME FISH RATINGS

Striper	🐟 🐟 🐟
Hybrid (Cherokee Bass)	🐟 🐟 🐟
Largemouth Bass	🐟 🐟 🐟 🐟 🐟
Smallmouth Bass	🐟 🐟 🐟
Crappie	🐟 🐟 🐟 🐟

STRIPER AND HYBRID

Although not safe to eat, these fish are heavily pursued for

WATTS BAR AT A GLANCE

Location: Hamilton, Rhea, Roane, Meigs, and Loudon Counties

Size: 38,600 acres

Length: 72 miles

Shoreline: 783 miles

Summer pool: 745 feet

Winter pool: 735 feet

Impounded: 1942

Featured species: Striper, Hybrid (Cherokee Bass), Largemouth Bass, Small-mouth Bass, Crappie

Other species: Sauger, Spotted (Kentucky) Bass, Bream, Catfish, Walleye

Description: A run-of-the-river lake with islands, steep, wooded banks, and rocky bluffs. Gizzard shad, threadfin shad, shiners, and minnows are the forage base. The lake's water clarity ranges from clear to stained. Watts Bar is monomictic (sedimentary rock composed of a single mineral) and is thermally stratified during the summer. There is diverse wood cover, including logs, which are common along the bank (with some washed onto the shallow flats), fallen trees, stumps, and manmade brush-piles. Bushes along the bank are a source of willow fly hatches in summer and attract many species of fish.

Advisories: Clinch River from Kingston to Melton Hill Dam: consume no stripers, bass, or hybrids. Tennessee River from Watts Bar Dam to Fort Loudoun Dam: consume no catfish, stripers, stripe, or hybrids. There is a precautionary advisory against eating large-mouth bass, sauger, carp, and smallmouth buffalo. Stripers and hybrids, while under an advisory, receive pressure from catch-and-release anglers. Unexpected natural reproduction has occurred in Watts Bar. They make up a strong fishery. Check TWRA fishing regulations for current advisories.

Main tributaries: Tennessee River, Emory River, Clinch River, Piney River, Ellis Creek, Caney Creek, Rock Creek, Hines Creek, Muddy Creek, Wann Creek, Wolf Creek, Cane Creek, White Creek, King Creek, Ellis Creek, Riley Creek, Hines Creek

Landmarks: Most of the lake is south of Kingston, northeast of Spring City, west of Knoxville, and southeast of Rockwood and Harriman, with access from I-75, I-40, US 70, US 27, TN 58, TN 68, TN 72, and River Road.

Operated by: Tennessee Valley Authority

See Appendix C for map information

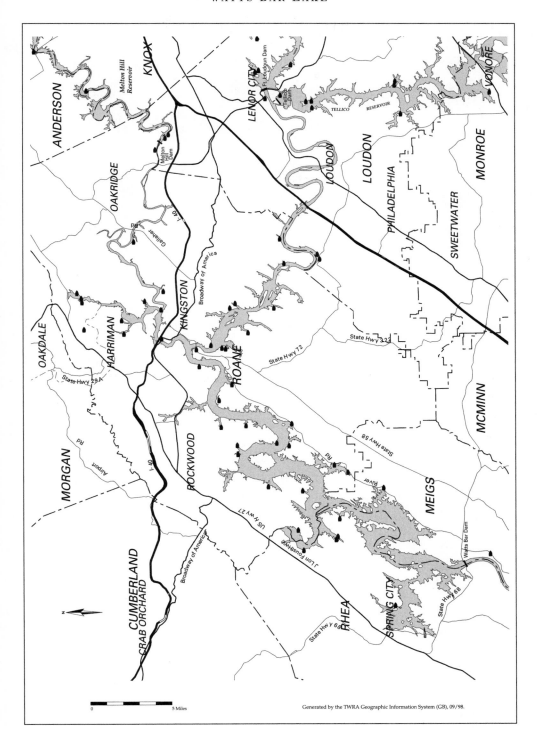

Generated by the TWRA Geographic Information System (GB), 09/98.

The popular Crippled Herring Spoon closely resembles a shad. Both baits work well in catching stripers and hybrids on Watts Bar Lake.

their fight. Most anglers prefer the hybrid because it has a longer, harder fight, but the striper grows to become the heavyweight in Tennessee. In cold weather, baitfish move upstream to stay in the warm-water discharge, and anglers concentrate near the steam plant in the Clinch River to get their rods bent.

The single most successful thing an angler can do to catch these true bass is to locate schools of shad, no matter the season. Striper and hybrid are pelagic and follow baitfish. They relate to structure, humps, and deepwater points when resting. The best time to catch them is when there is current.

Topwater baits are effective in winter, spring, and fall, but downlines and flatlines are top choices for live-bait fishing year-round (see Appendix A for description). Drifting and slow-trolling these rigs just below schools of shad, located with your sonar, is about as complicated as it gets. Look for striped bass and hybrids in the headwaters in January and February during their spawning runs. Two-pound skipjack are used for trophy-size striped bass. Hybrids prefer baitfish about 5 inches long.

Winter

When the Kingston Steam Plant opens the gates and discharges warm water, it's like someone rang the dinner bell. Starting in January, hybrids, stripers, sauger, crappie, and bass move to the warm headwaters of the steam plant.

J. D. Campbell from Harriman has fished this area for 45 years. He says, "Most of the hybrid and large stripers that we catch are caught on large creek minnows, skipjack, and large white jigs. Stripers up to 40 pounds are caught here through March. Fishing is fantastic from the I-40 bridge up to the steam plant. In February there are often 30 to 50 large hybrids caught per day fishing from the bank."

Freddie Phillips from Oneida is a regular wintertime angler below the steam plant, often limiting his fishing to hybrids, stripers, and channel catfish. He says, "Fishing the steam plant often fills the void of tough fishing conditions in our lakes simply because of the warm-water discharge. Anglers for 60 miles travel weekly to fish this area."

The most often used technique is large skipjacks, 17 to 20 inches long, cast on 7- or 8-foot rods, and fished on the bottom or drifted in deeper water just above and near the I-40 bridge. Other favorite baits are the ½-ounce white bucktail jig, Crippled Herring spoon, or Hopkins spoon.

Greg Jones from Lenoir City says the best winter fishing is between the bridges below the Kingston Steam Plant. On winter nights, anglers dressed warmly and in chest waders catch stripers and hybrids with topwater plugs like the Zara Spook and Red Fin. The catch rate at Bull Run Steam Plant is much less than at the Kingston plant.

Spring, Summer, and Fall

Greg Jones fishes for stripers three days a week below Ft. Loudoun, Melton Hill, and Watts Bar Dams. Jones says, "I fish live bait: threadfin, gizzard, and hickory shad [skipjack]. I use whichever they are feeding on. I like fishing the larger threadfin shad when they reach about 5 inches long.

"If they're feeding on hickory shad, I hook the shad in the back fin without any weight and drift them across the calmer water, not in the rough water. I catch better fish that way—between 20 and 35 pounds. When I'm drifting the hickory shad across the open water, the resistance of the water keeps it on the surface, and I can see the stripers make a pass at it. The first time some friends and I tried this, we caught 20 fish over 20 pounds in 4 hours. The three of us had fish on the line at the same time three times."

Jones will sometimes use a downline to fish the boils. He uses a 5/0 hook for threadfin and a 9/0 hook for hickory shad. "The ticket," he says, "is getting it to the bottom without getting hung."

Anglers who have a tendency to cast upstream or downstream suffer more snags. The water is about 14 feet deep below Ft. Loudoun and Melton Hill. The flats, where Jones fishes the unweighted skipjack, are about 7 feet deep.

"I run up to the discharge between two boils, cast about 10 feet in front of the boat into the eddy, free-spool about 6 more feet of line, and let the sinker drop straight down. If fish are in there and my bait is directly under the boat, I'll catch them within 100 yards of the dam. Some people drift 500 yards, but I stay close to the discharge." Jones prefers to fish between the number two and number three boils.

"If you fish behind the boils next to the dam, you can catch a lot of the smaller fish running between 5 and 12 pounds. I don't like catching them because they can hurt me. I fish 20-pound test so I can get the fish in quickly to keep them from becoming stressed. Trying to get them off the hook tears my hand up because they still have a lot of fight left in them."

To catch bait, Jones uses ⅟₃₂-ounce feather jigs with a No. 8 hook, called Pop Eye Flies. He ties three of these in series to catch skipjack. He catches only a few at a time because they are short-lived in a live well. "Live bait is key. Dead bait comes through the water like a helicopter and the fish are not going to hit it very well," he says.

"I fish from a flat-bottom boat so I can run up into the discharge and not get blown out like a boat with a V-hull or tri-hull. The flat bottom also allows me to get bait easier with a dip net next to the bank. You have to stay in your boat because there is a $600 fine for getting on the bank. The fine is for safety reasons because of people getting hurt and drowning. If there is no discharge, anglers should stay away from the area where the surge takes place. The surge at the beginning of a discharge has tossed people out of their boat. Watts Bar discharge is a little rougher than Melton Hill or Ft. Loudoun," says Jones.

He says that fishing below Melton Hill can get crowded, and if more than a couple of boats are fishing there, they spook the stripers downstream. Also the stripers leave when the baitfish leave in cold weather. More baitfish are below the dams in June, July, and August, but fishing is good in the spring and fall.

Jones uses a 7-foot Flipping Stick, 6500 Ambassadeur reel, and 20-pound-test monofilament line when fishing live bait.

LARGEMOUTH BASS
Largemouth bass angling is better on Watts Bar than most of the other lakes on the upper end of the Tennessee River. Its waters are nutrient-rich, providing an excellent forage base for bass. Wood cover is plentiful along the banks, and backwater and submerged structures, such as humps, sandbars, and islands, provide superb holding places for bucketmouth throughout the year.

Winter
Guide and pro bass angler Doug Plemons lives on Watts Bar Lake and fishes many tournaments there each year. His extensive knowledge of the reservoir is gained from more than 150 days on the water each year.

"Sometimes we have such mild weather in December you can still catch bass in the shallows," says Plemons. "January is probably the hardest month to catch largemouth bass. February can be tough, but we usually get several nice days, and the fish become active.

"When the water temperature is still in the 40s and the fish are sluggish, you have to fish for them really slow," he says. "I use a jig and pig on the

Doug Plemons displays the locally famous Little Petey crankbait that has won him many bass tournaments.

main-channel banks. I look for bluffs that begin to taper out with a lot of stair-step, rock ledges where bass like to hold in the winter. Any combination of black and brown works best for me. Some of the guys are partial to blue and black. Fly and rind work well for smallmouth—⅛- to ¼-ounce jig with hair and a small pork chunk.

"I fish that jig and pig in creeks, too—creeks that have rock banks and get the most sunlight. You want to fish those rocks that warm up more because water temperature is the key to finding fish in winter," he says.

Spring

"Early in the spring I like to use a suspending jerkbait," says Plemons. "It's very animated. The reason it's so attractive to bass is that you pull it down and, in its suspending state, it'll trigger a strike, especially in clear-water lakes. As the water begins to approach the 50° mark, and in the low 50s, the bass begin to move some. You start catching some of these prespawn bass in the creeks on rocky and stumpy banks. That's when you really start catching them on crankbaits and slow-rolling spinnerbaits. I catch a lot of fish on a home-made crankbait when the water reaches the mid-50s."

Plemons says a friend of his makes a crankbait called the Little Petey. It's a flat-sided, balsa crankbait with a lip made out of computer circuit board. "Pete Reynolds and his son Tony make them, and I've used it for years and won a lot of money with it. It's a shallow runner. And I think what distinguishes it so much is the sound that circuit board makes. It's very thin and creates a different sound cutting through the water and when that bill hits the rocks. I think it sounds more like a crawfish than the crankbait bills made of Lexan. These are difficult to get. They make them one at a time and they can't make enough to meet the demand. I'm lucky—I've probably got more Little Peteys than anyone."

Continuing with catching bass in the spring, Plemons says, "When the water warms to the upper 60s, the bass have the urge to merge. That's when you can catch stringers of large bass in shallow water. We can't sight for bedding bass in Watts Bar because the water isn't that clear, but we catch a lot of big female bass in April. I've caught prespawn bass as late as June."

Lime Coach Dog is Plemons's favorite color for the Little Petey. It has a lime back and chartreuse sides with a spotted pattern called lime coach dog. Next he prefers the White Shad that has white sides, a black back, an orange throat, and a chartreuse belly. "This color is one that smallmouth love," he adds. "The other color is called Horton, named for Knoxville pro angler Dewayne Horton. It's an orangish-bronze, kind of a crawdad-color scheme. Those are the best colored baits for spring. The primary food in early spring is crawdads. Biologists say that's because fish want something rich in protein. They need that protein for the spawning process."

Plemons casts the bait on creek-channel banks, making it bump into rocks and stumps. It runs about 5 feet deep. "Occasionally, if there are shad over what I call 'nothing banks,' where there is clay and no cover, I catch some big stringers of fish there. You have to get out there on the water to see what structure and cover the largemouth bass are using. Some of the better bass I've caught have been from these 'nothing banks.' A lot of fishermen believe bass have to have rocks and stumps to hold on, but it's the food the bass are after."

Plemons, like most springtime bass anglers, prefers prefrontal weather conditions. "That dropping pressure gives us good fishing. Also, a stable weather pattern is good. Several warm days in a row bring the fish up. I've even caught good stringers of fish in February after four or five warm days when the temperature reaches 68° or 70°. Sometimes those fish will come out of the winter mode to feed. One or two degrees in water temperature can mean the difference in catching bass and catching nothing. That's why you'll see bass anglers fishing the northern banks because they get the greatest amount of sunlight. The worst thing is where you have one front coming through after another. That really messes up your shallow-water bite.

"The first thing bass do in spring is stage. That's why you'll hear about big bass being caught on a primary point going into a creek, or even a secondary point. They are getting ready to move to their spawning areas. Once the water warms up, these staged fish scatter for the shallower banks. When you find fish staged on a point or ditch line, that's when you can have great days!"

Fluctuation in water levels can disturb the spawn. Usually if a fish is committed to a certain area, they don't retreat to deeper water during the passage of a front, he says. But if they drop the lake's water level or have a flood, the bass are forced to move.

Plemons says, "It's not uncommon for bass to spawn in late April and May on the lower end, and later in the upper end. After bass spawn, they don't bite very well because they are recuperating. Then they begin to move into deeper water. I've caught postspawn fish in the middle and lower end in June, but fish in the upper end haven't spawned yet because of the cooler water. All bass don't spawn at the same time. It's ridiculous to think that because the water temperature determines the spawn, and one side of the lake is not the same as the other. Current has a lot to do with the temperature, and there is less current in the lower end."

He says the middle of the lake has good bass fishing, the Bay Side, Blue Springs, and Rockwood areas are also good in March. There are some big smallmouth in this area, too.

"After June, the fishing can be exceptional in the upper end—from the Kingston area to Ft. Loudoun Dam," says Plemons. "The warmer the water, the farther up the river, the better the fishing."

Summer

Plemons says anglers should fish the humps, creek-channel ledges, and sandbars in summer. "The long tapering points and humps are best in the middle and lower parts of the lake. In the river, most people are fishing sandbars and creek junctions. The Tennessee River has better largemouth fishing than the Clinch or Emory Rivers.

"We catch most of our fish on deep-diving crankbaits that work between 8 and 15 feet and Carolina-rigged lizards and centipedes. You may have your boat in 30 feet of water, but the fish will be between 8 and 15 feet on the edge of a bar, hump, or ledge. I put my boat in deep water and cast shallow.

"To fish a sandbar in the river, cast upstream and work the bait with the current, keeping your boat in 20 to 30 feet of water. Bass position themselves on the ends of bars or on points facing the current. You've got to figure out which parts of the bar the fish are using. Are they using something as a current break, like a stump field, or does the current create a cut? You've got to figure where the bass are to catch them."

When the dam is generating, you usually get your best bite, he adds. "The shad become more active in current and move to the tops of the bars and humps, and the bass follow them," concludes Plemons.

Guide James Blair from Mt. Juliet says, "The secret to catching big largemouth bass on Watts Bar in July and August is to fish the drops and humps in the middle portion of the lake. I fish up the creek channels that are 15 feet deep and cast to the drop banks, or at least steep banks. Out in the lakes, the bass will be on the humps—that's what I like to fish most."

Blair says the best largemouth fishing is midlake to the dam. At Fooshee and Gillespie Bends, where the river makes a backward S, there are many humps. An angler can do as well in this 10-mile stretch as anywhere on the lake.

"Anglers need to get a map of the lake. That way they can see where the creeks and humps are, as well as the main channel," says Blair.

"The best way to fish the drop-offs and catch a big bass is with a 7- or 9-inch worm, a jig and pig, or extra-deep-running crankbait. I've found that a black-grape worm works best for me. If the water's clear, I'll go to a blue worm, but that red shad worm is good. I'm partial to black and blue, black and chartreuse, and solid black jigs with a No. 1 or No. 11 pork chunk rind. You wouldn't believe the big fish I catch on that black and chartreuse jig!"

Blair shares his secret about streamlining rind. "I lay the chunk flat on the boat. I shave the chunk completely off by cutting horizontally, then I find the eye for the hook in the head of the rind and cut the head to the shape of a bullet, being careful not to cut the hook hole. It looks like a rocket head with two tails; it gives so much more action that way."

Chartreuse and brown and chartreuse and green are the best colors for crankbaits, but if the water is clear, Blair casts a blue and silver bait. Keep in mind the bait has to get down to about 15 feet.

"If you cast parallel to the creek-channel drops and humps, you're better off," he says. "I find the creek-channel hump or drop-off with my sonar, keep my boat in-line with it, and cast straight ahead, making sure my lure gets down and stays on the drop-off. Early and late, I fish about 10 feet deep. I fish 15 to 25 feet during the brightest part of the day."

Blair says that live bait works well in the summer, but he prefers to use it only in the winter because the bass hit artificials so well in the summer. Shiners and creek minnows are his top two choices.

He adds that for summer fishing he uses 8- or 10-pound test. "I get a green- or gray-tinted line to reduce visibility."

Blair says, "I'll tell you one more secret. You can catch good-size fish by flipping the shoreline at night. I use a 14-foot Hawger pole that the line runs up the middle. I cut 6 inches off the tip to make it stiffer. I use 25- or 30-pound test on the little reel that comes with the pole.

"This is deadly on bass. I've caught plenty of 5- to 8-pound bass with this method. You just flip a ¼-ounce bug [a jig with the pig cut as described above] at the edge of the bank and hold on."

Fall

Fall is the time to make exciting catches in the jumps. Not only largemouth but also smallmouth, stripe, hybrids, and stripers can be caught scrambling for schooling shad. Shad-colored spoons, 4-inch Slug-Gos, topwater plugs, in-line spinners, and bucktail jigs (with a white, 4-inch trailer) are the best baits.

"When the big schools of shad begin to migrate into the creeks, the bass follow them," says Doug Plemons. "In October and November is when people go back to topwater baits. The shad are on those 'nothing flats' and this is where you can cast spinnerbaits, crankbaits, anything that imitates shad. Bass aren't necessarily structure oriented; they're looking for shad.

"Those that are good at flipping will catch some big bass around cover. The great big bass usually don't run shad like the smaller schooling-size bass. Your bigger fish are more structure oriented," says Plemons.

SMALLMOUTH BASS

Doug Plemons says, "Most of the smallmouth are from Thief Neck Island to the dam. We don't catch a lot of big smallmouth in the river, and that confuses a lot of people. We think of the smallmouth as a river fish. For year-round and night fishing, most of the smallies are caught in the middle and lower end of Watts Bar."

Guide James Blair is known for catching smallmouth when the best of anglers are skunked. He says, "Smallmouth are so unpredictable. You can catch them in 25 feet of water today with the temperature at 25° and go back tomorrow and catch them in 10 feet of water. You can't tell where they're going to be. I've chased those things all my life and I still can't predict how deep they will be."

Blair adds, "Watts Bar has some big smallmouth in it, but it is not well-known for smallmouth like Center Hill, Percy Priest, and Tims Ford—people just don't fish for them much. A smallmouth is harder to catch than a largemouth. You've got to know what you're doing to catch them consistently."

In general, when the water reaches the lower 50s, smallmouth prefer the gravel and rocky points between 12 and 20 feet along the channels of the Tennessee and Piney Rivers, Lowe Branch, Thief Neck Island ,and Half-Moon cutoff. As the water warms into the upper 50s and lower 60s, fish the 10-foot and shallower depths.

After May and through the summer, your best chances at smallies are at night, using jigs, drifting live minnows over humps, or casting spinnerbaits over rocky points and adjacent mud flats and sandflats. Willow fly hatches in July bring smallies to the shallows for fun with fly rods casting imitation mayflies.

By October, smallmouth are 10 feet deep or shallower along the channel. While nighttime angling is still productive, daylight anglers are enjoying the smallmouth, as well as cooler daytime temperatures. Fish will remain shallow until the water temperature drops below 50°.

Winter

James Blair says, "I fish the drop-offs and humps along the main channel. In the winter, small grubs and jigging spoons work, and you can always catch them dragging live minnows. Smoke and silver glitter or clear and silver glitter grubs are what I like best, and just about any color spoon will work in the winter. These fish are from 20 to 30 feet deep, but sometimes I have caught them as shallow as 15 feet.

"In November, you can catch them in the jumps in the mouths of the creeks and coves. I've seen them in the jumps in December and January. A friend of mine said the largest stringer of smallmouth he ever saw was caught on a Devils Horse, a topwater plug, when there was snow on the ground. Smallmouth can also be caught on the deep, gravel bars by dragging live creek minnows along the bottom. I've caught some big smallmouth that way," says Blair.

As the water gets colder, the smallies stay on the steep drops along the channel. A topo map is needed to find the humps Blair mentions. More humps are along the channel from Pearl Harbor and Red Cloud Campground down to the dam.

"Don't forget to fish the river-channel points, the creek-mouth drop-offs, and the bluffs," says Blair. "And you've got to use a very sensitive rod to fish the 'Tinker Toy' flies, those $\frac{1}{32}$- and $\frac{1}{16}$-ounce jigs. They'll eat that 'Tinker Toy' fly up in the wintertime, and they'll eat the float and fly, too. The clear water around the bluffs in the lower end is where you need to fish the float and fly. Fish it about 10 feet deep. You want just a little wind—just a ripple. Throw it against the bluff and let the wind-waves make the fly bounce up and down.

"You want to work these baits as slow as possible in winter. On the bluffs, casts parallel and let the 'Tinker Toy' fly fall. You'll barely feel the smallmouth take the fly—that's why you need a very sensitive rod." Blair uses 6-pound test on a spinning reel in winter.

Spring

Mike Curry from Chattanooga is a former guide who specializes in smallmouth. His knowledge of the waters from Watauga to Kentucky Lake, including all the Tennessee River, accumulated over the last 25 years, would fill several books. Curry is a three-time line class record holder and a holder of the Pickwick Lake–record smallmouth.

"If you are looking for trophy smallmouth and aren't going to Pickwick Lake, then Watts Bar is a good place to go," says Curry. Watts Bar doesn't have a reputation for large numbers of smallmouth, but it is known for large smallmouth. Curry says you aren't likely to catch smallies as consistently as you would largemouth, but the ones you do catch will be worth the effort.

Curry's experience is that the average smallmouth will weigh 3 to 4 pounds. "Of course, you may catch smaller ones but most will be in that range. It's not uncommon to hang 5-pounders, even 6-pounders. Watts Bar is one of the few lakes that has a population of smallmouth that size."

The area from the dam to Caney Creek above Thief Neck Island is where Curry suggests you fish for smallies. "The middle section of the lake probably offers the best fishing. I fish the main channel, Whites Creek, Piney Creek, and Caney Creek.

"I have a theory, not necessarily verifiable, that the huge population of baitfish and the heavy fishing pressure on Watts Bar causes smallmouth to suspend under baitfish, as opposed to being structure oriented, as they are in most lakes. I know some successful daytime anglers that fish the baitfish. They use a Cheater Fly, a carpet-yarn body on a ⅛-ounce leadhead on 4-pound-test line. They cast out and retrieve slowly. They aren't fishing near the bottom. They let it sink to a count of five or six.

"I start night fishing in March or April and continue until it gets so cold in November you can't stand it. An average trip lasts an hour before dark until noon the next day." A lot of the smallies Curry catches are caught on top-water baits right before and after dark and right before and after daylight.

"I've found that smallmouth are shallower at night than during the day. In July, they are going to be about 5 feet deeper than in the spring or fall. I think 10 to 12 feet is a good depth to fish for smallies."

Curry and two of his fishing buddies fish islands and humps that are about 7 feet underwater and deeper. "We move around a lot, trying to find out what the pattern is for that night. Some nights we catch a majority of fish on a Gitzit, but they won't touch a hair jig. The next night they may only want a hair jig, while some nights spinnerbaits are the only bait they want. They can be awful finicky this time of year."

When fishing three to a boat, each puts on a different bait to fish different types of structure at different depths and different areas, from creeks to the main channel, until they establish a pattern. If one bait gets more strikes, the other two will change to that bait.

The productive places they fish will be revisited during the night. A typical milk run starts with some choice points, moves to where the channel leaves a bluff and forms a little flat, then fishes stumps in a mud bottom, and finally moves to some rocky areas. They mix up structures and depths until they can determine where the fish are.

"We use a ⅝-ounce spinnerbait. I prefer a No. 4½ blade on ½- to ⅝-ounce baits. Any dark color works, but red and purple, solid purple, or black are my first choices. I switch to lighter weights, ¼- to ⅜-ounce baits, when fishing in water less than 4 feet."

Curry casts spinnerbaits with baitcasting gear using 20-pound-test line. The size of the line doesn't make much difference to fish at night, he says, and the heavier lines don't require retying as much. And you don't have to worry about breaking it in heavy cover. He uses lighter line when he switches to lighter spinnerbaits.

He prefers brown, black, or purple hair jigs from $\frac{3}{16}$ to $\frac{3}{8}$ ounce. He uses 10-pound test on a medium-action spinning rod for better casting and feel.

"I crawl a jig across the bottom, but my technique varies if the bottom is flat or steep. If the bottom is relatively flat, I let it hit bottom, pick it up, slow-wind it, and reduce the speed so it goes back to the bottom. On steeper structure, I let it hit bottom, pick it up, and let it drop while holding a tightline as it falls."

Fishing topwater early and late, Curry says he's really partial to a Zara Spook. "I work it fairly fast. A Red Fin works well, too. I let it sit for a moment then twitch it about five times and start a medium retrieve so the bait makes a V on top of the water. I look real close to see if a fish is following it. If a fish is short-striking or following, I speed up the retrieve, or stop and twitch it, and when I start winding it in, they strike."

Like most nighttime anglers. Curry's boat is rigged with black lights. He doesn't use them when fishing in 10 feet of water or less. "I'll turn them on if we are over 15 feet of water casting into 5 feet. I don't think it makes that much difference. As long as the fish have access to deep water, I don't mind using a black light."

The larger smallmouth bass seem to relate to underwater humps and underwater islands. Because of the traffic on Watts Bar, especially during tournaments, the typical points get fished 10 or more times a night. Curry says they try to find places that no one fishes.

In conclusion he says, "Your best shot at a big smallie will be the underwater islands where there are drop-offs, shallow structure from 7 to 15 feet deep that drops to 25 or 35 feet. The tops of submerged islands are good spots if they have stumps or rocks."

Summer

"The smallmouth are going to be deep, except early and late in the day and at night," says James Blair. "You'll catch them 25 to 30 feet deep in summer in the same places they were in the winter. You just need to speed up your presentation.

"I use $\frac{1}{8}$- and $\frac{1}{4}$-ounce jigs with the smoke and silver glitter or clear and silver glitter grub. I use the $\frac{1}{8}$-ounce jig down to 15 feet and the $\frac{1}{4}$-ounce deeper than that. I'll use 6-pound test for the $\frac{1}{8}$-ounce jig and 8-pound test for the $\frac{1}{4}$-ounce jig. When I've got a lot of line out, the 8-pound test has less stretch and gives me a better hook-set," he says.

Night fishing is the best way to catch them in the summer. "You've got to find out how deep they are to start with," says Blair. "I start fishing shallow, about 8 feet deep, and fish out to about 25 feet of water until I find where they are. About all the smallmouth will be at the same depth. There have been nights that the fish were at 22 feet, and if you didn't put your bait at that depth, you didn't catch any." Blair uses a black light and fluorescent line to detect the hits when he's night fishing.

The areas near Lowe Branch, Piney River, Wann Creek, White Creek, and Cane Creek are some of the best smallie areas on the lake. Blair says, "The area from the dam up the lake about 20 to 25 miles has the best smallmouth fishing in the lake."

Fall
"I love it when smallmouth get in the jumps during the last of October," says James Blair. "That's when they chase those shad an inch or two long. I use a small, 2-inch crappie Twister grub in clear and silver glitter or smoke and glitter. I let the grub fall about 10 feet before I ever move it. If the fish are in there feeding on the shad they've killed, they will knock the fire out of the grub. A Sidewinder spoon will work, too. I just let it flutter down."

In the fall the shad begin moving into the creeks. "During the day the shad will be about 30 or 40 feet deep at the mouths of creeks. You can find the shad with your graph. You can drop a spoon in them and catch smallmouth that way. I like the ⅛- and ¼-ounce Sidewinder. I want to match my spoon to the shad, in size and color, as close as I can. Late in the day the shad will come up and surface in the mouths of the creeks. That's when the grub works best."

Blair also night fishes in the fall using the same techniques he uses in the summer. The fish will usually be between 8 and 15 feet deep.

CRAPPIE
Watts Bar should make a crappie angler jump up and down with excitement. The latest data from the TWRA ranks Watts Bar among Tennessee's best lakes for angler catch-rate of white crappie.

Winter
Sherrill Smith from Oak Ridge guides for crappie on Watts Bar in a unique way. "I troll," he says. "That's the only way I fish for crappie. Sometimes I'll cast to a stump early in the spring, but in the wintertime, I troll.

"I get started fishing about the first of November when the crappie start schooling in deep water—about 17 feet deep. They hang close to the bottom, and you can identify them on your depth finder because there will be four or five together."

Smith uses a MinnKota Autopilot trolling motor and sets out three rods for each person in the boat. "We use my equipment because I have a way to cover a lot of water. I put out two 12-foot graphite poles, one in the front and one in the back, two 8-foot poles in the middle, and two 4-foot rods, one in the front and one in the back. We cover about 27 feet with one troll."

Smith prefers the graphite poles with glass guides because the wire guides create too much resistance for his line to slide through easily in cold weather. Four-pound test is his choice because it is thin and offers less resistance in the water, and his line doesn't bow as much as it would with thicker line. He says it's important that the grub be nearly vertical under the pole so that he can judge the depth it runs more accurately.

"I use almost exclusively ⅛-ounce leadheads. Sometimes I paint them and sometimes I don't. I don't think it makes much difference if the leadhead is painted or not. I use 2-inch Kalin grubs called Triple Threat. A grub has three colors. These Kalin grubs are made of a very soft plastic and are one of the best products I've ever used."

Smith selects grubs according to the amount of sunlight. In clear water on a bright day, he likes to use a dark color. On a cloudy day, he puts on a brighter color.

"I take tuffie minnows, too," he says. "There are times when I'll tip a grub with a minnow. It just depends on how well they are biting. If they're biting well, I go strictly with the grub. If the fishing is a little slow, I'll entice them with a tuffie minnow."

Smith trolls slowly. "If the water is cold, you've got to go really slow because those crappie are not going to come fast for your bait. If the water is warm, which it is in November, I go a little faster.

"I fish about 17 feet of water. When I make a troll, at the end I make a slow turn and come back over the same area," he says. "There is no cover, just a smooth clean bottom. I'll have the same leadheads on for the whole season. I may give a grub to a big rockfish but we don't lose them to stumps. You'll catch a variety of fish but mostly good-size, healthy crappie."

"I don't care how cold it is if there is no wind and you've got a cold, gray day. Those are the best conditions for crappie."

Smith fishes above Thief Neck Island in the Tennessee River arm. Riley Creek and Stamp Creek are two of his wintertime hot spots.

Spring

Smith uses his trolling method until about the middle of April when the crappie start going on bed. "I'll cast to some tree tops but mostly I'll troll in shallower water, about 8 feet deep. When I troll in shallow water, I switch to ¹⁄₁₆-ounce leadheads. I use the same 2-inch grubs. I'm catching the prespawn and spawning crappie."

He pours his own leadheads but uses a No. 1 hook for his ¹⁄₁₆- and ⅛-ounce jigs. "A lot of people use smaller hooks with their ¹⁄₁₆-ounce leadheads, but if you look at a crappie's mouth, you'll see he can get a lot in there. I have the best results from a Mustad No. 1F."

Sherrill Smith uses rod holders on both sides of his boat while trolling for crappie. He uses rods of different lengths to thoroughly cover a wide swath and keeps an assortment of colors to please the crappie.

Summer and Fall

"I don't fish for crappie much in the summer any more," says Smith. "I used to tie a 1½-ounce egg sinker about 3 feet up my line, then end with a plain hook and tuffie minnow. I'd fish between 18 and 25 feet deep on bluffs. I'd just drift around using my trolling motor, moving that heavy sinker up and down really slow. I wouldn't hit the bottom; I'd work it between 18 and 25 feet. When a crappie grabbed it, my rod stopped, I saw a little bend in it, and there he was."

He moves down-lake in the summer to fish the Blue Springs area. "Hog Back Ridge Cove and Whites Creek are where I fish in summer. If you fish during the week, you nearly have the lake to yourself. But on weekends, just forget it! It's loaded with water-skiers and so many people that it's hard to fish," he says.

"Don't overlook summer nighttime fishing. It's a good way to catch them when the traffic is less. Anglers fish under lanterns, along the channel, at points, bluffs, creek mouths, creek channels, and brush piles. They run 20 feet deep or shallower."

In the fall, crappie move back into the shallows, but not as shallow as they did in the spring. Look for them between 4 and 7 feet near their spawning areas. As the water temperature drops, the crappie ease back to run the channels.

"I start back trolling for crappie in the fall," says Smith. "You can see the number of fish you catch go up each week, until about the middle of November, when you can catch all you want."

CHAPTER 19

Melton Hill Lake

A Small Lake with Big Fish

Melton Hill's Bull Run Steam Plant is hot with wintertime activity because of its hot-water discharge. The warmer water attracts shad and their predators.

Dave Bishop, retired from TWRA, says, "Most guides don't fish much around the steam plants because these places are so widely known. There are a lot of people fishing from the banks, and they catch a lot of stripers." You can't launch your boat at Bull Run, but boaters can launch upstream and downstream.

Bull Run and Kingston Plants (on Watts Bar Lake) have a floating PVC line across the channel to prevent boats from going very far up the canals.

Bull Run's hot spot gets a lot of fishing pressure in winter. Bishop adds this caution: "We don't stock Melton Hill with striper. Some drift out of the Eagle Bend Fish Hatchery and others probably lock through from Watts Bar, where there is an advisory against eating stripers. There's a good chance there are some Watts Bar fish in there, and I would be reluctant to eat the Bull Run fish."

But stripers and hybrids aren't the only fish in this lake. The previous state-record northern pike was taken from Melton Hill, and Kevin Kloes caught the current state-record saugeye here in 1994. That saugeye weighed 10 pounds 0.4 ounces. David Lyons's yellow perch from Melton Hill tied the state record in 1996 at 1 pound 15 ounces.

This narrow, riverine lake is scenic and offers anglers good drift-fishing conditions. The interview with Sherrill Smith in

GAME FISH RATINGS

Striper	🐟 🐟 🐟 🐟
Hybrid (Cherokee Bass)	🐟 🐟 🐟
Sauger	🐟 🐟 🐟

the Watts Bar chapter tells you how he fishes for crappie on Melton Hill, also. In the sauger section of this chapter, he tells us how he fishes for sauger in this lake.

STRIPER AND HYBRID
Winter

Thermal pollution is the salvation of the cold-sensitive shad. When cold water weakens shad, a certain bacterium gets a grip on the baitfish, killing them by the zillions.

Predators enjoy a free lunch when this happens, but it is short-lived. Where shad concentrate and stay alive is better for the predator. The place on Melton Hill Lake where they concentrate is in the warm waters below the Bull Run Steam Plant.

Cold water makes the baitfish look for warm water and the steam plants provide it. This sets off the chain reaction beginning in January. The baitfish arrive after December puts a hard chill in the water, the predators follow their food, and the fishermen follow the fun.

MELTON HILL AT A GLANCE

Location:	Anderson, Knox, Loudon, and Roane Counties
Size:	5,720 acres
Length:	44 miles
Shoreline:	144 miles
Summer pool:	1,779 feet
Winter pool:	1,690 feet
Impounded:	1963
Featured species:	Striper, Hybrid (Cherokee Bass), Sauger
Other species:	Muskellunge, Bream, Stripe (White Bass), Largemouth Bass, Smallmouth Bass, Northern Pike, Catfish, Crappie
Description:	Melton Hill is a serpentine, run-of-the-river reservoir on the Clinch River. It has several small and large islands.
Main tributaries:	Clinch River, Hope Creek, Hickory Creek, Scarboro Creek, Sinking Creek, Beaver Creek, Bullrun Creek, Hinds Creek, Clear Creek
Landmarks:	Melton Hill is just west of Knoxville, north of I-40, east of Oak Ridge and Clinton, and south of I-75 near Lake City. Access points are below Norris Lake Dam, in Clinton, Oak Ridge, and Melton Hill Park, and at Melton Hill Dam.
Operated by:	Tennessee Valley Authority

See Appendix C for map information

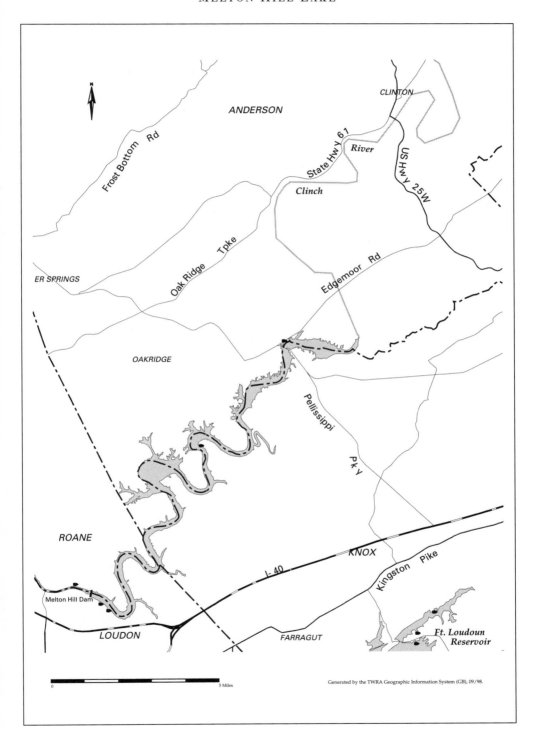

ANDERSON

CLINTON

Frost Bottom Rd

State Hwy 61

River

US Hwy 25W

Clinch

ER SPRINGS

Oak Ridge Tpke

Edgemoor Rd

OAKRIDGE

Pellissippi

Pky

ROANE

KNOX

I-40

Kingston Pike

Melton Hill Dam

LOUDON

FARRAGUT

Ft. Loudoun
Reservoir

0   5 Miles

Generated by the TWRA Geographic Information System (GB), 09/98.

Guide Roy Foster says freelining large skipjacks is the key to catching big stripers below Melton Hill Dam.

The most often used technique is large skipjacks, 17 to 20 inches long, cast on 7- or 8-foot rods and fished on the bottom or drifted. Other favorite baits are ½- and ¾-ounce Crippled Herring spoons and ½-ounce white bucktail jigs.

Stripers were introduced into Tennessee's waters for several reasons, but the foremost motive was to curtail the booming shad populations. Biologists also saw the opportunity to produce fish on a grand scale that were much larger than our indigenous species.

Freshwater stripers grow to over 60 pounds in Tennessee, as Gary Helms proved on February 13, 1988, when he landed a 60-pound, 8-ounce striper in Melton Hill Lake. This former state-record fish was caught on a skipjack nearly 2 feet long. Live bait, such as skipjacks, shad, shiners, and minnows, is most effective in winter, outperforming artificial baits significantly.

Many avid striper anglers claim small baits often work better after the water temperature falls into the lower 50s. You can catch 20-pound stripers on crappie minnows. When stripers move into warm water, they become more competitive, and no baitfish is safe. But if you are strictly a trophy hunter, skipjacks are for you.

Because the discharge areas around Bull Run Steam Plant are usually congested, you are often restricted to downlining bait rather than casting or flatlining. Also, the cold stripers are looking for a warm spot around the fire, and you have to be there early to get close to the hot spots.

Roy Foster of Nashville has been guiding for 30 years and recommends fishing below Melton Hill Dam for stripers. "I learned a big-fish technique while fishing below Melton Hill Dam. It's all bank fishing there. Anglers call TVA to find out when they are going to quit generating. They catch some skipjacks, go down the river about ½ mile from the dam and free-swim the bait on a 9/0 hook after the generation ends."

That's a big hook, but when your bait weighs 2 pounds, you need a big one. Think about the size of the striper that's going to hit that huge skipjack.

You have to hook the bait in front of the dorsal fin and "get a big bite of meat," as Foster puts it. "Free-swim the skipjack—let out as much as 200 feet of line. The bait will swim upstream, downstream, come into the bank, and go out into the channel. You just have to keep your eye on the bait and watch the slack in your line.

"When a striper gets around your bait, the skipjack goes crazy. It'll come to the top, jump, and do every thing it can to get away from that big fish. You know when you're fixing to get a hit. Once the striper hits your bait, don't let the fish run far. The striper will take the skipjack head first." Your hook is only 3 inches back from the head.

Live bait, such as shad, shiners, and minnows, is most effective in winter. Putting a shad on a hook is simple. Put the point inside the shad's mouth, up through the palate, and come out the nostril. Twist your hook a little to help it slide through the cartilage. Shiners and minnows are hooked through the chin and out the nose area, being careful not to hit the brain cavity.

Do not put your bait deeper than the stripers. They will not go down to get your bait but they will come up. If you're marking fish at 35 feet, fish between 30 and 32 feet.

Foster says, "Stripers will hit a small jig during the winter. Drop a jig 12 to 14 feet deep, place your rod in a holder, and let the rocking of the boat move the jig. Stay with the baitfish by watching your depth finder and controlling the boat with your trolling motor. Keep an eye on your rod, or when you look back for it, it may be gone!

"Hybrids won't hit a big bait in winter, although stripers may. You can catch stripers on big baits if you're in the right place. Big shad and skipjacks concentrate around the steam plants and that's where you can use a big bait," says Foster.

SAUGER

This is one of the easiest fish to fillet because of its rounded, torpedo-shape body, which goes right along with being one of the best tasting fish in Tennessee. The sauger belongs to the perch family. It looks much like its cousin, the walleye, but you have to use your imagination to see the resemblance to its other cousin, the yellow perch. All of these perches prefer cool water.

The sauger hybridizes naturally with the walleye to create the saugeye. The saugeye is also produced in large quantities in hatcheries so enough fry can be used for stocking. Melton Hill has the sauger and the saugeye.

Sauger have spots on their dorsal fins but walleye do not. The saugeye has more rounded spots on its dorsal fins than the sauger, and the blotches on its sides are fainter than those on sauger. Only the walleye has a white corner on the lower lobe of its tail. Sauger live about 12 years and walleye may live twice that long.

Winter

"I fish below five dams in this part of the state," says Sherrill Smith, "and I use the same technique each place because it works. I like to fish running water because I drift. When I get to the end of my drift, I crank up and run back upstream to make another drift. I'll drift ½ to ¾ of a mile. I have three or four places that usually hold fish. If I drift a few times without a hit, I move to another spot. Normally, I find fish in one of those places."

"Melton Hill is a shallow lake. It fluctuates about 3 feet and can fluctuate on a daily basis. But it doesn't have the fall drawdown like other lakes," says Smith.

He fishes the river where the bottom is sandy and smooth. "If I fished a rugged bottom, I'd stay hung up all day. Sauger like the sandy bottom in winter because they're getting ready to school up. They're usually about 15 to 17 feet deep. I've caught them deeper but normally they are in the 15- to 17-foot range."

He uses a 5½-foot baitcasting rod and a reel with 8-pound test. The smaller line creates less resistance in the water and allows more control over the bait's position. If there is a good deal of current, Smith increases the weight of the leadhead. He prefers a ½-ounce leadhead with a 4/0 Mustad wire hook. The hook bends when pulled off a snag, rather than breaking the line, and does less damage to the minnow. He goes prepared with leadheads up to 1½ ounces for swift water, but the ideal current is when it gives his boat the equivalent of a slow troll.

"Sauger like a bright color for some reason," says Smith. "They go for chartreuse, bright pinks, and reds, but sometimes they prefer blue or a darker color. I use Kalin's 3-inch Triple Threat Grub.

"I tip the jig with a minnow and then tie my stinger hook on. I use a No. 8 treble hook. I put the minnow on first, then tie my stinger line to the jig hook because the monofilament holds the minnow up. I don't know the name of the knot I use to tie the stinger hook, but I can loosen it with my teeth and slide it off to put the minnow on. The jig hook goes through the minnow's lip and the stinger hook is left loose, not put in the minnow.

"The line for the stinger hook is only about 2 inches or less. I keep it short because when you jig up and down, a longer line will let the stinger hook foul on your main line. When the action is slow, I'll put a minnow in the stinger hook. That usually gets me some action, and I like to use big minnows.

"Five-inch grubs work better in swift water," he says. "It must give them a bigger target so they can see it better, but for whatever reason, that's what catches them in fast water."

Smith says the sauger usually hits when your jig and minnow are on the way up. "A lot of times the jig hits the bottom and you don't know you've got a fish on. You lift and your rod feels heavy. You've got to lift your rod

straight up and keep pressure on
the fish. Chances are you don't have
the time or leverage to set the hook.
The fish is there and you've got to
start reeling it in with your rod tip
held high. The sauger has a bony
mouth and many times your hook
will just be hanging on a tooth. You
don't usually feel a hit; you just feel
the weight."

Smith says to lift your rod tip
about 2 feet when jigging and do it
slowly. "I put my rod tip about 3
inches from the water when the jig
hits the bottom. This gives
me more leverage than if I
had the tip parallel to the
water."

Smith watches two things
when he's drifting: his Lowrance LCD and his rod tip.

Smith concludes by say-
ing, "The sauger population
seems strong because more
bass anglers are catching
them casting crankbaits than they
have in a long time. I believe the
sauger numbers are better than they
have been in years."

*Sherrill Smith drift-
fishes, vertically jigging
large leadheads down the
Clinch River. He places
his stinger hook after the
minnow to keep the
stinger from fouling.*

CHAPTER 20

Fort Loudoun and Tellico Lakes

One Canal, Two Reservoirs, and Miles of Top-Notch Fishing

One of most memorable smallmouth trips that angler Doug Plemons has had on either Ft. Loudoun or Tellico Lakes actually occurred in the canal that joins these two long, run-of-the-river impoundments. An isolated rock pile surrendered two smallies to him in the 4- to 5-pound range, thanks to current in the canal that swept his crankbait into an ambush zone.

Landing smallmouth of that size was by itself an accomplishment, but catching them as he did—at the same time with one fish on each treble hook— made this trip unforgettable. While certainly a day to remember, it was only one of many for Plemons that has ended successfully.

Smallmouth inhabit both reservoirs—and are ballyhooed for their chunkiness—but it is largemouth that attract the majority of bass anglers to this area of Tennessee. Plemons himself fishes more often for largemouth, but at certain times of the year can't predict which fish will strike next.

Longtime fisherman Bill Crox is almost positive each time he sets his hook which fish has grabbed his jig. Crox is a seasonal, sauger angler who rates the water below Ft. Loudoun Dam as good as any he has fished—perhaps the best. White bass are also among the abundant species below Tellico Dam and are especially active in winter. Sometimes they are surprisingly big.

Largemouth, smallmouth, sauger, and white bass are discussed in this chapter, but numerous catfish and bluegill also inhabit Tellico and Loudoun. So do black and white crappie. Many techniques are discussed in other chapters that should help catch whichever fish is desired.

GAME FISH RATINGS

Largemouth Bass	🐟 🐟 🐟 🐟
Smallmouth Bass	🐟 🐟 🐟
Sauger	🐟 🐟 🐟 🐟
Stripe (White Bass)	🐟 🐟 🐟

LARGEMOUTH AND SMALLMOUTH BASS

Kingston resident Doug Plemons bass fishes about 100 days a year, but probably spends parts of the other 265 days either discussing bass, ordering homemade lures, or even helping make a few plugs. Plemons throws an assortment of artificial baits on Ft. Loudoun and Tellico but admits that he is best-known by friends as a crankbait angler. "A lot of people think that fishing a crankbait means just tying in on the line, throwing it out, and reeling it in," says Plemons. "There's much more to it than that."

Many techniques that Plemons uses on Loudoun—his favorite of the two lakes—also work in Tellico. A difference between the reservoirs is that Tellico, formed by the Little Tennessee River, has clearer water than Ft. Loudoun, which is formed by the larger Tennessee River.

Clearer water usually requires anglers to fish deeper. Water temperature also varies between the lakes, which is especially important during spawning seasons. Anglers should always check water temperature to help determine the stage of bass activity.

FORT LOUDOUN AT A GLANCE

Location:	Loudoun, Knox, and Blount Counties
Size:	14,600 acres
Length:	55 miles
Shoreline:	360 miles
Summer pool:	815 feet
Winter pool:	807 feet
Impounded:	1953
Featured species:	Largemouth Bass, Smallmouth Bass, Sauger, Stripe (White Bass)
Other species:	Bluegill and Catfish
Description:	A run-of-the-river reservoir. The upper segment flows through Knoxville. The lake widens as it winds toward Ft. Loudoun Dam near Lenoir City. Creeks, gravel points, and numerous coves and pockets are present. Rock banks and bluffs are common. A canal connects Ft. Loudoun Lake with Tellico Lake.
Main tributaries:	Tennessee River, Fourth Creek, Knob Creek, Little River, Lackey Creek, Sinking Creek, Little Turkey Creek
Landmarks:	Closest cities include Knoxville, Maryville, and Lenoir City. Nearby routes include TN 33, TN 115, TN 333, TN 332, and TN 444. The closest interstates are I-40 and I-75.
Operated by:	Tennessee Valley Authority

See Appendix C for map information

Winter

Although a crankbait expert, Plemons realizes that winter fish are sluggish and thus selects a lure he can work slowly—"right in their face." He is among numerous anglers all across Tennessee who catch winter bass with pig and jig combinations. "I fish the main river channel," he says. "I catch quite a few bass in the area where bluffs taper to a point. A lot of times, bass suspend around ledges where rocks stair-step to the bottom."

Plemons's favorite winter colors are black and brown. "Black works good by itself and so does brown, but I like to mix them to create contrast," he says. "It doesn't matter which color I choose for the jig or for the trailer, as

TELLICO AT A GLANCE

Location:	Loudoun, Blount, and Monroe Counties
Size:	15,860 acres
Length:	33 miles
Shoreline:	373 miles
Summer pool:	Not available
Winter pool:	Not available
Impounded:	1980
Featured species:	Largemouth Bass, Smallmouth Bass, Sauger, Stripe (White Bass)
Other species:	Bluegill and Catfish
Description:	The headwaters are below Chilhowee Dam in Cherokee National Forest. The reservoir widens as it flows north. Tellico River contributes long creeks before its confluence with the Little Tennessee River. Coves and pockets are numerous. Rock banks and bluffs are common. Standing trees and submerged cover are also common. A canal connects Tellico Lake with Ft. Loudoun Lake.
Main tributaries:	Little Tennessee River, Mulberry Creek, Citico Creek, Little Toqua Creek, Ninemile Creek, Ballplay Creek, Notchy Creek, Corntassel Branch, Fourmile Creek, Tellico River, Island Creek, Baker Creek, Bat Creek, Fork Creek, Sinking Creek
Landmarks:	Tellico Dam is near Lenoir City. The lake's headwaters begin below Chilhowee Dam in the Cherokee National Forest. Nearby routes include TN 115, TN 72, TN 33, and TN 444. The closest interstates are I-40 and I-75.
Operated by:	Tennessee Valley Authority

See Appendix C for map information

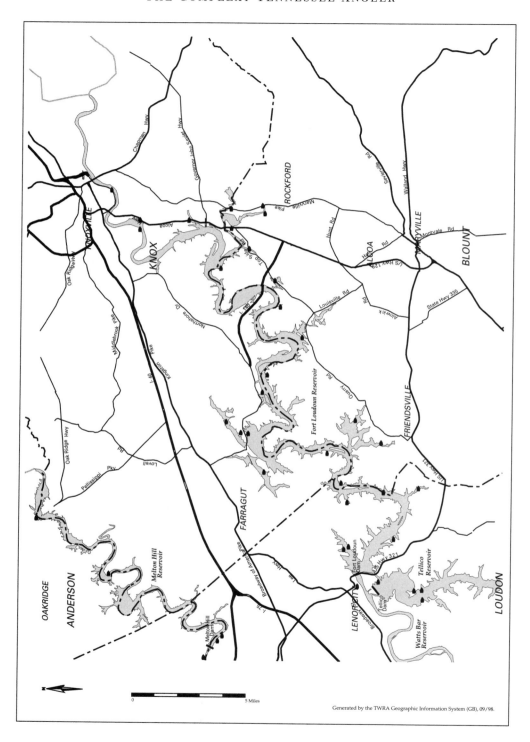

Generated by the TWRA Geographic Information System (GB), 09/98.

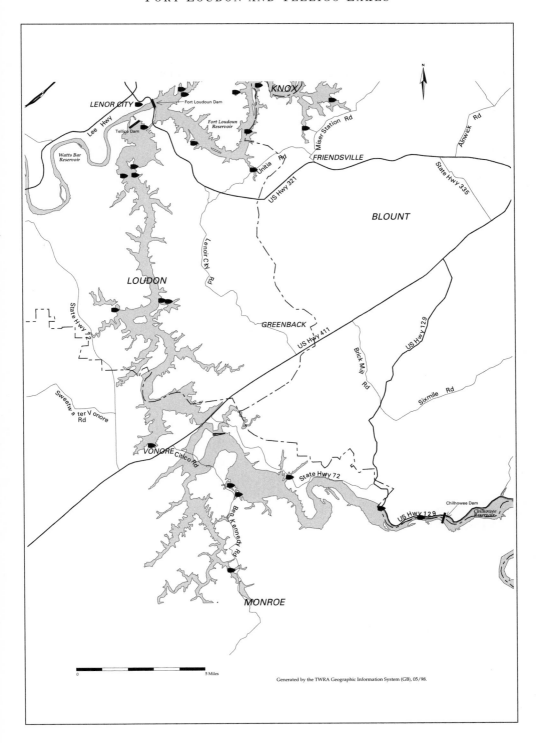

KNOX

LENOR CITY
Fort Loudoun Dam
Lee Hwy
Tellico Dam
Fort Loudoun Reservoir
Miser Station Rd
FRIENDSVILLE
Alnwick Rd

Watts Bar Reservoir
Unitia Rd
US Hwy 321
State Hwy 335

BLOUNT

LOUDON
Lenor City Rd

State Hwy 72

GREENBACK
US Hwy 411
Brick Mill Rd
US Hwy 129

Sweetwater Vonore Rd
Sixmile Rd

VONORE
Citico Rd

State Hwy 72
US Hwy 129
Chilhowee Dam
Chilhowee Reservoir

Ben Kennedy Rd

MONROE

0   5 Miles

Generated by the TWRA Geographic Information System (GB), 05/98.

Anglers who learn which baits to throw (and when to throw them) will learn that bass strike year-round. To get started, try slowly rolling spinnerbaits in cool water.

long as one of them is black and the other is brown. Some fishermen also include blue in the mix."

Plemons tosses ⅜- to ½-ounce jigs on baitcasting gear, depending on water depth and wind. He suggests throwing a hair fly and small pork rind for smallmouth and extremely sluggish largemouth. Downsize a fly and rind to ⅛ or ¼ ounce. "A lot of guys throw a fly and rind on straight bluffs," he notes. "Black, and combinations of blue and black, and black and brown are good." January has historically been Plemons's slowest winter month, whereas December has been fair, and February has provided the best cold-weather fishing. East Tennessee occasionally gets back-to-back warm days in February, which quickens the metabolism in fish and triggers a temporary movement to shallow water.

"When the water temperature changes, even as much as 2°, it kicks them into a search mode," says Plemons. "If we get consecutive warm days in late winter, bass move from the river channel into creek channels and shallower structure. One February, we had three consecutive days with temperatures in the mid-60s, and I went into a creek and caught three largemouth in the 6- and 7-pound class from brush only a few feet deep."

Plemons searches for stained water, which is why he primarily fishes Loudoun. He continues using black and brown jig and pig combinations, even when casting or flipping in shallow water. "Most bass caught during the dead of winter are caught on either a jig and pig or a fly and rind," says Plemons.

Spring

When water temperature warms to the high 40s or low 50s—usually by late winter or early spring—Plemons tosses suspending jerkbaits. "A lot of people think that jerkbaits are for topwater use only," he says. "But I like a suspending jerkbait because it imitates a sluggish minnow. It's animated and slow, and a lot of times fish can't resist it."

Plemons often throws a Suspending Rattlin' Pro Rogue, or a Suspending Husky Jerk. "Sometimes I add lead strips or lead dots to a jerkbait to make it suspend to my liking," notes Plemons. "I look for what the fish want, and then if necessary, I customize my lure."

His favorite Rogue and Husky colors include silver with a blue or a black back, and gold with an orange belly. "Largemouth and smallmouth hit suspending jerkbaits," he says. "Smallmouth sometimes nearly tear the rod out of my hands."

Suspending jerkbaits work best in clear water. "The clearer the water, the better a suspending lure works," says Plemons, who throws jerkbaits around bluffs in the main river channel and in "the first couple of gravel points going back in a creek."

Shallow-running crankbaits also catch fish when water temperature reaches the 52° to 54° range. Plemons's favorite crankbait this time of year is a Little Petey, a popular East Tennessee balsa wood lure made locally by Rockwood residents Pete and Tony Reynolds.

"I've won tournaments using the Little Petey," says Plemons. "It's a flat-sided lure that's real hard to find in local stores because it's so popular." While most anglers can't get the Little Petey, they can learn from it. "The lip on it is made from circuit board [computer board] instead of plastic," says Plemons. "I think this helps create a different frequency as it goes through water. I also think that when the lip bounces off rocks it makes a sound that better simulates moving crawfish."

Flat A Bombers or Shad Raps (a No. 7 in natural shad colors or crawdad colors or a No. 5 for finicky fish) are among manufactured lures that catch early spring bass. Plemons's favorite Little Petey colors include Lime Coach Dog, chartreuse with a lime pattern, chartreuse and khaki green, and an orangish-brown shade nicknamed "Horton" by local anglers.

Plemons searches for warm shorelines when water temperature reaches the mid- to upper 50s. He throws small crankbaits on spinning gear and 8- to 10-pound-test monofilament. He deliberately pulls his Little Petey into rocks, frequently starting and stopping his retrieve. "One degree in water temperature can make a world of difference," he says. "This is when I concentrate on rocky banks in creek channels where there has been lots of sunshine. Both Tellico and Loudoun have numerous rocky banks."

Tournament angler Doug Plemons uses a variety of baits to catch largemouth and smallmouth, but one of his favorite lures is a flat crankbait made locally.

Riprap near the dams and along shorelines—right in the backyards of homeowners—are also excellent places to catch hungry bass. "Crawdads are important to bass early in the year, and I think that when they're close to the bank this time of year, they're eating crawdads," says Plemons. "A friend of mine, James Nuckols, and I fished one bank in 1997, and in five minutes, we had a limit of five fish that weighed 26 pounds. We didn't find bass on every bank that day, but when we found this one area, we had a great time. I'm convinced the fish were eating heavily on crawdads. We caught every bass on Little Peteys."

Spinnerbaits are also good this time of year, especially for largemouth "around wood cover right on the bottom," says Plemons. Chartreuse or chartreuse and white are good spinnerbait colors in stained or clear water. "Slow-rolling the bait is very effective when the water is cool," he adds.

Many largemouth move shallow when water temperature reaches the low 60s, usually by early to mid-April. "They're getting close to spawning time and they really feed up," he says. Smallmouth are often caught on flats this time of year, or on gravel or rocky points. Rat-L-Traps and small plastic baits fished on light leadhead jigs are among lures that catch many smallmouth, says Plemons.

When fishing for shallow prespawn largemouth, Plemons throws floating worms or other soft, weightless, topwater lures. His favorite floating worm colors are white, yellow, and bubblegum. "I usually throw Trick Worms until late April or early May," he notes.

Plastic lizards, fished on a Carolina or Texas rig, are also among popular artificial baits that catch prespawn and bedding largemouth. Six-inch lizards in watermelon and pumpkin colors are as good as any lizard Plemons tosses.

Topwater action continues after the spawn, but Plemons begins using hard plastic that he can "walk" and "spit." Creeks with shallow structure and with secondary points are among his favorite postspawn largemouth areas. "This is the time of year when topwater lures are awesome," he says. "Fish are hungry after the spawn, and I find them in lots of places."

Pop-Rs and Zara Spooks are among Plemons's favorite lures. "These baits are good because they stay in a strike zone a long time when worked correctly," he says. "I walk the dog with them, moving them left and right as I retrieve. I also make them spit water to create commotion."

Plemons's favorite Spook color has a red and white body, while his favorite Pop-R is silver and black, with a bit of bone color after he customizes it. "Pop-Rs have a rattle in them," he explains. "I like to sand the paint off the sides of them so that they're thinner and the rattle is louder."

Topwater largemouth are usually active until at least early June in many areas. Plemons extends his topwater fun by moving up-lake as water temperature increases in lower sections. "The bass on Loudoun and Tellico pretty much do the same thing from year to year," says Plemons. "Knowing water temperature is always important to catching bass, especially in the spring."

Summer

Deep-creek or main-river drop-offs or humps become summertime hangouts for bass as water temperature rises. Plemons catches largemouth during the day with sturdy baitcasting outfits and deep-diving crankbaits or soft plastic baits fished on a Carolina rig. "Bass are usually holding 8 to 15 feet deep," he says.

Among his favorite crankbaits are Mann's 30+ and Norman's DD-22. Plemons uses 10- to 15-pound-test monofilament to get these big lures quickly into strike zones. The deeper fish suspend, the lighter the line he uses. Good lure colors include chartreuse and shad. He fishes chartreuse and other bright colors in stained water, while he uses shad or other natural colors in clear water.

"If fish are holding in the 8- to 12-foot range, I throw a DD-22," says Plemons. "If they're deeper, I usually go with the 30+. Having the right equipment helps. A lot of people can't use big crankbaits because they don't have the right rod. My favorite rod is a 7½-foot Castaway Launcher. It has strength in the butt and the midsection, but it doesn't have a real stiff tip."

Flexibility in the rod tip prevents bass from ripping lures loose, says Plemons. It also allows them to better inhale crankbaits. "That's why I don't like a flipping rod for this kind of fishing," he says.

When bass won't hit deep-diving crankbaits, vertically jigging lures often attracts strikes. "A lot of anglers here use ¾- to 1-ounce spoons or ½- to 1-ounce white flies around humps and ledges," notes Plemons.

Summer bass are also caught with plastic baits below Carolina rigs. A Ficht Fry—a French fry–type bait—and a Gambler Lizard are among Plemons's favorite plastic lures. He fishes them on a 24- to 36-inch leader below a 1-ounce sinker. Good colors include green-pumpkin, watermelon, and pumpkinseed. Plemons uses a 2/0 hook for a Ficht Fry and a 4/0 hook for a lizard.

Night fishing is also good, either on humps and drop-offs in main channels, or around points. Many anglers catch smallmouth at night around rocky or gravel points by slow-rolling "odd-colored" spinnerbaits, including purple, raspberry, or a combination of purple and chartreuse, says Plemons. Most night anglers throw a single silver No. 4 or 5 Colorado blade, he adds. These night blades usually have a pork chunk or grub trailer for added action.

Fall

As the water temperature begins falling, bass follow schooling shad into creeks. "October and November is when I like to use Rat-L-Traps and spinnerbaits," says Plemons. His favorite Rat-L-Trap color is a bright chartreuse that he can't purchase.

"This is another lure that I do some work to," explains Plemons. "I buy them, scrape the original color off, and then dip them into a chartreuse dye that's nearly blinding. This is an especially good lure for stained water. If the lake is clear, like Tellico normally is, a blue and chrome Rat-L-Trap shows up well enough that I don't need to alter a lure."

Sometimes Plemons fishes "nothing flats," which are mud flats that are often ignored. "Baitfish congregate on these flats, and the bass follow this shad migration every year," explains Plemons. Small crankbaits work great in these areas because "bass are sucking down minnows"

Black and brown, jig and pig combinations also catch hungry largemouth in fall around even the tiniest structure. "Many times the larger fish roam less and relate to structure more," says Plemons. "Flipping and pitching the jig can be extremely effective for these larger fish."

SAUGER

Veteran angler and guide Bill Crox has fished Tellico Lake since the TVA impounded it in the early 1970s, but he started fishing below Ft. Loudoun Dam in the early 1950s. "I can't name all the places I've fished in my life, but I think the sauger fishing is as good below Tellico as anywhere I've ever been," says Crox, who owns Twin Lakes Bait N Tackle, a Lenoir City store.

Fall and Winter

Sauger bite year-round, but are most vulnerable when they school in fall and winter. Spring and summer sauger anglers often troll deep-diving crankbaits in main channels. However, Crox only pursues sauger when they congregate during spawning runs. "I start fishing around October 15th," says Crox. "That's when sauger begin making their move, especially if there has been a lot of water flow. I usually quit by mid-March."

Good sauger fishing occurs from right below Ft. Loudoun Dam (the headwaters of Watts Barr Reservoir) to about 20 miles down-lake, says Crox, whose experience has helped him eliminate numerous poor holes. "Most fishermen put their boats in at the dam and work their way downriver until they find fish," he says.

Crox hits the same holes every year, most of which are well known by local anglers. All have landmarks that help with location.

Below the dam is the first good site. Crox catches fish there from mid-October to mid- or late November. Other excellent sauger holes—heading down-lake—include the old ferry site; the mouth of the Little Tennessee River; the "rock pile," which is riprap 2 miles below the dam; the "A-Frame hole," which is 1 mile farther downriver; and Staley's, an industrial plant about 3 more miles away. Crox is usually fishing around Staley's by late December or early January.

By late winter—usually mid-February to early March—big sauger

Guide Bill Crox believes sauger fishing below Ft. Loudoun Dam is as good as anywhere in America. He and son Randy have caught many limits using leadhead jigs tipped with minnows.

school near the I-75 bridge. "I catch some of my nicest fish down there," says Crox. When sauger action slows below I-75, he motors down to the "Barge Landing."

Tellico Lake anglers have their best sauger success between December and February by trolling "long-billed" lures. Most fishing occurs on the lake's upper end, says Crox, who prefers staying below Ft. Loudoun Dam. He uses a hair jig tipped with a minnow to catch hundreds of bottom-dwelling sauger, including many in excess of 15 inches.

"I'm including lots of small fish when I say this, but it's not uncommon for two people to catch 100 sauger in a day," says Crox. "Sometimes fish hit bam-bam-bam—one after another. I couldn't choose the one best month for sauger fishing here, but I could pick two of them. I have been keeping notes for many years and November and February are always the best months."

Jig colors are important. Crox always has a variety of colors with him and bases his selection on water clarity and the surrounding sky. New anglers must experiment to determine best colors. However, Crox's favorite color when it's overcast is white, while he prefers bright red when the sky is clear. "Whether it's cloudy or clear, my second-favorite color is orange," he says.

Numerous jigs catch sauger, but Crox uses a round "basketball" leadhead hair jig. Current helps him determine jig size. "Water flow is needed for sauger fishing to be any good," says Crox. "If three or four turbines are operating, I'll use a 1-ounce jig, but if only one or two are going, I'll drop to a ⅝- or ¾-ounce leadhead. If there is no generation, I don't go fishing because it's a waste of time."

Crox always tips his jig with a minnow. He hooks it underneath the eyes and through the gills. His fishing style is simple and works from October to March. "I drop my jig to the bottom and make about two cranks," says Crox. "I'm always drifting and I bounce my lure as I move. Sauger near the bottom won't chase a lure, so it has to be placed right in their face. I try to keep my jig anywhere from 4 to 12 inches off the bottom. I work it with an easy up and down motion."

A trolling motor is important because it keeps Crox in-line with his intended holes. Sonar helps him locate schooling sauger and he catches numerous fish over rock or sand. Some of his largest fish—egg-laden females—are caught in February and March over sand around the I-75 bridge. "The Tennessee River below Ft. Loudoun Dam has some of the best sauger fishing—in terms of size and number—as anywhere I've fished," says Crox.

Crox uses a short rod and light line, even when working a 1-ounce jig. "I use a 5- to 5½-foot rod and 6- to 8-pound-test monofilament on a spinning reel," he says. "A lot of times I catch fish when other people don't. I think I feel strikes better. Heavier line causes more friction in strong current, causing the line to bow. I fish as vertically as possible and I believe my reaction time to strikes is quicker with light line because it doesn't bow much."

Detecting a sauger strike often requires concentration or experience. "A lot of hits feel like a wet leaf on my line," explains Crox. "That's the best way to explain it. I'll bounce my jig and when it comes up, it just stops." Crox warns anglers, however, to always hold their rods firmly. "Sometimes a big catfish or striper grabs the jig," he explains.

STRIPE (WHITE BASS)

White bass bite year-round in Tellico and Ft. Loudoun. Plastic grubs, small crankbaits, and small spinners are among lures that anglers use to catch stripe, especially when they attack schooling shad on the surface in spring, summer, and fall.

It is in winter, however, when white bass fishing is excellent below Ft. Loudoun Dam (in the headwaters of Watts Bar Lake). Local angler Steve Nix always finds time for white bass when, he says, the fishing action is "unreal."

Ft. Loudoun and Tellico Lakes both have white bass, but one of the best times and places to catch schooling stripe is in the winter below Ft. Loudoun Dam. Small plastic grubs make ideal bait.

Winter

White bass usually begin running below the dam in December and stay active through February. Nix catches numerous, chunky stripe. "Every fish I caught in 1998 weighed at least a pound," says Nix. "I've caught more stripe in other years, but 1998 was a big-fish year."

February is Nix's favorite month. Sometimes he hangs rockfish while casting for stripe. White bass fishing is simple, although a bit dangerous. "I go right below the dam to where the swift water from the turbines meets the calm water," explains Nix. "I pull right to the edge of this and start drifting. I catch fish from where I start drifting all the way to the first buoy downriver." (Remember, always wear life jackets below dams, and never anchor over turbines.)

Nix uses light spinning gear and 4-pound-test monofilament. He normally tosses plastic grubs on ¼-ounce leadhead jigs. Sometimes he throws bucktail jigs. His favorite color is chartreuse. "As soon as my lure hits the water, I start retrieving," he says.

CHAPTER 21

Chilhowee Lake

The Hot Little-Known Lake in the Mountains

Chilhowee is a beautiful lake located on the Little Tennessee River between the Great Smoky Mountains and the Cherokee National Forest. This is a finger of a mountain lake known for largemouth bass, walleye, catfish, and trout, says Doug Peterson of TWRA. Chilhowee has four launching ramps along its northeastern shore that are usually only busy on summer weekends.

There are no guides serving the lake, but it has a few faithful anglers. It is a quiet and beautiful lake to fish.

You'll find Chilhowee to be a cold, clear lake with a few coves and creek mouths. Rainbow trout stocked by the TWRA are the anglers' favorite fish with bass coming in second. Bream, walleye, and catfish are present in good numbers, too.

Rainbows range from stocker-size to longer than 20 inches. Most anglers ply the upper end for trout and the lower end for bass. The area near the old ferry crossing in the upper end is where many anglers troll shallow-running, imitation-minnow lures. In-line spinners and small spoons work well on trout, as does live bait. Live bait and corn is more often used by bank anglers, and trolling is the preferred method for trout.

GAME FISH RATINGS

Rainbow Trout	🐟🐟🐟🐟🐟
Brown Trout	🐟🐟🐟
Largemouth Bass	🐟🐟🐟🐟
Walleye	🐟🐟

Chilhowee is also known for its trash line. The debris attracts many terrestrial insects, which fly anglers imitate and cast at the edge of the trash from summer to first frost. Streamers imitating minnows will catch rainbows looking for shad or minnows near the surface.

Largemouth bass in the 10-pound range have been caught in the warmer, lower end. Topwater baits are a good choice almost year-round because of the cool water. From July into September, spinnerbaits and live bait fished on Carolina rigs appeal to bass.

Catfish, bream, and other warm-water species prefer the lower end of the lake.

Walleye, a cool-water species, sometimes take the offerings intended for trout by trolling anglers. Live bait, spoons, and crankbaits, cast in the upper end and at the mouths of creeks, usually pay off for the serious walleye angler.

Just upstream is Calderwood Lake, a smaller version of Chilhowee. Its trout get much less fishing pressure, and it has a surprisingly good largemouth bass fishery. Although Calderwood's upper end is in North Carolina, it can be fished with a Tennessee license.

CHILHOWEE AT A GLANCE

Location:	Blount and Monroe Counties at the southeastern corner of the Great Smoky Mountains National Park
Size:	1,747 acres
Length:	10 miles
Shoreline:	Not available
Summer pool:	Not available
Winter pool:	Not available
Impounded:	Not available
Featured species:	Rainbow Trout, Brown Trout, Largemouth Bass, Walleye
Other species:	Bream and Catfish
Description:	Tapoco, a subsidiary of ALCOA, built this small, relatively shallow lake situated between two mountains. Almost a mile wide at its widest part, Chilhowee's water level fluctuates several feet with generation.
Main tributaries:	Little Tennessee River, Tabcat Creek, Abrams Creek
Landmarks:	The lake is situated south of Maryville, with access via US 129/TN 115 and Foothills Parkway.
Operated by:	Tennessee Valley Authority

See Appendix C for map information

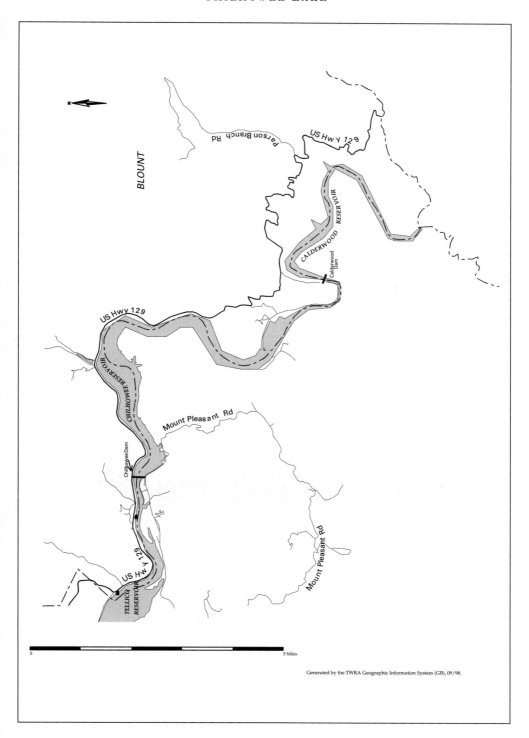

Generated by the TWRA Geographic Information System (GB), 09/98.

CHAPTER 22

Norris Lake

An Old Reservoir that Still Surprises

Other reservoirs have more stripers than Norris Lake, but few have as many that exceed 30, 40, and 50 pounds. Ezell Cox has had numerous good days fishing Norris, and a few great ones. In the winter of 1997, he caught two fish on the same day, both of which eclipsed 50 pounds. One of them is on display in Tazewell on the wall of Southern Outdoors tackle shop. It is a 58-pound, 4-ounce striper that was caught on February 12, 1997, with 17-pound-test monofilament, a well-placed gizzard shad, and the errorless fight of an experienced fisherman. It was a huge fish taken from one of the state's best big-rockfish reservoirs.

Norris is a scenic lake with both a fabled and controversial history. It is the Tennessee Valley Authority's oldest impounded reservoir. Many veteran anglers recall its youthful years when certain game fish—particularly crappie—were more abundant. Some anglers claim that voracious rockfish, stocked years ago by the state's wildlife agency, caused the decline in crappie numbers.

Other fishermen agree with the theory proposed by biologists who believe that the natural aging process of this impoundment has depleted it of vital nutrients important to the life cycles and reproduction of these fish. Regardless of the reason, Norris Lake is past its heyday; however, it is still a good lake that provides many pleasant surprises.

Walleye, largemouth, smallmouth, and big stripers are the species that attract most anglers to Norris—a

GAME FISH RATINGS

Largemouth Bass	🐟 🐟 🐟
Smallmouth Bass	🐟 🐟 🐟 🐟
Striper (Rockfish)	🐟 🐟 🐟 🐟 🐟
Walleye	🐟 🐟 🐟

deep and clear lake that at certain times requires anglers to either fish early, fish late, or fish deep. For those who learn its requirements, it's a fun place to be.

LARGEMOUTH AND SMALLMOUTH BASS

Jacksboro resident Dave Jones grew up fishing Norris Lake, becoming addicted to the bite and fight of its black bass. Nowadays, he is one of East Tennessee's most competitive tournament anglers, fishing some 260 days annually. He spends about 100 of those days on Norris Lake.

NORRIS AT A GLANCE

Location:	Campbell, Union, Anderson, Claiborne, and Grainger Counties
Size:	34,200 acres
Length:	128 miles
Shoreline:	800 miles
Summer pool:	1,780 feet
Winter pool:	1,690 feet
Impounded:	1936
Featured species:	Largemouth Bass, Smallmouth Bass, Striper (Rockfish), Walleye
Other species:	Spotted (Kentucky) Bass, Sauger, Stripe (White Bass), Crappie, Lake Trout, Muskellunge, Bluegill
Description:	This deep and sprawling reservoir has many tributaries and long hollows, and boasts a bevy of coves, pockets, and channels. The lake's maximum depth is more than 200 feet, and there are big fluctuations between summer and winter pools. Bluffs and rock, mud, and clay banks are common. Aquatic vegetation is sparse. Norris was the TVA's first impounded reservoir.
Main tributaries:	Clinch River, Big Sycamore Creek, Ball Creek, Williams Creek, Black Fox Creek, Flint Creek, Bear Creek, Straight Creek, Big Barren Creek, Dodson Creek, Hunting Creek, Poor Land Creek, White Creek, Clear Creek, Lost Creek, Mill Creek, Cuckle Creek, Big Creek, Cove Creek, Little Cove Creek, Powell River, Capps Creek, Davis Creek, Dossett Creek, Cedar Creek
Landmarks:	Norris Lake is north of Knoxville and near Clinton, Lake City, Caryville, La Follette, and Tazewell. Nearby routes include TN 32, TN 33, TN 63, TN 61, and TN 9. The closest interstate is I-75.
Operated by:	Tennessee Valley Authority

See Appendix C for map information

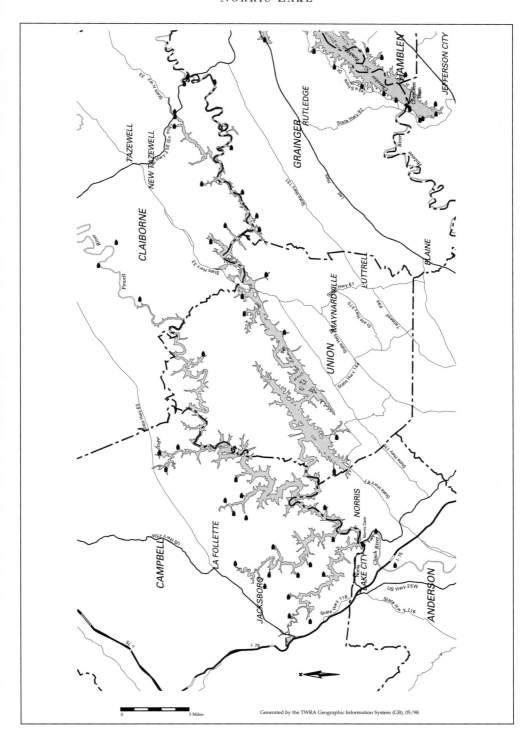

Generated by the TWRA Geographic Information System (GB), 05/98.

Tournament fisherman Dave Jones has fished Norris Lake for decades. Although this reservoir is sometimes a tough bass lake, it produces fish for those who know its secrets.

Jones catches smallmouth and largemouth from the same general locations. Because smallmouth are prone to hit smaller baits than sizes commonly thrown for largemouth, he uses medium to small lures to attract strikes from both species.

Jones is among anglers who recognize Norris as having two distinct halves—the Powell River side and the Clinch River side. He prefers the Clinch side over the Powell side because it has more submerged structure and has water color that is more conducive to bass fishing. Both sides have many bass.

Winter

Regardless of which side he fishes in winter, Jones tosses 2-inch plastic grubs in main river channels, especially where he finds color. Norris Lake is drawn down this time of year and Jones searches for drop-offs, points, or deep rock structure. "I locate most fish between 12 and 18 feet deep when the water temperature drops to about 50°," he says.

Jones maintains contact with the bottom by hopping his lure slowly across it. He threads his grub on a ¼- to ⅜-ounce leadhead jig. When water temperature falls to the mid-40s, usually between late December and mid-January, big fish hit. "I call 46° the magic number," says Jones, adding that large Norris bass are 5 to 8 pounds.

Pumpkin, green, smoke, or crawfish colors are good winter shades. Jones also throws small white grubs on ¹⁄₁₆- to ⅛-ounce leadhead jigs. He fishes light tackle on spinning gear with 6- to 8-pound-test monofilament.

When water temperature starts warming again in late winter—specifically when it reaches 52°—Jones throws crankbaits. "About two-thirds of the fish I catch from Norris hit crankbaits," notes Jones, who uses flat-sided lures that he makes himself. "I mainly fish rocky shorelines."

Many companies manufacture flat-sided lures, but Jones is among the Norris Lake anglers who make their own baits to help achieve desired action and depth. Red, shad, and a combination of yellow and green are common colors in Jones's lure collection. Anglers unable to make or obtain homemade baits should experiment with manufactured plugs.

He is a steadfast lure angler now, but Jones has caught many bass with live bait. Winter is a good time to use creek minnows or shiners on long gravel points, especially points close to channels. "I have caught a lot of smallmouth this way," he says. "If it gets too cold to catch fish on anything else, they'll always hit minnows."

Keep baitfish small—about 2 to 3 inches in length—and use a small splitshot to get live bait down. "Let it stay on the bottom for 15 to 20 minutes if necessary," says Jones. "Move it a little every now and then to attract attention."

Spring

As long as water temperature stays in the 50s, Jones throws crankbaits. As the water warms and bass move closer to shorelines before spawning, he tosses plastic grubs, small plastic worms, crawfish imitations, or 6-inch plastic lizards. Green and pumpkin are good soft-plastic colors. "Bass aren't chasing bait very much at this time, and I get away from crankbaits for a while," he explains.

Pockets or points are excellent early spring smallmouth sites. "I fish from 2 to 20 feet deep," says Jones. "I look for points that have gravel on the bottom. Norris has quite a few of these." Jones uses ½- to ¾-ounce egg sinkers above a 2-foot leader to help disturb the bottom and attract attention.

Knowing when bass go on bed is vital to catching fish. "I've watched the temperature every year," says Jones. "Smallmouth start going on bed when water temperature reaches about 55°, and largemouth start when it hits about 65°. On this lake, that means smallmouth are usually bedding in early April, and largemouth a couple of weeks later."

Jones fishes with plastic lizards and crawfish imitations after bass reach their beds. He also throws floating worms. Because Norris Lake is clear, Jones makes long casts to avoid spooking the fish. "I always throw past a bed and come back over it," says Jones, who works his worms with a tantalizing twitch.

Spinning gear and 6- to 8-pound-test monofilament is all that is necessary for soft plastic. "I fish with soft plastic until about mid-May," notes Jones. "After that, the fish move for a while to outcroppings, points, or humps 8 to 10 feet deep."

Early morning continues to provide topwater action around rocky shorelines for much of May, but once the sun gets up, the fish go down. By June, the morning and evening "bite" is much slower, and Jones goes deep for the remainder of spring and for all of summer.

Summer

Jones catches many bass with deep-diving crankbaits and small plastic grubs when fish move into their summer holding pattern. He especially favors the

Many East Tennessee anglers make their own flat crankbaits, which work well when water temperatures are cool.

Clinch River side of Norris this time of year because it has more submerged humps, islands, rocks, and other irregular features. "I catch quite a few limits of fish in summer around humps and other structure," says Jones. "Things can be pretty exciting."

Finding submerged structure is vital to catching summer bass, making sonar and topographical maps invaluable. Bass often congregate in deep, structure-filled areas and Jones usually catches several fish when he locates their hideout. "I expect to catch a limit even on a fair day," says Jones.

Mann's 20+ or 30+ are among diving crankbaits that Jones advocates for deep fishing. Chartreuse or natural shades such as shad are excellent colors. Jones tosses 3- to 4-inch twin-tailed grubs when working soft plastic instead of crankbaits. "I also throw 4-inch worms on either a Carolina or Texas rig," he says. "Sometimes I fish this vertical and sometimes I hop it across the bottom. This is pretty much how I fish until October."

Night fishing also provides steady action. Plastic worms and lizards, dark jig and pig combinations, and spinnerbaits catch many nocturnal bass around submerged structure. Jones usually throws a ¼- to ½-ounce purple spinnerbait with a single Colorado blade. He solicits many strikes by either slow-rolling it over structure or vertically bouncing it off structure like a yo-yo. "Spinnerbaits are especially effective for smallmouth at night," says Jones.

Fall

When surface temperature falls into the 50s—usually by late October—Jones pulls out his crankbaits. Largemouth and smallmouth are normally roaming the same areas. "I mainly fish rocky shorelines, just like I do in early spring," he says. "I always try to match the size of the shad that fish are eating."

Best fishing occurs in the upper third of Norris Lake, where water color is usually best for catching bass.

Jones tosses homemade crankbaits until the water temperature drops below 50°. Anglers should experiment with different manufactured lures, just as Jones and other Norris anglers tinker with homemade plugs. "The main reason I build them is to get the action that I want," says Jones. "I experiment with wobble and depth, looking for whatever triggers strikes."

STRIPER (ROCKFISH)

Tazewell resident Ezell Cox rarely has more than two species of fish in his boat at any time. If one isn't a gizzard shad and the other a striper, then some uninvited hungry fish has interfered with his trip by grabbing bait not intended for it. Few anglers are as dedicated to a single game fish as Cox, who began pursuing Norris striper in 1977 and who spends an estimated 250 days each year either fishing, scouting for fish, or catching bait.

Norris Lake is known for its large striper, which is why it is among Cox's favorite East Tennessee reservoirs. Nearby Cherokee, Watts Bar, and Boone are among lakes that have bigger rockfish populations. However, when Cox searches for trophies—as he loves to do—he heads to Norris.

A part-time guide, Cox is a "99 percent" live-bait angler. He has crankbaits stored in a small plastic tackle box for his customers or friends, but he seldom uses them. Gizzard shad is his bait of choice and helps him catch hundreds of stripers each year, including many that weigh more than 20 and 30 pounds, several that push scales past 40 pounds, and even a few 50-pound trophies.

Cox has patterned Norris Lake striper. He catches them year-round from places where experience has taught him they will be. Having the right equipment and gear, and keeping shad alive and fresh, are among the reasons why he is successful.

Cox catches gizzard shad below dams from several of East Tennessee's reservoirs using baskets designed specifically for bait catching. He also uses casting nets or dip nets below dams, creeks, or other reservoir sites where he knows that shad school shallow. "Good live bait is worth all the time needed to have the right size," says Cox. "When I'm after large stripers, I'll drive 120 miles round-trip to get shad that I know stripers will hit."

An aerated tank helps keep shad lively and fresh. Cox always keeps his storage water within 5° of the water temperature from which he catches his shad. "Their noses turn red and they lose their slime coat if I don't do this," says Cox, "They aren't near as good for bait when they lose freshness." Sonar is also vital. He says, "It's so important to catching stripers, that even with my knowledge and experience, I wouldn't go fishing without it."

Knowing where stripers are during certain times of the year and how to keep shad lively and fresh are vital to catching these wide-traveling fish. Angler Ezell Cox knows their movements as well as anyone.

Because Norris is deep and structure doesn't cause problems, Cox primarily uses 17-pound-test monofilament, which in clear water is difficult for stripers to detect. His rods are 8½-foot downrigger poles with medium to medium-light action. These long and flexible rods "absorb much of the shock of big fish," says Cox, and when worked simultaneously with properly set drags, his light line can withstand the fight of trophy-size fish.

Cox's favorite reels are Ambassedeur 6500 baitcasters, while his favorite hooks are 4/0 to 5/0 nickel-plated Gamakatsu Octopus hooks that are so sharp he doesn't have to set them. "The fish are aggressive and catch themselves," explains Cox.

A trolling motor and rod holders (Cox likes tube holders) are also necessary for his fishing style. Cox slowly trolls live bait while searching with his Lowrance 350A for schooling stripers. Sometimes he fishes shad vertically on Carolina rigs. Depending on bait size, he uses 1½- to 2-ounce Rubber Grip sinkers, which he can twist onto his line and avoid having to tie extra knots. He places the sinkers about 3 feet above his hooks.

Other times he flatlines his bait, releasing weightless line behind his boat. He often trails flatlines behind side planer boards, which swing his bait away from his vessel and widen his coverage. "Side planer boards also let me pull my bait into shallow water without spooking the fish," says Cox. Trolling motor speed helps control bait depth regardless of which technique Cox uses. His rods—usually no more than four at any time—are always positioned in holders.

Cox hooks shad through the upper lip most of the time. Fresh bait is so important to him that in the hottest months he replaces shad as often as every five minutes. How and where Cox fishes depends on the season, but except for only a few weeks, he has great results throughout the year.

Side planer boards, baitcasting reels, and strong graphite rods are among equipment that successful striper anglers use.

Winter

Rockfish inhabit both the Clinch and Powell River sides of Norris Lake. Cox fishes both halves, but primarily stays on the Clinch side because it's closest to his Tazewell home. Techniques that work well in one section are productive in the other, he notes.

In early winter—usually late November to early December—he locates large quantities of large fish in several areas between the lake's midsection to the dam. Stripers often school 30 to 40 feet deep this time of year, and Cox primarily catches them by slowly trolling what he considers small shad—"no more than 7 inches long"—on Carolina rigs.

From mid-December to early January, Cox usually trolls between Point 19 near Pilot Island up to Point 34 near Hickory Star Marina. "I'm in the main river channel, although several of the lake's major creeks come pretty close to where I'm trolling," he says. "I think shad come out of these creeks for the old river channel's warmer water. I try to locate schooling stripers first, but I look for shad if I can't find the fish. I use a cast net this time of year to catch my shad in the warmest creeks that I can find."

Fish attack bait aggressively throughout the winter unless the lake's shad are stricken by frigid water and schools suffer major die-offs. "When this happens, stripers go into coves and gorge on dying shad," Cox explains. "They become difficult to catch. This doesn't happen every year, but it does occasionally occur."

As the water begins to warm around mid-February, the diet of Norris Lake's rockfish changes. "They'll go from eating little baitfish to wanting shad as big as 20 inches long," says Cox. "This is the time of year when the stripers really start putting on weight. I catch big brood shad in Lost Creek in February and March."

Side planer boards come into use when stripers attack big winter shad. Many attacks occur near shorelines, which is why Cox slowly trolls flatlines 15 to 20 feet behind side planer boards and close to the banks in main-river or creek channels. The boards swing his weightless line near the shore as he slowly trolls.

"I use two rods with side planer boards," says Cox. "One is real close to the bank, maybe even hitting rocks, and the other one is out a few feet." Cox doesn't use them often, but Red Fins are among large crankbaits that rockfish ravage near shorelines.

Cox also releases two flatlines directly behind his boat while his planer boards comb the shoreline. He places small slip bobbers on each (some anglers prefer softball-size balloons) to help keep his bait in desired strike zones. Slip bobbers are easy to move along the line whenever he readjusts bait depth. More line behind a bobber makes bait run deeper. Cox will also raise and lower his bait by trolling in zigzag patterns.

Point 23 in Lost Creek is among the sites that provide excellent February catches for Cox, who does especially well around small springs that inject warmer water into the cold lake. As water temperature rises, Cox moves up-lake with the stripers, which are following shad toward warmer areas and moving closer to their eventual spawning sites. By the end of March, he is usually trolling around Point 28 near Bear Creek.

Spring

Big stripers keep moving up-lake as water temperature continues rising. Many fish enter Big Sycamore Creek, where they feed aggressively and where Cox adds to his angling technique. "I use the same rods and reels, but I return to Carolina rigs and fish vertically," he explains. "Big Sycamore Creek has mud flats, and when I find fish on these flats, I catch them with large shad."

Cox places 2-ounce egg sinkers 3 feet above his hooks and then drags these heavy sinkers through mud as he trolls in large circles. "I try to cover the entire mud flat, and some of them are several acres in size," says Cox. "Sinkers stir up the lake bottom and attract attention. My bait is well above the sinkers and that's what the fish see."

The Powell River side of Norris Lake has fewer mud flats than the Clinch River side, but these few make good angling sites when rockfish are on the move in early spring, says Cox. Capps Creek near Points 15 and 16 has excellent mud flats, he notes.

When water temperature reaches the mid-60s—usually around May 1 on the Clinch River side—Big Sycamore Creek turns oily and white. "I know the fish have spawned and that big stripers are ready to head back down-lake for cooler water," says Cox.

Water temperature on the Powell side warms less quickly than the Clinch side, which Cox realizes and uses to his advantage. Rockfish activity ceases for a while after the Clinch-side spawn, but stripers are gravid and hungry for several more weeks on the Powell River side.

As the fish move down-lake in the Clinch River channel and become aggressive again, they often suspend above humps and frequently break the surface to attack shad. "I fish vertically on a Carolina rig during this late-spring period, except when surface activity is good and I use flatlines and side planer boards," says Cox. Red Fins or Little Macs are among excellent artificial baits that catch breaking stripers.

Bank fishing is also good between March and June, notes Cox. Live shad, live bluegill, or cut bait catches stripers when fished on the bottom. "Bait, a 2-ounce egg sinker, and a 4/0 hook work great for bank fishing," says Cox.

Summer

As summer begins, big stripers inhabit cooler water. Between Points 19 and 24 are good sites. "I'm fishing about where I was in February and using a Carolina rig," says Cox. Summer stripers are deep, and Cox adds weight if necessary to his tightlines. He locates stripers while slowly trolling and keeping an eye on his LCR. "I keep my bait just above the schooling fish," he says.

Stripers school at various depths near shad, including around deep-suspending alewives that inhabit Norris. Cox finds many stripers suspending over points and near underwater cliffs. Occasionally, he chums an area. "I find a point and chum it with ground shad," he says. "I leave for a while after I chum and then come back to troll the point." Cox doesn't use them, but many summer rockfish anglers troll sassy shads and bucktail jigs. White, chartreuse, and pearl or gray are good colors.

As the summer gets its hottest between July and September, Cox fishes four rods vertically on Carolina rigs alongside the underwater cliffs that once stood as the Clinch River's original riverbank. Sonar is essential to finding these.

Cox often trolls near a cliff line where it drops quickly from its surface into deep water. He catches many big fish with 12- to 13-inch gizzard shad that he gets down with egg sinkers as large as 4 ounces, depending on the depth he needs to reach. "I troll right around the top of the cliff," he says. "I especially like areas where I find a layer of thermocline almost even with the cliff line."

Stripers stage near the cool thermocline layer, which Cox says isn't usually below 30 feet in midsummer. However, he also catches many fish alongside cliff walls in well-oxygenated water 30 to 45 feet deep. "I catch quite a few 40-pound stripers fishing underwater cliffs," he says.

Cox believes that cool water and good oxygen are the most important for rockfish, which is why deepwater areas around cliffs make prime summer rockfish holes. "This is the time of year when big fish really congregate because there's only so much cool water with good oxygen," says Cox, who advises summer anglers to cease fishing after they catch their limit, whether or not they keep any fish. Stress created by warm water and low oxygen is known to kill a high percentage of successfully landed fish, even after anglers release them.

Fall

Only two times exist during the year when Cox has a difficult time catching stripers. The first is immediately after they spawn; the second is the first several weeks after Norris Lake becomes cool enough for rockfish to travel widely. "Some fish may travel 30 or 40 miles in a day," says Cox. "They really scatter from about mid-September to mid-October.

"Cool nights and short days also cause the lake to homogenize by sometime in October. At this time stripers can be found at any depth and scattered over all of Norris Lake. That is what makes them so difficult to find."

Cox continues trolling the main river with gizzard shad on flatlines—two on side planer boards and two on weightless lines behind the boat. "Sometimes I run across a school, and every rod in the boat will go down, but then the fish will disappear, and I might not find them again that day," says Cox.

Some Norris anglers use downriggers in late summer or early fall to troll bucktail jigs, but Cox continues relying on shad. Bank fishing with live or cut bait is also a good way to catch stripers beginning in October until around the first of the year. Mud and clay banks in main-river or creek channels are places where Cox finds roving stripers.

As the water temperature continues to fall, stripers head to "skinny" water. "When the surface temperature is between 47° and 67°, stripers will migrate into very shallow water," explains Cox. "From mid-October to mid-November, I can find stripers in major creeks or up in the Clinch or Powell Rivers. They get into water that is only 1 or 2 feet deep and get behind rocks, stumps, or structure that breaks the current and makes good ambush areas. Shad are moving out of the cooler creeks and toward the warmer lake at this time."

WALLEYE

Lake City resident Babe Cox (no relation to Ezell Cox) began fishing Norris Lake in the 1940s. He remembers when walleye were much more plentiful than today and when he and other anglers caught them during annual spawning runs. Nowadays, most walleye are caught from the lake's main body. "Fishing isn't like it used to be when walleye spawned in the headwaters," says

Similar to the famous Flatfish, this Jet Lure is the favorite walleye bait of experienced walleye angler Babe Cox. Cox trolls Norris Reservoir starting in the late spring.

Cox. "We catch most of our fish now around rocky or sandy points that are a long way from the headwaters."

The native strain of walleye once abundant in Norris has dwindled, and Cox believes that today's walleye are mainly a northern species stocked several years ago to bolster the fallen population. This strain doesn't behave the same as native walleye, says Cox, who is among a small angling group that has adjusted to its different habits.

Cox misses the old times, but with his experience, still manages good outings every year. Anglers who duplicate his style should have good walleye trips, too. Perhaps eventually, with the help of management or more stocking efforts, Norris Lake's walleye fishing will be more like old times.

Spring and Summer

While Cox once caught walleye in March and April, he doesn't begin fishing for them until late May or early June now. He spends between 40 and 50 days each year pursuing walleye, ending his season in late August. "It's fairly hard to catch them even during their peak time, but outside of then, it's real tough," he says. Cox catches healthy fish when we he locates them. "They usually weigh from 2½ to 4½ or 5 pounds," he says. "My concern has been [in the late 1990s] that I'm not catching many young fish."

Cox uses the same angling method throughout his walleye season. He finds points and trolls slowly over them. "I especially like shallow, rocky, or sandy points," he says. "If there is a tree laying on the bottom, that makes a point even better. Fish often suspend in the ends of trees."

Numerous artificial baits catch walleye, including crankbaits and spinners designed specifically for catching them. However, Cox trolls a 2-inch Jet Lure trailed with a live night crawler. "A Jet Lure is similar to a flatfish. I've been using it for a long time," says Cox.

Cox rigs his bait presentation on a three-way swivel that keeps his lure near the lake bottom. He ties the main line to one swivel ring, a ½- to ⅜-ounce sinker (depending on fishing depth) to the bottom ring, and his lure to the top ring.

Cox ties his sinker on a 12- to 14-inch leader, while he trails his lure on a 30- to 36-inch leader. He ties a No. 2 single hook on a short leader and buries this stinger in the night crawler that is threaded on the main hook. "I bounce the sinker along the bottom," he says. "My lure runs a few feet above the sinker."

Cox only uses one rod to troll, a baitcasting outfit with 10- to 12-pound-test monofilament. Color is not a concern. "I don't think it makes any difference what color lure I use," he says. "I use yellow, orange, brown, chartreuse, pearl, and several other colors."

Walleye are caught in both the Clinch and Powell sections of Norris Lake, although Cox spends the majority of his time fishing the Powell channel. Early in his season, he often trolls 6 to 10 feet deep, but as air and water temperatures rise, he eventually trolls 18 to 28 feet down.

An exception to fishing deep in hot summer occurs where boat traffic has been heavy. "I look for places where boats have stirred up mud," explains Cox. "I'll troll 14 to 18 feet deep in these spots because walleye move shallower in dingy water. There's a lot of boat traffic on Norris, so finding muddy areas is pretty easy."

Cherokee Lake

Rated as Best Striper Lake in the State

TWRA began stocking striper in 1958. Known by many names—rockfish, striper, striped bass, and linesides—it belongs to the true bass family. The Cherokee bass, or hybrid (resulting from a cross of the female striper and the male stripe), takes its name from this lake, where it was first successfully grown, and is also a member of this family.

Other Tennessee members of this family include the white bass (stripe) and the yellow bass. All members of this family have strong schooling tendencies and feed as packs. They do not spawn in nests but drop their eggs in current without further care.

David Bishop, retired TWRA fisheries biologist in Region IV, was among the first involved with the striper stocking program in Tennessee during the early 1960s. In 1965 he suggested that Tennessee and South Carolina collaborate in crossbreeding the white bass with the striper.

He reported to the 21st Annual Conference of the Southeastern Association of Game and Fish Commissioners that three separate and successful crosses were made in 1965. Earlier experimentation proved that striper eggs and white bass sperm produced viable offspring, whereas striper sperm and white bass eggs were less successful. Subsequent back-crossing experiments (striper eggs and hybrid sperm) produced 50% deformed fry, while the other 50% appeared normal.

Bishop placed 35,000 hybrid fry in Frog Pond in April 1965, a part of Cherokee Lake that is only connected during summer

GAME FISH RATINGS

Striper	🐟 🐟 🐟 🐟 🐟
Hybrid (Cherokee Bass)	🐟 🐟 🐟
Largemouth Bass	🐟 🐟 🐟 🐟 🐟

pool. By November, a total of 5,017 hybrids up to 8 inches long were captured by seining. It was suspected, but not known at the time, that some of the fry escaped into the main lake. Proof came in February of the next year when nine hybrids weighing up to a pound were recovered in potholes several miles away.

This successful experiment paved the way for the TWRA's present hybrid stocking program. Bishop states, "The hybrid appears to have qualities superior to those of the striper. We have gotten better survival on fry and fingerling stockings and better growth in the first year or two. Many fishermen feel that the hybrid, pound for pound, will outfight the striper, but is not as good a table fish."

Ted "Yank" Kramer, a guide from Morristown, says that when fishing for Cherokee stripers, you never know when you will hang a hybrid, but as soon

CHEROKEE AT A GLANCE

Location:	Grainger, Hamblen, Hawkins, and Jefferson Counties
Size:	30,200 acres
Length:	59 miles
Shoreline:	463 miles
Summer pool:	1,002 feet
Winter pool:	920 feet
Impounded:	1941
Featured species:	Striper, Hybrid (Cherokee Bass), Largemouth Bass
Other species:	Smallmouth Bass, Crappie, Walleye, Sauger Catfish, Bluegill, Stripe (White Bass)
Description:	Cherokee suffers severe drawdown in winter. Banks are mostly rock and gravel. There are many rock bluffs and islands, and the bottom is rock, gravel, and clay. There is some development on the shoreline. The water is fertile and supports a strong forage base.
Main tributaries:	Holston River, Mossy Creek, Panther Creek, German Creek, Ray Creek, Springs Branch Creek, Spring Creek, Fall Creek, Kellar Branch, Poor Valley Creek, Cloud Creek, Stock Creek, Caney Creek, Honeycutt Creek, Dodson Creek
Landmarks:	Cherokee Dam is on TN 92 north of Jefferson Cityand US 11E. Access from Morristown via US 25E with Access north from US 11W.
Operated by:	Tennessee Valley Authority

See Appendix C for map information

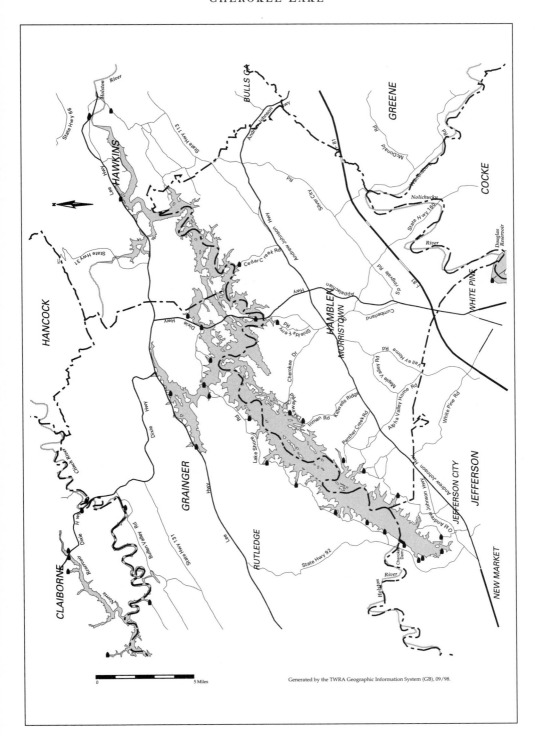

Generated by the TWRA Geographic Information System (GB), 09/98.

as you hook a hybrid you know it. It fights much harder than a striper. The hybrid doesn't quit fighting until it is exhausted.

STRIPER AND HYBRID

Often there is confusion about identifying the stripe, striper, and hybrid, especially when they are small. An experienced angler can usually look at the line patterns and quickly discern which fish he has.

The striper has a long, slender torpedo-shaped body with no back arch. Several distinct stripes extend to its tail and may be broken or unbroken. It grows to weigh over 60 pounds in Tennessee. The stripe has an arched back with only one stripe extending to its tail. Its faint lines may be broken or unbroken. The hybrid has an arched back with distinct stripes. Several lines extend to its tail and may be broken or unbroken. Generally, it has many broken lines. A quick feel of the tongue can separate the striper and hybrid from the stripe. The stripe has only one tooth patch in the center of its tongue, whereas the other two fish have two patches.

Ted "Yank" Kramer says some of the heaviest hybrids run nearly 20 pounds and stripers run nearly 45 pounds in Cherokee Lake.

"It's important to know the movements of the stripers through the seasons," says Kramer. "It's a lot easier to catch them if you know where they are. In the summer, the stripers move from around Point 27 downriver to the dam. In the fall, they begin moving back upstream. There are many schools of striper and hybrid in Cherokee, so you will find some in different places, but they will be in the same section of the lake and headed in the same direction."

Winter

"When the weather is miserable," says Kramer, "you can find the fish all the way from Rocky Hollow to Cherokee Boat Dock near Points 28 or 29. They are as thick as fleas. If you get out there early in the morning, casting a white fly or a Red Fin around the points, hold on because they are all over the place."

When he finds a school of fish with his sonar, he will drop a ¾-ounce Hopkins spoon to the bottom and lift it slowly, making the spoon flutter a little. You may want to follow his example of replacing the original hook with a larger one.

Kramer catches and releases between 300 and 400 stripers during the winter months.

Spring

"I use a 5/0 Kahle hook for large shad and fish with side planer boards. I use 17-pound test on my spool, I tie a barrel swivel to it, and then I put a 3-foot leader of 14- or 12-pound test below my swivel without any weight. I have about 15 feet of line between the hook and side planer. I attach my line to the

Yank Kramer frequently catches more than 300 stripers between November and April on Cherokee Lake. He uses a Dipsy Diver while trolling to get his jig to the proper depth. (Photo compliments of Yank Kramer.)

side planer and let about 13 feet of line. The planer acts like a float but it keeps the line away from my boat. The shad is out there swimming free. This is basically flatlining. Some guys use a float or balloon."

Kramer says he has caught a striper with a fly rod but doesn't recommend it. "I made a big mistake trying to catch one with a 6-weight fly rod outfit. The fish weighed about 7 pounds and it took me about 30 minutes to get it in." He caught it with a home-tied, feathered fly.

Springtime is a good time to fly fish for stripers and hybrids because they are shallow. Be prepared with 200 yards of backing on a good-quality fly reel and an 8- or 9-weight outfit.

Summer

"In the summer, the fish will concentrate near the dam because of the aerators," says Kramer. "In June, July, and August, there are plenty of fish there. I've caught them as deep as 90 feet, but it's a sin to catch them that deep due to the fact that when you bring them out of the water their bladders are hanging out of their mouths—those fish are dead."

He says, "There is good fishing around Black Oak Boat Dock, Mossy Creek, in front of the dam, and around some of the islands—some troll, some use live bait."

Kramer uses live shad on a downline to fish over humps. "I'll drop the rig to the bottom then raise it and drift around. You can do the same with a white fly or spoon."

In the summer, he takes his clients out to catch their limit of two stripers then goes bass fishing. The mortality is too high in the summer to release them. "First, they come out of deep water, and secondly, the water is too warm for them to survive. I have counted more than 100 dead stripers in one day. I don't like to see that."

Fall

"After summer, the fish begin to move upriver," says Kramer. "They start moving around the beginning of August and they can be found between Points 8 and 15. I keep track of their movements by keeping the data in my computer. I can track them almost to the week."

He recommends using live bait or trolling a Red Fin and Little Mac. Point 11, Point 15, German Creek, and Rocky Hollow are good spots in October.

"There's not much topwater action then; the water is too warm. In the fall migration toward the last of October, they may be anywhere from 2 feet deep against the bank to 45 feet deep. I've tried for 15 years to catch those fish when they are running shallow against the bank, but I can't get them to hit anything. I don't know what they are doing, but they won't hit anything. When I move into 17 feet of water, I can catch them on a white fly or Little Mac.

"As the water gets cooler, around Thanksgiving, that's when they come up between Points 15 and 21, and you can catch them on topwater early in the morning. You'll see 50 to 60 boats fishing for them," says Kramer.

"The biggest mistake anglers make is driving their boats right into the surfacing fish. You can tell where the surface activity is by watching where the gulls are working. But once a boat drives on top of the fish, they're down. It ruins the fishing for a lot of people. Most of the anglers leave when the action dies. I sit around for another 30 minutes until the fish come back up."

Kramer uses a 7½-foot flipping stick with 17-pound test and a 1-ounce white fly to make long casts into the breaks.

"A friend of mine freelines shad from a side planer to catch fish in the fall. You've got two ways of catching them; with live shad or trolling Bombers, Red Fins, or Little Macs. Most of the guys troll. The fishing will get better and better and better as the water gets colder."

Kramer prefers the fishing period that begins around Thanksgiving when the fish concentrate and start hitting surface lures. "They will hit anything you want to throw," he says.

"I'll tell you a trick about using 1-ounce Rat-L-Traps. I once scraped all the paint off a Trap with my knife to make a white lure. My client and I were catching fish with these white Rat-L-Traps when people in the other boats weren't catching any. Pretty soon I looked around and I saw all of them scrapping the paint off their Rat-L-Traps."

Upper Watts Bar dams are Greg Jones's "honey holes" for stripers and hybrids. *(Photo compliments of Greg Jones.)*

Kramer says to look for birds to find where the stripers and hybrids are hitting shad on the surface in the morning. The action will last until about 10 or 11 o'clock. After that, he relies on a Dipsy Diver to get his bait down.

The Dipsy Diver is about 5 inches in diameter and takes the bait to a desired depth. "The Diver has a snap where you attach your line. I let out about 30 to 40 feet of line with a 1-ounce white fly with a trailer behind the Diver. Then if I want to fish at 16 feet deep, I measure 16 feet of line between my rod and the Dipsy Diver, and I troll. If I'm reading fish on my sonar at 25 feet, then I let out 20 feet of line so my bait will be just above the fish. Stripers look up to feed, not down."

Another trolling tip Kramer offers for those who don't have a Dipsy Diver is placing a says place 1- or 2-ounce slip sinker above a large barrel swivel. If your main line is 20-pound test, he suggests tying on a 3-foot leader of 17-pound test, terminating with a white fly. The lighter-test line will break, preventing losing the entire rig to a snag. You can use a diving crankbait or other lures with this rig. This works well in the summer and fall," says Kramer.

LARGEMOUTH BASS

One of the first things you'll notice about the lake is the rolling, rocky shoreline. There is nearly 400 miles of it, and the islands alone make up over 60 miles of shoreline. Some homes along the shore have lawns that reach the water's edge.

Cherokee Lake has long running points and bluffs, as well as ledges, located next to deep water. Bass congregate on the bluffs from the US 25E bridge to Gilmore Brothers Dock and in the German Creek area. Numerous rocky islands and humps from Panther Creek to Fall Creek offer good holding places for bass. The waters near the dam are the coolest and best oxygenated during the summer and early fall.

Avid angler Jimmy Bunch from Talbott says, "It's pretty obvious that the bottom of Cherokee Lake is mostly rock, shale, gravel, and clay, but it's fertile. Fertile water is good for forage and, in turn, good for bass. That's why fishermen can haul so many bass out of here and it's still a great lake."

September is the last month of summer pool on Cherokee Lake. No matter the water level, anglers new to Cherokee Lake should use a topographic map to navigate these motor-eating, rocky waters. Threading in and out of the islands and rounding points can be very confusing, and makes another strong point for having a map of the lake.

Guide Tom Richards from Kingsport says, "There are several locations where you can launch your boat during the drawdown. If the weather is good, a lot of anglers back down the red clay banks and points to launch. There are a lot of long sloping banks that make launching easy, but I recommend using a four-wheel-drive vehicle if it rains. The ramp at the US 25E bridge is good but it makes for a long ride upstream to my hot spots. You can use the TVA Church House Landing ramp because when water is below the ramp, TVA dumps gravel and rock for a temporary ramp."

Winter

Tom Richards has fished Cherokee Lake bass, hybrid, and striper for many years. He says, "The one good thing about the deep drawdown on Cherokee is that it concentrates fish. In the upper end of the lake, above Poor Valley Creek, the shoreline is back in the old riverbed, and there are stump fields all over the place. Once you locate those stump beds, it's a largemouth bass smorgasbord.

"I flip a pig and jig hard against the stumps that stick out of the water. I want it to make a solid 'thump' sound on the wood. I let it fall down by the stump—if he's there, that'll get 'im," says Richards. He fishes this technique from mid-December into February.

"These stumps may stick out of the water a foot and extend 3 feet underwater and sometimes you can see the submerged stumps. You don't want to see the fish because they can see you then," he warns.

Richards uses a ¾- or ⅛-ounce jig with Zoom's artificial pork chunk in root beer and pumpkinseed colors. He says a lot of colors will work but those two colors have produced best for him. On dark days, he says to use a black, purple, or dark blue color. He casts a flipping stick with a baitcasting reel spooled with 10-pound test.

"I stay with the pig and jig, but if anglers want to use live bait, they certainly will catch fish. If you pitch a live shad on top of those stumps, or along the bluffs, you'll catch bass."

Spring

"The lake starts filling back up in March and April," says Richards. "I usually have a little trouble finding bass during that transitional period. When the lake stabilizes a little, I get on the bass with buzzbaits and Rat-L-Traps in the hollows, or anywhere there is shallow water that heats up during the day. Places like Rocky Hollow and Macedonia have a lot of rocks, and when they heat up, they hold a whole lot of fish."

Richards's method for locating springtime bass is finding stained, shallow water around big boulders and casting the Rat-L-Trap. "I've used many brands of lipless crankbaits, but nothing works as well as the Bill Lewis Rat-L-Trap. Topwater baits aren't as productive in the spring as they are in the fall," he adds.

Tom Richards knows the code for catching Cherokee's largemouth bass through the seasons. Soft-plastic baits should be in your tackle box for capturing Cherokee's summertime bass.

Summer

"When the water heats up in the summer, that's when I like to go worm fishing," says Tom Richards. "I catch my biggest fish in the lower end of the lake within a few miles of the dam. There are a lot of underwater humps at that end. I fish plastic worms and crawfish in about 25 feet of water along the humps. I like the cherry seed color with a chartreuse tail. I wear the fish out and I've done it for years—all summer long. Where most anglers make a mistake is by not anchoring; they move around too much. I anchor to cast worms and craws around the islands and humps.

"But early and late in the day, I fish crankbaits along the bluffs and banks. I want a crankbait that runs between 4 and 8 feet deep. My favorite places to fish are the bluffs. I cast parallel until my arm falls off. I put the trolling motor on medium or high and work those bluffs to death. I make a lot of casts but I catch a lot of fish."

One other trick Tom Richards uses to catch summertime bass is to cast a Crippled Herring spoon around bridge piers. He says, "It doesn't take long to determine if the bass are active around the columns. I cast at the leading edge and let the spoon flutter down. Then I hit the sides and then the back edge. Usually the bass hold along the columns next to the river channel."

Deepwater fishing is the order of the summer season that lasts from July into early October. When fishing deep water, your boat may be over water 50 feet deep or more. Bass hold tightly to the rocky structures of islands, points, bluff ledges, and humps, or they may suspend as deep as 30 feet. At these depths, a bass can inhale your lure without you feeling a thing. Strike detection requires that you watch your line for the telltale tick. Any tick or "heavy feeling" should signal you to sweep your rod and make the hook-set.

You'll need a medium-heavy rod and reel combination. The rod should be 6½- to 7 feet long to take up line stretch with your hook-set. FireLine or other fused lines with no-stretch qualities offer additional sensitivity and better hook-setting capabilities.

Summertime lures that entice less active bass are Texas-rigged plastic worms and crawfish on a 2/0 to 4/0 hook with a ¼- to ½-ounce bullet sinker. Natural-colored crawfish and electric-red with a chartreuse tail, red shad, and purple shad worms are prime colors.

Jigs work better on active bass. Plastic crawfish on leadheads worked along rocky areas, bluffs, and points next to deep water are productive. Some anglers have better success with hair jigs. Natural, crawfish-colored jigs (brown and orange) are good, as are purple or red jigs with the same-colored No. 11 pork rinds. Also try techniques employed by Jimmy Bunch as described in the next section.

Fall

Jimmy Bunch has been fishing Cherokee since the early 1980s. "We have a fall run of bass, both largemouth and smallmouth," he says. "Your lure selection should depend on the structure you're fishing. I love to cast a crankbait for largemouth, so I hit the sloping banks first. After all these years, I'm learning to jig fish so I can be effective on the steeper banks and rocky outcroppings.

"Occasionally I'll troll the points with crankbaits, moving as slowly as I can. That's a good way to get the gigantic smallies, but I prefer to worm fish for largemouth on points and bluffs rather than troll," he says.

"There are a lot of tournaments on Cherokee but there are plenty of places for everyone to fish. If you get on a good bank, you'll catch them. The fish are there. Just move up and down it. You can catch smaller ones closer to the bank, but the bigger ones are in 8 to 15 feet of water."

Bunch uses his sonar to locate objects on the bottom. "There are a lot of little bushes underwater. Most of them are gone because the water killed them, but as you look at the bank when the water is low, like it is in the fall, you'll see what I'm talking about. These bushes are spotty now and those are great places to fish—finding them is the hard part. Once you find them, keep fishing the area."

Most of the natural cover remaining in Cherokee is small bushes. Buttonbushes grow on the gently dropping banks and willows grow on the flats. There are stumps scattered throughout the lake. "You'll almost always find fish in them because there is so little cover in this lake," says Bunch.

He estimates there are more largemouth than smallies in Cherokee by about 3 to 1. But he is quick to add that some of the smallmouth are big, old, arm breakers. A TWRA survey of anglers indicated the average bass caught was 2.2 pounds and was 16 inches long. TWRA says that the smallmouth fishery is improving but doesn't equal the largemouth population, yet.

Crankbaits, covering depths from the surface to 15 feet, are needed to fish the variety of structures that Cherokee Lake has. Jimmy Bunch slings a wide assortment of crankbaits.

Bunch recommends fishing the upper end. "It's the best place to fish in the fall, from September through November. These are considered the best largemouth bass months," he says.

TWRA electrofishing studies show more largemouth bass are in the upper and middle portions of the lake, and this is especially true in the fall. Studies of smallmouth were inconclusive due to the small number of fish sampled, but more smallies were caught in the upper and lower portions in the fall.

"Old foundations, bridge pilings, rocky islands, and outcroppings are favored by both largemouth and smallmouth bass this time of year," Bunch says.

Various minnows, shiners, and shad make up the forage base for bass, and these fish are attracted to the sunlit, protected coves once the lake gets below the mid-50° range. The coves on the northwest side of the lake will have warmer water. May Spring Branch, Wa-Ni Village, Happy Hollow, Card'nal Cove, and Oak Grove are worth fishing. Casting baits that imitate the forage in size and color will probably be your best system.

One of the reasons Bunch likes crankbaits so much is that he can bump them along the rocky bottom. The bumping gets the bass's attention and entices it from between the rocks. Crankbaits may snag on a rock, but when the pressure is released, they float out of harm's way. Spinnerbaits and buzzbaits tie for his second choice of baits.

"I'll throw whatever I have," says Bunch, "until I give them what they want. A Zara Spook will be the ticket some days, and other days they don't want anything but a white buzzbait. It's a matter of offering them different things until one says, 'Yes, I want it!' Once I learn their pattern for the day, I go to fishing."

Often you can locate manmade cover along these banks using your sonar. At low water you can ride around and make notes of where brush piles and stake beds are.

"When parts of the lake are stained or muddy," says Bunch, "I can almost always find some areas that are not affected by run-off. When I fish stained or muddy water I don't change the type bait I'm using; I simply change color. I use blue, pearl, white, and chrome in clear water and chartreuse in stained. I'm a firm believer in the fire tiger and chartreuse colors. I've caught a tremendous number of bass on the fire tiger. I have 15 to 20 different colors of Bagley DB3 crankbaits because I crank more than anything else."

He says from Fall Creek (river-mile 81) upstream to Rogersville will have more stained conditions. "If you are fishing clear water and not catching fish, you can move up the lake to the stained water and catch 'em."

Cover is important to catching bass. One cove where Bunch fishes had an old fence post standing alone in the back where the water seemed too shallow. Bunch put his bait by it and hooked a bass. The bank was gently sloping with nothing to recommend it to an angler except that lone post. In cover-starved Cherokee, that's often all it takes to locate fish.

CHAPTER 24

Douglas Lake

An Excellent Largemouth,
Crappie, and Bluegill Reservoir

A few summers ago Rick Johnson was crossing Dandridge Bridge, which crosses Douglas Lake, when he noticed a commotion on the water that caused him to reconsider his plans. Instead of heading to work, he made a beeline to his fishing boat and spent the day fishing topwater lures. As fish broke the surface to attack schooling shad, Johnson enjoyed one of his best angling days ever. By day's end, he had caught and released more than 90 largemouth, and his thumbs were so raw from lipping bass that it hurt him to touch anything with his tender digits.

Floyd Coffey remembers catching 300 crappie a day and not thinking highly of this accomplishment. It was during a time when Douglas Lake's crappie population was large, but when few fish had enough length for reasonable anglers to consider them as keepers. Fishing Douglas these days is a different story.

Crappie populations are still good—in some years even excellent—but the average fish is much larger, perhaps in part because of size and creel limits established in the 1990s. To Coffey, someone who has fished Douglas for decades, the lake is East Tennessee's best crappie reservoir.

Largemouth bass and crappie attract numerous anglers to Douglas Lake and help create its reputation as a top-notch, warm-water fishery. This run-of-the-river reservoir also has numerous large bluegill, which bite for months, and rebounding sauger, which angler Danny Lee pursues with much success.

GAME FISH RATINGS

Largemouth Bass	🐟 🐟 🐟 🐟 🐟
Crappie	🐟 🐟 🐟 🐟
Sauger	🐟 🐟 🐟 🐟
Bluegill	🐟 🐟 🐟 🐟 🐟

LARGEMOUTH BASS

Rick Johnson lives beside Douglas Lake and has fished it since the early 1960s. He spends about 150 days fishing it each year. A part-time guide, Johnson favors the lake's midsection, which is the area closest to his Dandridge home.

Winter and Spring

Winter fishing begins for Johnson in late February when the lake starts to warm. For those who desire to fish during the coldest months, he advises working deep bluffs with large jig and pig combinations. Brown jigheads (crawdad colors) with black and blue pork rind are among popular midwinter lures, says Johnson.

DOUGLAS AT A GLANCE

Location:	Jefferson, Cocke, and Sevier Counties
Size:	36,600 acres
Length:	43.1 miles
Shoreline:	555 miles
Summer pool:	1,710 feet
Winter pool:	1,525 feet
Impounded:	1943
Featured species:	Largemouth Bass, Crappie, Sauger, Bluegill
Other species:	Stripe (White Bass), Spotted (Kentucky) Bass, Walleye, Catfish
Description:	A run-of-the-river lake that has much more water in it in summer than in winter and is subject to quick rises during wet weather. Shale points are common and are popular fishing sites. Large hollows, bluffs, rock banks, and mud banks are also common. There is much development on parts of the lake. Many fish are caught in spring along fescue-lined backyards in hollows, coves, and pockets.
Main tributaries:	French Broad River, Nolichucky River, Pigeon River, McCowan Creek, Diamond Creek, Allen Creek, Seahorn Creek, Spring Creek, Indian Creek, Swan Creek, Koontz Creek, Rimmer Creek, Shadden Creek, Muddy Creek, Clear Creek, McGuire Creek, Perry Branch, Flat Creek
Landmarks:	The nearest cities include Newport, Jefferson City, Dandridge, and Sevierville. Major highways near Douglas include TN 139, TN 92, TN 32, TN 113, and US 70. The nearest interstate is I-40.
Operated by:	Tennessee Valley Authority

See Appendix C for map information

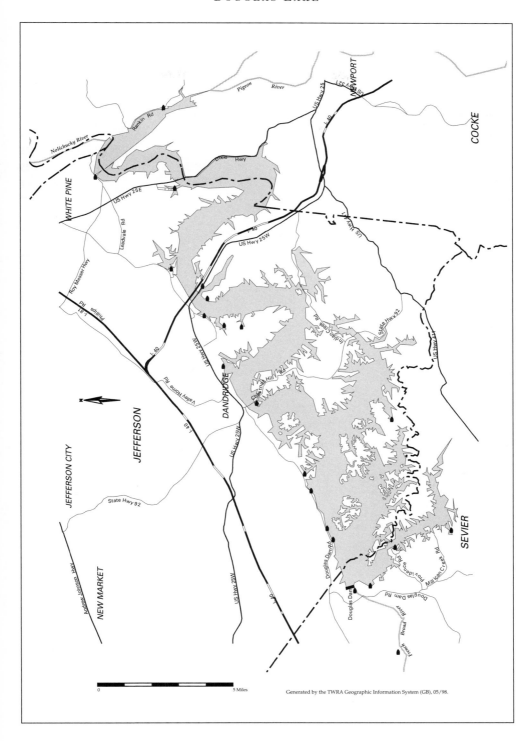

Generated by the TWRA Geographic Information System (GB), 05/98.

Coves filled with debris make excellent habitat for Douglas Lake's largemouth. Gold and black shallow-running Rapalas are among the lures that attract hits in these areas.

When Johnson starts fishing, he heads to main channel points and tosses crankbaits. "I know everybody has a favorite color, but I love throwing the No. 11 gold Shad Rap," he says. "All I have to do is crank right down the points. I make sure to hit the bottom while I'm retrieving."

Johnson knows from experience which points are productive. He advises newcomers to find "defined" points, those that are "sharp like a pencil" and drop off on both sides. "I've never seen anything like it when they're hitting here," he says. "I once took a doctor friend of mine, and we caught 98 large-mouth, and 30 of them weighed over 5 pounds. This was the best day I've ever had on Douglas. We were catching 10 to 15 fish on each point, and they were still hitting when we left."

The main river channel and Muddy Creek, a large tributary that Johnson considers an excellent part of the lake, have many points. "I never know for sure where the fish are until I start casting," says Johnson. "I throw across the points at different depths. I like to start by casting right up on the point near the shoreline and then moving back out until I locate fish. A lot of times I end up sitting in 15 to 20 feet of water."

While the No. 11 Shad Rap is a good lure, other crankbaits catch fish. Johnson also tosses shad-colored Fat Free Shads. He fishes a crankbait with a 6½-foot graphite rod and a baitcasting reel spooled with 12-pound-test monofilament.

Scouting Douglas is advantageous. "When the water is at summer pool, it's difficult to find the type of points that I've described," says Johnson. "Scouting in winter is a great way—the best way—to see just how sharp the points are and what the bottom looks like. I fish points that have shale on them."

Don't get discouraged by fishless points. "It's funny up here," explains Johnson, "I can fish all day and not do much, then hit a point and load the boat. It's just that way on Douglas Lake. I keep looking for fish until I find them." Johnson normally tosses crankbaits through March.

He catches bass from many places as the water rises. "I'll find them on main points, sides of points, secondary points in coves, or even dead ends of coves if the water has gotten back in them," says Johnson. Plastic worms and lizards—rigged Texas- or Carolina-style—catch many April fish.

Johnson's favorite worm color is electric red. Cotton candy, watermelon, or pumpkinseed and chartreuse are also good plastic lizard colors, says Johnson, who uses a 20-pound test, 4-foot leader with a ¼- to ½-ounce sinker for Carolina rigs. "Douglas always has stain in it, and fish like color here," he notes. "There aren't many times when you can see below 3 feet in this lake."

Johnson fishes plastic baits slowly. "A lot of fishermen raise and lower their plastic lizard," he says. "That's fine, but I like to wind real slow and stop about every three cranks, let my lizard sit for a few seconds, wind it some more, and stop. Sometimes I slow-roll spinnerbaits when I get in coves or pockets with submerged bushes or trees. White, fluorescent orange, and chartreuse and white are good lure colors," says Johnson.

In May, Johnson tosses topwater propbaits like Tiny Torpedoes and Crazy Shads. He also tosses shallow-running crankbaits, such as No. 7, 9, or 11 gold Rapalas. The slight wobbling motion in these lures attracts numerous strikes. Johnson tosses toward cover "anywhere from halfway back in a cove all the way to its end." He twitches first and then reels it slowly to the boat. "It will dive a foot or two," notes the guide. "I get quite a few hits doing this."

"Scum fishing" also becomes excellent beginning around the first of May, especially with Slug-gos, Flukes, or other soft plastic topwater baits. "When the water rises, it brings debris into pockets," explains Johnson. "I don't like so much debris that it's hard to fish a pocket. I want enough space to work my topwater lure. I'll cast to the bank and sometimes even actually on it, then I'll pull my lure real slow over the scum. I'll twitch it twice and let it settle, then twitch it twice more and let it settle again. I lose bass by throwing in this stuff, but I have to get fish on before I can worry about getting them in."

Johnson's favorite soft plastic topwater bait is a 6-inch "baby bass" Fluke. When working topwater, he uses spinning reels spooled with 8- to 10-pound-test monofilament and 3/0 Gamakatsu hooks.

Johnson often searches for floating pollen in coves or pockets. "I look for it on the surface," he says. "I can't tell you why bass get under this, but I'll fish it when I find it. If I come across a clean cove in May, I leave it alone. If the water is dead—I mean where nothing is moving—and there is pollen on

Angler Rick Johnson lives alongside Douglas Lake, and he knows that in the spring, bass feed around shorelines, some of which are in his neighbors's backyards.

the surface, I can almost promise you that bass will be there. I sometimes catch 6- and 7-pounders fishing this stuff."

Although he doesn't often use them, spinnerbaits, buzzed on the surface, work well around buck bushes and other cover.

Starting in June, Johnson catches 2- and 3-pound largemouth "in the breaks," as he did several years ago when he took a day off from work and landed more than 90 topwater fish.

"Douglas can have some fabulous surface fishing in June," says Johnson. "Most of the time I have to catch them early in the morning or late in the evening, unless it's overcast. Then I can catch them all day long."

Largemouth don't always surface, but Johnson has experienced many good topwater Junes. Sometimes Johnson spots fish surfacing 200 to 300 yards away. Zara Spooks, Tiny Torpedoes, and other topwater propbaits are among his favorite lures. When bass aren't surfacing, Johnson fishes points with plastic worms or lizards on Carolina or Texas rigs. He catches many fish suspending in main channels over points or humps.

Summer

July is one of Johnson's toughest bass fishing months. He begins night fishing this time of year. By August, however, action picks up as the Tennessee Valley Authority begins lowering Douglas Lake, forcing largemouth to congregate, notes Johnson, who fishes plastic worms on Carolina or Texas jigs into September. He spends most nights sitting on points in about 30 feet of water and tossing toward the shoreline.

Johnson prefers darker moon phases to bright night rays. Electric red is his favorite worm color, but purple, black, and blue are also good nighttime shades.

"I'm fishing points that have shale bottoms and sharp drop-offs on both sides," says Johnson. "I cast my worm and then retrieve it by raising and dropping it and raising and dropping it. If I stay out long enough, I hit a spell where I catch fish almost every cast. I'm not catching big fish—about 1 to 1½ pounds—but I'm having fun."

Larger fish are caught by tournament-serious anglers over deep humps with jigging spoons, notes Johnson. "Some of the best tournament anglers jig with heavy spoons on deep humps," he says. "They won't catch near as many fish as I do, but they'll catch big fish."

Fall

As the lake continues to fall and get cooler, largemouth hit crankbaits around points, says Johnson. However, if the water has fallen far enough to force bass out of the lake's creeks and coves, Johnson throws topwater lures.

Douglas lake is "just about cut in half" by the time the drawdown ends, notes Johnson. Bass become more concentrated because of this. "From September until about mid-November—when I quit fishing to go rabbit hunting—I catch big fish on buzzbaits," says the guide. "I average getting one hit every 30 minutes, but most every fish I catch weighs 5 pounds or more."

Fall is when Johnson locates bass on "lousy-looking" banks. "I fish mud banks or points that I wouldn't touch any other time," he explains. "A little bit of shale can help, but I primarily look for river points with gentle slopes and red mud banks."

White, chartreuse, and orange are Johnson's favorite buzzbait colors. He tosses a buzzbait large enough to create strong vibration. A shad-colored Zara Spook is also a good topwater lure, but most of the time Johnson favors buzzbaits. "I believe I like throwing buzzbaits in the fall better than anything else I do," he says. "Strikes are scary. Sometimes they'll maul my buzzbait right at the boat."

Don't overlook cover exposed by the falling lake. "If I see brush sticking out of the water, I cast over and around it," says Johnson, who works his buzzbaits with baitcasting reels and 12-pound-test monofilament. "Believe me, don't ever pass up brush."

CRAPPIE

Floyd Coffey has fished Douglas Lake since the early 1960s and has caught tens of thousands of crappie throughout the decades. He believes Douglas is the best crappie reservoir in East Tennessee and among the state's top lakes.

Winter

Coffey doesn't fish often during Tennessee's coldest winter months, but knows that they bite, especially minnows fished deep below bobbers. He also knows that they suspend in main channels over river or creek humps. "Usually they're 12 to 15 feet deep near the bottom," he says. "The best way to

Douglas Lake is among East Tennessee's best crappie reservoirs. Angler Floyd Coffey has fished it for decades and has much success using solid-bodied plastic lures with shortened tentacles.

catch crappie is to find humps and lower a minnow. There are a tremendous amount of humps in this lake."

Crappie also hit artificial baits, but Coffey believes that minnow fishermen have more success in winter than jig anglers, one reason why he doesn't fish the cold months anymore. "I'm older now, and I don't care about getting out in the cold, but I also don't have near as much success tightlining with jigs, and that's what I enjoy most about crappie fishing," he explains. "I fish for pleasure."

Occasionally, when East Tennessee gets back-to-back warm days, Coffey gets out and catches crappie with small plastic grubs and light leadhead jigs that he retrieves slowly over humps.

Spring

Coffey's fishing style doesn't change from season to season. He tosses solid-plastic tubes on tightlines and fishes main or secondary points in river or creek channels, sometimes venturing into large hollows, but never heading far back into creeks. "I just don't believe that crappie go way back into creeks," he explains. "I've read that and heard that, but I don't fish for crappie there and I never will."

Coffey's gear consists of a stiff 5½-foot graphite rod, a small spinning reel spooled with gold 4-pound-test monofilament, and—most of the time—a ⅛-ounce splitshot leadhead molded on a No. 4 hook and threaded with solid-plastic tubes. "They have tentacles just like hollow-tube jigs, but they stay on the hook better," says Coffey. "I use Hog Rustler solid molds, and it's important to shorten the tentacles on them a tiny bit to get the best action."

Best lure colors vary from day to day, depending on the lake's stain. Coffey tosses light colors in clear water and bright colors when the lake is dingy. Chartreuse, chartreuse and black, green metal flake, pink, and solid white are among his favorite shades. "If I could only have those five colors with me at any time, I'd be in pretty good shape," says Coffey.

How and where to work a crappie jig is key to catching Douglas Lake fish. "The thing I tell other fishermen is that if they learn to walk their bait on the bottom and do so without ever having slack in their line, they'll catch fish," explains Coffey. "Ninety percent of all the keepers I catch hit my jig when it's about a foot or so above the lake bottom."

"Walking the lure" means retrieving it slowly enough to attract hits, but quickly enough to keep it about 1 foot off the bottom, a rhythm that experience helps develop. Coffey reels his lure about 4 feet and then lets it fall back to the bottom. He continues this action, using the rod tip to control his bait. "I can detect more hits if I keep slack out of my line, but this will also keep the leadhead from turning over and getting hung up," says Coffey.

Sometimes hits are so light that Coffey sees them rather than feels them. That's why he prefers using gold line made by Stren. He catches more fish than many partners because he has mastered detection.

Coffey spends a lot of time fishing points, provided they have good structure. "I rarely fish brush," he notes. "I fish over shale mostly. Points that have shale are the best places to fish on Douglas Lake. In early March, crappie are usually on the end of the points, and I can actually catch bigger fish at this time than a few weeks later when they start spawning."

Gold line and line fished without slack are vital to Coffey's success, but so is the method he uses to work his lure. "I like to come up a point rather than go down it," he explains. "I can keep my lure closer to the bottom by bringing it up a slope."

Most of Coffey's late winter and early spring fishing occurs on the lake's midsection from Point 7 to Point 16. Crappie move on points as the water level rises toward summer pool. Fish segregate this time of year, with larger females found deeper on the points during the prespawn period, says Coffey. "When I start catching them together, I know they are ready to spawn," he says.

Douglas Lake crappie normally spawn between the end of March and the last of April. While anglers catch crappie spawning shallow, Coffey continues pulling them from deep water—often 10 feet or deeper. Many fish move off main channels into large hollows, but usually no farther than a couple of hundred yards.

"In terms of size, Douglas has had the best crappie [in the late 1990s] that I can recall," says Coffey. "I remember not too long ago catching 300 crappie a day but being lucky to have one even 10 inches long. It hasn't been a problem for several years to catch them 10 inches and longer."

Coffey quits crappie fishing for several weeks after the spawn. Midspring to midsummer are tough months for his fishing style, he says. Crappie suspend in the warmer months and tightlining becomes difficult. "This is when they're caught a lot by fishermen who troll," he says.

Summer

Crappie often suspend in main channels during summer. Little Wee-Rs and other small, diving crankbaits are excellent trolling lures. Coffey begins crappie fishing again in August when he heads up the lake to cooler water provided by the Nolichucky and French Broad Rivers. "I go to the upper end and fish riprap or rocky banks and even bridge pilings," says Coffey. "I'm tightlining, just like I always do, but I'm down 25 to 30 feet. I always look for rock and fish around it."

August fishing is not as packed with action as other months, but Coffey sometimes catches 10 to 15 fish during half-day trips. "I believe I could limit out on Douglas just about any time of the year if I fished from daylight to dark," says Coffey. "Douglas is a very good crappie lake."

Fall

As the TVA drops Douglas, Coffey heads back down-lake to fish shale points with solid-plastic molds, just like in spring. He catches many crappie between Seahorn Creek and McQuire Creek, which stretches from midlake to lower lake, respectively. He especially enjoys October and November action.

"This is the most consistent time of year to catch crappie," says Coffey. "I don't know why they go where they do, but I can plan on catching fish between 15 and 20 feet in October and November. Crappie hit harder in mid-October and all of November than at any other time of the year. That's the best six weeks of crappie fishing on Douglas Lake. It's my favorite time to fish for them."

SAUGER

While largemouth bass and crappie attract most anglers to Douglas Lake, the reservoir is also known for good sauger fishing. Jefferson City resident Danny Lee spends almost every weekend between December and March fishing for them. He catches sauger 15 inches and longer during most outings.

Winter and Spring

Successful sauger fishing for Lee requires that he follow the fish on their spawning migration to Douglas Lake's headwaters, which means eventually completing his season where the French Broad River becomes a definitive tributary. Some anglers pursue them several weeks longer, catching sauger with crankbaits in the Pigeon River, which is a tributary of the French Broad.

The best headwater fishing doesn't occur, however, until late winter or early spring. By then Lee has caught numerous sauger.

Lee begins his sauger quest on the main river channel between the mouth of Muddy Creek near where TN 92 crosses Douglas. Sauger are present here by December, and he catches many fish around the broken ends of bluffs where rocks spread out in the reservoir. Lee especially likes casting where the river flows closest to these rocks.

"I have to be careful," says Lee. "This lake is at winter pool, and it drops so much that it doesn't even look like the same reservoir it was in the summer, and there are many shallow rocks." Lee's favorite early winter bait is a 3½- or 4-inch plastic Gitzit that he inserts with a ³⁄₁₆- to ¼-ounce leadhead jig. Chartreuse is his favorite color, but he sometimes fishes smoke.

"I cast shallow and work my Gitzit down around the rocks," says Lee, who retrieves with a "popping" motion that he describes more as a sweep than a snapping action. Most sauger hit on the front side of the rocks, but he sometimes catches them on the back side.

As water temperature gets cold, usually by January, Lee stops casting for sauger and starts jigging for them. He also continues moving upstream. "I follow the fish," he says. "I don't ever fish slack water. I stay in the main river channel."

Lee's favorite plastic bait is the Umbrella plastic tube. Made in an array of colors, these tubes have tentacles and are the most popular with crappie anglers. Umbrellas work great for Lee because they are slightly larger than average crappie tubes and more appropriate for his jigging style. After cutting off the top of these tubes, Lee inserts ½- or ¾-ounce leadhead jigs through their open end. Strength of current determines which weight he uses.

Douglas Lake has a consistent stain. To help attract strikes, Lee paints his jigheads and purchases tubes with brilliant colors. Pink, white, and a combination of chartreuse and black are his favorite tube colors. Fluorescent orange, chartreuse, and hot pink are his favorite jighead colors.

Lee colors his leadheads with Powder Paint, dipping and baking them according to directions. Heat cures the paint to where it's almost impossible to even knock off. Lee clears the paint from each hook eye before baking the heads. Otherwise, he must take time to chip away dried paint before he can use them.

Selecting the best leadhead jig is important. Lee buys jigs with bait holders because these barb-like protrusions secure his Umbrella tubes. "Once all this is put together, I end up with a real pretty little lure," he says. "I take every color with me because on any given day sauger hit some colors better than others."

Tuffy minnows are also important. Lee always tips his hook with them. "The bigger the minnow, the better," he says. "Three- or four-inch tuffies are good." When sauger are biting short, as they are prone to do, Lee attaches a stinger hook to the jig.

Unlike many sauger anglers, Lee doesn't use a constant jigging motion. Instead, he drops his lure to the bottom, lifts it 1 to 2 feet, holds it for a few seconds, and then drops it again. He catches most of his fish between 15 and 25 feet.

During normal winters, when rain is infrequent and the lake is under constant fluctuation, sauger are easy to follow, says Lee, who fishes holes made the deepest by the reservoir as the TVA begins raising the water level.

Lee uses one rod while floating downstream. He favors a strong 6- to 6½-foot rod and a baitcasting reel spooled with 8- to 12-pound-test monofilament. "I like the flipping switch on a baitcasting reel because I can lower line when the lake contour changes without using two hands," he notes. "I like having a free hand to do other things."

Douglas Lake's Point 18—an area 18 miles from Douglas Dam—"is a famous place for sauger," notes Lee. Many anglers follow sauger into the French Broad River and even upstream into the Pigeon River in late winter and early spring. Shad Raps, Rapalas, or other baitfish imitations catch numerous sauger at this time, notes Lee, who quits sauger fishing in March to pursue bass.

BLUEGILL

Floyd Coffey catches crappie with the best of them, but after the spawn, he becomes a bluegill angler. "This is the best bluegill lake in East Tennessee by a wide, wide margin," says Coffey. "On average, I catch them bigger than my hand."

Spring, Summer, and Fall

Because Coffey has fished Douglas Lake for decades, he knows where many bluegill beds exist. "I have found lots of them on clean shale points," he says. "When I'm searching for a new bed, I look at the bank to get an idea of what the bottom is like. If the bank doesn't have many trees or bushes, I know there is a good chance bluegill are bedding nearby."

Clean banks in short hollows or pockets attract bedding bluegill. Many fish nest 6 to 12 feet deep, although they are sometimes shallower, especially in May. "I catch a bunch when I find them," says Coffey. "I have sat in one spot and caught 100 big bluegill."

Coffey catches bedding bluegill from "the first full moon in May" through September. "They spawn every full moon," he says. "I know I'm in business once I find a bed."

Floyd Coffey (back) and son Steve believe Douglas Lake is the best big bluegill lake in East Tennessee. Finding bluegill beds is as easy as finding a shale point with little or no cover on it. Bluegill school on these sites for months.

Many anglers catch bluegill by fishing worms or crickets deep below bobbers, but Coffey favors retrieving crickets on a slow tightline. "I walk my bait right over their bed," he says. "I let it go to the bottom and then reel it a foot or so above a bed, just like I do when I'm crappie fishing. I reel it about 4 feet, let my cricket fall to the bottom, reel it some more, and let it fall again."

Worms work fine, but Coffey favors crickets. He uses a 5½-foot rod with a spinning reel spooled with gold line. A No. 6 hook and No. 6 splitshot crimped a foot above the bait is perfect for bluegill fishing, he says. Mashing the hook's barb helps Coffey remove bluegill quickly and keeps his action fast.

Although he returns to crappie fishing in fall, Coffey notes that bluegill are caught around piers, bridges, and rocky points—really rough rocky points—in November and even later. Use the same tightlining methods for the best results, he says.

CHAPTER 25

Boone Lake

*Touted as the Best Striper and
Hybrid Lake in the State*

If you can fish only one lake in the state for stripers and hybrids, Boone Lake should be your choice.

Dave Bishop, retired fisheries biologist from TWRA, says, "Boone Lake's 4,500 acres were first stocked with striper in 1972. Years later, when the stripers reached the 25-pound range, they begin to change their behavior—they slowed down and became more solitary. As they got older, their numbers decreased. I don't know for sure if they would become more solitary if it wasn't for attrition."

The reason stripers in Boone are so large is that they weren't discovered until they had become large. Anglers now know of Boone's big stripers and are putting a lot more pressure on the lake. But striper/hybrid/bass guide Tom Richards of Kingsport takes a different slant on big fish: "I think there will always be some big stripers—those over 40 pounds—in Boone. At least until the anglers learn how to fish for them. Not many people have learned the fine art of catching big fish. None of my 50-pounders were caught when anyone else was around. One gasoline motor, one noisy trolling motor, or even a depth finder can shut down the big fish. I think there will always be some big fish in Boone."

Richards is credited with catching more freshwater stripers over 50 pounds than anyone. He has 13 notches in his rod handle for each fish over that weight.

GAME FISH RATINGS

Striper (Rockfish)	🐟🐟🐟🐟🐟
Hybrid (Cherokee Bass)	🐟🐟🐟🐟🐟
Smallmouth Bass	🐟🐟🐟
Trout	🐟🐟🐟

Two state-record hybrids were caught by his guide service, and Boone Lake has held three of the last four state hybrid records.

But just because Boone Lake has superior striper and hybrid action, don't think that's it. You can satisfy yourself with smallmouth bass, largemouth bass, stripe, catfish, crappie, bream, and trout.

STRIPER (ROCKFISH)

Richards has been a guide on Boone Lake for more than a decade. He has grown up with stripers and hybrids and has learned their behaviors as they developed into trophy-size fish.

"The secret to catching trophy stripers," says Richards, "is to fish with a plan. Decide what you are going to do first and if that doesn't work within

---

BOONE AT A GLANCE

Location:	Sullivan and Washington Counties
Size:	4,520 acres
Length:	33 miles
Shoreline:	130 miles
Summer pool:	1,263 feet
Winter pool:	1,258 feet
Impounded:	1952
Featured species:	Striper (Rockfish), Hybrid (Cherokee Bass), Smallmouth Bass, Trout
Other species:	Largemouth Bass, Stripe, Catfish, Crappie, Bream
Description:	A run-of-the-river lake that has much more water in summer than in winter. Debris lines may become water hazards after heavy rains and when water levels change. Watauga and South Fork Holston River arms run clear in summer. Banks are mostly rock outcroppings with many bluffs. Stump fields are still present. There is much development on the shoreline. The water is fertile and supports a strong forage base of gizzard shad, threadfin shad, shiner, alewife, and minnows.
Main tributaries:	Watauga River, South Fork Holston River, Candy Creek, Muddy Creek, Beaver Creek, Indian Creek, Wagner Creek, White Branch, Knob Creek, Snyder Creek, Gammon Creek, Boones Creek
Landmarks:	The lake is located north of Johnson City, with access via I-81, US 11E/19W, TN 36, TN 75, and TN 34.
Operated by:	Tennessee Valley Authority

See Appendix C for map information

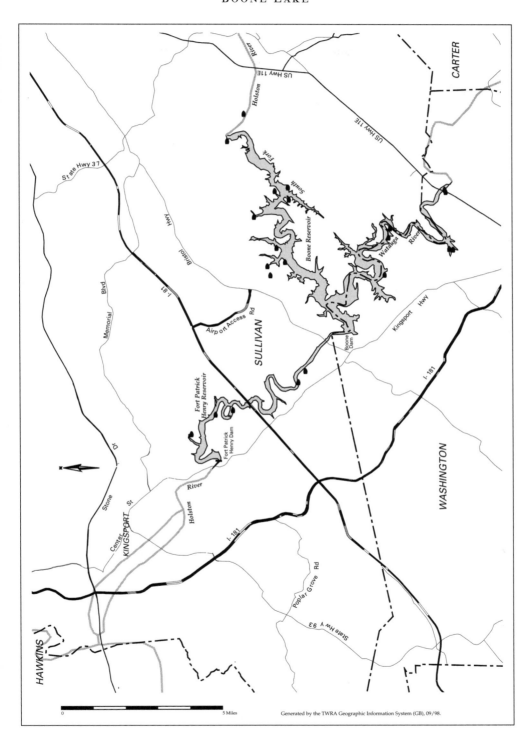

0   5 Miles   Generated by the TWRA Geographic Information System (GB), 09/98.

Tom Richards (center) has caught more stripers over 50 pounds than most fishermen because he has studied the fish's behaviors. These are some of the artificial lures he uses for catching stripers and hybrids through the seasons.

a reasonable amount of time, go to plan B. Most striper waters in Tennessee have trophy fish, so all you need is a good strategy to catch them." He defines a trophy fish as one that weighs over 30 pounds.

Richards began striper fishing on Boone as soon as the stripers reached legal size. He got hooked on stripers back in the 1970s, and in the past two decades, he has pursued them with an outstanding obsession.

"I've studied the small stripers, and as they grew big, I observed how some of their behaviors changed. You might say we grew up together. I learned I had to change my fishing techniques if I was going to catch the big ones."

Tailrace Tactics for Trophies: "All my trophy stripers," says Richards, "come from the tailrace or river. I've never caught a fish that weighed 50 pounds in the main body of the lake. I catch plenty of 20-pound fish in the lake, but not the truly giant stripers." Most of his fish over 50 pounds were caught on the Red Fin.

During periods of generation, the oxygenated water attracts the big fish from the main body of the lake, but probably the most important attraction is the abundant food supply of stunned or chopped shad swept to the waiting stripers.

"If you've had experience with trout or smallmouth fishing in streams," says Richards, "you've got the basics for catching stripers in tailraces. Look for anything that breaks the current. That's where the fish will be. Rocks and rock piles are common below the dams, and that's where you should fish."

The eddies behind rocks are where the fish hold and dart out to snap up shad as they float by. "The stripers are expecting food to come with the current so cast your bait upstream so that it passes close to the rocks." Richards cautions you to keep the slack out of your line, reel fast, and give your bait a little action.

He also says, "The best of us are going to lose a few big ones. The current plus the fish's fight puts a lot of strain on your line and the fish's mouth. All that pulling can make a hole in the lip so your hook can slip out. That's why you have to keep constant pressure on it. When you feel your line go 'thump, thump, thump,' that means the fish is shaking its head trying to throw your hook. Don't try to horse it then, just maintain your tension.

"After you land your striper, be sure to retie your lure. Your line takes a lot of abuse during the fight along the rocks." Richards uses a 7-foot rod and 17-pound-test line on an Ambassadeur 6500C reel for tailrace angling.

Lake Tactics for Trophies: "Depending on the season, I'm on the water an hour or two before sunup. Unlike most anglers, I don't start my big engine. I use the trolling motor. And unlike most anglers, I catch big stripers close to the launch."

Richards says trophy stripers are easily frightened. "People don't realize how spooky these fish are. Folks come to launch their boat, turn on all their lights, start the big motor, let it warm up, and then run up and down the lake looking for a place to fish. They aren't going to catch trophy stripers. This is especially true on Boone Lake, where the best fishing begins right at the ramp. I don't fire up my big motor until I'm ready to come home."

Richards explains what this commotion does to big fish: "People come up to me saying, 'What are you doing? I've seen you catching big fish and I can't catch one.' The reason they haven't got a fish is because they have set a bomb off in the striper's living room. How long would you hang around if someone tossed a grenade through your window? Boy, someone is expecting a lot to think I'm going to hang around!"

Describing his strategy for a day, he says, "First, I throw a topwater bait. No sense working any harder than you have to. It's easy to throw, and if they're hitting, what could be simpler?"

Richards analyzes it this way, "Topwater baits stay in the sight zone longer. If you are fishing a ledge, the bait stays in their sight longer if you fish perpendicular to it. A lot of times the stripers are holding under ledges and they know shad are above them in about 3 feet of water."

Stripers don't think about how or when to attack. It's all instinct and conditioning. They are conditioned to ignore shad breaking along the bank, but the one that breaks above the striper and heads for deep water is an invitation to dine. "That's why parallel fishing is not as productive as fishing perpendicular to a ledge. The shad are vulnerable away from the bank over deep water."

Richards's observations of baitfish play a big role in catching stripers. "You'll see people cast a Red Fin and work it with a retrieve and pause technique. That's not the way shad swim. Crank it fast or slow, but 90% of the time, your best bet is a steady retrieve," he continues. "If the bait stops, that's not what the striper expects. That's like sitting down to eat a T-bone steak that tastes like chicken. You like chicken, but you aren't expecting it. You'll think something is wrong with it, so you won't eat it. The same way with a striper seeing a twitch and pause retrieve—it isn't natural. Have you seen an injured shad? It gets up on the surface and scoots, leaving a wake behind it. It's moving fast and then it's gone. That triggers the striper's instinct to strike."

Richards wants a topwater bait to produce an unbroken **V** across the surface. He also wants it to cast a big shadow and make a lot of noise. Richards claims big baits mean big fish. "That's why I use a Red Fin or ThunderStick," he says. "They're big and sound loud."

He will cast topwater for 15 to 20 minutes. If he doesn't catch anything, he goes to the next phase of his plan—a combination of planer boards and flatlines.

"Planer boards are like diving lures that go sideways," he says. The diving bill points horizontally rather than vertically. "I can run up to eight boards at a time. When you're trolling with an electric motor, stripers spread out to the sides to get away from the boat, then move back to whatever structure they were on. With the planer boards, I get the bait out and away from the boat so it runs right over the stripers. Planer boards give you more opportunities to catch fish."

If Richards doesn't catch one on the boards, then there are other opportunities. "I run two flatlines. Flatlines are two lines trolling live gizzard shad about 100 feet behind the boat. The main function of these lines is to get the bait way back. Fish are not smart creatures. As soon as the boat goes over them, if you're using a trolling motor and not your big engine, they forget about it and move back to where they were. Then here come those big gizzard shad you're trolling. This covers the area where the fish are going to merge after the boat passes."

Sometimes he doesn't put any weight on the flatlines. The bait will be 6 to 8 feet deep when trolling slowly. If you go slowly enough, the weight of the swivel will take the bait to the bottom. The purpose of flatlining is to get the bait far enough away from the boat and at a depth a foot or two above the stripers. (See Appendix A for description.)

To prevent twisted line, Richards places a No. 4 barrel swivel about 4 feet from the hook. He also uses a No. 4 swivel with the planer boards. The way he has it rigged, the line stays with the board when you set the hook. The

No. 4 swivel won't slip through the eye on the planer board, therefore preventing it from sliding back on the fish. The lightweight board doesn't interfere with playing the striper.

With planer boards and flatlines, Richards has bait covering a 100-foot-wide path as he trolls. He also employs downriggers. He sets his bait so it runs above the stripers, which he has located on his sonar. Sometimes he uses lures on the downrigger, but live bait is usually more productive.

To catch the trophy stripers, Richards recommends using big gizzard shad. Big shad eliminate anything under 15 pounds. "I've found that I catch three or four fish real quick or else it's going to be a long day. If they don't hit soon, I go for little fish, those 20 pounds or less, because they are easier to catch when conditions aren't right for big ones."

Spring

"The thing to look for on Boone in the spring is for water temperature to reach 52°," says Richards. "This is when they turn on. From 52° to 70° is the best time for casting topwater plugs. Nighttime is the best time, too. The fish are going to be shallow, chasing threadfin shad and alewife. The alewife is a deepwater forage fish, but it comes to the surface to spawn on shallow banks at night in the spring. When they're spawning, that's what makes night fishing so good.

"In the daytime, I prefer live baits on planer boards and flatlines," says Richards. "Threadfin and gizzard shad work better than the alewife does because the stripers and hybrids are used to the alewife being deep."

The places that warm first are the long hollows and coves. "Friday Hollow, Long Hollow, Candy Creek, and places like that warm up first," he says. "At night I fish the flats on the main channel adjacent to those big coves. During the day I fish in the coves. The upper end of the rivers will remain cold for a long time because they are fed by cold mountain waters from South Holston and Watauga Lakes."

Stripers and hybrids are together until they get the urge to spawn. "They spawn at different times and a lot has to do with their size. The 12-pound hybrids may go with 12-pound stripers. Males go upstream first and hold on points waiting for females. There's a prespawn that occurs in late March and early April, but the true spawn takes place in late May. If you're in the main lake catching 4- to 6-pound fish, that's a good indicator that the big fish have gone to spawn," he says.

Females reach sexual maturity at the beginning of their fourth year. Males begin maturing at the age of two years; nearly all are ready by the age of three. During spawning, the striped bass run upriver to the tailraces. Spawning begins when the water temperature is between 55° and 65° and peaks when it is between 60° and 67°. During spawning, the larger female is surrounded by a number of smaller males. No parental care is provided for the eggs, and they drift downstream and hatch in a few days, depending on the water temperature. The eggs must remain suspended in a current until they hatch, one to three days later. In still water, the eggs sink into the silt and the embryos die of suffocation. Landlocked areas are poor for reproduction, although it occurs sometimes.

If you specifically want to catch hybrids, Richards recommends casting a smaller bait, such as a 3-inch Chug Bug, instead of a Red Fin. You'll catch more fish with the smaller bait, but if you're looking for Mr. Big, cast a 5-inch Chug Bug.

"About the second week of May, you can go to the dam at night and catch hybrids. There is light around the dam, and the stripers shun it, but the hybrids seem to like it. I've caught anywhere from 17 to 50 hybrids, weighing more than 15 pounds, in 4 hours using live bait at 34 feet deep. You need to anchor and put more lights on the water. Use live alewife and hold on!" he says.

Summer

Richards says that hot weather drives the fish deep in the lake or up the rivers. This makes them less accessible to most anglers, but it is a blessing to the angler who knows where the hot weather sanctuaries are.

He says, "Hot weather sanctuaries can be underwater springs, cool mountain rivers, or deep water, which is naturally cooler than the surface. Stripers seek these areas when the water temperature exceeds 75°. Although stripers in excess of 30 pounds will often move to sanctuaries when the water temperature rises above 65°. Not all bodies of water have these cool areas, and this suggests that there may not be any fish over 30 pounds."

Richards points out if your lake has hybrids, they offer some exciting action because that cross-bred species can tolerate warmer temperatures and poorer water quality compared to the striper. You can catch hybrids surfacing in water in excess of 75°.

"Concentrate on the rivers feeding into the lake. Mountain rivers range from 48° to 55° in August. This is ideal for stripers," says Richards.

"As the river runs into the lake, you will find a trash line where they meet. I concentrate my efforts 100 yards to 1 mile below the trash line, fishing in rather shallow water 12 to 16 feet deep.

"Shad make the best bait. Use the largest you can find because fish 20 pounds and larger will be feeding on shad 9 to 12 inches long."

He suggests locating underwater springs. This can be done two ways. Check old maps of the area for farmhouses before the land was flooded. Springs were the usual source of drinking water. The other way, somewhat easier, is to run the lake late at night and early morning looking for small patches of fog on the surface. The patches may be no more than a 20-foot circle of fog, but it's a sure sign of cooler water. A thermometer will also be useful in these endeavors.

"Concentrate on the vertical drops," he says. "Bluffs and cliffs with steep dirt banks above them often hold wet-weather springs. They offer excellent cover from the bright sun while providing shady ledges and caves. Fish these areas by trolling shad 60 feet behind the boat and casting live bait to the small breaks in the bluffs and cliffs. These small breaks often run several feet below the surface and offer great cover for the fish."

Late summer is the time most striper anglers cast lures from the surface down to the thermocline to seduce fish. Jigs and topwater plugs are the two main baits that anglers prefer.

White bucktail jigs are a mainstay lure. Richards says, "Cast your jig where the water is about 10 feet deep if you have marked stripers 13 and 20 feet. Let it settle, barely pump it off the bottom, and let it settle again. Repeat this until you pass the area you expected to contact the fish. Stripers feed up and you have to work down to them. This technique bounces the bait so it falls toward the fish.

"If stripers are feeding near the surface, cast your jig beyond the fish, bringing it back with a rapid, steady retrieve. If your lure returns empty, cast again, letting it settle a few feet, then repeat your retrieve. If that doesn't produce fish, vary your speed and imitate an injured shad."

Stripers stay under a school of shad and rise into the school to feed. After less than a minute, the fish descend for a while before hitting the shad again. Letting your lure fall is intended to arouse a strike from the deeper fish.

The above techniques are the ones Richards uses when fishing Devault Bend and farther down-lake.

"Night fishing for big stripers means more success during the summer," says Richards, "because stripers become more active and boat traffic is light.

"A period of good activity begins just before sunset and lasts for about two hours. The sunset feeding occurs over deep river-channel points at about 15 feet [Deerlick Bend, Pickens Bend, Flourville, and Devault Bend]. Your sonar will show you their location. Jigging a Crippled Herring spoon or drifting live or cut bait just above the stripers is most effective."

There is a two-hour lull after the sunset action before the activity begins anew near the shoreline, usually in a cove. At approximately 11 o'clock, the stripers move to within 20 feet of shoreline to forage on schools of shad. The shad's poor night vision leaves them susceptible to easy predation. Jigs or spoons, jigged vertically or cast, and topwater baits are most productive. Live bait about 4 feet under a float also works, and this is also an excellent time for fly fishermen to cast 2/0 and 3/0 streamers.

Stripers find comfortable temperatures up the Watauga River. This may be more to your liking as well because the fishing is best there.

"I go up the river early in the mornings," says Richards, "when I can find the fish in the shallows and catch them on a jointed ThunderStick. It seems like the stripers have seen too many Red Fins and have gotten tired of them. But any angler should be able to catch fish if their lure imitates a minnow."

He says fish the Austin Springs Bridge area early and late to catch stripers, but if you go by boat, be very careful of the shallow-water flats. "Every year at least a hundred people leave their lower units on this flat. It'll be from 2 to 6 feet deep with lots of stumps and brush. Anglers in boats can get to river-mile 15, about a half-mile below Saylor Island at Watauga Flats, and bank anglers can enjoy fantastic fishing there by taking Herb Hodge Road that runs along the river."

Richards says the jointed ThunderStick is great for bank anglers, but live trout can't be beat. He cautions that you cannot use trout you've caught, only trout you buy, and you *must* have a receipt *with* you. Smoky Mountain Hatchery at Hampton is the nearest place to buy trout.

After the morning bite is over, he moves downstream to cast live shad or cut bait and a Crippled Herring spoon. "I prefer a ⅓- or ½-ounce in silver or silver with a blue back. Of course, I have rods rigged with a jig and a topwater bait."

It's hard to beat tailrace fishing for striper during dog days. Boone Dam tailrace waters come from the bottoms of the lake, where the water is much cooler. The generating turbines send stunned and chopped shad downstream. These enriched waters ring the dinner bell for many species, including striper.

Richards says, "Boone's tailrace is shallow and rocky—wicked to your prop and lower unit—so try bank fishing, for this and one other reason. If you want to catch giant stripers—I mean fish over 40 pounds—fish the tailrace from the bank. To catch the big fish from a boat, you will have to do it within your first few casts. Your motor will spook them and they'll leave the area."

To work the tailrace from the bank, Richards situates himself about 15 feet from the edge of the water so his first dozen casts are retrieved close to the bank. He suggests wearing subdued colors so the fish can't see you. "If you wear a white hat or shirt, the fish will see you and move away from the bank," says Richards.

"Stripers like rocks; that's why they are called rockfish. I fish the shoreline riprap before working farther out. If I don't get a fish within about 12 casts, I start working the rocks out in the stream."

Richards says to make your bait pass exactly over the top of the rocks. Cast upstream and reel your bait so that it looks like it's swimming when it goes over the structure. Stripers will be in the backwash behind the rocks facing upstream. Once you get your bait to wobble by those rocks, you should hang a fish. If a fish didn't hit the bait going over, cast so it goes a little past the structure. The striper may look at it three or four times before he hits it, but if he's there, he'll take it by casting to one of those positions.

"Stripers get close to the boils. A lot of people think of a boil as being all turbulent and forceful, but right where it's coming straight up is the easiest place for the fish to hold. There is a lot of force once you get away from the boil, but it's relatively calm near it," he says.

That's where he casts a ¾-ounce bucktail, lets it sink, then bumps it along the bottom. "Carry a pocketful of jigs," Richards warns. "The bottom is going to eat its share, too."

Richards says the worst thing you can do is try to horse a striper in. "You've got to think about the strain that small hook is putting on that fish's mouth. Not only do you have the fish pulling against you but you're fighting the current, too. That's enough force to rip the tissues, and then you've lost a big fish."

Fall and Winter

You can also locate schools of striper deep in the small, main body of the lake from September into October, but your best prospects are up the rivers.

Put in at Bluff City's public ramp to fish the South Holston arm, and at Johnson City Yacht Club (at Austin Springs) or Sonny's Marine in Flourville (east of the junction of Routes 36 and 354) to fish the Watauga arm.

"During the fall and early winter, a variety of techniques will work to entice stripers to hit," says Richards, "but nothing works as well as live bait. The best live bait according to experienced striper anglers is shad.

"These fish are bite-size, abundant, and nutrient-rich. They are defenseless, so they find safety in large numbers. They spawn heavily, filling lakes with tiny fry that quickly grow into edible forage. These fish school tightly, becoming a mass that predators find hard to identify and attack."

He says stripers first have to break up these tight schools so they can select individual targets. To break up the group, stripers will herd a school into areas with few escape routes then slice through them, causing the school to break formation and scatter. Once the bait scatters, they become targets and are quickly picked off.

Richards says, "You will also find that stripers are concentrating on small baits in the fall and early winter, and this can make fishing tough. For some reason they tend to ignore larger baitfish.

"You've probably heard an angler claim they were in an area with fish surfacing all around, but could not get one to hit, even after throwing everything but their tackle box. This happens when stripers are feeding on fish less than an inch long. But there are some tricks you can use to coax a strike."

He says you have to give stripers what they want, and if it's small shad, that's what you give them. The first thing you have to do is catch shad in a cast net with a ⅜-inch mesh. You need a round or oval bait tank with circulating, aerated water. Insulated tanks will serve you and the bait better.

There are several ways to fish small baits, but pulling two flatlines, one 40 feet and the other 80 feet, behind the boat works well. In fall and early winter, the stripers are feeding shallow, so you can place a float about 4 to 6 feet above the shad. No weight is added to the line.

"Also, rig a rod for casting a shad to any fish breaking the surface. You need a light-action spinning rod with an extra-light tip for casting the nearly weightless bait. Six- or eight-pound-test line and a No. 12 treble hook are suitable for lake fishing. The small hook will not damage the shad, yet will give you greater striper-hooking ability. Remember to set your drag loose," he warns.

"The last thing you will need is a weighted float. These commercially prepared devices are available in most bait shops and sporting goods stores. They are made of Styrofoam with a small lead weight added for greater casting distance. Hook the bait, with just one barb of the hook, through the nostril. This avoids injuring the bait and causes it to track straight in the water instead of spinning and twisting your line," Richards concludes.

These techniques work on stripers, hybrids, and white bass equally well. In the winter when the water gets below 40°, the stripers and hybrids become lethargic.

HYBRID (CHEROKEE BASS)

The hybrid is the result of crossing a female striper with a male white bass (stripe). The hybrid was thought to have an average life expectancy of about five years, which is about the same as that of a stripe. But they actually live much longer and attain a weight of more than 23 pounds. The fast-growing, long-lived striper can live a maximum of about 30 years. The average hybrid will weigh about 8 pounds, but in the rich waters of Boone Lake, some weigh over 20 pounds. Not enough data have been collected nor has enough time passed to learn the true growth and longevity of hybrids.

For further comparison, the average stripe (white bass) weighs about 2 pounds, with a maximum around the 5-pound mark. Stripers grow to over 60 pounds in Tennessee, but a 125-pounder was caught in the Atlantic Ocean.

Tom Richards says, "My guide service has held the state record on two different occasions. Steve Carigger caught the first record while on a guide trip. That fish weighed 19 pounds 4 ounces. My client Norman Hutson caught the next record. His weighed 19 pounds 10 ounces."

The TWRA first stocked Boone in 1972 with hybrids and stripers. Now they are stocking hybrids one year and stripers the next at a rate of 25,000 fingerlings per year. This works out to be five fish per acre, which is the rate at which most Tennessee lakes are stocked.

Through the Seasons

"The best fishing of the year, under normal weather conditions, begins in March when the surface temperature warms to 55°," says Richards. "At this time I concentrate my efforts near the mouths of feeder creeks in the midsection of the lake. The reason I like the midsection during the early season is because Boone is created by two rivers, Watauga and South Holston. Both of these rivers are cold mountain waters that flow from the bottoms of South Holston and Watauga Lakes. Hybrids prefer the warmer water found around these smaller creeks.

"By March, the lake will be near full-pool, and I will start fishing the gradually sloping, pea gravel and gravel points. If I'm fishing for hybrids, I avoid the clay banks because hybrids don't use them as heavily as stripers do."

He says, "From 9 at night until daylight, I concentrate on fishing the shallow points with a topwater plug. The best color is chrome with a blue back. There are several ways to fish this bait, but none works as well

Boone Lake is also known for its hybrid fishery, and the Tom Richards Guide Service has held two state records. Richard's striper-and-hybrid rig is a downline with a small treble hook.

as reeling in the lure on the surface with a slow, steady retrieve. This retrieve creates a small wake that closely imitates a shad on the surface. The 7-inch Red Fin is a popular lure for stripers, but I prefer smaller baits like the 3-inch Chug Bug, because the hybrid has a smaller mouth than the striper. Hybrids naturally have a tendency to hit smaller baits."

He recommends casting as close to shore as possible because the fish will be holding in no more than a foot of water, waiting for stray baitfish to swim by. If your bait falls directly on top of the fish or out in deep water, the fish will ignore it.

"There always seems to be an exception to the rule and here is one. On nights with a full or bright moon, fish usually avoid the shallows, and top-water fishing is slow to nonexistent. During these few nights I switch to using a deep-running crankbait. My first choice is the Spoonbill Minnow by Rebel. I retrieve it with the same slow, steady action. I have better luck casting to the shady sides of points.

"One of the biggest mistakes I see people make is positioning their boat too close to the shore they plan to fish. Stay as far from shore as you can and still make your lure hit right at the water's edge. I keep my boat about 30 yards out when I can."

Another point to keep in mind is that you shouldn't let your boat's wake wash onto the bank you intend to fish. Shut down your gasoline motor at least 100 yards away and make your final approach using your trolling motor.

He adds that it's important to fish facing the moon rather than having it at your back. Yours or the boat's shadow will spook the fish. Try to keep the dam behind you so your lure will move with the current. Even if there is no current, stripers and hybrids expect injured shad to move in that direction.

Richards says, "A slow presentation is preferred because the water is cool and the fish are still sluggish. Once the sun has been up an hour or so, stripers and hybrids will stop striking surface lures as they move for the protection of deep water. When that happens, I switch to a ½-ounce bucktail jig.

"I cast the jig to the shoreline and allow it to fall about 5 feet, then sharply jerk the rod tip from a 9 o'clock position to 12 o'clock. This causes the jig to jump toward the surface. Quickly, I reel in the slack line, while lowering the tip back to the 9 o'clock position. Keeping the line taught, I allow the bait to sink again and repeat the procedure. The fall and jump of the jig imitates a dying alewife or shad. I guarantee this action will catch more fish than a steady retrieve," he says.

SMALLMOUTH BASS

It may be difficult to think about casting for bronzebacks when stripers and hybrids are hitting, but Boone has a strong smallmouth population. As Tom Richards explains how to catch them, you will become excited about trying his simple techniques for a 7-pound brown bass.

Winter and Spring

In the winter, smallmouth are from the midsection of the lake up into the Holston and Watauga Rivers (more so on the South Holston side), anywhere from Wagner Bend to Bluff City.

Richards says, "Look for smallmouth on brush piles and logs. The transitions from bluffs to the sandy gravel flats are also good places. Use live bait: threadfin shad or shiners on a No. 1 hook without a sinker and 6-pound-test line. Let the bait swim freely. For some reason, I've found that the smallmouth in this transition zone only want live bait.

"Another technique I use is putting a minnow on a Carolina rig and fishing it just like you were fishing a plastic worm. This works best on the flats and ledges, but this bait rig works just about everywhere on Boone."

Between the twin bridges (river-miles 33 and 34.5) close to Bluff City is another hot spot. Richards says he catches an enormous number of smallmouth bass on threadfin shad. But it depends what size bait you use as to what size smallmouth you catch. He recommends using 5- to 7-inch shad for trophy smallmouth bass.

"Up the Watauga River arm," he says, "you begin catching smallies about the Volunteer Parkway Bridge to Watauga Flats. Be sure to fish Hyder Bluff." Richards says look for the same sand and pebble flats as on the South Holston side, and fish them the same way.

Summer and Fall

"I've found smallmouth in the summer in two places," says Richards, "up the rivers along the bluffs and on the humps in the main body of the lake. Between Point 3 and Point 5 in the lower end of the lake, there are a number of humps you can find with your sonar. Look around the sides of the humps and you'll mark fish. Ninety percent of the time they will be smallmouth bass and they'll stay there all summer. I vertical jig for them or drop live bait on them. I really got into them with that Crippled Herring spoon."

On clear days Richards uses the ⅓-ounce silver or silver with a blue back Crippled Herring spoon; on cloudy days he switches to the gold color in the same weight. He uses 3- to 5-inch threadfin when he uses live bait. If he's trophy fishing for smallies, he'll put on 7-inch shad.

"When the water cools in the fall, the smallmouth become very aggressive on top. I just ride around in the boat looking for surface action. I use binoculars, too. A lot of people who see this action think they are stripers in the jumps, and smallmouth will be mixed in with stripers sometimes, but 80% of the time, the jumps in the river are smallmouth. Sometimes I'll wait by a bridge. Sooner or later smallmouth will come up and break the surface at a bridge in the fall. I cast the 3-inch Chug Bug or the Crippled Herring spoon."

He says, if they are aggressive, you can get close enough to cast the Chug Bug into the action. When you can't get your boat close without spooking them, cast the spoon. You can cast the ⅓-ounce spoon a long way.

"When it hits the water, I count 'thousand-one, thousand-two,' and crank five times fast. Then I repeat that sequence to make the spoon yo-yo, but I'm not letting it sink more than a couple of feet before I bring it back to the surface. The smallmouth are concentrating on the little shad on the surface," he concludes.

TROUT

Richards says that rainbow trout have taken over the upper ends of Boone. "We're catching some brown trout in the 25-pound range. I'm not an expert on trout, but I fish for them like I do for stripers and I'm catching trout. I

Smallmouth bass anglers should not overlook Boone Lake's bronzeback fishery, especially in the summer.

catch them on topwater baits and trolling by with live bait. I catch them with every striper technique, including planer boards. They are teeming up the rivers."

One simple way to catch brown trout is to put a threadfin shad on a No. 10 treble hook, a splitshot for weight about 18 inches above the hook, and cast to the bank from a boat. "This works from the Volunteer Parkway Bridge all the way up the river to the swinging bridge in Bluff City," says Richards. "Summer is the best time. The big browns are in the South Holston arm. The Watauga arm has mostly rainbow trout."

Anglers who fish for hybrids in front of Boone Dam in May and June often complain about trout getting in the way. Both Richards's technique and the techniques described in the Dale Hollow chapter for catching trout near the dam will work here. The trout action in the river arms is from July until the water temperature starts to drop in the fall.

CHAPTER 26

Fort Patrick Henry Lake

A Small Impoundment with Good Marks

While anglers may not want to travel a long distance to fish Ft. Patrick Henry Lake, results from a study conducted by the Tennessee Wildlife Resources Agency indicate the impoundment has a decent largemouth population and quite a few bass that grow to better-than-average size.

In 1996, the state's wildlife agency (TWRA) studied Ft. Patrick Henry with electronic fishing gear. Nearly 40% of largemouth collected "consisted of fish greater than 15 inches," according to Doug Peterson, a TWRA biologist. "The results revealed a surprisingly good largemouth bass fishery."

Biologists also collected smallmouth, but not enough for a proper evaluation, noted Peterson. Largemouth, however, received good marks—actually approaching a trophy fishery. Although the study turned up few young bass, adult largemouth have many baitfish to pursue and few threats from predators. Nearby Boone, South Holston, and Watauga Lakes attract most anglers.

Ft. Patrick Henry is 872 surface acres impounded on the South Fork of the Holston River. While it doesn't spread out like many typical Tennessee reservoirs, local anglers catch largemouth, smallmouth, bluegill, rock bass, catfish, trout (in the headwaters), and even a few big hybrids and large stripers that have escaped from adjacent Boone Lake.

GAME FISH RATINGS

Largemouth Bass	🐟 🐟 🐟 🐟
Striper (Rockfish)	🐟 🐟 🐟 🐟
Hybrid (Cherokee Bass)	🐟 🐟 🐟 🐟
Trout	🐟 🐟 🐟 🐟

Ft. Patrick Henry is a small, run-of-the river reservoir with a few embayments and a horseshoe bend inside Warriors Path State Park. Much of it is lined with bluffs.

Stripers and Cherokee bass also provide anglers with occasional action. "We don't stock them in Patrick Henry, but somehow some of them have managed to get in there, probably from Boone Lake," explains Peterson.

For tactics on catching rockfish and hybrids, study the techniques of Boone striper angler Tom Richards, a well-known East Tennessee fisherman (see the Boone Lake chapter). Methods for catching largemouth, smallmouth, and catfish in run-of-the-river impoundments are discussed in other chapters.

Bluegill and rock bass are also among species that inhabit Ft. Patrick Henry. Rock bass bed around stumps in spring, while bluegill stack against bluffs in summer, according to Peterson. Crickets and night crawlers fished on small hooks and light sinkers are good baits for both species (see the Center Hill chapter for ideas on fishing bluffs). Rock bass also hit small crawfish, crawfish imitations, or any number of small crankbaits or spinners.

Trout fishing is also good below Boone Dam. Corn, salmon eggs, night crawlers, artificial fish eggs tossed on light tackle, or artificial flies worked on fly rods catch trout. Any number of small crankbaits, spoons, or spinners work well, too.

FORT PATRICK HENRY AT A GLANCE

Location:	Sullivan County
Size:	893 acres
Length:	37 miles
Shoreline:	130 miles
Summer pool:	1,075 feet
Winter pool:	980 feet
Impounded:	1953
Species include:	Largemouth Bass, Smallmouth Bass, Hybrid (Cherokee Bass), Striper (Rockfish), Catfish, Bluegill, Rock Bass, Rainbow Trout (in the headwaters)
Description:	The lake is a short, run-of-the-river reservoir lined with bluffs.
Main tributary:	South Fork of the Holston River
Landmarks:	Fort Patrick Henry Dam is near Kingsport. The closest interstate is I-81.
Operated by:	Tennessee Valley Authority

See Appendix C for map information

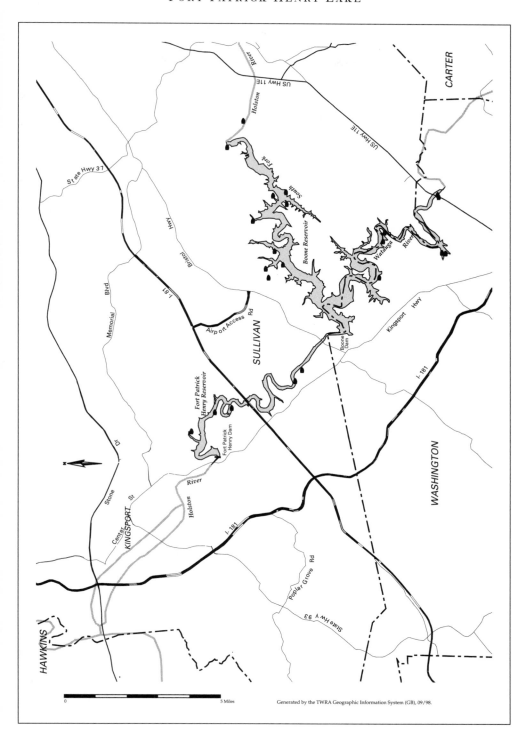

Generated by the TWRA Geographic Information System (GB), 09/98.

0   5 Miles

South Holston Lake

The Under-Utilized Surprise

When researching all of Tennessee's major reservoirs, South Holston proved to be a most surprising lake. It has a strong fishery.

Most of South Holston Lake is in Tennessee, with a narrow arm of the South Fork of the Holston River reaching into Virginia. This mountainous lake is cold and deep, with cold-, cool-, and warm-water species present. This chapter will delve into the warm-water smallmouth bass, the cool-water walleye, and the cold-water rainbow trout.

Because the lake lies among East Tennessee's mountains, it has little cover, but is rich in structure: humps, points, bluffs, main channel bends, and deep but short creek coves.

WALLEYE

Tennessee's native walleye is a river species that has a difficult time maintaining its numbers in an impoundment. Siltation covers the rock-and-gravel spawning areas once swept clean by current. Loss of habitat means the loss of population. Our walleye migrates up rivers to spawn. This usually takes place in March and early April in the tailraces of our dammed, run-of-the-river reservoirs.

In *The Fishes of Tennessee* by Etnier and Starnes, they say males reach the spawning area first, then the walleye group by sexes until they spawn. Courtship and spawning consists of "butting and pushing." Two males usually accompany the female. She releases eggs approximately every five minutes and completes her duties in one night. Males hang around for two weeks performing

GAME FISH RATINGS	
Walleye	🐟 🐟 🐟 🐟
Rainbow Trout	🐟 🐟 🐟 🐟 🐟
Smallmouth Bass	🐟 🐟 🐟 🐟 🐟

their duties. They also say that our southern, riverine strain of walleye was apparently genetically superior in growth to northern populations. Stocking programs using the northern strain have supplanted our southern strain.

Winter

"It's not unusual to find 80 to 150 feet of water right off the bank in South Holston," says guide Tom Richards from Kingsport. "This lake is very clear. It's not very fertile, and it doesn't have a strong forage base. It does have alewife. The alewife is a deep-running baitfish and it draws the predators deep. The key to fishing this lake is fishing deep.

"The only thing I vary from season to season is the depth I fish. I troll year-round, and I do some casting and vertical jigging, but I troll a lot. In winter I fish open water over humps. Walleye suspend about 20 feet over these humps and the humps are 60 feet deep."

Richards says success drops off in winter when the water temperature drops to 40° or below. "If we have two or three days of unseasonably warm weather and the water temperature rises, you can catch fish."

SOUTH HOLSTON AT A GLANCE

Location:	Sullivan County and Virginia
Size:	7,580 acres
Length:	24.3 miles
Shoreline:	118 miles
Summer pool:	1,385 feet
Winter pool:	1,330 feet
Impounded:	1950
Featured species:	Rainbow Trout, Walleye, Smallmouth Bass
Other species:	Brown Trout, Largemouth Bass, Bream, Catfish, Crappie, Stripe (White Bass), Sauger
Description:	A highland lake located in mountainous terrain. The lake has many rocky bluffs with a rock, clay, gravel, and shale bottom. The water quality is good, but not rich in nutrients.
Main Tributaries:	South Fork Holston River, Little Creek, Fishdam Creek, Riddle Creek, Big Creek, Sharps Creek, Little Jacobs Creek, Big Jacobs Creek, Harpers Creek, Spring Creek
Landmarks:	The lake is just east of Bristol. Access from US 421, TN 44 on the west, and Big Creek Road on the east.
Operated by:	Tennessee Valley Authority

See Appendix C for map information

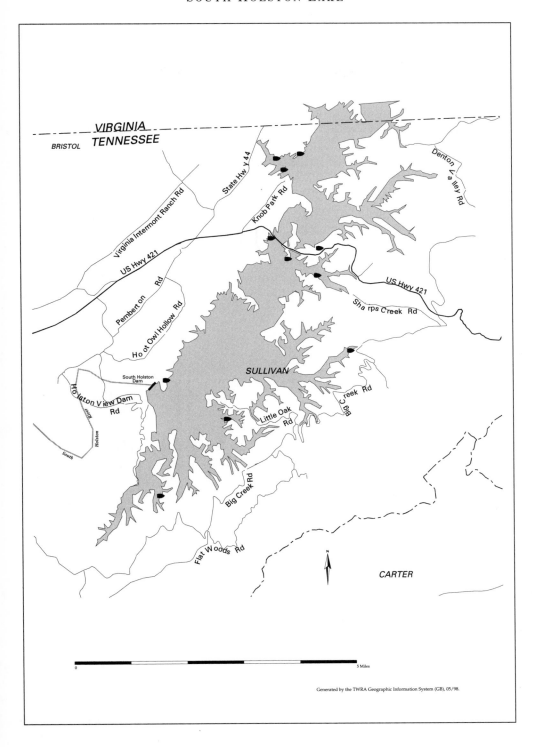

Generated by the TWRA Geographic Information System (GB), 05/98.

Spring

"Spring is the best walleye fishing in the world on South Holston and Watauga," says Richards. "Those little Rapalas that are about 3 to 5 inches long are the bait. Go up the river until you can see shoals. Cast below the shoals at night, and I'm telling you that you'll have some fantastic fishing."

As the water comes up (the drawdown on South Holston is about 50 feet) in late spring or early summer, the fish move back to the main body of the lake near the US 421 bridge.

"A few years ago I learned there is some excellent fishing when the water is in the trees," he says. "The walleye are still aggressive for topwater baits in May and June. They'll hit any imitation minnow. My favorite for this is the ThunderStick.

"For some reason, they concentrate right under submerged trees that still have leaves. It's difficult to fish, but I saw a technique on TV that works. Pull your line back under your spinning rod so it makes a bow and let the rod shoot your lure under the tree. You can skip your lure across the water, but using the bow is more accurate. Walleye stay in the trees until the last part of June or first of July," he says.

Summer

"In July the walleye start going down," says Richards. "I switch to the deep-diving ThunderStick that runs about 8 feet deep. I fish the same areas as I did in June and a few points with old trees and stumps. I've had good success with the Hot Lips Express, too. Firetiger and baits with chartreuse and orange work better than the chrome or shad-colored baits.

"In the dog days of summer, I go back to deep-trolling from 40 to 80 feet in the main river channel from the US 421 bridge to the dam.

"Also, at night I'll pull up to a bank that has a gradual drop-off—at least gradual for South Holston Lake. I look for a point that has stumps on it. I go into the bank, tie my boat to a tree, with the back of the boat over 70 feet of water. I put lights on the water and wait about two hours while the lights attract baitfish. Then I start vertical jigging with ½- to ¾-ounce spoons. The Crippled Herrings don't come in exactly the colors I want. I use that powered color, dip my spoons in bright chartreuse, orange, and other wild colors, and bake it on. I drop those bright-colored spoons to the bottom. I bring it up and let it drop again. I get my strike on the fall. I catch some bodacious walleye this way," he says. Dog days are walleye days on South Holston.

Fall

"In the middle of September, walleye start moving back upstream," says Richards, "and they start coming up shallow again because the water temperature is starting to fall. Now, the walleye aren't concentrating like they do when they move to spawn in the spring, but they are looking for food and current. There is a lot of current when they are dropping South Holston to winter pool.

"This is the time I go back to trolling. In early fall I troll a lot of different depths. I use the Hot 'n' Tot Pygmy and tip it with a minnow or night crawler. That's my favorite bait from fall until it starts getting real cold. Later in the fall I troll from 16 to 40 feet deep. They are gorging themselves for winter, and the fishing is fun."

RAINBOW TROUT

"The best trout fishing is during the hottest part of summer," says Tom Richards.

Tom Holland, a tournament trout angler from Blountville agrees that summer is the heart of the season. Holland lives near South Holston Lake, but also fishes Watauga

The clay points on South Holston Lake are key to locating rainbow trout in the spring and fall. Power Bait on a small salmon-egg hook is a favorite among trout anglers.

Lake using the same techniques and strategies for catching rainbow trout. He says his largest 'bow weighed 6 pounds, but he catches many in the 3- to 5-pound range. He says, "You'll catch a lot of stockers in the spring, but if you troll, you'll catch better fish. The largest fish are caught night fishing in the summer."

Winter

Tom Holland says, "You can't fish for trout in South Holston from December 1st through all of February—the season is closed."

Spring

"Trout season opens March 1st and the fishing is best from the banks," says Holland. "The technique is fairly simple. You fish right on the bottom, using what I call the universal trout bait, night crawlers and corn, minnows hooked in the tail, and Power Bait. I fish the shallow, muddy points in the spring between 8 and 12 feet deep."

He slides on a small egg sinker and then crimps on a BB splitshot several inches above a No. 8 or No. 6 hook. The BB shot keeps the egg sinker from sliding all the way down to the hook. He doesn't use a barrel swivel. He says to cast out as far as you can with 4- or 6-pound test. He says, the best fishing in the spring is around Sharps Creek near the US 421 bridge.

"I don't usually fish from a boat in the spring, but when I do, I troll. I troll a silver ½- or ¾-ounce sliver or copper Hopkins spoon or Little Cleo. The fish are going to be 12 feet deep, up and down the lake. I troll the river channel from Sharps Creek down to the dam. You'll have your best luck staying in the river channel next to the cliffs."

Summer

Holland begins night fishing in April and says the heart of the season is June, July, and August. "I tie up to the bank, back out to about 150 to 200 foot of water, and drop an anchor. That's a lot of rope, and it's hard pulling that anchor up the next morning.

"I fish on the river channel along the cliffs. I don't like sloping, shallow points. I tie up on a cliff between points. The trout school up, run down the cliff, turn around, and run back," he says.

Holland sets out black lights at dark and waits for the fish to gather. "Sometimes they hit right away, but most of the time they start hitting around 10 o'clock. It also depends on the weather. The hotter the weather, the later they begin to hit—around midnight. They bite until daylight."

Night crawlers, corn, Power Baits, and minnows are fished straight down. In April the fish are 12 feet deep; in May they are about 18 feet; in June they run about 20 feet; in July they're 25 feet; and in August they'll be about 40 feet. It's hard to find a school when they are 40 feet deep.

Holland says he has never used sonar; he counts off the number of feet of line to reach the depth the fish are running in that month. He may put out a couple of rods with different depths to zero in on their depth. Once he knows that, he catches trout.

His summertime hot spots are the dam; Points 1, 3, and 4; Grandpa's Knob; and Riddle Creek. He suggests getting a map and fishing the river cliffs.

South Holston Lake's tailwater offers some grand trout fishing in the summer, according to an article by Larry Self of Mosheim in *Tennessee Angler* magazine.

Self says, "Fly fishing popularity has increased in these waters thanks to efforts of Trout Unlimited, and the tailwater is a good place to begin. Brown and rainbow action is strong, with the section just below the dam being the place to start. Anglers will find fishing good downstream for several miles. The downstream waters get less pressure and there is the bonus of more wild trout."

Sulphur flies in size 14 imitate the Sulphur fly hatch from spring through the summer. Self says the "housefly" is another top trout attractor. The black body has a touch of white craft hair for the wing. Size 18 or smaller works well on wild trout. The Gold Rib Hare's Ear and a Pheasant Tail in size 14 or 16 are good wet flies, and he suggests using Hendrickson nymphs, too.

He recommends a 6-weight rod, 9 to 9½ feet long, to cast a good distance, but a 5-weight rod, a foot or two shorter, is better when casting where the banks are closer together. He says a 7½-foot 5X leader and a 2-foot 7½- or 8X tippet is a must for the more wary trout.

Fall
Tom Holland says, "In the fall I start trolling again and then fishing from the bank in November until the season shuts down."

SMALLMOUTH BASS
Tom Richards fishes for smallmouth in South Holston the same way he fishes for them in Watauga (see the Watauga Lake chapter). Smallmouth behavior and movements are the same through the seasons on both reservoirs.

Winter, spring, and fall are the times to fish the float and fly along the bluffs and the humps in the lower portion of the lake. In the summer, follow his instructions for fishing humps, pea gravel banks and points, and night fishing (in the Watauga Lake chapter).

Fall
Cofounder of the National Smallmouth Trail, Terry Pierce from Elizabethton says he casts a 4-inch grub to fish 20 to 35 feet deep. He prefers a purple or bluegill-colored grub on a ¼-ounce leadhead to fish the points during the day and uses ¼-ounce crawfish-colored jigs at night. He says to make sure the jig bumps the bottom as you work it down the point.

Short worms (4 to 6 inches long) and jigs are excellent for fall fishing on ledges, drops, and rocky points close to deep water. Smallies don't travel far up creeks during any season, but you should fish the secondary points near deep water.

CHAPTER 28

Watauga Lake

The Highest Headwaters in Tennessee

Look no farther than Watauga Lake for exceptional trout, smallmouth, and walleye angling. If you could be happy catching these three species, you would love to live on this lake.

The cold Watauga and Elk Rivers begin high in the Unaka Range of the Blue Ridge Mountains to feed this deep basin formed by a 318-foot dam in a gap in the Iron Mountains. The Wilbur Dam, below Watauga Dam, holds back a small impoundment of 72 acres. The Wilbur Dam was rebuilt in 1928, making it one of the oldest in Tennessee. While the Little Wilbur, as it is known locally, is not covered in detail in this book, it has the same species as Watauga Lake, with rainbow trout being the most popular.

Watauga Lake does not rank in the top 50% of the lakes for any species, according to the latest TWRA catch-rate results. But that is based on creel surveys, and the other lakes have much more fishing pressure. Watauga is certainly worth fishing; the advantage is that you'll share the lake with only a handful of other anglers.

Of the lakes covered in *The Compleat Tennessee Angler*, none outranks Watauga for its beauty. Its steep, forested, mountainous embankments and deep, green water make it an exquisite background for photographing your catch.

This is the home for the state's record lake trout, caught by Eddy Southerland on April 2, 1994. Southerland's laker weighed 20 pounds 0.79 ounces. Watauga was once stocked with ohrid trout and holds the state record for that fish, 14 pounds 5 ounces. Richard Carter

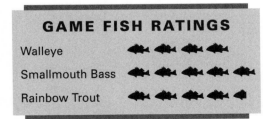

GAME FISH RATINGS

Walleye	🐟 🐟 🐟
Smallmouth Bass	🐟 🐟 🐟 🐟 🐟
Rainbow Trout	🐟 🐟 🐟 🐟

caught it in March 1986. The ohrid trout is a lake-spawning species similar to brown trout. The TWRA experimented with this trout, and although it grew well in Watauga, it is no longer considered for stocking.

WALLEYE

Tom Richards of Kingsport knows the lakes in eastern Tennessee as well as anyone. "I learned how to fish Watauga for walleye and took that information and applied it to South Holston Lake. One of the best-kept secrets in Tennessee is the walleye fishing on Watauga Lake."

Winter

Richards says, "In winter you want to fish below Butler Bridge. The walleye hold in the lower portion of the lake off the points that run into deep water. Here they have deepwater access and they can move shallow along the points to feed. They are lethargic then.

WATAUGA AT A GLANCE

Location:	Johnson and Carter Counties
Size:	6,430 acres
Length:	16.7 miles
Shoreline:	106 miles
Summer pool:	1,975 feet
Winter pool:	1,815 feet
Impounded:	1948
Featured species:	Walleye, Rainbow Trout, Smallmouth Bass
Other species:	Crappie, Bream, Catfish, Largemouth Bass, Stripe (White Bass)
Description:	A highland reservoir in mountainous terrain. The cold, deep lake has many rocky bluffs and a rock, clay, gravel, and shale bottom, but has very little natural cover, except for trees falling from the steep, wooded banks. The water quality is good, but not rich in nutrients.
Main Tributaries:	Watauga River, Elk River, Little Stony Creek, Bunton Creek, Gregg Branch, Big Dry Run, Little Dry Run, Roan Creek, Doe Creek, Cobb Creek, Copely Branch
Landmarks:	Watauga lies east of Elizabethton about 5 miles, with access from US 321, TN 67, TN 167, and Wilbur Dam Road.
Operated by:	Tennessee Valley Authority

See Appendix C for map information

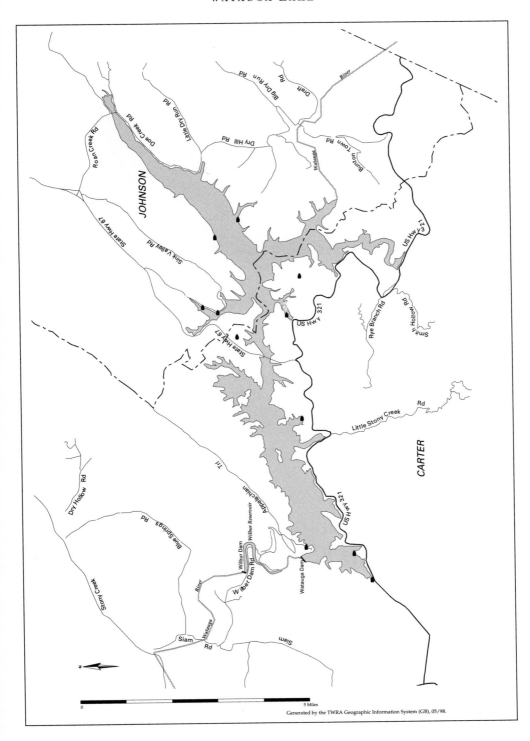

Generated by the TWRA Geographic Information System (GB), 05/98.

Near the dam, the long, low-angle points are good spots for catching walleye and trout with minnows, but crawfish appeal to smallmouth bass.

"There are alewife in Watauga—probably the strongest population in this part of the state. These are deepwater fish and they draw the game fish down with them," he says.

The best method to catch walleye is by vertical jigging or trolling, according to Richards. "You need to fish about 40 feet deep or deeper. There are a lot of different baits you can use; that's a matter of preference. Deep-diving crankbaits, jigs, or live bait all work. The main thing is to fish from Butler Bridge down to the dam."

Spring

"In the spring," says Richards, "they move into the rivers to spawn. That's when you go up the rivers to fish in 2 feet of water. The lake is still low, and a lot of the riverbed is exposed and gives you good access to the walleye.

"After they spawn, they move back down the lake. But before they go deep for the summer, they hang around the trees along the shoreline. This is the time to cast topwater or shallow-diving crankbaits that imitate minnows. My favorite is the ThunderStick. You can enjoy some bodacious fishing for about three weeks before the water gets too warm for them.

"I skip it across the surface, and if the limbs aren't too close to the water, I shoot it under the tree by pulling the lure back with my left hand to make my rod into a bow. I turn loose of the lure, being careful to avoid getting hooks in my fingers, and let it fly under the tree. Shooting a lure is more accurate than skipping. Walleye stay in the trees until the first of July sometimes," he says.

Summer

"During June and July, while many other lakes are settling in for the summer doldrums, this gin-clear mountain lake comes to life," says Richards. "Sure the months of April and May are good, and September through November offer some great fishing, but June and July are when Watauga kicks out record numbers of walleye in the 1- to 4-pound range. Some larger and smaller fish are taken, but the gold mine of 1- to 4-pounders draws Tennesseans and non-resident anglers alike.

"This great fishing didn't always exist. TWRA stocked Watauga with alewives back in the 1980s as a food source, and it definitely worked. The fishing has improved steadily over the last several years, and walleye in the 10-pound range are not rare," he says.

Anchoring in 25 to 40 feet of water at night and turning on the lights to attract bait works with seductiveness. Richards begins vertical jigging just off the bottom. "It usually takes a couple of hours to draw the baitfish in, but it pays off in fish caught. It is well worth the time spent waiting."

Richards recommends night fishing the points around Butler Bridge. "Move up on one of these points and tie a rope to a tree on the bank," he says. "Then use your trolling motor to move away from the bank until you're over water 45 or 50 feet deep. Drop your anchor off the back of your boat and then pull both of your lines tight. You want your boat to stay put. Next you need to put your lights on the water. The best time to get started is between 9 and 10 P.M., so the fishing will get real good between 12 and 1 o'clock."

There are a number of lures that will work equally well, including Crippled Herring spoons, Hopkins spoons, Silver Buddies, Sonars, and Johnson Silver Minnows. The important thing to remember is color: chartreuse, orange, fluorescent green, and yellow. You can buy the spoons, then apply colored tape, spray paint, or the bake-on powder to achieve the desired color.

"Lower your spoon to the bottom, take in a crank or two of line, and start jigging. This is the best method I have ever used for catching walleye," says Richards.

Fall

"Walleye fishing is best above Butler Bridge," says Tom Richards. "There are a lot of humps in the lake and those are good places to fish. I fish them just like I do the points except I can't tie to the bank. The only drawback, if you consider smallmouth a drawback, is that you'll catch these bass there, too. The top of the hump may be 40 feet deep, and the ones that hold fish best are the ones that have one side that runs up nearly vertical and a gradual drop-off on the other side. Also, the better humps will have a creek channel running beside it.

SMALLMOUTH

"The way to smallmouth fish on Watauga is the same way I fish on Boone. Watauga has more humps. The key is to get off the banks and get over the deep water, especially for smallmouth."

Fall, Winter, and Spring

"That float and fly is the ticket from fall through early spring," says Richards. "I've used it for four years and I've absolutely torn the fish up. You've got to get on those deep bluffs and fish about 20 feet deep. You need a long pole. What I do is pile the line up behind me in the water, make one hard cast that jerks it out of the water, and before the line gets tight, I stop it in midflight. This swings the fly close to the bank, but the float is out from the bank. This lets the fly fall down along the face of the bluff underwater, then slowly swing under the float. The best way is to get beside the bluff and cast parallel.

"The best fishing is on the main lake right at the dam—anywhere I can find humps in 30 to 50 feet of water. Throw that fly around those humps. You need to take the float off to get as deep as the fish are in winter. The float and fly works on the bluffs, whereas just the fly works on the humps," he says.

Richards suggests that you find bluffs that are close to shallow water with pea gravel and bedrock. These are the spawning areas, and smallmouth don't travel far from these areas during the nonspawning times of the year. They move more vertically than they do laterally.

"In the spring they are more aggressive and they move into the shallows to spawn. Use the small fly, as I've described, or use a small spoon. I like that small Crippled Herring spoon, and I've had good success with topwater baits. I keep a rod with a topwater bait ready to cast during the fall and spring when they come up shallow. It's not unusual to see schools breaking the top, especially in the fall."

Richards says once the water drops to 40° in the winter, he only fishes after there have been a few days of warm, sunny weather. The fish are lethargic, and you must fish slowly with small baits such as the float and fly.

Summer

"In the summertime, take the float off and use the fly over a hump," says Richards. "This works year-round. Most people don't have patience to let that little fly settle to the bottom. They weigh $\frac{1}{32}$ or $\frac{1}{16}$ ounce. You can go to a $\frac{1}{8}$-ounce fly, but no more. It's got to be a duck feather jig.

"The ideal situation is to find a point with a gradual drop to it where the end of the point hits a river channel and then a hump. These places are golden! These are difficult to find, but you don't have to know but three or four of these places to fish all day. It'll take a day to fish them right, especially with those lightweight flies."

Smallmouth bass are hot on cool-water Watauga Lake during fall. Sonar units are a must for locating the deepwater humps that attract walleye and smallmouth bass.

Smallmouth like bluffs with a pea gravel bank with stumps or big boulders nearby. He adds, "Smallmouth bass only move from their spawning area on the gravel or boulder banks to the nearest bluff. And humps are the same; they've got to be close to a spawning area. Those fish are not roaming all over the lake; they're a home-body fish."

He adds that you can use the same nighttime technique for smallmouth bass that works for walleye. Tie to the bank and anchor over 40 feet of water to jig for bass (see the walleye section in this chapter for details).

Richards says the only difference between Watauga Lake and South Holston is that the greater wood cover in Watauga. "The wood holds smallmouth good, so be sure to fish it."

TROUT

Watauga has rainbow, brown, and lake trout. "Nobody has figured out how to catch that lake trout," says Tom Richards. "But I'm a man on a mission; I'm going to figure it out. All that have been caught in the past few years were caught trolling at 100 feet. In the coldest part of winter—the last of January and first of February—is when they spawn. They'll be shallow and take surface baits then. I've never caught a big one. My heaviest was about 15 pounds. But I'm going to figure out how to catch them. That's my next goal."

Tom Holland from Blountville says to use the same techniques he uses on South Holston Lake for catching rainbow trout. Watauga is open to trout fishing year-round.

Rainbow trout are one of the major attractions on Watauga Lake and Little Wilbur Lake (immediately downstream).

Winter

"Watauga Lake is deeper than South Holston," says Holland, "and it's known for lake trout as well as rainbows and browns. I fish for rainbow trout just like I do on South Holston. I fish on the bottom of the shallow, muddy points with night crawlers, corn, Power Bait, and minnows. Rat Branch is one of my favorite places. I slay them there."

He recommends fishing shallow in the winter, spring, and late fall, but says you'll catch your trophy trout fishing at night along the cliffs in summer.

"I catch trout casting a Little Cleo along the bank when they are shallow. I prefer fishing the bottom, but casting can be effective. Silver- and gold-colored Little Cleos work best. You can cast them along the cliffs, too. You've got to put the bait at the depth the fish are," he says.

Spring, Summer, and Fall

Holland says the fish behave the same on Watauga as on South Holston. (See the South Holston Lake chapter for techniques and types of structure to fish during these seasons.)

"I love to fish Little Wilbur," Holland says. (Little Wilbur is a small impoundment of 72 acres just below Watauga Dam that's about a mile long.) "I've got one on the wall from Little Wilbur. It's a great cold-water reservoir. I've caught a lot of breeders out of there on salmon eggs. I used to fish every weekend while I was in college. It's cold-water, hard fishing! It's beautiful, but hard fishing because the water is so clear. There are some monsters in there and below the Wilbur Dam [headwaters of Boone Lake]."

Appendices

APPENDIX A:
POPULAR FISHING RIGS
AND ARTIFICIAL BAITS

BLADE BAITS (Left): Cicada, Silver Buddy, and Sonar are versatile and popular thin-metal vibrating baits. Use them for casting to schooling fish on the surface, for casting into deep water and working along the bottom, and for jigging vertically. Great for stripers, hybrids, stripe, bass, sauger, and walleye.

CAROLINA RIG (Right): Place an egg sinker on the main line and then tie a barrel swivel below the sinker. Sinker weight is usually determined by water depth or current strength. Tie a swivel below the egg sinker and then tie a leader—usually 2 to 3 feet in length—below the swivel. Use a hook suitable for the bait in use, which, depending on what fish is being pursued, might be anything from a plastic worm to large, live shad. Most bass anglers place plastic worms, lizards, and crawfish on the hook in a Texas style (top). A Carolina rig (bottom) allows live or artificial bait to suspend above the sinker and lake bottom. The sinker often makes noise and stirs the lake bottom to attract attention.

CATFISH RIG: This is a Carolina rig with a 5/0 to 8/0 Kahle hook tied to the end of a leader. Well-known catfish angler Jim Moyer recommends using a 1/0 swivel with 2 to 5 feet of leader. Bait should float and move with the current. Keep the main line tight to detect bites.

FLAT-SIDED CRANKBAITS: The Little Petey (left) is an example of a flat-sided crankbait. These baits are thin, creating a distinct sound as they cut through the water. Crankbaits are efficient year-round. Cast them in the spring and fall, and troll them in the summer and winter.

TROLLING CRANKBAITS: The Hot Lips Express (right) is a good example of a deep-diving trolling bait. It has cams on its long bill that help deflect snags. The Hot 'n' Tot is another favorite trolling bait. Crankbaits are effective in summer and winter when fish are holding along ledges, drops, edges of flats, and along submerged channel banks.

DOWNLINE (Left): This consists of strong line, often 17-pound test or stronger, usually weighted with an egg sinker above a barrel swivel. A 3-foot leader terminates with large hooks, often 3/0 to 6/0. Sinker weight is usually determined by current strength. Line needs to be as vertical as possible. This is an excellent method for fishing live bait for striper and hybrid.

FINESSE RIG OR SPLITSHOTTING (Right): Often used in winter when fish are sluggish in clear water, or whenever fish are inactive or finicky. Place small splitshot

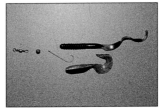

(one or more) 12 to 18 inches above a hook baited with a small lure, such as a plastic grub or worm. Use round split-shot (without ears) to prevent line twist, or use a small barrel swivel above the splitshot to prevent line-twist. Hooks should be appropriate for the bait size, but are usually small. Finesse fishing is often tossed with spinning gear spooled with 4- to 6-pound-test monofilament.

FLATLINE (see Downline): This is similar to a downline, but without the sinker. Flatlines drift bait behind the boat, often as far back as 75 to 100 feet. How far back is determined by needed bait depth. This is an excellent live-bait method for striper and hybrid.

FLOAT AND FLY: Flies (small feather or hair jigs) are often tipped with minnows and then fished beneath a float. This rig most commonly catches suspended, less active, cold-weather smallmouth bass. There are times when unadorned flies work better than those tipped with minnows or pork trailers. Ultralight rods in the 7-foot range catch fish, but 8- to 12-foot rods are more appropriate because there are several feet of line between fly and float. Light line—usually 4- to 6-pound-test monofilament—is best for this fishing style. Float and fly anglers usually use $\frac{1}{16}$- or $\frac{1}{32}$-ounce flies.

KENTUCKY RIG OR TIGHTLINE (Right): Used primarily for crappie fishing. Attach an egg sinker to the end of the line. About a foot above the sinker, loop the line to form a 6- to 8-inch leader and tie the loop in position with a surgeon's knot. About 18 inches higher, form another leader. Attach appropriate-size hooks to the leaders by threading the leader loop through the eye of the hook, opening the loop, and sliding the hook through the loop. Bronze hooks are not as stiff as gold hooks and bend more easily, so they will come free of snags before breaking the line.

MASON METHOD (Left): When fishing for bluegill or shell-cracker, Kentucky Lake angler Garry Mason slides a small round cork onto his line and positions it with a conical-shaped peg that accompanies the cork. The cork can be easily moved up or down to adjust fishing depth. Mason prefers a $\frac{1}{48}$-ounce jig when after sunfish. He often fishes with crickets, but sometimes threads the small jig with tiny plastic baits. He uses ultralight spinning gear for this method.

PLASTIC BAITS (Right): More popular than hard baits, soft plastic baits are also more versatile in retrieves and fishing at varying depths. They come in numerous shapes, ranging from natural crawfish, lizard, worm, and shad to unnatural but fish-attracting forms. These baits can be fished on the surface or crawled along the bottom and are effective year-round.

PUSHING OR PULLING A SPIDER RIG: Used primarily to catch crappie, the spider rig is aptly named because it requires multiple rods for use. These rods resemble spider legs when dangled over the corners or sides of a boat. Many anglers place rods across the bow and/or stern. Rod holders are vital for fishing this technique because anglers must manage several rods (usually three or four) simultaneously.

A popular spider rig setup has a ¼-ounce jig tied to the end of the line with another ⅛- or ¼-ounce jig (depending on wind or current strength) tied approximately 18 inches above the bottom jig. Sonar is vital when fishing this method. Check it often to find crappie depth or lake bottom.

Some anglers prefer to tip jigs with minnows. The crappie will help determine needed colors for jigs. Vary bait colors and combinations until a successful lure is found.

Pushing/pulling methods work best when anglers mount trolling motors amidships. Used with a spider rig setup, pushing and pulling allows anglers to cover wide areas quickly. To push or pull, position a boat so that it moves broadside. Forward or Backward thrust will exert a push or pull motion.

SINKING DIVERS: A sinking diver like the Dipsey Diver (left) gets your bait deep for trolling during the summer and winter. It can be tracked straight or to the side. Often used in conjunction with side planer boards for fall and spring trolling.

SLIPFLOAT RIG: This is a simple way of being able to change fishing depths quickly. By sliding a slipfloat and an accompanying stop (usually a plastic, rubber, or wire stop) above a splitshot and hook. Placement of bait can be made without having to cut and retie line. Place the stop at the desired depth. Line will slide through the float until it hits the stop, positioning bait at the desired depth and allowing anglers to make long casts more easily.

SPINNERBAITS AND BUZZBAITS: Spinnerbaits (right) are potent year-round baits because they can be fished at all depths and speeds. Buzzbaits are topwater baits and work best in spring and fall when fish are near the surface.

SPOONS: These slabs of metal imitate shad and other forage fish. The Crippled Herring Spoon (left) compares ideally with the shad in color, size, and action. Spoons can be jigged vertically (good for summer and winter angling), cast for long distances (to reach schooling fish in the jumps), cast in the shallows, or trolled during the spring and fall.

STINGER HOOK (Right): Commonly used on jigs to catch fish that are hitting short. A small treble hook, usually No. 10 to No. 2, is tied to the eye of a main hook with monofilament. Make the leader for the stinger hook long enough so that it trails the main hook. Embedding the stinger into the bait (usually a soft plastic lure or live bait) helps keep it near the bait's tail. Embedding the stinger is not necessary, but is often done with minnows.

SUSPENDING BAITS: The Rogue (left) is the best-known suspending bait. These neutrally buoyant baits stay in place when you pause your retrieve. This technique entices bass to hit. Suspending baits are most effective in late winter and early spring.

TEXAS RIG (Right): A bullet sinker is most commonly used for this rig. Sinker weight is usually determined by water depth or current strength. Place the sinker on the main line before tying on an offset hook. Pierce the head through a selected plastic bait (worms, crawfish, and lizards are common plastic baits used on a Texas rig). The hook should exit about a ¼ inch

below its entrance point. Pull the hook down so that it becomes even with the back of the bait. Where the apex of the curve of the hook meets the underside of the plastic body is the point where it reenters the lure. Only the tip of the hook is embedded in the plastic body, which helps make it weedless around branches, stumps, and other cover or structure where hooks easily snag.

TROUT RIG: Tie a small barrel swivel to your main line and attach a 2-foot leader to the other end of the swivel. Tie a No. 12 salmon egg or bait hook to the leader. Place a small splitshot just below the swivel, another small splitshot 3 inches below the first one, and another 3 inches below the second splitshot. Bait the hook with a Power Egg, corn, worm, or insect. This works best on ultralight tackle and 4-pound test.

WALLEYE OR RIVER RIG: This is a Carolina rig but is used with live bait rather than with soft plastic baits, common in bass fishing. It is used most commonly for walleye and sauger.

Thread a slip sinker (egg sinker is preferred to the bullet type) on the main fishing line. A Lindy walking sinker also works in place of a slip sinker. The weight needs to be heavy enough to stay in contact with the river or lake bottom. Sinker weight is determined by current strength. Next, tie on a barrel swivel (between ½ and ¾ inch in length should work).

Tie a leader to the swivel. Many anglers use lighter monofilament for the leader so that it will break when snagged and only the leader will be lost. An appropriate leader length is between 12 and 18 inches. Tie on a No. 1 to 2/0 Aberdeen hook to the leader.

Many baits will catch fish. Shiners, small shad, tuffies, and night crawlers are commonly used. If pursuing big fish, use big bait. Soft-plastic baits work, but are not as popular as live bait.

APPENDIX B:
TELEPHONE NUMBERS FOR
FISHING GUIDES

We appreciate the fishing guides who provided us with information for this book. All the guides referred to, mentioned, noted, and quoted in this guide are listed here with their telephone numbers and specializations. They have been arranged alphabetically and may be listed under more than one lake. Please understand that other excellent guides reside across the state. Check with local docks, marinas, and bait and tackle shops for additional guide information.

Barkley

Dayton Blair	(615) 754-1256	largemouth bass, stripe, crappie
Jim Moyer	(931) 358-9264	catfish, largemouth bass

Boone

Tom Richards	(423) 246-7628	striper, hybrid, bass

Center Hill

Gene Austin	(615) 871-4109	bass
Dayton Blair	(615) 754-1256	bass, walleye, crappie
Jim Duckworth	(615) 444-2283	bass
Dwayne Hickey	(931) 668-3008	muskie
Tim Staley	(615) 597-8501	bass

Cheatham

Dayton Blair	(615) 754-1256	bass, walleye, crappie
Donny Hall	(615) 383-4464	catfish, bass, crappie

Cherokee

Ezell Cox	(423) 626-9547	striper
Ted "Yank" Kramer	(423) 587-4931	striper
Tom Richards	(423) 246-7628	striper, bass

Chickamauga
Billy Joe Hall   (423) 775-0951   largemouth bass

Cordell Hull
Ralph Dallas   (615) 824-5792   striper
Jim Duckworth   (615) 444-2283   bass, sauger

Dale Hollow
Gene Austin   (615) 871-4109   bass, walleye
John Cates   (615) 952-4294   smallmouth bass
Jim Duckworth   (615) 444-2283   smallmouth bass

Douglas
Rick Johnson   (423) 397-4135   largemouth bass

Ft. Loudoun
Bill Crox   (423) 986-9687   sauger

Great Falls
Dwayne Hickey   (931) 668-3008   muskie

Kentucky
Kenneth Bennett   (901) 364-3038   bass, crappie, stripe
David Harbin   (901) 925-2952   bass, striper, catfish, sauger, crappie
John Hunt   (931) 296-1297   crappie
Billy Hurt Jr.   (901) 427-7066   bass
Bob Latrendresse   (901) 584-2041   bass, crappie, bluegill, shellcracker
Garry Mason   (901) 593-5429   bass, crappie, bluegill, shellcracker
Steve McCadams   (901) 642-0360   bass, crappie, bluegill
Jim Perry   (901) 642-8870   crappie
Glenn Stubblefield   (502) 436-5584   bass, crappie, catfish, bluegill, stripe

Norris
Ezell Cox   (423) 626-9547   striper

Old Hickory
Gene Austin   (615) 871-4109   largemouth bass, crappie, striper
Dayton Blair   (615) 754-1256   bass, catfish, striper, crappie, sauger, stripe
James Blair   (615) 754-1256   bass
Ralph Dallas   (615) 824-5792   striper
Jim Duckworth   (615) 444-2283   sauger, bass
Roy Foster   (615) 356-2298   striper
Donny Hall   (615) 383-4464   catfish, bass, crappie
Harold Morgan   (615) 227-9337   crappie

J. Percy Priest
Gene Austin   (615) 871-4109   bass, crappie, striper, hybrid
Dayton Blair   (615) 754-1256   bass, catfish, crappie, Cherokee bass
James Blair   (615) 754-1256   bass

Jack Christian	(615) 672-0194	bass
Jim Duckworth	(615) 444-2283	bass, crappie
Roy Foster	(615) 356-2298	striper, hybrid
Jeff Hudson	(615) 849-2694	striper, hybrid
Harold Morgan	(615) 227-9337	crappie

Pickwick

Steve Hacker	(256) 383-1058	smallmouth bass
David Hancock	(901) 689-3074	bass, crappie, sauger, smallmouth bass
David Harbin	(901) 925-2952	bass, striper, catfish, sauger, crappie
Lou Williams	(901) 989-5367	bass

Reelfoot

Billy Blakely	(901) 253-6878 or 538-2972	largemouth bass, crappie, bluegill

South Holston

Tom Richards	(423) 246-7628	walleye, smallmouth bass

Tims Ford

Gene Austin	(615) 871-4109	bass
Terry Smith	(931) 967-7127	bass

Watauga

Tom Richards	(423) 246-7628	walleye, smallmouth bass

Watts Bar

Ezell Cox	(423) 626-9547	striper
Sherrill Smith	(423) 483-1547	crappie

Woods

Clyde Hill Jr.	(931) 967-6463	bass, crappie

APPENDIX C:
MAP INFORMATION

Anglers can improve their success more quickly by learning how to read maps effi-ciently. All species of fish have a certain favored habitat. Good map-readers can elimi-nate unproductive areas before they get on the water. The following are government agencies and private businesses that sell maps:

Tennessee Valley Authority
TVA Map Store, 311 Broad Street, Chattanooga, TN 37402-2801; (800) 627-7882
A large store with a variety of maps, including topographic maps of TVA reservoirs. Navigation books are also available. Costs vary. Catalog is essential and free. Office hours are 10 A.M. to 4:30 P.M. EST, Monday through Friday. The Map Store is located just off I-24 in Chattanooga. Take the same exit as the Tennessee Aquarium and go to Broad Street. The store is in the Haney Building, across from the Children's Museum.

U.S. Army Corps of Engineers
Maps Division, P.O. Box 1070, Nashville, TN 37202-1070; (615) 736-7864
Topographic maps are available for Corps of Engineers impoundments. One-page order form is available and free. Office hours are 8 A.M. to 4 P.M. CST, Monday though Friday. The Maps Division is on the sixth floor (room 670) of the Estes Kefauver Building (fed-eral building) at 801 Broadway, next to the U.S. Post Office.

Tennessee Division of Geology
Maps and Publications, 401 Church Street, Nashville, TN 37243; (615) 532-1516
Topographic and index maps are available. *Tennessee Atlas & Gazetteer* and *Tennessee County Maps*—both excellent for directions—are available. Call for prices. Office hours are 8 A.M. to 4 P.M. CST, Monday through Friday. The office is on the 13th floor of L & C Tower. Ask for the pamphlet entitled "Topographic Map Symbols."

Fishing Hot Spots
(800) ALL-MAPS
Provides numerous topographic maps for many states, including Tennessee.

Local Map Stores
Check the local Yellow Pages for map stores. These stores can usually obtain maps designed specifically for anglers. Many local sporting goods stores, department stores, and bait and tackle shops also sell fishing maps.

APPENDIX D:
TELEPHONE NUMBERS FOR
LAKE INFORMATION

Ofttimes, having generation schedules will help you plan fishing strategy. For instance, some species will not be active unless there is current. Thus, knowing when there is current will increase your chances of catching fish. The more you know about a lake before you go, the better prepared you will be to fish it.

TVA
Obtain information about TVA reservoir levels, generation schedules, and so on, by calling (800) 238-2264 and selecting the desired reservoir from a menu. Computer users can obtain information through the Internet (www.lakeinfo.tva.gov/).

Corps of Engineers
The Corps's reservoir information for individual lake levels, generation schedules, and so on, can be obtained by calling the following telephone numbers:

Barkley: (502) 362-8430
Cheatham: (615) 883-2351
J. Percy Priest: (615) 883-2351
Old Hickory: (615) 824-7766
Cordell Hull: (615) 735-1050
Center Hill: (931) 858-4366 or (615) 548-8581
Dale Hollow: (931) 243-3408

The Internet address for the Corps's reservoirs in Tennessee (part of the Corps's Nashville District) is www.orn.usace.army.mil/pao/lakeinfo/home.html.

APPENDIX E:
TWRA LAKES

Tennessee's large public lakes with their excellent fishing have made the state an attraction to anglers across America. While not as well known as the TVA or Corps of Engineers impoundments, and certainly not as large, lakes managed by the Tennessee Wildlife Resources Agency are like jewels in a crown. They add luster to an already magnificent fishing state.

Ranging in size from 15 to 500 acres, these 17 lakes are located in west and middle Tennessee. Each one receives management care that helps perpetuate game fish populations, and occasionally each is stocked with catfish. These lakes are perfect for families. No swimming, skiing, or personal watercraft are allowed on them. Fishing piers, along with rental boats, are found on most of the lakes. Picnic areas are common.

The following is information about each lake, including telephone numbers where anglers can obtain more information.

Brown's Creek Lake
Size: 167 acres
Species: Largemouth Bass, Crappie, Bluegill, Shellcracker, Blue and Channel Catfish
Location: Henderson County, 10 miles south of I-40 in Natchez Trace State Park. From I-40 take exit 115. Follow TN 114 south to Brown's Creek Lake Road.
Telephone: (901) 423-5725
Facilities: Boat launching ramps, fish attractors, fishing pier, boat rentals, rest rooms, picnic areas, vending machines

Carroll Lake
Size: 100 acres
Species: Largemouth Bass, Crappie, Bluegill, Shellcracker, Blue and Channel Catfish
Location: Carroll County, on TN 22 between McKenzie and Huntingdon. From I-40 take exit 108 (TN 22). The lake is approximately 20 miles north.
Telephone: (901) 352-0654
Facilities: Boat launching ramp, fish attractors, fishing pier, boat rentals, bait and tackle, picnic areas, rest rooms, concessions

Jimmy Holt and Glenn Smith tape Tennessee Outdoorsmen *TV shows on TWRA lakes because the fishing is great!*

Coy Gaither/Bedford Lake
Size: 47 acres
Species: Largemouth Bass, Crappie, Bluegill, Shellcracker, Blue and Channel Catfish
Location: Bedford County, approximately 14 miles east of Wartrace and Shelbyville. From I-24 take exit 105 (US 41) toward Manchester 0.4 mile. Go right on 16th Model Road and 5.9 miles to Bedford Lake Road. Go 2.5 miles to lake entrance.
Telephone: (615) 857-3214
Facilities: Boat launching ramp, fish attractors, fishing pier, boat and trolling motor rentals, bait and tackle, picnic tables, grills, campground, rest rooms

Davy Crockett Lake
Size: 87 acres
Species: Largemouth Bass; Crappie; Bluegill; Shellcracker; Blue, Channel, and Flathead Catfish
Location: Crockett County, approximately 4 miles west of Humboldt off TN 152. From I-40 take exit 80B (US Highway 45) north to Humboldt. Stay on bypass west of Humboldt. Turn right on TN 152W.
Telephone: (901) 784-3889
Facilities: Boat launching ramp, fish attractors, fishing pier, boat rentals, picnic area, playground, rest rooms

Garrett Lake
Size: 183 acres
Species: Largemouth Bass, Crappie, Bluegill, Shellcracker, Pickerel, Blue and Channel Catfish
Location: Weakley County, approximately 7 miles east of Dresden off TN 54. Take TN 190 north off TN 54. Go right at the split and follow directional signs to the lake.
Telephone: (901) 423-5725
Facilities: Boat launching ramp, fish attractors, fishing pier, picnic area, picnic pavilion

Tennessee Outdoorsmen *cameraman John Key gets into the act with a TWRA lake blue catfish.*

Glenn Springs Lake

Size: 310 acres
Species: Largemouth Bass, Crappie, Bluegill, Catfish
Location: Tipton County, on Glenn Springs Road 12 miles northeast of Millington. From Memphis take US 51N from I-240. Go left on Drummonds Road, then turn right on Glenn Springs Road. Go 1 mile to lake entrance.
Telephone: (901) 835-5253
Facilities: Boat launching ramp, fish attractors, fishing pier, boat and trolling motor rentals, bait and tackle, picnic area, rest rooms, concessions

Herb Parsons Lake

Size: 177 acres
Species: Largemouth Bass; Crappie; Bluegill; Shellcracker; Blue, Channel, and Bullhead Catfish
Location: Fayette County, approximately 8 miles north of Collierville off Collierville-Arlington Road.
Telephone: (901) 853-4193
Facilities: Boat launching ramp, fish attractors, fishing pier, boat rentals, picnic area, playground, rest rooms, vending machines, concessions

Lake Graham

Size: 500 acres
Species: Largemouth Bass, Crappie, Bluegill, Shellcracker, Blue and Channel Catfish
Location: Madison County, approximately 5 miles east of Jackson on Cotton Grove Road. From Nashville take I-40 exit 93 to US 412. Follow US 412 to Cotton Grove Road. From Memphis take exit 85. Turn right onto parkway and follow signs.
Telephone: (901) 423-4937
Facilities: Boat launching ramp, fish attractors, fishing pier, boat and trolling motor rentals, bait and tackle, picnic area, rest rooms, vending machines, concessions

VFW Lake in Lawrence County is small, but offers plenty of room for families to fish and picnic.

Laurel Hill Lake
Size: 325 acres
Species: Largemouth Bass, Crappie, Bluegill, Shellcracker, Blue and Channel Catfish
Location: Lawrence County, approximately 15 miles west of Lawrenceburg. Take Peter Cave Road off US 64 to lake entrance. From the Natchez Trace Parkway take the Laurel Hill Lake exit (Brush Creek Road) to lake entrance.
Telephone: (615) 762-7200
Facilities: Boat launching ramp, fish attractors, fishing pier, boat and trolling motor rentals, bait and tackle, picnic area, rest rooms, grills, vending machines, primitive camping area

Maples Creek Lake
Size: 90 acres
Species: Largemouth Bass, Crappie, Bluegill, Shellcracker, Blue and Channel Catfish
Location: Carroll County, approximately 4 miles north of I-40 in Natchez Trace State Park. From I-40 take exit 116 (TN 114) to Maples Lake Road.
Telephone: (901) 423-5725
Facilities: Boat launching ramp, fish attractors, fishing pier, boat rentals, picnic area, rest rooms

Marrowbone Lake
Size: 60 acres
Species: Largemouth Bass, Crappie, Bluegill, Shellcracker, Blue and Channel Catfish
Location: Davidson County, on Marrowbone Lake Road near Joelton, approximately 20 miles north of Nashville. From Nashville take US 41A (Clarksville Highway). Take a left on Eatons Creek Road. Then take a right on Grays Point Road.
Telephone: (615) 876-9050
Facilities: Boat launching ramp, fishing pier, boat and trolling motor rentals, bait and tackle, rest rooms, picnic tables, concessions

VFW Lake

Size: 22 acres
Species: Largemouth Bass, Crappie, Bluegill, Shellcracker, Blue and Channel Catfish
Location: Lawrence County, approximately 12 miles west of Lawrenceburg off US 64. Take TN 241 off US 64 to VFW Lake Road just past the TN 240 junction. The lake may also be reached from Natchez Trace Parkway; take the Napier Road exit.
Telephone: (615) 762-9009
Facilities: Boat launching ramps, fish attractors, fishing pier, boat rentals, picnic tables, rest rooms, vending machines

Whiteville Lake

Size: 158 acres
Species: Largemouth Bass, Crappie, Bluegill, Shellcracker, Blue and Channel Catfish
Location: Hardeman County, approximately two miles south of Whiteville off US 64.
Telephone: (901) 254-9014
Facilities: boat launching ramp, fish attractors, fishing pier, boat and trolling motor rentals, bait, picnic area, picnic pavilions, playground, rest rooms, snacks and drinks

TWRA lakes are typically stocked with largemouth bass, catfish, bream, and crappie.

Williamsport Lakes and WMA

Whippoorwill Lake: 24 acres*
Blue Cat Lake: 63 acres
Goldeneye Lake: 15 acres
Shellcracker Lake: 53 acres
Species: Largemouth Bass, Bluegill, Shellcracker, Blue and Channel Catfish
Location: Maury County, approximately 10 miles west of Columbia on TN 50 and 2 miles east of Natchez Trace Parkway.
Telephone: (615) 781-6622
Facilities: Boat launching ramps, fishing piers, boat rentals, bait and tackle, rest rooms, concessions

*Must be 16 years of age or younger to fish Whippoorwill Lake. Adults may fish if a youngster accompanies them.

GLOSSARY

BAITFISH: Also called forage fish. Includes threadfin shad, gizzard shad, skipjack, alewife, shiners, and many types of minnows. These are excellent for live bait and cut bait.

BAR: A long submerged ridge in a lake.

BAY: A large indention in a lake's shoreline.

BELL SINKER: A pear-shaped sinker that comes in various weights with a brass eye for your line tie.

BREAK: An abrupt, horizontal, or vertical change in otherwise constant stretches of bottom or structure. On a topographic map it is the interruption of the smooth flow of contour lines.

BRIDGES: These have many potential fish-holding areas. Deep water is usually nearby and the vertical pilings and riprap are associated with a sloping bottom. Bases of pilings frequently have a lip—a breakline. The base of the pilings may be undercut by erosion and may have logs trapped there. Pilings are also a break in the current and form two edges that fish like. There will be an eddy downstream of the piling and seams on both sides.

BULLET SINKER: A conical or bullet-shaped weight with a hole through the middle. Commonly used with a Texas rig. One of several types of slip sinkers.

CHANNEL: Refers to the streambed. Tennessee's reservoirs have a main channel, referring to the riverbed, and creek channels, which are tributaries to the river.

COMFORT ZONE: Area or strata of water where conditions such as temperature, pH, and so on, fall within a fish's tolerance range.

CONDITIONS: Light, wind, weather, water clarity, oxygen, pH, and many other aspects affecting fish.

COVE: An indention of a lake's shoreline, but smaller than a bay.

COVER: see *structure.*

DOCKS, MARINAS, AND BOAT SLIPS: Manmade structures have cover, pilings, or other objects that accommodate the food chain. Lights are often on at night, providing another good reason to fish these places.

DRAWDOWN: The dropping of a lake's elevation to accommodate storage of winter rains and help prevent flooding. Drawdown begins as early as June on some reservoirs.

DROPLINE: A short length of line extending from the main line with a baited hook or lure.

DROP-OFF OR DROP: Where the bottom makes a quick descent. Drops are often associated with flats and ledges.

EDDY: An area of swirling or reversed current, usually behind an object such as a boulder, point, or downed tree.

EDGES: Where two dissimilar features meet. Edges can be sharp or diffuse. Differences in temperature, pH, light, dissolved oxygen, chemicals, gravel and sand, rock and wood, aquatic plants, and current are examples where edges form.

EGG SINKER: Egg-shaped sinker with a hole lengthwise through the middle. Commonly used with the Carolina rig. One of several types of slip sinkers.

FISH ATTRACTOR: Manmade cover used to attract various species of fish and their food chain from algae to baitfish. TWRA marks their attractors with buoys.

FLATS: Submerged flood plains along the main channel and feeder creeks. These are frequently fertile areas containing the food chain and spawning grounds. They figure prominently as habitat on flatland lakes because logs, aquatic plants, and debris accumulate on them. In deeper lakes, the flats become narrower and their role diminishes. The edges of flats, especially at breaks, are important places to fish. A flat on one side of a channel point increases the likelihood of locating fish. Large flats often have depressions or old pond sites; these are places you don't want to miss.

FLIPPING: A method of underhand casting at close range around cover and structure.

FLIPPING STICK: A long, heavy-action rod (usually 7 or 8 feet) commonly used for bass fishing.

FLOAT: Also called a bobber. A buoyant strike indicator that holds bait above the bottom.

FORAGE: The act of predators eating baitfish.

FORAGE FISH: See *baitfish.* Also called Forage Base.

FRONT: See *weather front.*

GEAR RATIO: Number of times the spool or bail revolves for each complete turn of the handle. This is a measure of a reel's line retrieve.

HABITAT: The environment suitable to the needs of a fish.

HYBRID: The offspring of two related species. Two common hybrids in Tennessee are saugeye (walleye X sauger) and Cherokee bass (striper X stripe).

HUMPS: Often called submerged islands. They come in all sizes and depths. Those along a channel probably attract more fish, especially if the peak reaches within less than 10 feet of the surface and has some form of cover on it. Hill-land lakes are deeper and have more humps than flatland lakes. These features are particularly excellent nighttime fishing spots.

JIG OR LEADHEAD: A lure composed of lead, with a fixed hook, and frequently adorned with hair, feathers, rubber skirts, or plastic.

LEDGES: They form a step-down along a bank or bluff. Ledges are often associated with migration routes. Flatland reservoirs will have mud ledges along the channel and along feeder creeks. Ledges in the deeper lakes are commonly rock.

MIGRATION ROUTE: The path fish take when they move from deep water to shallow water and back. Fish are said to be migrating when moving along this route.

MONOFILAMENT: Fishing line made from of a single strand of synthetic material.

PATTERN: Establishing the whereabouts of a species during a certain time of the year or under certain conditions.

PITCHING: (See *flipping*) Similar to flipping, but casts are usually longer.

PELAGIC: Fish that live in open water and do not relate to cover. Striper, hybrid, and stripe are pelagic species.

pH: The measurement of acidity or alkalinity in water (seven is the neutral point).

PHYTOPLANKTON: Minute aquatic plants.

PLANKTON: Made of phyto- and zooplankton. Beginning of the aquatic food chain.

POINTS: An extension of land into a lake. Some are pointed and others are rounded. Rounded points are called rounds.

POUND-TEST: The breaking point of fishing line. Measured by the number of pounds of pressure required to break it.

PRIMARY AND SECONDARY POINTS: The former is on the main channel of a lake and the latter refers to the points found beyond the primary points up a creek or cove.

RIPRAP: Construction rocks placed along a bank to prevent erosion.

RUN-OF-THE-RIVER RESERVOIRS: Pools formed by dams along a major river system. In Tennessee, the Cumberland and Tennessee Rivers are the two major systems. These lakes rarely stratify because of current. Dams along tributaries of the major river systems form tributary reservoirs.

SLOUGH: Backwater area of a lake.

SONAR OR DEPTHFINDER: Electronic device that transmits sounds waves, detects the echoes, and displays these echoes as fish, bottom, cover, and so on, on a graph or flasher.

SPLITSHOT: Small, round, lead weight crimped on fishing line.

STRIKE ZONE: The area in front of a fish where it will pursue baitfish or lures. Inactive fish have a smaller strike zone than active fish.

STRUCTURE (vs. COVER): These two terms mean different things, and many of us use them interchangeably. You may consider a log as structure, as many do. There is no one accepted definition, but to avoid confusion, we will adopt the following definitions for our use here. Structure is the bottom from the shore to the deepest part of a lake or river. Structure is part of the bottom like a point, hump, or flat. Simply put, it is the shape of the bottom. *Cover* refers to all the other things that may be in the water. This would include tires, logs, weeds, trees, docks, bridges, brush piles, and so on.

TAILWATER: The area immediately below a dam.

THERMOCLINE: The layer of water with a steep gradient change of temperature (½° per foot) between the warm upper layer (epilimnion) and the colder bottom layer (hypolimnion).

TOPOGRAPHIC (TOPO) MAP: A map with contour lines representing elevations.

TRAILER: Plastic grub, worm, lizard, skirt, pork frog, pork chunk, live bait, and so on, attached to a lure or hook to entice strikes.

TWRA: Tennessee Wildlife Resources Agency.

WEATHER: Often a strong factor influencing fish behavior. Conditions can change drastically with the passage of a weather front.

WEATHER FRONT: The line between two air masses, usually a cold one meeting a warm one. Warm, moist air is ahead of the front with cold, dry air behind it. The barometric pressure is lower ahead of the front and fish are active. A change in the wind direction lets you know the front has reached you. After the passage, the barometric pressure rises, the sky clears, and the temperature drops. Fish become inactive and bury themselves in heavy cover. Active fish will be on top of structure looking for forage. Less active fish may suspend or concentrate along breaklines or close to cover. After three days of constant weather conditions, fish become active again. Observations of other conditions and how you interpret them will determine your fishing success.

ZOOPLANKTON: Minute aquatic animals.

INDEX

FOR MORE OF VERNON SUMMERLIN
AND DOUG MARKHAM

Photo of Doug by Vernon

Tune in to *Outdoors with Vern & Doug* on the Tennessee Radio Network. They talk with anglers and other outdoor guests on their one-hour radio program. Contact TRN at (800) 346-9467 for a station near you.

Tennessee Angler magazine is a monthly all-fishing publication edited by Vernon Summerlin. For more information contact *Tennessee Angler,* 5550 Boy Scout Road, Franklin, TN 37064.

Doug Markham is a regular guest with Jimmy Holt and Glenn Smith on *Tennessee Outdoorsmen* on WDCN Public Television Thursdays and Saturdays, and rebroadcast statewide. Contact WDCN for other stations and times at (615) 259-9325.

Doug Markham is author of *Boxes, Rockets and Pens—A History of Wildlife Recovery in Tennessee,* published by University of Tennessee Press.

Cathy and Vernon Summerlin are authors of *Traveling the Trace—A Complete Tour Guide to the Historic Natchez Trace; Traveling the Southern Highlands—A Complete Guide to the Mountains of Western North Carolina, East Tennessee, Northeast Georgia, and Southwest Virginia;* and *Traveling Tennessee—A Complete Guide to Tennessee.* All are published by Rutledge Hill Press.

Photo of Vernon by Doug